Dreaming the Present

Dreaming the Present

Time, Aesthetics, and the
Black Cooperative Movement

· ·

IRVIN J. HUNT

The University of North Carolina Press Chapel Hill

This book was published with the assistance of the Authors Fund of the University of North Carolina Press.

Set in Charis by Westchester Publishing Services
Manufactured in the United States of America

The University of North Carolina Press has been a member
of the Green Press Initiative since 2003.

Library of Congress Cataloging-in-Publication Data
Names: Hunt, Irvin J., author.
Title: Dreaming the present : time, aesthetics, and the black
    cooperative movement / Irvin J. Hunt.
Description: Chapel Hill : University of North Carolina Press, [2022] |
    Includes bibliographical references and index.
Identifiers: LCCN 2021041569 | ISBN 9781469667928 (cloth) |
    ISBN 9781469667935 (paperback) | ISBN 9781469667942 (ebook)
Subjects: LCSH: Cooperative societies—United States—History—20th
    century. | Social movements—United States—History—20th century. |
    African Americans—Economic conditions—20th century. | African
    Americans—Social conditions—20th century.
Classification: LCC HD3444 .H86 2022 | DDC 334.0973—dc23
LC record available at https://lccn.loc.gov/2021041569

Cover illustration: Betye Saar, *Weight of Persistent Racism (Patented)*, 2014
(mixed media assemblage, 25 x 9 x 7 in / 63.5 x 22.86 x 17.78 cm). Courtesy
of the artist and Roberts Projects Los Angeles, California; photo by Robert
Wedemeyer.

for
Anna and James,
who reminded me, this is light

Contents

List of Illustrations, ix

Introduction, 1
The Only Way Out Was In

1 Sustained Incipience, 20
W. E. B. Du Bois and the Negro Cooperative Guild

2 Planned Failure, 69
*George Schuyler, Ella Baker, and the Young Negroes'
Cooperative League*

3 Pluripresence, 136
Fannie Lou Hamer's Freedom Farm

Conclusion, 193
Trouble in the Water

Afterword, 201
*This Bridge Called the System: An Interview with
Stephanie Morningstar*

Acknowledgments, 211

Notes, 213

Index, 251

Illustrations and Map

Illustrations

Crisis magazine offices, circa 1918, 23

Advertisement car of Roddy's Co-operative Stores, 28

"Two of the Memphis Cooperative Stores," 33

Copy of Ralph Bunche's typescript, "The Negro Cooperative Guild," 36

"Colored Co-operative Store at Buffalo, New York," 80

George Schuyler with Mr. Massey outside the offices of the Co-operative Wholesale Society of Great Britain, 83

Ella Baker addresses a group from the podium in Hattiesburg, Mississippi, 1964, 86

Flyer for joining the Young Negroes' Cooperative League, 89

Hamer on the Farm, 144

Hamer in her home, 144

Man and boy posing before Freedom Farm headquarters, 145

Girl looking at camera on Freedom Farm, 146

Three girls stand before a food sign and repurposed kitchen equipment, Freedom Farms, 146

Workers on Farm, 147

Children holding up crop inventory sign, 147

Map of Mississippi, 153

Fannie Lou Hamer Daycare Center welcome sign, 154

Freedom Farm Cooperative housing development, Ruleville, MS, 168

"Miles Foster checks on first crop of cotton," 169

Freedom City Housing, 179

Freedom City Soil, 179

Map

Sunflower County, 152

Dreaming the Present

Introduction

The Only Way Out Was In

· ·

They lay
kissed by seafoam, sand
on
their skin, dream they knew
no way not to be dreaming
—Nathaniel Mackey, *Nod House*

But if the future did not arrive, the present did extend itself.
—Toni Morrison, *Song of Solomon*

I began this book in search of alternatives to hope, alternatives I was seeking in a period of history, or at least in my lifetime, when they seemed most needed. I mean hope in the futural sense, not hope as I've heard it used by one of this book's stars, Fannie Lou Hamer: "hope me something," as in give me what I need to live, to flourish, now. That's hope in the eminently present sense. That, it turns out, was the hoping I found in what these bards christened as the Black cooperative movement. And I have translated that nowness, that now-hope, into shapes of time.

This is a book about time, political time, the kind of time that opened up out of a startling question I heard a bevy of artists asking: Where can we move to if not to a better tomorrow? How do we make a movement that in no way relies on the promise of brighter days? For me, this question issued at least two others. One: What kind of language on the page and on the ground, written and lived, avoids the pretentions of universalist progress, the screen through which movements are most often read, the sign under which they are most often found? And two: Dreams are often considered the precedent for freedom, but what if freedom was the precedent for dreams?

When I first saw writers talking about cooperatives, I was sitting on the floor in the cold and dim stacks of Columbia's main library. I was randomly browsing huge, leather-brown volumes of Black newspapers and magazines from the 1900s. With a sort of puzzled awe, I read headlines in tall angular font like "Co-operation Seen as Best Way Out"; even catchier ones, nearly marching off the page, like "Consumers' Cooperation, The American Negro's Salvation"; and plenty, fittingly enough, announcing a "Co-operative Movement," a "Cooperation Replacing Individualism," and most boldly, "A New Era."[1] I didn't know what these cooperatives were but I was clearly thinking of everything that they were not: the lavender-lush health food store I couldn't afford to shop in, the patioed apartments gentrifying Harlem that I, even if I wanted to, couldn't afford to live in, and the credit union on Saint Nick's I had no money to join. I suspect I thought, crouched in a kind of optical stutter, what a lot of people think today when they hear of a co-op: a group of people working together for economic advantage, certainly not the effort, as I'd later learn, to "doom to extinction" the global "capitalist system with its by-products of war" and "unemployment," certainly not a "new era" in the Black diaspora.

Those words of "doom" were the scythe of George Schuyler in December 1932, seeking to bury global capital just as he himself said he felt about buried, a month before the worst year in the Great Depression but the best years in the history of Black cooperatives, when common need brought people together. As the most widely recognized African American journalist at the time, Schuyler, from his perch in upper Harlem, was writing in a West Indian magazine, drumming up members for his and Ella Baker's Young Negroes' Cooperative League. At this point their League was young, only two years old, but it bore the weight of generational ambition. The cooperatives the League established shared, as Schuyler noted, all of the hallmarks of most of the left-leaning cooperatives emerging around the world at the time and will emerge from this book: "organized buying power" with the goal of "service instead of profit," of "mutual respect instead of hatred," of nothing less than a "new social order."[2]

Sleuthing through archives across the country, I eventually discovered that this new order was promoted and portrayed by writers as famous as Ann Petry, Langston Hughes, Margaret Walker, Richard Wright, Zora Neale Hurston, Amiri Baraka, Alice Walker, June Jordan, and more; writers as unappreciated for their writing as journalists James Farmer, Zalmon Garfield, or Alethea Washington, and as wholly forgotten as Ben Fowlkes, an owner of a bookstore in Birmingham, Alabama. In 1907 Fowlkes published a volume of ballad poems titled *Cooperation: The Solution of the So-Called Negro Problem*. This was a rhapsody to Black co-ops and their founders in 228 fine-print pages. Who would have imagined that a supermarket shelf could amuse and "captivate," exciting a torrent of jump-rope rhymes, like "They carry oysters, salmons and clams, / They carry Swift's best premium hams, / They carry Van Camp's pork and beans, / American and imported sardines"?[3]

Yet it was the founders of Black cooperatives, those who not only aestheticized them, from fretwork to shelf-work, but who also established them around the country, who attracted me the most. I found it staggering just how many cooperative organizations were founded not by businessmen, union organizers, or merely concerned citizens, but by some of the most influential Black artists of the twentieth century. I say artists in the broad sense of both oral and written work, and in the unusual sense of the performance art of activism. Of these artists, none was more ambitious than W. E. B. Du Bois, George Schuyler, Ella Baker, or Fannie Lou Hamer, all of whom, in Schuyler's words, sought to usher in much more than cooperatives: they called for "a new social order," a cooperative movement across the Black diaspora. By calling them artists, I hope to upset the kind of gendered logic that goes, "with exceptions (and unlike Du Bois), Baker did not express her ideas in essays, academic monographs, or novels but rather through institutional action."[4] This is not only factually untrue, it also serves as a sore reminder that rarely has Baker, like Hamer, been given literary attention. Such attention might compel us to ask: What happens when institutional action becomes novelistic? Bracketing for the moment the sticky problem of the division between activism and art, artistic production and political formations, my questions is even more basic than the last. What happens, as Brittney Cooper has asked, when we account for all that these Black female intellectuals like Baker and Hamer said, especially as we celebrate all that they did?[5]

In 1877, England's thriving Rochdale Society of Equitable Pioneers, a bearded bunch of thirty ex-Chartists, Owenites, temperance campaigners, and weavers first codified the word "cooperative" as the antonym to "competition" in their *Rochdale Rules*. This slim pamphlet is still widely used today as the basis for some of the most far-reaching experiments from the International Cooperative Alliance to the largest collection of cooperatives in the world, Mondragon in the Basque Country of Spain.[6] These *Rochdale Rules*, none more vaunted for Blacks than "let each member have only one vote, and make no distinction as regards the amount of wealth any member may contribute," became a guide, a kind of new North Star, for Black cooperatists in the 1900s.[7] Since then a cooperative has been defined as a business whose patrons (producers, consumers, or workers) equally own and democratically distribute the collective surplus, from revenue to, as Schuyler insisted, "respect."[8] Although Black cooperative members often quoted in their bylaws the *Rochedale Rules*, mutual aid societies, like Sarah Allen's Benevolent Daughters (1796) and Richard Allen's and Absalom Jones's Free African Society (1787), were the cultural blueprints for Black co-ops. They, after all, were "the earliest Black community institutions."[9] One cannot overstate how critical these blueprints were for the ability of Blacks to feed and protect themselves, mourn their dead, provide for the survivors, and contest capitalist notions of property.[10]

But go back to Schuyler's flag-waving words, three words loudly waving the same flag, "doom to extinction," and there you'll find what cooperation means distinctly for me: an alternative temporality, a strange experience of time, social movement time, outside capitalist clock-time and its ascending linearities. To doom something to extinction, to end an end, is not really redundant so much as self-undermining. It is more the undoing of oneself than the repetition of oneself. It is essentially to extinguish any total and totalizing project like "doom." George S. Schuyler, once radically anarchistic but now remembered as radically right-wing; Ella Jo Baker, his compadre and increasingly popular model of ecumenical leadership; W. E. B. Du Bois, their predecessor; and Fannie Lou Hamer, Baker's fellow field-worker in the civil rights movement, someone who lived her life on her sleeve— each one of these bedevillers presents cooperation, from the 1890s to the 1970s, as the dual operation, the "co-operation," of a grand utopian goal, like dooming global capital, and the cancellation of this goal, its collapse, its doubling-back, like bringing "doom to extinction."

While we're here, I should say that I offer this rhetorical example mainly for brevity. The representation of nonprogressivism was not limited to a rhetoric. It was active in the way these insurgents organized their cooperatives, interfaced with the law in bylaws and charters, planned and held their meetings, spoke with each other in letters and live dialogue, delivered speeches, fashioned themselves in photographic portraits and flyers, told stories, and reflected on their activities on the page and on tape. By close reading this material as modes of extraordinary perception, I'm merely extending the defining labor of Black studies to finally defetishize the literary artifact and uproot the assumption of a "universal poesis."[11] I am tempted to call this, what they said and did, as others have called it: a praxis.[12] But I hesitate when I look again at the meaning of praxis, most influentially defined by Antonio Gramsci, as the passing of philosophy through the crucible of common sense, only to emerge beyond it (common sense), crowned with a "single," "coherent," and "higher conception of life."[13] While the language of their performance remained tied to that of the masses, as is the case for a praxis, the language was ultimately too crafty and nonintuitive, too diffuse and unselfconscious, to fit that crown of "unity," "awareness," and as Cedric Robinson has added, "dialectical development."

This language of social movements, an exact and exacting lexicon I have traced and magnified, fits what I like to call a quicksilver aesthetic.[14] The aesthetic choices of my actors were, like quicksilver, organic (organic in the Gramscian sense of emerging from social contestation), prompt, and rapidly changing. Against the impulse for completion, their aesthetic cut two paths. Beside the narrative of emancipation ran a narrative of its foreclosure, a progressive time beside a nonprogressive time, in which the "only way out" was in. And I can't say enough how much this just baffles me, their inner-will and insight to inaugurate a movement without the expectation it would take them somewhere better, somewhere else. I do not mean to suggest these cooperative movements had no interest in going anywhere, only taking place. They indeed had a destination: new locations in a present heretofore unseen, less the victories of tomorrow than those already of today. Here I'm thinking of Baker who suggested there's a victory in the attempt to counter capitalist relations in and of itself. Reflecting on her life at seventy-five, Baker said, "I really didn't have a career but my forte, if we can call it that, was believing that whatever you did, you did because it was important to try."[15]

A Tale of Two Arguments

The question, again, at the core of this book is: What might a movement look like freed from the dictates of progress? I offer three replies in successive chapters: a continual beginning, a deliberate falling apart, and a simultaneity, a kind of all-at-once-ness. These embodied temporalities ultimately come down to a reimagination of the present and its limits.

One half of my argument unsettles how twentieth-century cooperatives are usually perceived. So first, a quick precis. Formally, cooperatives initially emerged among the national agrarian fraternal organization, the Grange, between 1870 and 1890, then again among Black agrarian workers who comprised Black populism roughly between 1886 and 1896, to use historian Omar Ali's time frame.[16] All of these cooperatists contested low wages, high interest rates, and depreciated commodity prices. But in the case of Black populists like the one-million-member Colored Farmers Alliance and Co-operative Union, founded in 1886, the contest was for land among the landless and an expanded logic of property based on "guaranteed access to natural resources" instead of the "independent ownership of them."[17] This insistence on collective, self-run property recalls some of the predecessors to Black cooperatives. It recalls the fugitive Black communes, like the Dawn Settlement in Ontario, Canada, established in 1837, or the Combahee Colony established on a tear drop of an island, Port Royal, South Carolina, during the Civil War. The "Combees," as they called themselves, were freed through Harriet Tubman's raid on the Combahee River. The Combahee River Collective, a socialist feminist organization, took its name from this act of liberation in 1977.[18] And this collective recalls something common to all Black cooperative bloodlines: the intimate communion between freedom and deprivation, mobility and loss, the fact that Tubman's raid for the promise of freedom within the new colonial state was also a raid on an ongoing practice of mutual aid. Then there are the swamps—if not the most numerous then surely the most seismic predecessors to Black cooperatives were the swamps on which fugitive slaves took up residence. As you'll see, Du Bois depicts the swamp in his first novel as the haunted territory of all Black cooperative economies, and as a ghost he couldn't shake.

From this point on through the 1900s, cooperatives of all colors are usually said to follow a politically conservative line. Indeed, the bulk of them did. John Harold Johnson, who founded *Ebony Magazine* in 1945, avidly cheered Black mutualism and told *Fortune Magazine* "I don't want to destroy the system—I want to get into it."[19] In part, statements like that are why few have recognized, in the words of Barbara Ransby, those cooperatives that operated as a "direct challenge" to capital's legitimacy.[20] Black cooperatives in particular are remembered as economic stopgaps or benign integrationist measures, harmless pools of futility that did not add up to anything like a radical interruption to capital and property, that did no more than clip "the twigs of the capitalist tree," as Rosa Luxemburg famously wrote.[21] The cooperative life gathered here, however, proved to be purposeful and disruptive zones of social movement experimentation, seeking to transform the racial, gender, and imperial foundations of liberal inclusion.

The second half of my argument reconsiders the largely spatial tradition of social movement studies, characterized by an emphasis on where movements happen: in "repeated public displays" of typically extravagant action—sit-ins, marches, strikes, boycotts, and demonstrations on "streets, agoras, squares, cities."[22] No doubt, to quote Hagar Kotef, "space is often what is at stake in civic resistance," and "not just for free movement but for a designated common place."[23] My actors, however, reconfigured a movement, one of the most stubbornly invariable materializations of collective action in scholarly discourse, as reconstructions of time, as a mode of presence, a manifold of presents. "The Negro youth must awake to the challenge of the HERE and NOW," wrote Baker in 1933, fully capitalizing those words from a clichéd phenomenon into something larger, something on the order of a metaphysical question. These presents could be as disconnected as Hamer's pluripresence, in which she claimed to emerge, like some chthonic deity, in the North and the South at the same time. They could be as partial as Du Bois's sustained incipience, in which he made the state of being born a veritable state of being, or as anarchic as Schuyler's and Baker's planned failure, in which the coherence of their organization and its governing body were fundamentally meant to fail.

Cooperatives were uniquely poised to facilitate an expansion of the possibilities in the present. Beneath the gunsights of the state, cooperatives were deceptive and disruptive within, rather than outside, capitalist exchange. Unlike the alternative agendas in the most progressive political parties of their day, the socialist and communist parties, my authors dreamed not of the future but of the present. It is in the former orientation that we have mostly imagined them. For this reason, Black artists on the left have been predominantly portrayed in terms of their vexed involvements with communist and socialist party agendas.[24] But, as we know, the fenced vision of a universal future espoused by these parties is what pushed many Blacks away. What I wanted to know is where then did they go? As it turns out many went to co-ops, Indigenous outside choices.

Radical Black cooperatives in the twentieth century belong to a long tradition of clandestine maneuver. "On then Black Americans," exclaimed Du Bois in 1919, "and remember the pass-word—*Organization and Cooperation!*"[25] As themselves a secret password, these Black cooperatives doffed their hats to an act of dissemblance performed in the nineteenth century in mutual aid societies. There members were required to adopt special salutations and, yes, secret passwords. The Colored Farmers Alliance, for example, even used a private language. And to enter one of their funerals, one would have to show a doorkeeper "a sprig of evergreen" pinned to "the left lapel of [one's] coat."[26] The dangerous aims of these cooperatives could more easily fly under the radar of state surveillance by the early 1900s because the federal government started using cooperative businesses to offload its welfare responsibilities.

I don't mean to underemphasize the red record and terminal risks to the life of cooperatists, but a long list of federal endorsements ironically granted radical Black politics partial, if not enduring, clemency, or maybe the better word is "invisibility." A number of federal decisions signaled broad support for cooperatives: Theodore Roosevelt's 1908 Country Life Commission, which recommended the development of a cooperative credit system for farmers; Woodrow Wilson's 1916 Federal Farm Loan Act, which provided support for cooperative banking; the 1922 Capper-Volstead Act, which exempted agricultural cooperatives from antitrust laws; and President Roosevelt's hydra of New Deal agencies, that for the first time in American history tried to give the "consuming public" an equal voice next to business and labor.[27] Cooperatives meant one thing for the state—cheaper welfare relief—and an empowering thing for radical Blacks—local alternatives to global capital. For them, cooperatives meant the rebuke of evolving technologies of globalization: imperial expansion, manifest destiny, and by the start of the twentieth century, a settler colonialism on new frontiers across the seas.

By the 1930s, the decade that witnessed a rise in more African American cooperatives than at any other equivalent time in U.S. history, the educator Alethea Washington could comfortably say, even in the specialized *Journal of Negro Education*, "we are certain that many journal readers are interested in the cooperative movement. It is likely that a number are participating in consumer cooperative projects and credit unions." She could not have made the same pronouncement by the end of the 1970s when Black cooperatives began to dwindle. Yet this conventional plotline I myself just drew (it's almost irresistible) is bucked by the very discourse I was privileged to hear. There they called into doubt biological time, or as Althusser once put it "ordinary time," where life comes to an end. There Fannie Lou Hamer mystically said when asked about the civil rights movement, "I don't think you would say it is dead, but every so many years things change and go into something else." I've tried to sketch the logic of that "change" and other-else, those transformations of political time, under which no one, referring to a movement, "would say it is dead," unless in dying and dying again (and again) it came ecstatically alive, as you will see in the Young Negroes' Cooperative League. There in the cooperatives, the imagination assumed an unusual role: not to reveal what could be. To reveal what is.

Beginning from the Beginning

My principle contribution is a new iconography of social movement time. My protagonists all spoke of their cooperatives as initiating an historical break, as assuming the essential makeup of a novelty, or as Ezra Pound wrote of literature, "news that stays news." They said their cooperatives were either extending or even inaugurating movements, each of which they then proclaimed to be unprecedented in African American history, a "first," "new."[28] And I have taken them at their word, not in its factuality or accuracy, but in its semantic content, which again and again (a recursion that itself points to something other than a wish to be right) announced dramatic departures from any long and continuous time, the very kind of time into which social movements across the humanities and social sciences continue to be written.

This persistent and defining form of duration (long and continuous) is part of the standard definition used implicitly or expressly by most, from Giorgio Agamben, Charles Tilly, Hagar Kotef, and others to Jeff Goodwin and James Jasper, a duo who defines a movement as "a collective, organized, sustained, and noninstitutional challenge to authorities."[29] "Sustained" is the most important of these words, for it distinguishes a movement from other forms of collective insurgency, like riots or rebellions, and it functions as the prerequisite for organization. It accumulates, this emphasis on a "sustained" duration, in this common definition of a social movement, but it appears to have deeper roots. It appears to be a consequence of the imperative to contest the pejorative claim that social movements, to the extent they arise spontaneously, are unconscious and irrational. The genealogy of this contestation can be traced back to at least as early as Lenin's pamphlet *What Is to Be Done? Burning Questions of Our Movement* from 1902. "Our task," rifled Lenin on behalf of the working class, "is *to combat spontaneity*," lest "political consciousness" be "completely overwhelmed." Since then, as Belinda Robnett shows in her critique of the sexism in rational choice models, rarely has the question ever been why spontaneous eruption is innately irrational and continuity the reverse.[30]

The "burning questions" shaping the discourse on movement formation and viability often reinforce the opposition between consciousness and ephemerality, organized planning and passion, reason and speed. In their penchant to evidence the rationality of their players, these questions tend to be about the comparative value between charismatic and grassroots or "bridge leaders." Apropos to faceless movements like Occupy or dispersed ones like Black Lives Matter, these questions also address the comparative value between a movement that is leaderless and one that is "leader-full." When it comes to what makes people feel a movement will be feasible, these formative questions often tilt toward the importance of seeing new political opportunities in state structures, like a congressional seat,[31] or seeing preexisting opportunities in Indigenous structures, like a seat in a church.[32]

The rise of movements, in this latter logic, is governed by resource availability rather than resource regeneration, not to mention redistribution.

I am going to bypass the profound intricacies of these arguments because all I want to say is that the emphasis on rationality and organizations predetermines the temporal shape of a movement as a rise and a fall, as an "emergence and decline," foretold from the start.[33] One can see such chronicles of a fall foretold in increasingly popular tragic emplotments, the kind of plot where the canker is ever in the wound. The reason for this stubbornly alpine shape is that it is, in the end, the lifespan of a movement's organizations that delineates its span of time. Thus even in a study about "bridge leaders," Robnett's seismic study on the formative role Black women played in the civil rights movement as they connected people across lines and nodes of power, the demise of the movement was still the "demise" of a central power, a central organization, the Student Nonviolent Coordinating Committee.[34]

The only burning question out of this bunch for me is what happens to the time of a movement when rationality no longer guides the meaning of organization, coherence, or continuity, when rationality no longer guides the story's plot? The organization might look like a deliberate discoherence, as I show in the case of the Young Negroes' Cooperative League. Continuity might look like a sustained incipience, a "continual advent," in the words of Stephen Best, as I show in the case of Du Bois's Cooperative Guild.

I am not contesting the methods or conclusions of these fore-referenced scholars on the history of social movements. I am simply approaching the question of what a movement is and how to assess its success from a different place. I am less interested in the history of Black cooperatives at large than in the aesthetic choices and sensibilities that made some of the most radical cooperatives possible over the course of the twentieth century, that allowed them to exceed and confound adaptive structures of an abiding anti-Blackness.[35] My authors' claims to being first might very well look like facts plucked from the air, a dismissal of the historical record, a willful forgetting (they all knew of each other, after all), a presentism. But I am less interested in historical fact than in the making of history at the moments of its emergence, uncertain, unset. To quote Myra Jehlen, "a history before the fact" is what I wish to tell.[36] I say "wish" because suspending the determination of how the movement ended or whether it ended at all, writing from the viewpoint of its advents, often felt like drawing a landscape under a lightening flash: cut short, incomplete. But writing from the advents is how I have taken up (or been taken by) nonprogressivism as a method.

I am interested in what Zakiyyah Iman Jackson forcefully calls "an inquisitive practice of description that neither presumes we already have an adequate epistemological model for comprehending the nature and stakes . . . nor presupposes that a sufficient political framework for intervention already exists."[37] I take as my departure into the idea of the social movement E. P. Thompson's *The Making of the English Working Class*, a study that records with seismographic sensitivity the way class tensions produce an evolving idea of class (rather than the reverse), and the way class as an active and self-created category can be seen as synonymous, indeed interchangeable, with the category of the social movement. The social movement is "the conflict where classes are formed." My sole assumption is that the Black cooperative movement did not arise at an "appointed" let alone at an anointed time, but was, to quote Thompson, "present at its own making," its eyes wide open dreaming eyes wide open.

That simple formulation, to be present at its making, shucks off a number of binaries in conventional social movement theory that blind us to the nuances and newness of what my authors carried out under the name of a social movement. The biggest binary to go is, in this regard, the top-down application of movement theory, and with it the notion that an inarticulate mass and an articulate minority, that grievances of the masses and the aspirations of the articulate, form the conjunction necessary to make movements move. This is the thinking that supports the role of a vanguard, and it is still prevalent in a Marxist strain of movement theory as if it were impossible to imagine a dialectic detached from the tension between class consciousness and objective class. The reason Thompson has been a powerful guide for me is that, like C. L. R. James and Ella Baker, he considers movements as essentially headless classrooms, where people try "to make sense of and transform their own situation," where, as James wrote to Martin Glaberman, regarding James's work with Grace Boggs and Raya Dunayevskaya, "we were acting and taking part in what were not large and expensive features of the class struggles against the bourgeoisie, what was in reality small and rather political," but where the organization "gives you a consciousness of yourself meeting the problems that capitalist society poses to you as a person."[38] The movement is a record of those gifts. Nonprogressivism as a method means withholding historical judgment of the actors, means tracing, in words that bear repeating, how "their aspirations were valid in terms of their own experience." No other reading practice has put a greater strain on my capacities as a thinker, but no other seems more urgent.

The Only Way Out Was In   11

The story of social movements over the course of the twentieth century, particularly those on the left, toggle between the grim and the glorious. That toggle about overall achievements has everything to do with the fact that the stories start at the end, rather than at the beginning. Nowhere is this debate about a movement's merits more crowded than in discussions of the civil rights movement. For some, it remains so obviously a disappointment, given its goals of economic redistribution, that every grim assessment can be made merely in passing: "a vision of global class revolution," writes Robin Kelley, "led by oppressed people of color was not an outgrowth of the civil rights movement's failure, but existed alongside, sometimes in tension with, the movement's main ideas."[39] For others, this view must be wholly rebuffed. Indebted to the work of Jacquelyn Hall, Charles Payne reprises with impeccable detail the voter registration campaign in Greenwood Mississippi, the retraction of a federal injunction to cease the racist interference with the campaign, and the subsequent departure of many organizers in the spring of 1963.[40] He then writes, "It is common for scholars to drop the Greenwood story at this point, referring to its 'collapse' or 'demise.' How true that is depends on what we take the movement to be. If we understand it as being fundamentally an attempt to focus national attention, those characterizations can at least be defended. If we understand it as Myles Horton or Ella Baker or Septima Clark would—Are people learning to stand up and fight their own battles?—they are way off the mark."[41] Both these ways of understanding the movement, Payne's and Kelley's, have one thing in common. They are based on an end it delivered, a self-education or a spotlight, an end that furthermore is determined in retrospect. The arc of the movement is decided too soon by virtue of it being decided too late.

You may be interested in knowing that at big debates over a movement's success, the Black cooperative movement isn't even awarded an honorary seat. Despite the central role cooperative economics have played in radical Black thought and continue to play today in cultural studies under the banner of "mutual aid," historical studies of it are scarce. It is still a country of one, Jessica Nembhard's *Collective Courage*, unless we include Du Bois's study from 1907. And as Nembhard observes, "When there is a narrative, the history is told as one of failure."[42] It is precisely their low position in the pecking order of insurgencies that make cooperatives especially fit for the question, what happens to time when it no longer accords to a politics of ends? I address this question most forthrightly in chapter 1, where I attempt to move beyond a politics of ends, but also beyond its presently favored alternative, a politics of means (prefiguration).

The Disappearance of the Present

In his 1989 influential essay "Between Memory and History: Les Lieux de Memoire," Pierre Nora wrote, "We speak so much of memory because there is so little of it left. . . . We speak no longer of 'origins' but of 'births.' Given to us as radically other, the past has become a world apart."[43] Nora was reflecting on a particularly modern obsession with archivization, which emerged by degrees since the early twentieth century in response to a sense that the narrative of American and Western European progress, origin stories, retrievable origins, living memories, and all has been deeply and irrevocably disrupted. If these disruptions registered the feeling for a certain tradition of white historiography that we are living in a present divorced from the past, then a different set of disruptions have registered the reverse within Black studies, that we are living in a past divorced from the present.

David Scott puts this well. Reflecting on the unmistakably modern skepticism toward the language of emancipation, following the collapse of anticolonial revolutionary projects, Scott describes the present as an "accumulation of aftermaths." The present, in short, is bereft of itself. Before the failed promises of historical materialism, "we are left with . . . [only] *aftermaths*,"[44] a present "stricken with immobility and pain and ruin." Evoking José Muñoz's notion of the present as an "impasse," Scott remarks that "a certain experience of temporal *afterness* prevails in . . . what feels uncannily like an endlessly extending present," which is also to say feels like no present at all. Scott implies that the present feels bereft not only because in its endlessness there is nothing to make it distinctly felt but also because there is nothing in it except the past. This book hopes to reimbue the present with some of its own content, to show some of the ways it was felt then, and may be felt now, and felt as something other than catastrophic time.

Of course, my claim that the present as felt then, among my authors, may extend to a present as felt now, among us in Black studies, depends on how I account for where we are on the matter. So let me back up. Scott's macabre image of an "accumulation of aftermaths" reminds me of a song by Sza and Chance the Rapper, "Childs Play." In this slow, interstellar, witch house meets soul meets macabre love song, two Black people, older now and disconsolate with diminished expectations, remember "building a fantasy" of play in a "backyard." The Black woman remembers playing Nintendo's *Street Fighter*, a game that for her meant slaying ("finish him," she recounts the command) a patriarchal and racial calculus to save from a tragedy both

Othello and Desdemona. Her memory releases a whirl of others: "memories keep playing back," they sing in unison. "Just wonder how it used to was, how it used to was." The final phrase, "how it used to was," suggests that even the fantasy of redemption is now, and has always been, enveloped by the past. "How it used to was," instead of, say, "how it used to be," suggests that even in the past there was never a present to inhabit, never a space to be. "How it used to was" expresses the sense that the past is all, at all times, that the present never touched down. In this case the ironic thing about the memories that play back is that "play back" does not mean recur, but recede. Here human time is not human memory, to recall Elisa Gabbert's lapidary phrase from her essay "The Unreality of Time."[45] Human time, if anything, is human pre-memory: nothing ends to be remembered. I say all this because "how it used to was" captures part of the understandably growing pessimism in Black studies, the increased recognition that we are living on aftermaths piling by the hour, and our angels cannot close their wings.

The concept of prefiguration, "living the future now" because one's life depends on it, as Tina Campt says, has largely emerged to correct this diminishment, this virtual disappearance, of the possibilities in the present. In prefigurative politics, how-it-used-to-was has been displaced by, let us say, how-it-were-to-be, a past imperfect displaced by "a future real conditional" (Campt again). According to Carl Boggs who coined the term, prefiguration is a kind of rehearsal, the performance in the very making of the movement of what one hopes social relations will be.[46] So "the future real conditional or *that which will have **had to** happen*" is more accurately considered prefiguration with an added must, prefiguration-plus, "a future that hasn't yet happened but must."[47] It is what "embraces and exceeds" current conditions inside the inner regions of an eruptive present. One can see why prefiguration has been so attractive. Weaving between melancholy and hope, without donning the bright complacency of a presentism, it severs all ties with the belief in historical progress and works hard not to reinstitute another upward telos.

"Works hard," I say, because anti-progressivism is what it promises, not always what it does. For all its beauty, prefigurative politics still holds formidable barriers. The problem I see in many of its iterations is that the present does not manifest a fulsomely futural time, but an empty one, a fact that makes me think perhaps it is not "the future [that] remains to be won," as Kara Keeling contends.[48] Perhaps it's the present. As Joshua Chambers-Letson notes, the transformational capacity of minoritarian performance "has often been conceived of as a discourse on futurity, in which the present is often condemned."[49] Instead of the past flooding the present it's now the future that floods us (favorably), as if the present offers no integral content on its own. Let's consider the prefigurative language of a text that largely made it possible to speak of prefiguration in the first place. José Muñoz's *Cruising Utopia*. The past for Muñoz is "the no-longer-conscious" that endows the future with all its potentiality. When the no-longer-conscious is resituated, not importantly in the present, but in the future as the not-yet-conscious, this process performs a historical materialist critique of the present's limits and of certain abiding genealogies of oppression. Despite the way the "past does things" while "in play with the present," the past and the future are really the only operative terms. They are the "then and there," as Muñoz's quip goes, against the here and now. If the present, drenched in political pragmatism, has any potentiating power it takes it from the future. For Muñoz, it seems, the present is habitable only to the extent that it is not actually present, to the extent it takes the shape of "forward-dawning futurity" (29). That seems to apply even to the presence in the present participle "cruising." While Campt speaks of something here to "embrace" while also to exceed, Muñoz's eyes are firmly on the latter, the "excess" that exceeds itself and the present, itself in the present.

The present, in short, seems to have become less a category of time than a container for it.

I have another concern. I wonder if this kind of excess of excess, rewriting the present under the sign of tomorrow, is motivated by the very target of our critiques, a hidden and beguiling metaphysics of progress. Consider Kara Keeling's incandescent exegesis of alternative temporalities, *Queer Times, Black Futures*. Keeling states that the future is a "temporal disruption," which "exceeds its expression."[50] The future, for her, is another word for a surprising surplus and for pre-cognitive feelings (affects at a granular level). As such, the future "points toward a different" onto-epistemic "regime." Two conflicting concepts of time are being described here, a tension that shows just how sticky and tricky the universalist logic of historical progress is. On the one hand, the future is now and on the other it is a better time to come. We can see the latter in the word "toward," the future as the lived time of forward movement, a future that thus retains a certain linearity. We can see the former, the future as now, in what Keeling later describes as the "felt presence of the unknowable." The future in this sense is actually a sobriquet for a particular kind of existing content, an immanence that however "unknowable," however unspeakable and unspoken, is disruptively here.

To talk about a future expressed but inexpressible, a future that we know is here, at least in part, but will take us time to come to know is to scratch in a line of ascending development. Let me put this differently. To really and lastingly make itself felt, the "felt presence" of the future needs another time to show itself, a better time; or, to put it more concisely, it needs *time* to show itself. For all intents and purposes, the future bears a meaning that just hasn't crystallized yet, a meaning, to return to Muñoz, that is as much forward as "forward-*dawning*." All this is to say, the shadow of the object, the future we've lost, still falls on our very refusals of it.

Proffering an outside that is declaratively inside makes difficult labor, finding an "inwardly elsewhere," to steal Nathaniel Mackey's term, that is not also upwardly mobile. My hope is that this book makes a small contribution to this collective, needful work. My phrase "dreaming the present" alludes to the urgency of recovering the present not purely as brutal, limited, or pragmatic, but also and more so as oceanic, like dreams: nonprogressively expansive beyond what may be immediately visible (or ever visible at all). What most distinguishes these cooperatives from other radical spaces is also what makes them most remarkable: the present is not what they dreamed of escaping. The present is what they dreamed.

This book is thus more a complement than a reply to a larger search for temporalities beneath the crystal stair of teleological time. That search has produced such difficult delights as Stephen Best's "metaleptic history," through which one can better understand what it means to appear only in and by way of a disappearance, "where the slave makes himself once over from the stuff out of which he had been made," a disappearance. It has engendered such tidal insights as Homi Bhabha's "time-lag," a slowing down of modernity that reanimates the dead and remakes the past; Michelle Wright's "Epiphenomenal time," an inclusive now-time with loose connections to causality and tough connections to all of us; Zakiyyah Jackson's "superposition," a refreshing alternative to liminal and interstitial ontology; Soyica Colbert's "contrapuntal time," combatting linearity in a way that weaves a decentered web of affiliations; and I could go on, and on. Yet of all the ways of being in time outside teleology, ways of being in the present have still received the least elaboration, the least space on our canvas. The Black people and people of color who comprise this book struggled, as I believe we struggle, with the blessing that history has never made space for them. As the light got colder than it was when I started, I urgently tried to see what else happens to time when Blacks in turn make space for themselves.

The Chapters

In a time when revolution might feel foreclosed yet never more urgent, how does one work toward impossible ends? How does one persist? With my first chapter, "Sustained Incipience," I explore these questions in the context of W. E. B. Du Bois's lifelong fight to launch domestic and transnational economic cooperatives. I unearth the work of the Negro Cooperative Guild (est. 1918), a multistate, grassroots organization that survived long past its formal dissolution and helped to establish at least ten consumer cooperatives and one cooperative bank.

Expanding the focus on Du Bois's engagement with cooperatives well beyond its customary treatment in the 1930s, and examining meeting notes, editorial columns, photographs of cooperative grocery stores, and letters, I show that Du Bois fashioned a movement that was principally about beginning. Despite all the cooperative stores Du Bois helped to start, he refused to develop them. He then extolled only the inception of his efforts throughout the remainder of his life. Where some might see stasis or delay, I see what Jericho Brown calls "the foreday in the morning," a continual commencement that leaves Brown with the awe, "My God / We leave / Things green." I see an activism of *sustained incipience*: a nondialectical embodiment of time in which continuously beginning a movement is the end goal. While refashioning our reception of this don of dialectics, I show why sustained incipience escaped two dilemmas still hobbling social movement theory: the binary choice between spontaneous and organized action and hierarchies between the leadership and the social base. As I disentangle Du Bois's cooperative philosophy from his socialist vision, I tilt the scholarly emphasis from Du Bois the towering socialist mapping "world revolution" to Du Bois the hardscrabbler, less certain of how to proceed, less confident in progressive time, humbler. I probe the mysteries of motivation beneath the floodlights of total terror.

The second part of the chapter explores the affective economy of this nondialectical time. I reconsider the recent turn in political theory to love as a counter capital affect, helping us endure when hope has lost its salience. I offer the concept of *necromance* to attend to the ways the popular configuration of love as life-giving often overlooks how in the history of slavery and liberal empire love operates as life-taking. Distinct from necromancy, *necromance* is not a process of reviving the dead but of bringing subjects in ever closer proximity to the dead. Grounded in a reading of W. E. B. Du Bois's romantic novel *Quest of the Silver Fleece*, particularly its vision of a cooperative economy and its response to the evolving meaning of love in American culture at the end of the nineteenth century, necromance is both a structure of feeling and a form of writing. The plot of extraordinary adventures to which this love belongs is less a romance than a necromance. Moving into Du Bois's Atlanta Studies and his reflections on the limits of sociology as a discipline, I demonstrate that necromance contests the common conception that in order for grievances to become social movements they must be framed to create feelings of anger or outrage, not melancholic grief.

Cultural scholars, like Lee Edelman, Jack Halberstam, Jared Sexton, and Christina Sharpe have been asking a tart question: How do we live and plan for a day that will never come? In my second chapter, "Planned Failure," I ask, How do we live and plan for a day that must not? I uncover George Schuyler and Ella Baker's Young Negroes' Cooperative League, founded in Harlem in 1930, reaching the West Indies by 1931 with over three hundred members. I prove Baker to be far more radical than she has been received and Schuyler far from the conservative for which he has been remembered. They were anarchic, interrogating the basic legitimacy of the state. Reading, among other things, manifestos, pamphlets, conference brochures, Schuyler's serial novel, letters, financial records, and Baker's unpublished essays beside her teaching material for free classes she designed, I argue that Baker and Schuyler were trying to figure out how we live and plan for a day opposed to that life and plan.

From this conundrum, I puzzle out a concept of performed temporality that I call *planned failure*. We can see this performance perhaps most visibly in their bizarrely impractical membership requirement: nobody older than thirty-six could join the League, but Schuyler was thirty-five at the time of its founding. This meant that they would lose their president less than a year after they began. Reversing the terms through which we have come to understand Black social movements as failed plans, *planned failure* designates the intended demise of the original plan under the assumption that to maintain the form of the organization (by which I mean both the political group and political subject) is necessarily to reinforce the very problems one sought to escape, intersecting hierarchies of gender, race, and class. As an ungovernable generativity, planned failure registers Schuyler and Baker's anarchic suspicion of centralized planning and their wish to redefine the Black public sphere around self-governing enclaves, instead of charismatic leaders. Unsettling the remarkable dominance of the tragic frame to interpret political action, I show the principal role the ecstatics played in their conferences and writing.

I end with chapter 3, "Pluriprescence," where I return to "the insight that we are always outside of history," as Stephen Best remarks, to help me recount the work of Fannie Lou Hamer.[51] No other figure in the book better elucidates the way in which these Black cooperatives sought ways to survive the double afterlife of slavery: the burden and the denial of legal personhood. How does one survive the exclusion and the imposition of normative subjectivity, especially as this paradox manifests in the law?

Hamer, for her part, founded her Freedom Farm Cooperative as a zone to reinvent relations of property and its temporal dynamics. Her 680-acre Freedom Farm provided food, health care, scholarships, free housing, and jobs to poor whites and Blacks primarily in Mississippi but also in Chicago and its surrounding areas. Curiously, she incorporated the Farm as a nonprofit, a business owned by no one but discussed and advertised it as a cooperative, a business owned by all. Reading a range of documents from speeches to grant proposals, I demonstrate that this production of tension in property rights was very much deliberate. She needed some form of private property as a Black woman seeking to protect her private space, to keep her body a body, and to preserve her newly formed commons. But she also needed to detach private property logics from its Lockean tradition. As an ex-sharecropper, Hamer's personal experience reflected the fact that John Locke's labor theory of property reinforced plantation slavery and settler colonialism more than any other property theory in American history.

I have called her production of mutually exclusive property rights and its embodied traversal *pluripresence*. No other word sufficiently names her disconnected but simultaneous inhabitance of space and time, her all-at-once-ness. As a kind of juricraftsman, Hamer used bylaws for by-ends, deploying the law to protect what the law itself cannot legitimate, personal privacy without private property and a commons without ownership. Hamer forged a social movement as a sort of stillness, a movement based on refusing to move: simultaneous emergences across great distances, flash by flash. Together these chapters partially account for the lived transformations of political time, lives expended and the lessons they bare. As you read this book and its modes of presence, I hope you'll see how one of the most forgotten mass movements in American history is profoundly speaking to the challenges of our times.

1 Sustained Incipience

W. E. B. Du Bois and the Negro Cooperative Guild

. . . .

back

at

some beginning it seemed . . .

—Nathaniel Mackey, "Song of the Andoumboulou: 58"

Infancies of Light

The spring before Du Bois started his Negro Cooperative Guild in 1918, he sent out a clarion call to begin a new cooperative movement. "I want to begin the work as a great movement and not piecemeal," he wrote to John Jefferson, dashing a similar message to others. "We could work through the churches and fraternal orders, but only after we have made a success-ful beginning."[1] We can imagine Jefferson wondering, But what makes "a successful beginning"? We can speculate that maybe Du Bois is saying that he wants everything and everyone in place and not "piecemeal." That speculation complies with the Du Bois we today have come to know, the institutionalist, settling for nothing less than an organized attack on capital-ist institutions through socialist ones. In this line, the opposite of "piece-meal" is a grand plan with grand foresight. His Pulitzer Prize–winning biographer David Levering Lewis describes him as a titan of foresight: "the premier architect of the civil rights movement." Likewise, in a recent, am-bitious study by Bill Mullen, Du Bois is pictured as someone sagacious enough to "map" not only the world, but a blueprint, a "typology," of "World Revolution."[2]

I see a different Du Bois—call him a shadow Du Bois—in his largely missed and dismissed work on cooperatives (dismissed as reformist and pro-vincial). Let's return to his call and its wish for a successful start. What might make it most successful, a specific kind of start, say an organized one? If we're true to the word, the problem there is that such a start would take time to evaluate, which means then we're no longer talking about begin-ning but reflecting. Perhaps then the most successful thing, in an oddly cir-cuitous way, would be to simply begin. I think it makes more sense to read his call as saying that the work will begin as a "great movement" only if the beginning is the entirety.

This chapter puts forth an argument for seeing Du Bois's activism around cooperative economics as fashioning a social movement that would be principally about beginning. It would be more than the "right [to experiment and] to fail," as Vaughn Rasberry brilliantly argues in his conception of Du Bois's activism, because this was not "en route to a genuinely emancipatory sequence."[3] It would be more than "the movement of *repeating the beginning*" after the disasters of the communist states, as Slovoj Žižek counsels us to do, "to 'descend' to the starting point and follow a different path."[4] All that is about returning to the state of being born, when this was about birth as a state of being.

What we will see is that Du Bois practiced something I call a *sustained incipience*, something that reminds me of what the poet Elton Glaser calls "infancies of light." For him, the image names shoots of grass in a cemetery.[5] For me, it names the quality of light from a particular kind of survival. Sustained incipience is a critical life practice: not only a place, not only a housed establishment or diasporic web of these establishments, as Du Bois would prod by 1946, but a practice of democratizing time.[6] It was a practice of configuring time as the dual operation, the co-operation, of beginnings and ends, such that the motivation to persist would not be determined by counterattack. The ends toward which political actors worked were always already met as soon as the work began, but because the beginning did not cease, the very notion of meeting ends, and therefore a politics of ends, was thrown into question. We will see Du Bois eventually refusing to move forward on the plans he garnered all the resources and the people to execute. I have called this practice sustained incipience in order to describe an activism and a daring that in the context of teleology would otherwise look like stasis and delay.

I offer an account of Du Bois's activism by embedding it in the conditions of normalized violence confronting African American communities, as well as in the fraught conjunction between capitalism and cooperatives, businesses owned by their patrons. I offer an answer to a slog of questions: How does one work toward impossible ends? How does one persist? What kind of cooperative model inspires persistence among those who face nightmarish backlash, the lethality of growth? To the extent that Du Bois's movement was new, it was because it broke with dialectical histories previously charted by other leaders in the cooperative movement, but also on a more personal level it was Du Bois breaking with Du Bois, the socialist firmly invested in Marxist historical reason. As I unravel the history of the Guild and its afterlives, I will show why I think Du Bois's form of activism fundamentally changes how we understand social movements today.

Roddy's Cooperative Stores

The story of the Guild really begins with a reign of attacks on Black cooperatives at the end of the nineteenth century. The biggest of these attacks occurred in 1889. The largest producer cooperative in African American history, the Colored Farmers' Alliance and Cooperative Union, was disbanded at its headquarters in LeFlore Mississippi by what the Black press almost uniformly called a "massacre." It had more than a million members across "every Southern state," making it the largest Black organization in U.S. history at the time. But when a cackle of pistols, an echolalic glee in the hollow of hate, took the lives or banished its primary leaders, members, and their children, it ended.[7]

Three years later in 1892, proprietors of a consumer co-op in Memphis, Tennessee, the People's Grocery Store, were lynched for amassing competitive profits. As historian Mia Bay notes, this "rocked Black Memphis," the American South, the African American press, and Ida B. Wells. Because one of the dead was Wells's close friend, Thomas Moss, it was this event that was the catalyst for her anti-lynching campaign, another moment that proves the long tessellation between cooperatives and African American letters. But she was also, like Du Bois, tired of enduring the perils of prosperity—the white reaction, as she would report from a mouth in the mob—to Blacks "getting too independent."[8] Beside these events, Du Bois knew well the scattered record of attacks on snuff-size co-ops: buying clubs, newspaper stands, insurance groups, so many miniventures, shrugs and perseverances, pinched into darkness.

The enormity of this loss is what Du Bois marks when he and his research team admit in their study on *Economic Cooperation* a confession that could be mine: "The faith of our people in standing by co-operative enterprise in face of the signal failures of cooperative undertakings among us here, is most remarkable."[9] Perhaps no one knew better than Du Bois the blazing binds of success, the pyromania of envy and entitled control. Against the demise of a mainly nineteenth-century Black cooperative movement, Du Bois would spend the better half of his life inciting its resurgence, trying, as he said, to "foster and encourage" it. To his *Crisis* readers, he proclaimed, against all odds, "whatever happens you CANNOT fail as long as your shareholders are true, and they will be true as long as they share in the profits

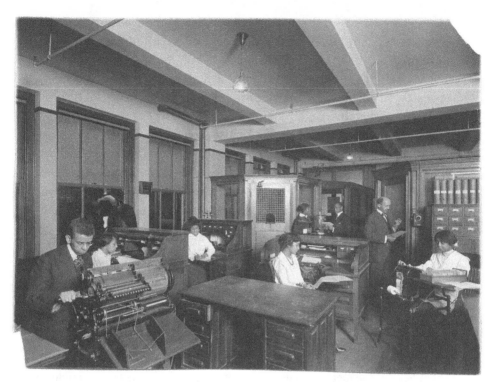

Crisis magazine offices, circa 1918. Du Bois is standing second from right. Portrait Collection—W. E. B. Du Bois (Item: SC-CN-79-0036), Photographs and Print Division, Schomburg Center for Research in Black Culture, New York Public Library.

according to their purchases. Don't be afraid!"[10] We must remember how vulnerable cooperatives were despite government sanction. Co-ops were open targets: legally incorporated, easily slain. That's why, as I show at the end of this chapter through a novel, essays, and a forensics of ephemera, Du Bois would rely on an affect more fit for these conditions than the futurity of expectant hope.

For the moment, however, hope was enough. In a hot and sticky August in 1918, Du Bois and a dozen community leaders gathered for the long-awaited occasion of finally establishing the Guild. The conference was held at the headquarters for the *Crisis* magazine. A loft in the center of Harlem, it bore all the signs of safety and safekeeping: thick, skyward walls; enormous, massy windows rebutting the buzz of Fifth Avenue; thin, hanging lamps like upside down communion cups with infancies of light; and all around the desks, floor, and steel front door a variegated white like the surface of the moon. It was naturally here where all seemed possible, here, as Du Bois rejoiced, in a "fine big office building with elevators, light, and air,"[11] where

James Peter Warbasse, the most prominent figure in the country on economic cooperation, joined the principal of Bluefield Institute Richard Page Sims, president of the NAACP Memphis branch Bert M. Roddy, African American archivist Ruth Anna Fisher, "the first woman ever to be given a key to the British Museum," and a cluster of other preeminents, all to form the Negro Cooperative Guild.[12]

The idea of the cooperative was mischievously simple: "the phenomenon of a group of people buying and selling to themselves—buying necessities at cost and selling them back at retail prices," as Du Bois contended. The difference between the two prices would be returned as dividends so as to make the group, Du Bois cheered, "its own *middle-man*." Attracted to the idea of reappropriating the surplus as coin and sociality, the Guild still had to think about the points of distribution. Jobs, schools, "pageants," "parades," factories, land, "medicine," and "hospitals" were all floated possibilities.[13] Comprised of six state secretaries from the Big Apple to peach country, with Fisher as vice president under chairman Du Bois, this big band of eight declaimed "the object of this Guild is first to study co-operation, secondly, to start co-operative stores and thirdly, to combine those into manufacturing and importing establishments."[14]

Yet besides the fact that these plans would soon be halved and humbled, their scope had already been narrowed by Du Bois's approach to the conference: "small and informal," wrote Du Bois to one attendee, "but I'm expecting it to be the beginning of bigger things."[15] The key word was "beginning" without definite ends, for this would be the leitmotif of everything from Du Bois's purview to the open-endedness of the conference, set at 2 P.M. on Sunday, that day's close and the next day's schedule to be decided on ad hoc. Despite or in part because of this mystical openness to such an anticipated, pre-celebrated meeting, announced in the *Crisis* almost monthly since January, droves across the country, both invitees and onlookers, were positively elated. Warbasse, president of the Cooperative League USA, received his invitation less than a week before the conference day, yet shot back a promissory upon receipt of the letter: "I shall be in New York at the office of the League on the 26th, and shall be glad to attend a meeting at your office to discuss co-operative organization among colored people. Please leave word at the league office as to the time when you would desire my attendance."[16] A rush of folks kept asking when the event would occur, and when it passed by, letters gusted in asking what was just missed.[17] Everyone could feel it, as much "the beginning of bigger things" as bigger things beginning.

But when the conference was over, Du Bois seemed set on mystifying the contents of the congress: the contentions, the personal fears and projections, the ideological range between the extremes, say, of George Mitchel, the egalitarian and self-effacing secretary for Pennsylvania, and Charles Lane, the clownishly patronizing secretary for D.C. Lane was someone who non-sequitured to Du Bois in a birthday message that same year, "a lawyer friend told me that living among colored people had made me much more tolerant and mellow than I would have been had I not had this experience."[18] From such a plurality, mirror to the spectrum of cooperative belief, one would easily expect less consensus than concession, less agreement than grief. But unlike Du Bois's reports of the famed Niagara or Amenia conferences, in which he boasted that barbed differences ultimately fused into a singular vision, Du Bois measured out in droplets his reflections on the Guild's making.[19] In all his published works, he did not even name the members.

How bizarrely brief for the sole organization of "our economic way out, our industrial emancipation."[20] Someone by the name of C. W. Banton wrote Du Bois asking for "the results of the cooperation meeting," results which were "mentioned in this month's *Crisis*," he pointed out. Banton was president of D.C.'s Commercial Study Club and intent on helping to fulfill the Guild's first goal, the establishment of study groups. To Banton, as to all, Du Bois was curt: "the results of our meeting in New York was the formation of the Negro Cooperative Guild."[21] Du Bois then listed its three objectives, rather unnecessarily, for, as Banton had already told him, they were "mentioned in this month's *Crisis*" (the September issue).

Did Du Bois intend to stoke desire through mystification? In the November *Crisis* he asked in a report of the Guild, "What is this thing which may be the greatest result of the war? Whatever it is, it is worth study. The Negro Cooperative Guild . . . [is] encouraging study."[22] For all the promise the Guild beheld, a slim crystal of hope on the wreckage of war, the Guild, like cooperation, would attract the masses through enigma. The allure of this enigma—a conspicuous concealment of who the leaders were—was that it signified the openness of the movement, the freedom of movement, but most of all, the subordination of a new leadership to an old social base.

By the start of 1919 the Guild was in full if zigzag motion. Since returning to West Virginia, state secretary Richard Sims had been "trying to get together a group of men that will be interested in such a movement and at the same time select some good reader who will direct their study."[23] By January he had done it. Four teachers, one the prominent Jones W. Scott, English professor and president of the West Virginia Teachers' Association of Colored Teachers, "agreed to conduct study clubs in their city."[24] But the problem was that Scott intended to take this into a liberal capitalist agenda. That would have made Du Bois positively bristle.[25] In a 1911 speech to the Huntington YMCA, Scott said, "I have often wondered what a vast difference it would have made in the general progress of the Huntington Negro if there had been among the early comers a few capitalists, a few professional men."[26] Scott wasn't alone. One John H. Pilgrim "proposed . . . to form a cooperative enterprise . . . in the nature of a Joint Stock Company chartered under laws of Liberia."[27] Despite the interest this international ambition must have piqued for Du Bois, who was, after all, concluding preparations for his first Pan-African Conference, he all but reprimanded Pilgrim: the Guild is "not a profiteering scheme and it is quite different from a Joint Stock Company." But Du Bois was sure to enclose "reading matter" and request that Pilgrim "act as State Secretary for the Canal Zone."[28] All these prospects were promising, but they needed to be recommenced.

The Guild took credit for creating five cooperative stores. It is the sheer size of this claimed achievement that makes Du Bois's focus on its beginnings, rather than on what the stores became, so peculiar. When Bert M. Roddy, secretary for Tennessee, left *Crisis* headquarters to return to Memphis, he "entered upon an active campaign," Du Bois wrote, "for the introduction of co-operation throughout the South." Roddy did introduce a chain of five Citizens' Co-operative Stores, but Du Bois would boast that the Guild inspired and produced them. "Twelve representatives came from seven states and adopted a tentative program," Du Bois said to the Twentieth Century Fund. "Out of this came the establishment of several local efforts," including Roddy's meat markets.[29] Du Bois's boast was a sham. Contrary to the implication of the phrase "out of this came," the construction of Roddy's meat markets began long before the gilded gathering, not immediately after it. To be sure, the first stores physically opened in the spring of 1919, a year after the conference, but in July 1917 Roddy apologized for the delay in correspondence and shared his recent accomplishments: "I guess you have wondered why you have not heard from me any further with references to the Citizens' Co-operative Movement, . . . the charter is now drawn and the application signed, . . . we are planning for a county wide campaign which will open next week."[30]

It's a little unbelievable, isn't it, that Du Bois would appear to so boldly and publicly lie? It'll be hard but I'm going to try to convince you that there was something deeply honest in it. The vagueness of Du Bois's language, "out of this came"—I think of it as a word-eddy, a sort of circular pursuit of a lost time—implied the Guild at once inspired and produced the stores, and that implication reveals something central about Du Bois's activism: motivation and production shaded into each other. No doubt, these reports have been misleading. They rebuff the best efforts at historical precision: "we know that at least two cooperatives grew out of that meeting," writes economic historian Jessica Nembhard, "Citizens' Co-operative Stores in Memphis and the Cooperative Society of Bluefield Colored Institute." Nonetheless, the reports, like the letters, the ad hoc meetings, and the excursions to come, may hold their power in their break from positivist causality. Emblematized by the eddy "out of this came," Du Bois's activism severs the line between cause and effect.[31]

Du Bois wrote in the December *Crisis* of 1919 that "among those present [at the Guild meeting] was B. M. Roddy of Memphis, Tennessee, who returned home and entered upon an active campaign for the introduction of co-operation throughout the South—beginning naturally enough with Memphis."[32] The most important part of this statement is the easiest to miss: Roddy "returned home." Whatever role the meeting played in materializing Roddy's efforts, the first thing it did was inspire a return, a return to a local, decentralized "campaign." "In the vicinity of each store is a Negro co-operative guild composed of stock holders of the Company," who "keep abreast of cooperative literature, open discussions and offer suggestions." By implying that Citizens' arose in August 1918 from his loft, Du Bois effectively reverse-marched its development, affixed it to the tense of the present continuous. Or as he said with one word in the *Crisis*, affixed it to the tense of an "introduction."

When Du Bois published the summary of Roddy's stores in the *Crisis*, he drew his readers' attention to their beginnings quite forcefully. Above the essay he posted the following picture: a boxy, black Ford, faces left on the page, the name of Roddy's establishment branded on the side, and stamped beneath, like a logo, in white bold caps: NO. 1.

The image is dizzying. The letters on the car pull our eyes one way; the direction of the car pulls them the other. We might ask why a vehicle, not the store itself, would be pictured first, the store occurring only on the second page. And why, if by December, five stores were already operating, five to the pride of plodding Roddy, would our focus be funneled solely to the first? Roddy gave a speech at the National Negro Business League Convention, in which he mentioned "this month [August 1919] Cooperative Store No. 5 was opened." In fact, he proudly mentioned it twice, and the second time was followed by a "hearty applause."[33] Was Du Bois again suggesting that the

Advertisement car of Roddy's Co-operative Stores. W. E. B. Du Bois, "Roddy's Citizens' Co-operative Stores," *Crisis* 19, no. 2 (December 1919), 48. Jean Blackwell Hutson Research and Reference Division, Schomburg Center for Research in Black Culture, New York Public Library.

cooperative itself was a type of motion, a temporal tension between the past and the present? The image of the Ford, the slim distinctions between inspiration and inception, and inception and finality captured in the phrase "out of this came" all point to the notion not of back-stepping into a modernist nostalgia but of conceiving a program as perpetually just conceived.

Tomorrow Again

The impression may linger that these recursions of potentiality are less an activism than a fear to act. It may also be objected, rather justifiably, that Du Bois was trying simply to evade the state, its technologies of surveillance encroaching faster than a comet by the 1920s and 1930s as J. Edgar Hoover consolidated the FBI. As I have argued elsewhere, cooperative economics as a counter surveillance strategy is certainly at play. But here I am after a broader or, to put it better, a more granular activism that both enfolds and gives way to clandestine maneuvers.

So a brief remark on my approach, which has been largely determined by the nature of cooperative economies themselves. Polymorphous mechanisms for the democratic dissemination of the surplus, cooperative economies are at once local and fringe. Their protean and peripheral nature, along with their procedures of countering capitalist accumulation (asset locks, dividends, one-vote per person no matter the size of the purse), invite a kind of Foucauldian analysis. Foucault strips down the mechanisms at work in relations of power and resistances, revealing how power became organized less and less around a unified and repressive sovereign than around productive and intricate schemas, how power not only takes you, but makes you. Foucault therefore focuses on the strategic field of resistance and power "at its extremities," its "capillary" and "local" forms, rather than its consolidated and centralized ones, its seemingly benign forms over its putatively obvious ones. I follow these resistances into zones they seem unlikely. For I am analyzing an activism immanent in the interstices and borders of power, a borderline activism in constant friction with capitalist enterprise.

Thus whether Du Bois intended this activism or not is beside the point, for its "intention, if it has one, is completely invested in its real and effective practices." Because of its embeddedness in power through a range of discursive forms, embodied and textual, from a social gathering to a Word-eddy, sustained incipience is "individual and nonsubjective" at the same time. Further: the very seriality of Du Bois's gestures endows them with a consistent but not uniform structure. My approach is not to extract and partition Du Bois's intentions and desires. It is to make new sense, not rational or commonsense, of their effects, and of the mechanism behind their compulsion to repeat.

The simultaneously personal, impersonal, and repetitive nature of Du Bois's activism brings me to the second reason for my approach: the productive force of normalized violence. This violence issues from at least two places: strategies of backlash that effectively tarmacked previous efforts and lives; and Du Bois's own attempt to consolidate power through organizations, institutions, and a centurion of leaders. Because sustained incipience is an effect of a violence that takes on its own life, we may consider it a fugitivity, "a desire for and a spirit of escape and transgression of the proper and the proposed." Transgressive by nature, fugitivity "moves outside the intentions of the one who speaks and writes, moving outside their own adherence to the law and to propriety." One example of fugitivity Fred Moten hears in Du Bois is, of all things, the way he speaks, the very sound of his voice. Moten listens to a recording of Du Bois and hears him speaking with a whistle under his breath as he reflects on the lynching of Sam Hose. "Every sibilant sound is subject to the rude extension of a whistle."[34]

This is the last thing one expects to hear from someone who exerted such control over his speech.

Du Bois pronounced his letters with the sparest of breath. He tapped out syllabic sound so that words took on the aura of clipped evocation, vowels withdrawn, consonants discontinued, each phrase a seductive fuse of intimation and fact. Thinking of this whistle in relationship to fugitivity and pornographic terror, Moten describes it as a "transgressive scar." "What I'm after," he says, "is some recognition of the accidental, contingent and extra-intentional nature of the voice's essential quality, some acknowledgement of the transgressive scar on the body of the instrument."[35] As a partial and unwitting effect of violence, the violence of others and Du Bois's own, we may consider his activism a wild assembly of "transgressive scars." His speech was the soundtrack, the audible analogue, to the micro-dramas of his sustained incipience.

Following Moten, I'm after some recognition of how the ethics of cooperation Du Bois himself prescribed might have commandeered an extra-intentionality, sounding subtleties of gesture over dynamos of action. Much more attention has been paid, after all and for good reason, to Du Bois's grand acts on the global stage. But we can see that self-doubt and failure ultimately cohered as a productive, regulating ideal—not a defect—in his social movement strategy. After forty years of effort, Du Bois wrote to sociologist Ira Latimer in 1932, "Of course, I think the cooperative movement is the way out . . . but I do not know how to get it properly started." This was a startling admission not only because Du Bois had already done so much, from launching the first national conference on cooperative economics in 1898, this on the gales of the just-established International Cooperative Alliance (1895), which prevails today, to gathering and connecting scores of cooperatists. It was startling also because at no other point in American history up to the 1930s had cooperatives become so prominent. Whether you were a producer, consumer, or worker cooperative, these were your golden years so far as numbers are concerned. More than one-third of producer cooperatives since 1790 arose in the 1930s. Because cooperatives saved the government money on unemployment relief, they received droves of federal grants through the 1933 Wagner-Lewis Relief Act. And right there in New York, Du Bois had only to walk a few blocks from his Fifth Avenue office to witness what Nembhard calls, perhaps punning on the New Deal, the "great deal of activity": the Harlem Consumers' Cooperative, Harlem's Own Cooperative, the Modern Cooperative Association, the Active Citizen's Cooperative Association, the 137th Street Housing Corporation in

Harlem, and, farther up the state, the Lackawanna Consumers' Cooperative in Buffalo.[36]

In the realm of cooperative economics, Du Bois's self-doubt, to which we have paid little attention, was his greatest ally. Because he refused or repeatedly failed to develop his cooperative commonwealth, a global federation of housed cooperatives,[37] fating him for an astonishingly long time, pre-century to mid-century, to always begin again in every facet of cooperative life—theory, plans, action, until all rush-fused into a gesture—cooperatives could emerge anywhere by any hand. And as perpetual beginnings, they could not be demised, they could only prevail: always the beginning, never the fall.

Roddy, for his own part, appeared to have taken this logic to heart. He expressed this by rewriting a popular poem of the times titled "Unsubdued." When the bank that granted the initial funds for his grocery stores, Solvent Savings Bank and Trust Co., the only Black-owned bank in Memphis, was forced to close for fines of alleged embezzlement, he wrote a mournful essay and sent it to Du Bois. "A Bank Fails for a Million," he called it, and he decided to end it with a revision of a popular poem by Samuel Kiser. His revision read, "They are old, they are bent, they are cheated / Of all that youth urged them to win / But count them not with the defeated / For tomorrow again, they begin."[38]

Keiser wrote "Unsubdued" (1911) in the I-voice, but Roddy's speaker switched that to a "they," and instead of closing with Keiser's "name them not with the defeated," Roddy wrote, "count them not."[39] Rodney's changes, taken together, "count" instead of "name," "they" instead of "I," signify the unruly time of an unruly collective, not only unaccounted for by the poet's location, but impossible to count. Roddy asserts that to "again . . . begin" is a principle of political action that, like the phrase itself, a deviation from the norm of "to begin again," abides as an off-beat, rejuvenating and vital, beneath the stern rhythm of workday clock time. Unlike the phrase beginning again, again beginning lacks an origin from which to measure its duration. The again beginning, awkward as that sounds, a suggestively awkward sound, is an extension, a sustainment, of a start that started yesterday, always yesterday, since "they" begin not tomorrow, but every tomorrow, tomorrow and tomorrow and "tomorrow *again*." This beginning from a past that is here in every present, this, if you will, sustained incipience is the inconspicuous machination, inconspicuous as the move from "name . . . not" to "count . . . not," the indivisible machination, indivisible as the switch from "I" to "They," the mighty machination against capitalist time.

The Ghost of Ralph Bunche

For the first few years, Roddy's stores were a model or about as near a model of cooperative ethics as Du Bois would touch. But eventually they would prove their fraught connection with capitalist firms. Roddy was not clamoring after money but generational solidarity. He fought for an equal distribution of resources and profits, along with jobs for present and future generations. At the 1919 convention of the National Negro Business League, he said to his audience, clapping with gleeful approval, "Now, possibly, the question may be asked: Why is it that you limit your shares of stock to blocks of one to ten shares? Now, in the corporation we will sell no man more than ten shares of stock, no matter whether he was able or offers to buy more than ten shares or not; but we will sell to the humblest man or woman as many as ten shares—the same number that we would sell to the wealthiest Negro in our town; our object is to place our stock in as many Negro homes as we possibly can, and to make our enterprise COOPERATIVE in fact as well as in name."[40] By mentioning the importance of keeping the stock inside the home, which would then be passed to posterity, Roddy was talking about an "asset lock." That means locking into place a set amount of capital. By preserving the cooperative as a collective good to be passed on to future generations, asset locks prevent "demutualization" or degeneration to a capitalist firm. Without the lock, employee-owners would be tempted, especially near retirement, to sell their shares to investors.[41] The point was to transmute the "stock" of private property into a protected commons.

Such voluntary resource sharing without the risk of overuse was what Roddy stressed in his speech. He claimed that his stores displaced the debtor relation of plantation shops by relationships of reciprocity. And reciprocity, as he imagined it, should be thought over a longue durée, generationally. Roddy insisted, "We are trying to make every Negro home feel . . . that some of the money they are spending will come right back to them in the form of dividends at the end of the year, plus the equally if not more valuable privilege of helping to provide employment for their own boys and girls."[42] The members might indeed "feel" some money would come back, but there was no guarantee. Roddy's point was that the most important return on their investment was not the cooperative firm and its revenues, but an affective tie to even more than the living: the yet to be born.

Nevertheless, Du Bois found significant fault with Roddy's stores. "We [the Guild] regret that the stores thus auspiciously established have not adopted the full cooperative principle, namely one vote to each shareholder."

TWO OF THE MEMPHIS CO-OPERATIVE STORES.

"Two of the Memphis Cooperative Stores." W. E. B. Du Bois, "Roddy's Citizens' Co-operative Stores," *Crisis* 19, no. 2 (December 1919), 49. Jean Blackwell Hutson Research and Reference Division, Schomburg Center for Research in Black Culture, New York Public Library.

Voting rights were instead scaled to the number of shares held. The "principle" of direct democracy was the regulating motive to invest and stay involved in a cooperative, the "coordination mechanism" as some economists call it. Du Bois was already stepping away from his idea of centralized leadership through a Talented Tenth. Horizontal rather than vertical collaboration, for which cooperatives were known, ideally creates "relations based on trust more than on direction, thanks to the fundamental role of intrinsic motivations and procedural fairness."[43] Roddy went on to build a total of thirteen stores, all of which appeared to close in 1928, but for Du Bois looking ahead in 1919, the canker was in the wound.

The poultice might have been the aesthetic of the stores' interior, two of which were photographed, full page, in the *Crisis* report. Du Bois cautioned Roddy in a letter, "it must be a matter of honor among [the members] to use [the stores] for every single thing that they can even in spite of temporary and incidental disadvantage."[44] By all appearances the stores' aesthetic tried to solicit just that honor by adopting an aesthetic of the infinitely inchoate.[45]

The resemblance between the pictures of Roddy's stores, which themselves recalled pictures from other periodicals, suggested they were part of a bigger genre of cooperative aesthetics. These images implied almost uniformly that the experience of the co-op denatured the allure of shopping, the buzzing frenzy of options for newly nuanced needs. With their repetition of "basic goods," as Du Bois would insist, "flour, meal [and] meats . . . sugar, coffee, teas, etc.," an echolalia of cans neatly queued and stacked on shelves behind the cashier, then pyramidized like a Warhol in the middle of the shop—with this repetition cooperative stores left you supplied, if not satisfied.[46] They attempted to change the requisites of personal satisfaction, along with the borders and basis of the wanting self. Could you slake your desires with just a few things? Could you question and revise what you really needed? Could the desire to support others, the merchant, the members, the future's future members, occupy as much space as the desire to support yourself?

Such attraction of loyalty is what the layout of the co-op attempted to achieve by winnowing down the profusion of wants. Through a copy and paste of needs, it effected a line, however arbitrary and shifty, between desiring and needing anything. Its dynamics of design was a minimalist modernism, an emphasis on balanced and clean similitude, a zone hermetically sealed from the contaminants of capital. If hulking department stores or large chain groceries intoxicated its customers with a bounty of glossy differences, laminated and limitless distinctions, that zesty appeal of personal freedoms, then the small consumer co-op detoxed its members with deglossed similarities. It floated that uncanny sense of the common good, that overdrive or outer-will to do for the other of oneself. Cooperative stores, like Roddy's, seemed to believe that if the reflet sheen of buying could be dulled to the tenor of daily life, then people would see beneath the goods a civic republicanism of endangered service. If consumerist needs could be contained and copied, copied and recopied, almost to the point of parody, then those same needs might start to feel nugatory and unneeded. This was the paradox of the "unselfish" consumer co-op: a movement downward and inward spelled an enormous movement out.

No wonder they called themselves the Guild. Since medieval times guilds were groups of producers or merchants that agreed to a limit on "the possibilities of profit, and, hence, [to] *a self-limitation of needs*."[47] Yet this Guild that stood for a thrift of desire, by spring of 1920 had Decembered into dusk. Vice President Ruth Fisher left New York to study at the London School of Economics. Richard Sims, along with other state secretaries, were still "interested in training persons in the cooperative idea," but Du Bois, with the pressures of his Pan African conferences, felt forced to leave "without further encouragement . . . perhaps the most promising of my projected movements."[48] Referring to both the cooperative movement and his Guild as one entity, Du Bois said, decades later, "It *temporarily* failed."[49] Around the same time he wrote a letter asking for funds for the cooperative movement, and here of all places, he was equally double-tongued about its duration. "Would it not be possible," he wrote, "for the Twentieth Century Fund to make an investigation into the economic plight of the Negro in cooperation with our proposed institute and with the idea of exploring the possibility of a distinct movement toward consumers cooperation among Negroes? Such a movement is already under way not only in the North but in the Southeast and Southwest."[50] When I first read this I had to ask, If the movement already exists why explore its possibility? Perhaps the exploration of possibility is the movement that exists.

In closing, I'd like to turn to a somewhat haunted study by Ralph Bunche. This was a study on the "tactics" of *Negro Betterment and Interracial Organizations* that Bunche drafted in 1940. Bunche won the 1950 Nobel Peace Prize for having finally achieved an armistice between Israel and its bordering Arab States, momentarily ending the Arab-Israeli War. No one tendering his accomplishments would have thought to mention that study on tactics he prepared a decade prior for Carnegie Corporation's immensely influential

The Negro Cooperative Guild

The Negro Cooperative Guild was a brainchild of Dr. DuBois.
On August 26 and 27, 1938, a conference of those interested in
establishing cooperative enterprises among Negroes throughout
the country, was held at the office of the _Crisis_. The call
was issued by Dr. DuBois. Twelve representatives from seven
states attended and an organization was formed under the name
of the Negro Cooperative Guild. This association adopted a
three-point program: (1) To induce individuals and clubs to
study modern consumers cooperation, its extent, methods and
objects; (2) To hold an annual meeting for encouraging the
establishment of cooperative stores; (3) To form a central
committee for the guidance and insurance of such stores.

There is no evidence that the Guild ever advanced very far
beyond ~~the organization stage~~ this first conference, though Dr. DuBois is
still ~~preaches~~ a staunch advocate
~~and~~ cooperative ~~enterprise~~ enterprise for
Negroes.

fifteen-hundred-page survey of Blacks in America, *An American Dilemma*. Written from a summarizing, all-of-the-above perspective, *An American Dilemma* controversially occluded all-of-the-below, like Bunche's study itself, given merely a footnote. Across the span of two paragraphs, Bunche provides a kind of snapshot-chronicle on Du Bois's Guild. And this snapshot provides a magical synopsis on all the issues of duration in question throughout this chapter.

One issue above all—how to write a history about the process of beginning, how to ascribe a birth and death date to something that coldshoulders the very effort to place it in sequential time—surfaces in Bunche's fastidious edits and marginalia. For a snapshot, it is shocking to see all the trouble Bunche went through to mark and remark the scarcest, almost negligible, nuances of time, yet he appeared to have the same difficulty as I with giving the Guild a timeline. Bunche's edits become even more shocking when we consider that he very likely copied out this plot summary, letter by letter, from Du Bois's 1940 autobiography *Dusk of Dawn*, which relays everything exactly in this order but without any of the punctuation or the enumeration Bunche inserts. Bunche turns infinitives into imperatives, turns a present that has not happened yet into a future that must happen now, he turns periods into semicolons, three finalities into three phases, and then numbers each of them, all as if to retrofit a tail wing of historical ascent. One wonders how Bunche could give such precise and sensitive attention to the duration of the Guild (he pencils in "very" to qualify "far"), yet at the same time overlook the document's only error, a glaring error at that: his statement that the Guild was born "On August 26 and 27, 1938."

How did 1918 become 1938, a one buckling to a three? Was this an accident, an impression, or an alien sleight of hand? Having written this scrimp, no more than a scrimp, in 1940, did Bunche on some level believe the Guild just began? Because the archive has offered me no time or place of death regarding the organization, I wonder if Bunche somehow knew of "evidence" that the Guild "advanced far" but not "very far," or, contrarily, if he were saying by his phrase "no evidence," saying quite suggestively, that there was no evidence whatsoever to distinguish the distance of "far" from that of "very far." On a historical odometer they would have registered the same. I hazard from Bunche's failure to pinpoint the Guild's beginning and hence the Guild's end a guess that the beginning could not be pinned. By 1940 the Guild was formally long gone but somehow still going.

Beyond Prefiguration: W. C. Matney and "The Comet"

Du Bois himself had intimated that his "most promising" movement along with the Guild was somehow still moving. His intimation raises questions about the measure and meaning of longevity to social movement organizations. The rule and ruler of duration is by far the most commonly applied criteria of a movement's value and validity, an almost trans-disciplinary fetish.

It has become, however, increasingly popular to rethink longevity along the lines of what is known as "prefiguration": beginning to experience what we want to become, living what's yet to arrive. Coined by sociologist Carl Boggs in 1977, prefiguration is "the embodiment, within the ongoing political practice of the movement, of those forms of social relations, decision making, culture and human experience that are the ultimate goal."[51] Prefiguration is what literary scholars might call, following philosopher of language J. L. Austin, a "performative utterance" in the flesh, a consequential action in and of itself. These are ritualized statements, like "I swear" or "You're under arrest," that can come only from certain contexts. This politics of means, a kind of now-politics, we could say, arose as a contrast to a politics of ends, which tend to chart social movements as an arc. Nick Srnicek expresses this arc-view perfectly when he says, summarizing leftist movements since the 1990s in Europe and the U.S., "a common pattern emerges: resistance struggles rise rapidly, mobilise increasingly large numbers of people, and yet fade away only to be replaced by a renewed sense of apathy, melancholy and defeat."[52] Hoping to be a corrective to despair and an intervention into dominant schemes of social movement time, prefigurative acts are "synecdochic expressions of social movement goals."[53] But they have their critics. According to Achille Mbembe, for example, this means-magnified politics paints time as a "simple sequence in which each moment effaces, annuls, and replaces those that preceded it, to the point where a single age exists within society."[54]

In this section I hope to show why sustained incipience is an alternative to prefiguration, and what this alternative means for the movement's leadership structure. Sustained incipience names a recursivity where starting a social movement is not the end goal but the end and the goal, where the means are the beginnings and the beginnings are the ends in a continuous recommencement. The difference between a prefigured future and sustained incipience is that the first ascribes a completion to the political act, whereas the second is gestural with no desire to be complete.[55]

No matter how one pictures a movement emerging in time, that picture will simultaneously be one of its leadership. As Michael Hardt notes, "Modern revolutionary theorists continuously grappled with the problem of leadership, of strategy and tactics. Their solutions generally fall into two groups, both of which pose a dialectic between spontaneity and authority."[56] Hardt, for instance, offers his own solution to this dilemma, and it has the added benefit of proclaiming to elaborate Du Bois's vision, who was, Hardt says, "certainly right that people are not innately capable of collective self-rule and that democracy is not and cannot be spontaneous."[57] Hardt's solution? A contingent relay between spontaneous self-rule and gradual centralization. This relay would be fluidly performed by what he and Antonio Negri famously dub "the multitude": "a radical diversity of social subjectivities that do not spontaneously form together but instead require a political project to organize."[58]

Hardt is adding nuance and fluidity to the temporal logics that sociologists Michael Schwartz and Naomi Rosenthal described in their momentous essay from 1989, "Spontaneity and Democracy." "In one view," they write, "'continuity and emergence, planning and impulse, organizational strategy and individual spontaneity are polar tendencies' in social movements. In the other, spontaneity and structure are neither discontinuous or opposed."[59] Rosenthal and Schwartz argue for "the *intermingling* of spontaneous and planned action," a relative equivalence. Instead of an intermingling or relay between gradualism and spontaneity, between the ongoing and the gotgoing, what would it look like to see them as metonymic, the leadership in the base, the base in the leadership, bearing the same relationship to each other as a comet's tail to its head?

A comet: this was the image Du Bois plucked from the sky, as we will see, to project onto the present-present continuous a combined but not equivalent spontaneity and organization. Here the leadership and the social base do not so much form a single collective body but something akin to a transpersonal feedback loop, where their beginning and their ends are indivisible but different. As it applies to Du Bois, the problem with the common resolutions above to the erroneous split between "planning and impulse" is that they are trapped in their own impulse to estimate the comparative value of the leaders and their tail, as though they could combine to make a mathematical fraction.

Though helpful in their own right, such approaches are indebted to what Pheng Cheah calls the "central principle" of historical materialism, its birthmark if you will: the organization. As an operation and historiography that purports to project and summarize a trajectory of class struggle, historical materialism, Cheah points out, holds that "the dynamism of matter comes from the activity or process of organization, the ordering of things through dialectical relations of mutual interdependence such that they become parts or members of a whole, where each part is an organ with its designated function within an integrated or systemic totality."[60] The organization is the structural analog to the totality of performances that regenerate, adrenalize, and sometimes sunder relations of production over time. In our context, the organization can be seen as an order of things where each part in an integrated whole is either a leader or a follower bearing a prescribed, even if contingent, duty, often with the mandate of gender, racial, and sexual regulations. Now we will see Du Bois, against his own impulse, look at the emergence of a social movement and its coeval structure of participation phenomenologically, not axiologically, not through a measure of relative value, but through a vision of relative light.

In the late 1930s, less than a decade after Roddy's stores closed, a student-run co-op at Bluefield Institute was shut down.[61] Helping to get this store off the ground was by Du Bois's estimate his second greatest concrete accomplishment. This corner room of a shop had an enormous reach, operating enough business to fund the student newspaper and wrest its independence from the tightening school budget. Founded in 1924 by Bluefield instructor William Clarence Matney, the venture attracted rhapsodies up and down the East Coast by 1928. "A splendid piece of work," said Harvard economist Frederick Nichols. A "very worthwhile contribution to the general business education," said the U.S. Department of Commerce. "Exceptional," exclaimed the president of the American Cooperative League. And accolades from local papers and lay observers soon followed.[62]

At no point did any figure working with Black cooperation receive more praise and backing from Du Bois than William Clarence Matney, a disabled vet with a daybreak smile. This was someone who seemed to see the present in two dimensions, the present future and the present fact. He offered what at first seems like a pretty bizarre answer to a question on his Harvard Business School application, asking him if he had "present self-support." He wrote, "disabled ex-soldier." If he meant he had a pension, it would have been clearer to say that. But it was as though his disability, a present fact, confessed a present future of a hidden strength, an inner "self-support." Perhaps he was slyly critiquing operations of ableism yoked to a liberal regime of institutional recognition. His sneaky refusal to construe his disability as an incapacity in general, or an "enfeebled intelligence" in particular, presents him as already beyond what Roderick Ferguson calls the "regulatory affirmation" of the minoritized: institutional inclusion that works by way of "ascribing ability in some instances and disability in others."[63]

Maybe because Matney thought or sensed that cooperative ethics encourage a refusal to be enlisted in mechanisms that give proportional rank to reason, capacity, and worth, he took early leave from Harvard. He left the university to direct the Commercial Department at Bluefield Institute, his alma mater. There he committed himself to a radical vein of cooperative philosophy with near monastic devotion. Du Bois took note, eventually crowning him three *Crisis* awards for commendable public service, best essay in economics, and best essay of the year 1928. The applause effectively silenced his bygone Harvard record, in which one dean declared, "he was not a strong student with us" and placed him on probation.[64] Du Bois was not only augmenting Matney's resume, he was seeking on Matney's behalf a scholarship from Warbasse so Matney could study cooperative economics abroad (in France, England, or a Scandinavian country). A year after "the state of West Virginia . . . forbade [the] continuance" of Matney's Bluefield cooperative, Du Bois gave Matney even more support.[65] He lettered to Warbasse in 1929, "I want very much to start with [Matney] as a nucleus a movement for co-operation among American Negroes." The die was cast for a new phase of Du Bois's cooperative plans, the 1930s, but despite widened public interest it would strikingly resemble panurgic yesteryears.

In Du Bois's letter to Warbasse, the role that Matney will play is decisively indecisive. If Du Bois wants to use "[Matney] as a nucleus," does he mean he wants to start alongside him, before him, or start inseparably with him as one nucleus?[66] Nor is Warbasse's role all that much clearer. According to the plan, as the "experiment" unfolds, at it starts without a starter, these three men would disperse across the country, deliberate, and galvanize. "I should think that Harlem would be the best starting point and that the experiment should be accompanied by a series of lectures by Mr. Matney, yourself and myself covering a whole year and bringing together a large and interested body of intelligent colored people. I believe that three years' work of this sort would start a cooperative movement which would in time transform their economic situation and be an asset for the rest of the country." Two years study, three years assembly, a quinquennium of incitement by way of seduction in which no one predominates is also a period in which roles can be revised, removed, reversed.

This would not be a leaderless movement, but a movement in which the leadership remains in question and fluid. This fact is captured in Du Bois's closing words: "I am writing to ask if you have any advice or suggestion as to how this problem could be inaugurated." On one level the movement *is* "this problem" and on many more the problem is the leadership. And this was not to be solved but sirened, not fixed but sustained, through, again, a generation of doubt.

If Matney was messiah, he was messiah unborn. He was a "nucleus," a ghostly coming-into-life, which gives his power to revive a movement the paradox of waiting for the movement to revive itself. Psychoanalyst Wilfred Bion offers instructive insights into the potential effects or the potential reason for framing a social movement as perpetual parturition. In his 1961 study of different strategies of leadership, he considers the deferral of the future golden day, the state, say, of justice and non-exploitation, as a means of protecting hope. In this formation, which he names the "pairing group," "the feelings thus associated in [this assemblage] are at the opposite pole to feelings of hatred, destructiveness, and despair. For the feelings of hope to be sustained it is essential that the 'leader' of the group, unlike the leader of the dependent group . . . should be unborn."[67]

Du Bois said, "[cooperative] enterprises are peculiar instances of the 'advantage of the disadvantage'—of the way in which a hostile environment has forced the Negro to do for himself."[68] Cooperatives were born in a predicament of almost total confinement. Here where hope easily buckles to despair the sources of encouragement, the motivation of the masses, may be found in delay, or so the application of Bion's logic suggests. "Only by remaining a hope does hope persist," Bion writes. "It is a person or idea that will save the group—in fact from feelings of hatred, destructiveness, and despair, of its own or of another group—but in order to do this, obviously, the Messianic hope must never be fulfilled."[69]

But the most interesting thing about the metaphor of nucleus is that it is both a start and start as such, a beginning as motion and as concept. Listen to the awkward wording of Du Bois's wish: "I want very much to start with him as a nucleus a movement for co-operation among American Negroes." Du Bois basically says, I want to start with a start. Important for motivation, then, is not only that the messiah remain unborn but also that the movement be conceived as just beginning. Subjectivity is transformed from a coherent whole, a body with a nucleus, to temporality itself, a nucleus without a body.

As Du Bois fashioned an amorphous leadership for the movement, reminiscent of the Guild, Matney got impatient. To Matney, Du Bois was Hamletting. Hesitant, Du Bois delayed the next step of establishing a cooperative, be it worker's, producer's, consumer's, or, as Du Bois professed was needed, a multi-stake-holding combination of all three. "I feel," goaded Matney in February 1930, "that now is the opportune time for definite organization to execute the promotional work of Co-operation among Negroes and to see the program vigorously pushed to success."[70] Matney had good reason to believe the venture would be successful: "I am receiving requests almost daily for information on the organization and operation of cooperative undertakings," he wrote. "In many cases local situations are outlined and personal advice and assistance is requested." And in case Du Bois had any doubts about the reach of these inquiries, Matney, speaking from West Virginia, assured him that "Some requests come from as far South as New Orleans; as far north as New York . . . as far west as Chicago and St. Louis."

Matney ended the letter with a herd of anxious questions. He was anxious about the possibilities for funding and for scholarship to study cooperation abroad. Rather than corroborate Matney's urgency, Du Bois merely forwarded a letter from Warbasse, stating that Matney did not need more study of European cooperatives: "Mr. Matney is pretty well equipped and if he is to go ahead here in the U.S. the sooner the better." Warbasse, also urging Du Bois to act, ended the letter by suggesting a scurry of viable cooperative markets: "housing[,] banking, movie show, school, theater, coal and milk distribution," and so on.[71]

Matney and Warbasse were not alone. A decade later in 1941, John Brown Jefferson, someone Du Bois now long ago selected as a possible state secretary for his Cooperative Guild, expressed similar concerns. Brown submitted to Du Bois a comprehensive plan for a distribution cooperative of raw fabrics and clothing, which eventually would purchase land to farm its own materials, and establish credit unions and an exporting agency, all to "solve the problems of non-employment and poverty that now impedes the progress of a submerged and harassed race."[72] Du Bois outright rejected the plan, explaining "I do not believe that you can at present base a cooperative effort among Negroes upon imports and exports. . . . This might work after the war." Brown was shocked at the reluctance to materialize a plan, citing grassroots work being "organized in Los Angeles," and finally restating the same advice as Matney's: "Now is the time for preparation, the time to effect complete organization. There can never be a period more auspicious. Delay invites failure." For in the eyes of the very actors Du Bois selected to accelerate the movement, Du Bois, with tragic irony, had gone too far with his principle of thrift, that pedal pump of self-denial.

This hesitance looks different when we take rather seriously Du Bois's description of Matney, and by extension the leadership, as a "nucleus." That word was far from a toss-off. Nucleus formed the basis for his title of his 1920 apocalyptic short story "The Comet." When it was coined in the seventeenth century, "nucleus" originally meant the flaring core in a comet's head. The title may also describe how the story feels to read: a fire in the brain. It is more than difficult to follow. Because it lacks transitions, we whiplash from one scene to another. The story stages a combustion of temporalities, yet it's precisely this duration that makes a perfect match for the *short* story form.

The story depicts an environmental catastrophe that nearly ends the world. It depicts the affective fallout of the Red Summer of 1919, the influenza pandemic of 1918, and the fact that the white death rate at the height of the pandemic equaled the annual Black death rate in cities alone between 1906 and 1920.[73] Du Bois was playing with the superstition that comets augur disaster, a belief prevalent among German culture of the eighteenth century and exploited by H. G. Wells to rather utopian effects in his speculative fiction novel *In the Days of the Comet* (1906).[74] Everyone in the short story expects the head of a comet to strike New York City. But in the end, like Wells's novel, only the tail falls; but unlike the novel where the tail's gasses redeem the people, here the tail obliterates the city. This is an allegory, you might have guessed, of the relationship between the leadership and the social base, in which the focus on the leadership, the nucleus, makes the strike of the tail the real surprise. To view this phenomenologically is to see that the leadership functions as a kind of misdirection (not indirection: misdirection), and together these collectives conspire to produce unpredictability, the affective correlate to sustained incipience.

Though what strikes is just a tail, it kills everyone in its wake except the narrator Jim Davis and the wailing woman he rescues, Julia. At first she is terrified to be saved by a Black man. But after coming to the conclusion with baffling speed that they are the earth's sole survivors (not even a day has passed), she exalts him as "All-Father of the race to be" and herself as "Bride of Life," "mighty mother of all men to come."[75] Driving home the idea of messianic time, Jim sees himself as a reborn messiah and Julia his sibylline wife, for "it was as though," she divines, "some mighty Pharaoh lived again."[76] No sooner do they announce their union, this dubious flash-formation of postrevolution bliss, equality, justice, freedom, a bliss already undermined by Du Bois's reiteration of its patrifocality, undermined, too, by an implacable feeling that this is all too implausible, all a comic stretch of the melodrama of melodrama—no sooner do the lovers trumpet "The world is dead!" "Long live the—" than a "Honk! Honk!" coming from her father's Benz deflates their spiritual high. Julia's father pulls her away with alarming ease. She never looks back. Jim reconnects with his wife (is it his actual, previous, or also somewhat fictional wife? Is the cyclical time of marriage goosed here as well?). His wife carries the "corpse" of their son. His death is the final stamp of the story's message that, as Saidiya Hartman contends in her reading of the work, "the stranglehold of white supremacy appears so unconquerable, so eternal that its only certain defeat is the end of the world, the death of Man." Because the story asserts a basic equivalence between the status of Black life and the status of the slave, both treated as commodities rather than as workers, both totally fungible, Hartman claims that "some might even describe it as an ur-text of afro-pessimism."[77]

One could equally describe it as the ur-text of Du Bois's political orientation. Going back to the "corpse" of Jim's son, one could call the corpse the symbol of dashed messianism to the extent the son is the reproduction of Jim. The story does not only caution against fantasies of messianic resolution, being saved from or for a new era. It imagines what times looks like without messianism and rejects nearly every option. At the story's start Jim "stood a moment on the steps of the bank, watching the human river that swirled down Broadway," a river of universal, inexorable, one-way growth, teleological time rejecting Jim like a flume.[78] "Few noticed him. Few ever noticed him save in a way that stung. He was outside the world—'nothing!' as he said bitterly." By the end we as readers have jolted from progressive, cause-effect time, to an irruptive, causeless time, then finally to a sort of non-time of accumulating aftermaths, where nothing seems to change but the number of deaths. Remember that what struck was never the comet, but its "tail," a trail of aftermaths from which the world thought it was safe. The feel of this speedy story, never allowing us comfort in any time, at any time, calls into question and unsettles the veracity of every time. No single experience of time is trustable.

One might object, however, that the short story is actually about history as recursions and forward leaps, oscillations or even stasis. But that reading assumes a backdrop of linearity. It can only be charted when progressive clock time remains the gold standard of measurement. The temporal implications of "The Comet" and their implications for leadership are far more demanding. If no single mode the story depicts accurately represents historical time, if each experience of time is existentially dubious, then the temporality to consider is the one that lay outside the narrative: the beginning, the nucleus. In terms of leadership, eschewed from the story is not the comet's tail, the social base, but the nucleus, the leadership, which disappears into space.

From the viewpoint of "The Comet" and Du Bois's letters to Matney, what to Matney and others was a frustrating hesitation could also be an adage: leaders should help to start a movement and just as quickly abscond from view. Because the leadership and the base shade into each other without becoming one another, because, to return to our original question, they are effectively metonymic, the leaders, the story holds, should eventually disappear into a base of Blackness no less bound than outer space. Instead of movement actors divided hierarchically between the usher and the procession, we might think of them through Du Bois as co-conspirators, metonyms, generating surprise and its material impact.

Non-Dialectical Time: The Conjunction

It is probably clear by now that the Du Bois I've unearthed was as much intent on changing the world as he was on changing time. I said at the beginning Du Bois fashioned the cooperative movement as non-dialectical, and I would like to explain this, along with the stakes this approach holds for the lives of the movement participants. For Du Bois, the cooperative surplus, from its revenue to its affects, has an awkward relationship to capital: it neither dialectically negates exploitation nor does it propose to be complicit with it. Despite residing inside capitalist structures (the circular flow of commodities, the general equivalence of money, state lands, private lands, contracts, charters, and so on), the surplus exceeds capitalist control. Let us look at the two terms Du Bois uses to describe the cooperative's relationship to a capitalist economy: a "conjunction" and "in the midst," a conjunction that is in midst of capitalism. "We believe," Du Bois said, "that, if carefully and intelligently planned, a co-operative Negro industrial system in America can be established in the midst of and in conjunction with the surrounding national industrial organization and in intelligent accord with that reconstruction of the economic basis of the nation which must sooner or later be accomplished."[79] This statement comes from his 1936 "Basic American Negro Creed," which according to him expressed the collective beliefs of himself and young Blacks he interviewed across the country. To think of a "system" as not merely in conjunction but also in the midst—a conjunction in the midst of another system is different from thinking of it as holding it together, conjoining it, different of course from complicity.

To be a "conjunction in the midst" is another way of saying to be in the midmost, not just in the middle but, to use a funny old word, in the middest. A conjunction in the midmost region of a system can be identified only if it is also a break. Otherwise it would be seamless and self-same with the systems that surround it. The cooperative is not only the joint, the "conjunction": it is also the break within the joint, the midmost. The cooperative refuses dialectical extremes. While determined by the surround of capital, giving it shape as a conjunction, it exceeds those determinations, breaks free of them, as it were. Against the beginning of his sentence, the beginning of his *sentence*, that part about careful and intelligent planning, Du Bois is imagining an alternative to the historical materialism that Engels found in Marx, though Marx never used or explicitly endorsed the term, and which has since been identified as the virtual namesake for Marxist historical reason writ large. In contestation here was not historical materialism in all its forms, as for instance those envisioned by Walter Benjamin as a "weak messianism," but a hierarchical version that designates a progressively amplifying ricochet of class conflicts and the necessity of negation for the very emergence of material life. As Pheng Cheah remarks, "Marx suggested that human beings indirectly produce actual material life when we produce our means of subsistence through labor. Material reality is therefore produced by negativity."[80] All this is to say that what makes cooperative economics cooperative, for Du Bois, is that it opens an alternative not just to class struggle but to the supremacy of negation.

The reason Du Bois presents the cooperative movement as an alternative to that amplifying ricochet relates to the conditions of normative racial violence. We may remember that it was the aftershocks of these conditions and more that led Jacques Derrida in *Specters of Marx* to proclaim the need to think non-dialectically if we are to think let alone have a future at all. Du Bois's midmost conjunction is analogous to life in the aftershock, what Derrida quoting *Hamlet* calls "time out of joint." To figure the future from this vantage point of disjointedness, from what Derrida says is "the joining of a radically dis-jointed time, without certain conjunction," or as Du Bois suggests, a time with a certain break, "is not [to figure] a time whose joinings are negated, broken, mistreated, dysfunctional, disadjusted, according to a dys- of negative opposition and dialectical disjunction." For Derrida to negate this negation, this negative condition, is not to create a new future, but to reiterate the same, and what's more, it is to miss the opportunity to embody the madness of this broken time, a "time . . . run down, on the run and run down," he says, a time "deranged, both out of order and mad."[81] The point is to affirm the breaks so a different future, the future as such, might actually come, for what is the future but a break from the present? Cooperation in Du Bois was a kind of madness as it activated a fugitive time, sadly run down but somehow, still, on the run.

In this vein, Du Bois broke with the ascending linearity in popular theories of cooperation. He broke with the proclivities to project a cooperative future as though it were inevitable, a destiny waiting either at the end of human evolution, as in Peter Kropotkin's *Mutual Aid: A Factor in Evolution* (1902), or at the end of class conflict, as in Laurence Gronlund's *The Cooperative Commonwealth* (1884). This was the book from which Du Bois creatively stole the name for his desired state: "a cooperative commonwealth." Whereas Kroptkin argued that animal life survives through reciprocal "altruism" not Darwinian competition, Gronlund thought that the American railroad strikes of 1877 marked the start of revolution, and there "in the fullness of time we shall have a labor revolt that shall not be put down."[82] In this context, it is no wonder most have read Du Bois's cooperative ambitions as an evolving sequence of rectangular unfoldings. His philosophy of cooperation has been interpreted as either "the ability of the trained elite to generalize an agenda for the community," or as the abstract belief that "a peaceful transition to socialism in America could be gained through the development of economic cooperatives."[83]

He had profoundly important reasons to depart from these projections. To address the stakes for movement actors, we might return to Derrida and note that Derrida and Du Bois are not after the same sort of present or thinking of the danger to their lives in the same way. For Derrida the problem of negation is that it imprisons the present, turning political actors into the property of a preexisting script, an expectation, a plan. Derrida wants to hold out for a true event and a radical alterity. Du Bois wants to hold out for life. For Derrida one must affirm the conditions of impossibility because the eventness of an event, the future, cannot be seen in advance or recognized once it comes. In this light, the impossible is the life we cannot imagine, but paradoxically it is also the life we have been living since the failure of the Communist states. For Du Bois the impossible is Black life overbrimming with duress.

Du Bois's affirmation of the negative, from structural foreclosures to mechanisms of displacement, culminated in a move that many Black leaders considered totally mad: the affirmation of segregation. When Du Bois proposed "deliberate, and purposeful segregation for economic defense," he left the NAACP wincing in their leather armchairs, for the NAACP's most basic and enduring policy was their legal attack on segregation in any form.[84] Yet Du Bois was convinced that "the attack upon these hidden and partially concealed causes of race hate, must be led by Negroes in a program that was *not merely negative,* in the sense of calling on white folks to desist from certain practices and give up certain beliefs: but in the sense that Negroes must proceed constructively in a new and comprehensive plan of their own" (emphasis mine).[85] Slogging through segregation was the only way to get out of it. In concrete terms this meant intensifying already existing "self-governed" enclaves, already existing "economic solidarity,"[86] and the buying "power of the Negro as a consumer."[87]

Du Bois may not have explicitly called for Blacks to abandon all acts and forms of negation, but his strategy of transvaluing segregation assumes at least an epistemic and ontic shift from negating the negative to affirming it. What better slogan could there be for such a shift than his famous description of the political economy of Black cooperatives: "the advantage of the disadvantage"?[88] In case anyone wished to downplay in his defense how firmly he felt about this shift, he told everyone from *Crisis* readers to his Fisk University students, "there is no alternative,"[89] "there is no other way."[90] What was odd about this unremitting echo is that there must have been another way, or there wouldn't be any need to encourage it: there is the path they are on and the path he wants them on. We can explain the paradoxical non-choice of this outside choice as Du Bois implying that negating the negative would reiterate the same, not procure a new way to the other, not procure, that is, another way. By phrasing his path forward in the negative, by never saying "this is the way," but "there is no other way," he suggests that his affirmation of negative conditions does not project an opposite of positive conditions. Rather, the affirmation sinks into the very pores of negation, finding life and a living inside death and the deadening. "Either we do this," he said, "or we die."[91] Du Bois was essentially saying, the closer you confine us the less confined we'll be.

Sustained incipience is non-dialectical because it affirms for Blacks not what they wish to lose as they ricochet to something better, but what they have now and in a new mode of having do want to keep. Frederic Jameson drives home better than Derrida what historical materialism entails for us personally: a loss of life. That fatal surrender implores us to remember, he says, the people we will "lose in the course of so momentous a transformation."[92] Du Bois's movement affirms not what Black people do not have since "unexpectedly new" they do not see it, but what they have now and in a new mode of having do want to keep. Dialectical reason offers the self as libation of sacrifice to the power of hope. This is a "hopefulness" that, as Kathi Weeks argues, "sustains" the undaunted through "fear and anxiety," half-slept anxiety and unsleeping fear that awakes us to the "prospect of our own 'perishing.'" This perishing "in a different future, a future in which neither we nor our children . . . would exist," may mean "to become more" by way of becoming nothing.[93] Or it may mean to become nothing by way of becoming more, and that ambiguity is what may wake us up at night. Either way, Du Bois's cooperative movement refuses both. It asks is there a self for the duressed that need not be overcome?

It follows, then, that the non-dialectical nature of cooperation made it distinct from the very socialism it stood beside in Du Bois's texts. Because they move together they, as their reception shows, are easily conflated. Negri and Hardt define socialism as "state ownership and control over the means of production and equality of income," that is, "the public management of economic activity and a disciplinary work regime." Mark Van Wienen claims that Du Bois believed in such a socialism, which modeled a way of "using the parliamentary and legal procedures already available." One of two things follow: cooperation does not fit within Du Bois's socialism, or Du Bois's socialism, despite his own testimony, does not fit within this frame.[94] Although he defined socialism as equitably governed labor Du Bois casts cooperation as inherently ungovernable, ungovernable because not despite its surrounding governance. One method of "economic independence," he wrote, "consists of such a cooperative arrangement of industries and services within the Negro group that the group tends to become a closed economic circle independent of the surrounding white world." As cooperation becomes more cooperative, not necessarily older or more widespread, just more itself, its independence augments from the very regimes of labor that work to control it. The important point here is not that cooperatives sustain their autonomy (they do not and never have), but that they, by inherent design, "tend" toward this. Despite the history of socialist states developing cooperatives, Du Bois cautions against subsuming cooperatives beneath such state projects.

For Du Bois cooperation, and the cooperative movement, signals something deeper than working inside the conditions of the possible, not to say the pragmatic: that deeper thing is autonomous since non-dialectical, and it is given by the very idea of withinness, of conjunctive resistance, of working "in the midst of" (to keep with Du Bois's words). In his essay "The Union of Color" (1936), Du Bois argued that the political economies of cooperation was a "third path" for "Asiatic and African worlds." The path stood between alignment and "war" with European capital, a middle distance in which "we can stop the dependence of colored consumers upon white exploitation" and "establish new ideals of mutual respect which shall not be exclusively and continually white ideals."[95] Du Bois published the essay in the Indian journal *Aryan Path*, and some have viewed it as a bourgeois adoption of Ghandian *swadeshi* principles, the means through which a nation achieves self-determination by producing its own goods and boycotting foreign ones. Bill Mullen, for instance, sees Du Bois's focus on consumption rather than production as Du Bois's "hostility" to both attacks on private property and to framing an Afro-Asian alliance as fundamentally anti-imperial. Instead of reading this third path as a liberalism, a pragmatism, or a "patience," as Mark Van Wienen sees it, something "opposed to the cause of social disruption and the immediate revolution championed by the insurrectionists," we could read it as a radical break from dialectical opposition, from voluntary "war," which, as Du Bois suggests, predetermines ones "ideals."[96] It is the "third" because it deviates from the opposition between what is here and what is not, between the present we have and the future we want. The condition of duress, to filch a phrase from Derrida, "is not simply negative or dialectical: it *introduces* the possible; it is its *gatekeeper today*; it makes [the possible] come."[97]

Necromance

> But for now, before that,
> Sleep of ages, again as if starting
> from scratch.
>
> —Nathaniel Mackey, "Song of the Andoumboulou: 58"

When we think of how to work toward impossible ends, how to persist, sustained incipience reminds us that there is a self to affirm because it survives the impossible and impossibility is the origin of the new. Du Bois merged the desire to last with the imperative to let go, to elasticize a nowness over the long haul. Emanating from the political economy of cooperatives, this timely alternative forced Du Bois to rethink and reengage movement participation as well as formation from a perspective more democratic than he practiced elsewhere. Cooperative ethics compelled him to ask, particularly because of their fraught connection to capital, what might the timescale of democracy look like? To purloin a term from rhetoric, it looks like an anaphora, the echo of the same word in successive clauses, anaphora, from the Greek word that means *a hauling back* or *bearing again*—like an anaphoric time, where phrase upon phrase begins from the beginning. It may be staggering to think this (I stagger as I think it), but the cooperative movement in Du Bois may be the surprising pivot from negating the future that can happen to affirming the future that can't. In this section I explore this pivot and its affective attachments.

Political sympathies have limits. When a movement declines, it is often because we have reached our limits, the limits of our sympathies with plans, posterity, hope, with even our own dreams, with everything that preserves the sense of having a future despite not having one and so preserves the wherewithal to avoid the quiet descent. The quiet and the descent are really the muted plea of only five words: *I can bear no more,* or maybe five words and a phrase, *I can bear no more, even dreams have limits.* This point of return (and for many, there is no return) in political plotlines obviously applies with particular poignancy to a practice of activism about bearing things again, from the beginning, not only sustaining the incipience: allowing the incipience to be *sustained.*

Few have described this problem of perennial burnout with more light and lucidity than two field-changing political theorists, Alex Williams and (again) Nick Srnicek. They claim that "We [have] lost the capacity to build a better future. . . . From the alter-globalisation struggles of the late 1990s, through the antiwar and ecological coalitions of the early 2000s, and into the new student uprisings and Occupy movements since 2008, a common pattern emerges: resistance struggles rise rapidly, mobilise increasingly large numbers of people, and yet fade away only to be replaced by a renewed sense of apathy, melancholy and defeat."[98] The renewal this duo notes is a historical one. It is a renewed pejorism. The belief that the arenas for freedom are narrowing, will keep narrowing, a betrayal of progress learned from movements across the entire twentieth century primarily in Europe and the U.S. In other words, these two rising stars could be talking about the dangers, and for most the turnout, of all the cooperative movements I explore in this book. And as I will discuss now, Du Bois essayed an answer to a fundamental question for the Black cooperative movement as a whole, a question that is as pressing for us today as it was for them then. If the usual cynosures of hope and faith have lost their salience, then what affective resources can we rely on to disentangle ourselves from, or at the very least counter, psychically, physically, structurally counter, relations of progress and capital?

A new rise of scholarship has been answering with love. We can rely on, they say, knee-deep at the crosscurrent of literature and political economy, the redemptive powers of love. For all the distinctions in these arguments, they appear to reiterate a deeply historical notion that what love redeems is life from the clutches of death. It is interesting how explicit this assumption tends to be, yet how rarely its limits or logics are really questioned. "Love makes us feel more alive," says bell hooks, with something like awe, in her recent vade mecum on how to challenge capitalism and its permutations of patriarchy: deploy "a love ethic" that in challenging "our cultural obsession with death" will necessarily bring to its knees "patriarchal thinking."[99] "Love in the Time of Death" is the title Jennifer Nash gives her final chapter in her profoundly moving clarion call *Black Feminism Reimagined.* Nash posits a "love-politics," a relationality extendable to strangers, that can transform the law from a site of injury and social death to a stage for "vulnerability and witnessing." Through a fretwork of concepts from Patricia Williams, Judith Butler, Christine Straehle, and others, Nash contends that a love based on an "empathic looking," attends to the personal specificities of a Black woman's experience, which would otherwise be assimilated into generic categories of injury.[100] Although I cannot render the full complexity of Nash's argument, the part I want to stress is that if this love were activated in the judicial system it would make the law "survivor-centered" and ultimately safeguard Black women's lives.

It is this historical antagonism between love and death, death and love, that Hardt and Negri have famously worked up, as they themselves have said, into nothing less than a trilogy on how, naturally enough, to unclutch the hold capital has placed on the meaning of life and its conditions of possibility. A kind of unflappable biopolitical infinitude, love, according to them, is power upon power, indeed, power over power: "the power that the common exerts and the power to constitute the common" ad infinitum.[101] Capable of generating "infinite subjectivities" to use Alain Badiou's phrase from his *In Praise of Love,* love for Hartd and Negri is a resource without restriction. It therefore balks at the usual fate of social movement burnout, where people simply run out of energy and trip into despair. Beginning with the idea sounded in 1675 by Benedict Spinoza that "love is joy," opposed specifically to "melancholy," and thus augments "the body's power of action," Hardt and Negri have recommended particular forms of love over others—for example, love that celebrates irreducible difference over likeness. But in the end they exemplify the long history that says through love above all else we are heart-wired to life.[102]

Hardt and Negri are bucking a tide in social theory that configures love as a limited reservoir. Following Freud's economic model of the psyche, social theorists have considered the political affect of love a "quantitative magnitude," in Freud's terms. Extending Freud's notion that love is a libidinal attachment encompassing everything from "sexual love with sexual union at its aim" to "self-love" and "love for parents and children, friendship and love for humanity in general," too, social theorists often argue that "human beings possess only finite libidinal energies for cathecting social objects."[103] Detaching love from melancholy is one way Hardt and Negri suffuse the affect of love with something akin to the infinite.

There's a "love beyond death" proclaims Slavoj Žižek in *Incontinence of the Void* (2017). Žižek finds in love the structure of the struggle for a truly communist state. Žižek riffs off Lacan's division between empty and full signifiers, roughly equivalent to the local and the universal or the categorical and the particular, with each needing the other like color and light. From here Žižek argues that an authentic statement of love would be, I do not love you because of your particulars; I love your particulars because I love you. According to Žižek, in "authentic" or Lacanian love, one is constantly surprised by the details of one's lover, since they always stand in excess of the perfectly cohesive and self-identical person with whom one is actually in love. In transferring this romance to anticapitalist activism, we learn to appreciate small and mundane forms of political action. "An authentic sequence persists as long as its agents are surprised by the fact that 'this' (a series of often pragmatic and modest measures) is 'that' (advancing the universal Cause)—that, for instance, bringing water and electricity to a poor village is part of a Communist project."[104] For all his doomsday harmonics, Žižek toots a love that sounds rather hopeful, quintessentially equipped to deliver us "beyond death" and the feeling of fading away: political defeat.

Quest of the Silver Fleece

I want to explore a love counterpoised to this redemptive romance, a love that does not insist on negating and ultimately overcoming, nor fatalistically resigning, to the results of what Achille Mbembe has famously called "necropower." The *"generalized instrumentalization of human existence and the material destruction of human bodies and populations,"* necropower results in a panoramic of *"death-worlds,"* "new and unique forms of social existence in which vast populations are subjected to conditions of life conferring upon them the status of the *living dead.*"[105] Today among the left love appears more and more inherently ordained to overturn the necropolitical dimensions of political sovereignty and the pessimisms that it excites. And no wonder, considering how nearly totalitarian Mbembe's original conception was of this biopower gone mad. We see him totally and, I must admit, hypnotically giving himself over to the logic of his argument, following it to its outer shores in which the right to kill has become so sweeping that "to a large extent, resistance and self-destruction are synonymous," the freedom of self-severance now the last freedom left.[106] One suddenly feels desperate to step outside this logic, as though attempting to breathe in a heavily hot room. That outside space with all the air we need has purportedly been love.

Yet what if this love came from the inside of a necropolitical reality, gave us breath inside it? Enter Du Bois's *The Quest of the Silver Fleece*. Drafted in 1905 as *Scorn*, then wholly reworked and published six years later, Du Bois's first novel was something he also thought of as "an economic study." Accordingly, scholars have frequently placed it in a lineage of either the broader muckraking tradition or the plantation (or "anti-plantation") novel.[107] We should also consider it as belonging to a line of work that conveyed cooperation itself as a love plot, that configured cooperatists as bearers of love, from Ben Fowlkes tome of lyric poems *Co-operation: The Solution of the So-Called Negro Problem* (1908) to Toyohiko Kagawa's Christian treatise *Brotherhood Economics* (1936), cited later by Du Bois as somewhat of a muse.[108]

As to the geographic context, what better place for Du Bois to set his "economic study" than rural Alabama at the end of the nineteenth century (also the setting for Fowlkes poems)? "I do not think," Du Bois said in 1906, "it would be easy to find a place where conditions were on a whole more unfavorable to the rise of the Negro."[109] His Victorian romance imagines the construction of an alternative to the systems of credit and wage-labor: a cooperative economy based on cotton production. The novel reflects again the definition of a cooperative as the unification of small resources that would be powerless on their own and the distribution of their surplus (in this case, love), according not to the level of investment as in a corporate firm, but to the level of one's involvement in its production and use.[110]

Quest is almost carnivalesque in its repertoire of characters and labyrinthine plots, so for the sake of orientation, think of this romance as a bundle of triangles. Du Bois conveys a series of tense, triangulated relationships between two or two sets of characters, whose hypotenuse is always the slave plantation. There's the triad between the Cresswell family (Southern plantocracy) and the Taylors (Northern finance) working in tension with each other over the sale of cotton grown by Black sharecroppers; the triad between two teachers, Miss Smith and Miss Taylor, at an experimental "Negro school" in Alabama. Smith imagines the school as the start of a new "nation—a world," in fact. Taylor abhors that very idea. But the relationship in question for us lies at the bottom of this bunch, the love between Zora Cresswell and Bles Alwyn. Zora was raised in a swamp on the Cresswell plantation and meets Bles after he becomes a student at Miss Smith's school.[111] The novel traces the battle between all these clattering plans for the future of Blacks in America and ends with one winning (or nearly winning) out: the school and an interlocking cooperative society that Bles, Zora, and a warren of others construct. From a total two hundred acres rented from the Cresswells with plans to purchase, they draw up a blueprint for a new society: "twenty-acre farms" sold to members for "promise[d]" labor, "one hundred acres for the school" and "the public good," "a little hospital," "a cooperative store," "a cotton gin and sawmill," "all sorts of industries" whose "trustees" would be "chosen" by buyers of the land plots—in sum, a veritable prototype for Du Bois's cooperative movement.[112]

The bigger point for us in thinking about sustainable political affects is that Du Bois uses the logic of cooperative production on a landscape of slavery to rethink the nineteenth-century romantic marriage plot. In the process, he envisions a love so strikingly bizarre and so heavily haunting that it is almost comic. Here's the love in its fullness, when Zora, the novel's hero, stands alone in a room overlooking a marriage ceremony among the white characters, and then decides, rather strangely, to marry the cotton her cooperative produced, "shimmering" as though a ghost. She has called this the Silver Fleece, but here she calls it "dead love": "Zora, almost forgetting the wedding, stood before the mirror. Laying aside her dress, she draped her shimmering cloth about her, dragging her hair down in a heavy mass over her ears and neck until she seemed herself a bride. And as she stood there, awed with a mystical union of a dead love and living new born self, there came drifting in at the window, faintly, the soft sound of far-off marriage music."[113] The passage reads like it was written by a nineteenth-century wedding planner with a morbid sense of humor. Zora's hair is the most literal and most visibly plentiful expression of her body and it feels like a dead body, "a heavy mass," a fact underlined by the note that she must "drag" it to move it. And this self, adorned in long, cascading filaments of decay, ever more morbidly, has effectively betrothed the dead. So no matter how "living" this "new" self is, it is also, indistinguishably, akin to something dying. If characters in nineteenth-century marriage plots wed for social esteem or for romantic rapture, neither case applies. Here Zora's marriage continues a process of mourning, best expressed by the chapter's tart quip of a title, "The Marriage Morning."

As that title suggests, Zora's love emerges from a necropolitical expanse. The town is named Tombsville and the cotton is grown on a swamp. Swamps were the paradigmatic historical sites of escape for fugitive slaves. Think of the more-than-perilous and less-than-refuge 2,000 square mile "Great Dismal Swamp," overlapping North Carolina and Virginia. It housed the largest number of American maroons. Archeologist Dan Sayers suggests that like other swamps, the Great Dismal offered the blessing that here Black bodies could "decompose without . . . a trace." Here living without a trace of life was what it meant to stay alive.[114] Because Zora's love would not be possible without its surrounding necropolis, because a necrologic inheres in the love through and through, the closest word I have arrived at to describe it is "necromantic." It's an intimate necromancy not in the sense of reviving the dead, but of bringing subjects in ever closer proximity to the dead. The plot of extraordinary adventures to which this love belongs is less a romance, then, than a necromance.

As a resource for activism, necromance contests the common conception that in order for grievances to become movements or collective behavior they must be framed to create feelings of injustice or outrage.[115] After all, grief and its entourage, mourning and melancholy, are rarely considered sources of political action.

As not only a form of writing but a structure of feeling, necromance is an effect of a particular kind of production, and thus an intangible and unpossessable surplus. It largely suspends relations of property, as captured when Zora attempts to mentally describe the Silver Fleece/the "dead love" as her own but cannot: "It belonged—" she stammers, suddenly derailing her sentence as if the Fleece decrees it.[116] The kind of production I have in mind is a certain transvaluation: transforming things that are lost into losses that are things. This cannot be more explicit than when the narrator says, "[Bles] must at least see the grave of his hope and Zora's, and out of it [the grave] resurrect new love and strength."[117] I am thinking of things as the promiscuous mingling of subjectivity and objecthood, things as fugitives, escapees, from the confinements of being made either into objects or purely into subjects.[118] Such a thing is precisely what the Silver Fleece signifies in both its personification (rendering it a concept, a person, a product, all of the above) and in its futurity, its supersession beyond present conditions. The Silver Fleece is here but always elsewhere as the thing the characters "quest." "Ressurect[ed]," to return to the passage above, their love surfaces from a transvaluation of loss, not to recover it but to make something "out of it," something as unpossessable as the loss itself. I am trying to get at the fact that these things do not fill in a loss or retrieve a loss as a presence, but invent a new presence (the Silver Fleece) from the airy substance of a loss.

That substance is its fugitivity, or to use a cumbersome word its unpossess-edness, preserved and thereby remembered in a new thing as a new thing.

Remarkably, Du Bois does not imagine this love as something inside a person to be given through a process of exchange to someone else. It is not something one possesses, which in turn makes that person all the more self-possessed. Rather, we see it float from Bles's and Zora's cooperative labor with the haunted land. Du Bois describes the bond between them as practically turning them into ether, adrift like the "atmosphere" above their cotton crop, as they toil on the soil together, suffering and sacrifice in toiling silhouette: "But beside and around and above all this, like subtle, permeating ether, was—Zora. [Bles's] feelings for her were not as yet definite, expressed, or grasped; they were rather the atmosphere in which all things occurred and were felt and judged . . . insensibly they were drifting to a silenter, mightier mingling of souls."[119]

It is difficult to overstate how odd, given prevailing conventions, this impersonal love is. As Victorian mores waned, representations of love in pop and high culture at the end of the nineteenth century typically presented love as displacing the world, whereas here a haunted love displaces Zora and Bles.[120] Depictions of love also increasingly became deeply personal and subject-bound.[121] Its inter- and inner-subjective nature has served to (nearly up to today), as the late Lauren Berlant argues, "manage ambivalence," manage, that is, all libidinal excess over the flattening circuits of exchange. These circuits render equivalents and commensurabilities just to live another day.[122] One may say, in carrying out the implications of Berlant's argument, that by designating "the individual as the unit of social transformation" and by reducing "the overwhelming world to an intensified space of personal relations," love in its normative form has habitually rendered another general equivalent, analogous to the liquefaction, the dematerialization, of money into credit at the turn of the century.[123]

Necromance is bizarre for yet another reason, one that also makes it coextensive with the cooperative ethics of equal distribution: because it is non-subjective, it does not attach to certain objects or subjects over others. Du Bois's necromance reminds us that the construction of love as life-giving often disavows the way it operates as life-taking. David Eng, for instance, contends that the intensified scholarly focus on love as central for the process of redress against colonial violence has mostly unwittingly, but sometimes by design, enforced colonial divisions (gendered, racial, sexual, and so on) between the loved and the unlovable, reflecting the way the redemptive powers of love have been unequally distributed in a history of liberal empire and colonial rule. In "Colonial Object Relations," Eng demonstrates that in the reparative process envisioned by Melanie Klein, who continues to guide so much contemporary political theory, love is not assigned to an already valued object that is worthy of repair. Instead, love produces the valued object by affording it repair in victorious splendor over and above a devalued one, that which, for Klein, lies outside the mother and the motherland. The repair that love enacts, as Eng notes with a bracketed addition to Klein's words, "revives [dead] objects." Those are the objects that the ego itself has destroyed.[124] While this revival could be called necromancy in the original sense of the term, blowing life into dead, it should not be conflated with necromance, which brings subjects into intimate encounters with the dead.

Eng contends that in the exercise of love for a restoration of life, in the subject's choice of what to love and idealize or what to hate and aggress, is also a choice of what to keep buried, what to judge as deserving or underserving of life. This is significant, Eng concludes, because "it is those to whom repair can be offered that become the very sign of the human—of liberal value and valuable life in which intersubjective relations might be invested and cultivated."[125] Surely not every construction of love as uniquely intent on pulling one back over the threshold falls into the liberal traps of hierarchizing lives, but Eng helps us appreciate how necromance escapes those traps. For in the end the problem comes down to reparability, something interwoven with the effort to intensify "intersubjective relations," as Eng says. This is the effort to enlarge spaces for psychological depth, individual uniqueness, personal autonomy, to secure the overall expansion of the self through another, even or especially when that self becomes other. By sending Zora and Bles adrift, necromance functions as a sentiment of attachment without ever becoming an attachment of sentiment that sticks to some over others.

Adrift is precisely how Fred Moten and Stefano Harney envision love in their momentous study on subjugated knowledge, *The Undercommons*, which closes with a celebratory turn to what they call "hapticality, or love." As "the touch of the undercommons," hapticality is the "capacity to feel though others" (no misprint), "for others to feel through you, for you to feel them feeling you, this feel of the shipped is not regulated, at least not successfully, by a state, a religion, a people, an empire, a piece of land, a totem."[126] Against the mutual alienation of modern-day laborers, haptic love redeems a special kind of intimacy that refuses to reinforce logics of possession, even those of self-possession, the very hotly contested notion that in the face of infringements we have a self to possess. Hence this feeling "through others" is also one we have despite or, awkwardly, "though others," despite the persistence of the notion of self-possessed individuals, purported to hold and exchange sentiments as if items of merchandise. What makes hapticality momentous is that it envisions the most deeply personal of affects as simultaneously impersonal, so extensively vaporizing the borders of subjectivity that one might say, with Moten and Harney, quoting Du Bois's *Quest* almost word for word, that it "sets me adrift."[127]

Du Bois's linkage of love to economic cooperation certainly had its critics. Du Bois's longtime friend George Streator dispatched a total dismissal of this affective economy. "Flimsy" and insufficient, Streator charged in a letter from 1935. "Your cooperation program would be based on sympathetic interest of Negroes in themselves. And this is a flimsy interest. . . . There is no such thing as a Negro LOVING his race in the matter of capital investment and profit."[128] Streator basically echoed, albeit with slightly more sting, the same suspicions articulated by one of Du Bois's characters in *Quest*, a character allegorically named "the practical Carter." "Can you put trust in that sort of help?" Carter asks Bles. "We can when once the community learns that it pays."[129] Du Bois did no better than Bles to defend himself. He sidestepped the charge through a general statement on unselfishness and then sidestepped himself through a slide into the third person, distancing himself doubly from the matter: "Streator and Du Bois are not the only unselfish people among Negroes," he said.[130] Alternately, his defense could not have been more apt. By effectively scare-quoting not only himself but his whole manner of living, manner of loving, he appears to have so absorbed the drama of *Quest*, the drama of a love that is out of body in body, that all these years later the drama's almost a reflex, a quick gestural reply. Streator's point about the easy exhaustibility of love might hold if this love originated inside the subject. In this case, Du Bois's flights of imagination, page to page, was his best and last defense.

Necromance operates as an estrangement of love from the liberal constitution of the person, someone endowed with the ability to fully grieve and repair her wounds. It does not initiate the reparative process, but stems from it epiphenomenally. As "the atmosphere in which all things occurred" and the project of which one is always in "quest," it is coextensive with the cooperative production of something here and elsewhere. In this way, necromance is the process of remembering that which we cannot remember. We cannot remember what we have lost ironically because we're never allowed to forget, surrounded by "an atmosphere in which all things occurred." This is the paradox necromance presents: the inability to forget what we cannot remember. Necromance certainly pushes us toward melancholy, but not the kind Hardt and Negri oppose with their biopolitics, the kind rather that propels us to act. Nonetheless, necromantic love poses the same problem raised by credit and its proliferating futurity: as Ian Baucom puts it in his study of the entanglements of credit and loss, "the problem of the unseen, the problem of nonappearance."[131] Or to return to the way Du Bois says it in *The Quest of the Silver Fleece,* necromance is the sensation of the "silent" and the "insensible." If the politics of love in Du Bois and elsewhere has been construed as an effort to "produce social revolution as a kind of affect that is as viscerally felt as romantic longing," as Erica Edwards has observed, revolution as something longed for, then necromance, by working inside existing conditions of irrevocable loss, registers the feeling that the revolution is already here.[132]

It Has Its Disadvantages

Necromance registers the grief in Du Bois's vision of cooperative economics. Cooperatives for Du Bois were a product of confinement, nearly all-determining, seemingly unending. In a plaintive tone, he told the American Economic Association in 1905 that "there are persons who see nothing but the advantages of this course [cooperation]. But it has its disadvantages. It intensifies prejudice and bitterness. . . . Then too this movement narrows the activity of the best class of Negroes, withdraws them from helpful competition and contact, perverts and cheapens their ideals—in fact provincializes them in thought and deed."[133] "This movement," it seems, is a flight through loss, an adventure in mourning inexorably without end. Freud would call this mourning melancholia, indefinite because "one cannot see clearly what it is that has been lost."[134] Although Freud did not publish his seminal essay on mourning until 1917, Du Bois had begun reading Freud closely by 1905, when he confessed the indelible impact of Freudian psychoanalysis on his view of collective behavior. It is perhaps Du Bois's recent plunge into Freud that explains why after all his remonstrations about the way cooperatives "withdraw" Blacks from the world—why his mood, his perspective, suddenly toggled into optimism, which thus appears to lack base. "Yet it is today," he continued, referring to the cooperative movement, "the only path of economic escape for the most gifted class of Black men and the development in this line which you and I will live to see is going to be enormous."

How did the litany of complaints about a narrowing present turn so quickly to a prophecy of better tomorrows? In some ways, the quickness of this turn betrays the unlikelihood and untenability of an optimistic outlook. In other places, his optimism was more howl than stutter, but no more convincing: "at the present rate we will have in this country a mass of people of colored blood acting together like one great fist for their own ends, with secret understanding, with pitiless efficiency and with resources for defense which will make their freedom incapable of attack."[135] A speech-act to break through a bedrock of segregation, this, we might consider, was Du Bois's "fist," a fist vengeant and backhanded. To evoke another image from Du Bois's short story, "The Comet," whose main character escapes from "the lower vaults" of a bank as the world burns, Du Bois was essentially saying, the more you hold us down, the deeper the vault, the more concealed the vault, the colder and thinner the air of the vault, the more cohesive and disruptive we will be when we rise.[136] Steely, though, as it may have been, the sentiment concealed a weary underside, a vulnerable act of mourning, mourning for the loss of other exits, less "narrow," unideal, secretly unlikely. His one "way out" was all hemmed in.

Whereas Du Bois found freedom, hastily, fantastically, in some state-backed socialisms outside the U.S., mainly the Soviet Union and China, the socialist project of cooperation at home was much more compromised. Most scholars descry Du Bois embracing cooperation with a renewed vigor during the 1930s, descry him hopeful and bolstered by the policies of the New Deal, which, according to Doug McAdam, were "responsible for nothing less than a cognitive revolution within the Black population regarding the prospects for change in this country's racial status quo."[137] But although he wanted to believe that exploiting New Deal provisions was possible for African Americans, the very hyperness of his yearning, unanchored in a clear direction or even a clear example of how Blacks would take advantage of the New Deal, foretold a different prospect.

He believed cooperatives must request aid from the Tennessee Valley Authority (TVA), an agency established during the Great Depression that provided substantial funds for farmers of that region. "By taking advantage of the TVA," Du Bois wrote in a 1946 *Pittsburgh Courier* column, "and the other great developments of power throughout the United States which are bound to come, the home industry could be established in the country districts, where each home would have its garden and raise the food which it needs. It could establish communities where education, art and industry could go hand in hand."[138] This recommendation, laden then leadened with a congeries of coulds, probably did more to highlight the dual directionality of co-operative economics, the jointure of opposite production scales as in the oxymoronic "home industry"—did more to intimate what it struggled to reach than it did to persuade his readers of prospective government aid. For, again, missing from this hyper-could was any practical how or concrete precedent.

But maybe that was the point. Emphasizing what could happen detached from practical method not only functioned to acknowledge the political limits but, in a way, also stretched them. Such prospects without instruction served two seemingly contrary aims: acknowledging that these prospects "could" also *not* occur, while reviving a sense of potential untethered to its realization. Du Bois's statement of encouragement implicitly acknowledged a wide halo of restrictions (the possible bind of government aid, the missing avenues to actualization, and the ghosts of failure evinced by the conditional "could," by the undervoice of *could not*). But coupled with a staunch insistence on potentiality, this crosscut directive suggested the paradox of uncontingent power, powered by contingency. Du Bois asked his readers to envision two mutually exclusive states—beginning and ending, potential and foreclosure—as mutually transformative.

This vision was infallibly melancholic. To pirate David Eng and David Kazanjian's words in their reinterpretation of this psychic eclipse, Du Bois stages melancholia as "adamant refusal of closure," thereby transforming it into a "creative process."[139] They explain that "it is precisely the ego's melancholic attachments to loss that might be said to produce not only psychic life and subjectivity but also the domain of remains. That is, melancholia creates a realm of traces open to signification, a hermeneutic domain of what remains of loss."[140] If melancholia produces the remains on which we live and through which we live on, then those remains for Du Bois are the losses suffered on and off the plantation, if one can say there is a difference. He had one particular loss in mind, though, as he thought about building a "cooperative commonwealth." During Reconstruction Blacks entrusted their savings with the Freedman Bureau, which eventually lost by embezzlement all their money, all that collective buying power. "It is difficult to over-estimate the psychological effect of this failure upon Negro thrift," wrote Du Bois. The remains of this loss, this wound, would include the forcibly closed system of cooperatives and the necromance they engender. Du Bois's powerful position of grief revised against common sense the inactivity of the melancholiac, whom in the eyes of Freud was at best of little influence, at worst catatonic.[141]

This Freudian version of mourning recalls a passage on grief by Josiah Royce, the idealist philosopher at Harvard University whose work and probably lectures significantly influenced Du Bois. David Levering Lewis, Anthony Appiah, and others have noted Du Bois was attracted to Royce's "Kantian certainty that humanity felt the need to be loyal to society's highest morals."[142] Lewis and Appiah, however, overlook the implications that for Royce this need evolved out of grief, an energizing, not an "enervating," force. The "cause which the world regards as lost . . . the faithful view as ascended to a higher realm, certain to come again in renewed might and beauty."[143] These flights of imagination transport us back to *Quest*, specifically to the mirror scene, where Zora does not know where she ends and the fleece begins. One is tempted to call this a hallucination. That scene, like Royce's statement, dramatizes the question of what happens to one's politics when the lost "cause" is not lost to historical time but to current sight, when "one cannot see clearly what it is that has been lost." Necromance records a blindness that adrenalizes a way of acting in uncertainty, not in being "loyal" to a known transcendent cause. Freud describes the descent into the dusk of melancholy as the moment that "the shadow of the object [falls] upon the ego." Rather than trying to retrieve whatever has been lost, flesh out the shadow, necromance uncomfortably and, in regard to the issue of burnout, endlessly preserves the form of the loss as a disembodied outline, a hallucinatory trace.

Shadowy Outlines

I have been considering necromance as an affective economy that emerges from cooperationist spaces, be they cooperatives themselves or descriptions of cooperative life. Sarah Ahmed defines an "affective economy" as an arrangement of fleeting or nebulous emotions, an arrangement that "does not reside positively in the sign or commodity, but is produced only as an effect of its circulation."[144] Signs, commodities, and for that matter, dreams, bodies, homes, and so on, are the matter around which the affect is formed and refracted, one could say, into existence. As an economy of intimate affects (namely, melancholia, romantic love, deathliness, and deadliness) necromance is also a method of activism. It is a way of approaching one's most intimate desires that may or may not be permanently lost. Those desires for Du Bois, freedom and justice, lay ambiguously on the ground and on the page as it were, rendering necromance a method of both study and political action. The significance of necromance for social movement studies is that it reflects a way of acting on one's political desires without a clear idea of those desires. It reflects the feeling that one's deepest desires lack essential content. So when those desires are freedom and justice, necromantic activism reflects a way of leaving the grammar of emancipation uncomfortably open, permanently unset.

We can see this necromantic approach in Du Bois and his research team's very first study of cooperative economics, conducted out of Atlanta in 1898, *Some Efforts of American Negroes for Their Own Social Betterment.* Their venture was terribly difficult. They had to investigate cooperatives through institutions that bore different names and often presented themselves as having different natures. The sites of cooperatives, in other words, were sites of loss, sites of tentative possibilities. Reminiscent of Freud's image of a shadow that falls like a sheet upon the psyche, they had to discern the body of cooperative life from the shadow it cast. One reason for this movement by misdirection was that economic cooperation, which in this study was defined as a tryptic of reciprocal exchange, resource sharing, and the attenuation of the system of credit and debt, was often unsystematic, open-ended, even random. So in looking for cooperation in institutions like the church, for instance, they had to discern the unsystematic from the formalized. Although Du Bois had departed from British sociologist Herbert Spencer and his influential analogies between laws of genetics and laws of social processes, although Spencerian sociology was for Du Bois a bygone era, he and his fellow social scientists still wanted to definitively account for that which left no definitive account, left, that is, only a shadow.[145] Listen to how they—or I should say how Du Bois, as the author of "the results of the investigation"—discusses "relief" and "charity," two shadows of cooperation thrown down by the church. On the one hand, in the church, "much is done by individuals, and *perhaps the larger part* of the charity is entirely unsystematic and no record is kept of it."[146] On the other hand, "from this data it is clear that Negro Churches are becoming *centers of systematic relief* and reformatory work of Negroes among themselves."[147] The greater portion of church altruism is systematic while also unsystematic. This is less a contradiction, it seems, than a code: body is code for shadow, systematicity for the irregular. What is left is code for what is lost.

That cooperation is precisely what is both lost and formless—formless since lost—becomes increasingly obvious the deeper one gets into their study. Measuring or approximating the lost is one of their ambitions. "The actual expenditure of the organized agencies is not large," but "when we remember that . . . much of the unorganized and spasmodic work is unrecorded it seems that the work being done is both commendable and by no means insignificant in amount."[148] Two forms of measurement, two "amount[s]," are being combined in this semi-explanation, this twist and turn: the certain and the incalculable, each signifying the other. Instead of simply subordinating that which can be measured to that which cannot, Du Bois conflates them so that neither one means what they purport to mean, so that the amount of money spent, the number of co-ops built, conceals in unformalized practice the amount of cooperation. The traces of this practice conceal its breadth and impact, which itself can only be described through a double negation: the work is "by no means insignificant."

Du Bois's derivation of cooperative life splintered, at the very least, the crutch of causality. Consider the circularity of this sentence: "Economic and cooperative action became the business of the beneficial society and secret society; and benevolence, of special associations and institutions; finally, cooperative business and insurance sprang from the beneficial societies. How curious a chapter is this of the adaptation of social methods and ways of thinking to the environment of real life."[149] Curious, indeed. Cooperation somehow "became the business," and in turn the business somehow "sprang" from cooperation. Cooperatives have donned the nature of a ghostly shadow, traces of the dead, emerging in different forms through a process akin to transmogrification.

This necromantic maneuver of the cooperative movement is summarily reflected in Du Bois's issues with his field of sociology. In an unpublished essay written sometime after 1905, "Sociology Hesitant," Du Bois laid bare the limits of his discipline, the limits of discipline, to capture the nature of cooperative gatherings, "unorganized and spasmodic work." The essay upbraided the prevailing methodology of sociology, which for Du Bois was a positivist free-for-all that, to boot, failed to account for the ineluctable facts of chance. He defined or redefined sociology as "the science [that seeks] to measure carefully the limits of Chance in human conduct." "Looking over the world," he wrote with characteristic sweep, an ironic sweep given his argument, "we see evidence of the reign of Law; as we rise, however, from the physical to the human there comes not simply complication and interaction of forces but traces of indeterminate force until in the realm of higher human action we have Chance—that is actions undetermined by and independent of actions gone before." As much as this was an opening to transform the meaning of sociological investigation it was also a mourning of what the science could not do, what he could not capture or observe with the science.

The mourning is not obvious but it is also not far from view. It is what I see in light of what he wishes not to retrace, but retraces inevitably by his own logic: "a shadowy outline." Spencerian sociologists could only limn a shadowy outline of the meaning and rhythm of human deeds to be filled in when scientific measurement and deeper study came to the rescue.[150] But measurements and deeper study never came to rescue Du Bois from always already losing the "unrecorded," to quote again from *Some Efforts*. The work of Spencer "and his imitators" was "limited because their data was imperfect—*woefully* imperfect: depending on hearsay, rumor and tradition, vague speculations, travellor's tales, legends and imperfect documents, the memory of memories and historic error" (emphasis mine).[151] If these limitations were woeful, woefully symptomatic of refusing to interact with the living subjects of concern, then how much worse must it have felt for Du Bois who frequently went "house to house" yet encountered similar limitations. He also had to depend on "the memory of memories." Worse still must have been the uncertainty of whether his living subjects, like cooperation, were alive or dead, were anything more than a "shadowy outline."[152]

A mourning also lingers in the very first example, a very haunted example, Du Bois uses to define the limits of knowledge as the limits of chance. "That there are [such] limits is shown by the rhythm in birth and death rates," he says. To further define these limits "in the realm of human conduct," Du Bois summons terms from musicology, calling the "conjunction" between law and chance—"Law and Chance working in conjunction"—a meeting of a "primary rhythm" and "secondary" one. Each rhythm could ostensibly be ascribable to chance or law, depending on the circumstances. Speaking shorthand, he says, "a primary rhythm depending, as we have indicated, on physical forces and physical law; but within this appears again and again a secondary rhythm which, while presenting nearly the same uniformity as the first, differs from it in its more or less sudden rise at a given tune, in accordance with prearranged plan and prediction and in being liable to stoppage and change according to similar plan."[153] It only takes him a few sentences, heartbeats, before he returns, as if by compulsion, to his first example: "an example of primary uniformity is the death rate," he repeats. If the "death rate" is a "sudden rise at a given tune," then is Du Bois hearing a dirge? Is he sounding one out? Is he waxing elegiac for "the deaths that both make up and disturb the rate"?[154] Without a solid partition between chance and law, without inhabiting anything more than a "conjunction," Du Bois appears foredoomed to retrace little more than "a shadowy outline."

It must have been hard. Let's return to *Some Efforts*, where Du Bois writes, "This study has to review chiefly the activities of organizations [secret societies] whose main object is not benevolent but who incidentally do much work to promote the social welfare."[155] He has to find cooperation where it is codified and secret, as if through a shadow or a password, which gives new meaning, a darker meaning, to his cheer, "On then Black Americans, and remember the pass-word—*Organization and Co-operation!*"[156] He had to find cooperation through something it is not: associations such as secret societies that "incidentally," circumstantially, never intended but needed to produce cooperative life. I want to magnify the emotion of that unassuming word, that toss-off—"incidentally"—along with his phrase "the main object." In full, I want to magnify the reason the promotion of social welfare is *incidentally* the *main object* of secret societies.

The word "incident," at the time Du Bois used it in 1898, meant a light. "An illumination," "falling or striking upon a surface often in photographic contexts." A light that fell "from without."[157] As an incident cooperation was an outside light maddeningly accessible only from the inside, the matter, the "main," of what it was not. How might it feel to track something through something it is not? How do you track and tabulate distant and amorphous offshoots, rhythms, "a sudden rise at a given tune," knowing that where you begin may not be the beginning, but a cross-reference in infinite regress?

Of course, Du Bois would not explicitly assume that something originates in something incommensurate, something whose resemblance is "incidental" and remote, whose fleeting effects were driven by an ostensibly different cause. If the sociologist has to study the organized, the lasting, the objectively measurable, even or especially when searching for the opposite, then Du Bois is also admitting a wish to do otherwise, to be otherwise, to reside at the inceptions and extensions and flight of his desiderata. The "main object" is the hapless but only access point to another unnamed object, and this unnamed since unnamable, since ever evasive of object-life. Without the comforts of causality, Du Bois presents cooperatives as grievously spasmodic: tiny combustions of circumstance and need. As an outside light, they linger in the air like specters of the sun. On the field of sociology, we watch Du Bois stoop with the longing of always arriving at the ending's end, there in the grievous post-heat and suspended body-hum from a dashed and endangered crowd, a beginning gone elsewhere to begin again. In the pensive nook of his office, at more than one remove, he must effectively imagine and reconstruct the story from the darkening blur of a film fade.

2　Planned Failure

George Schuyler, Ella Baker, and the Young Negroes' Cooperative League

. . . .

After ecstasy what?

—Nathaniel Mackey

To set out for rehearsals in that quivering quarter-hour is
to engage conclusions, not beginnings . . .
Deprivation is made lyrical, and twilight,
with the patience of alchemy,
almost transmutes despair into virtue.

—Derek Walcott

Live not for battles won.
Live not for the-end-of-the-song.
Live in the along.

—Gwendolyn Brooks

You Know Nothing Lasts for Me!

Du Bois's cooperative movement was a perpetual advent in full accord with the old saw that a movement must endure. George Schuyler and Ella Baker's cooperative movement would be markedly different. Theirs was made to discohere, never made to last. Their Young Negroes' Cooperative League reflected Du Bois's Guild as a national coalition with transnational reach based on the creed of people over profit, but it differed in its defense of failure as an option, differed in its shift from grief to guffaw.

In 1977, at the age of seventy-three, Ella Baker tells this joke about life on the edge. A good part of the joke is how surprising it is, how brightly it breaks through her somewhat listless tone. She's being interviewed by Sue Thrasher and Casey Hayden in her upper Harlem apartment at Lenox Terrace. For most of these three-hours her words sound scratchy, crumpled and thin. She's tired. And seems far away. She's easily lost in the slur of traffic and wind that ever so often trails in through the window. So it's with a rote remove that she recollects her collaboration with George Schuyler on Black cooperatives during the Great Depression.

"We called for a meeting of young people for the formation of the Young Negroes' Cooperative League," she says. "I was the 'executive secretary,' or whatever."

"For how many . . . ?"

"Huh?"

"For how many years?"

"Only a couple of years." Then suddenly with jubilation, "you *know* nothing lasts for me!"[1] She doesn't just state this. She unzips this. She laughs half-throated. And her interviewers chuckle, albeit a bit awkwardly. If she's been somewhere else for the greater part of the last hour and forty-nine minutes, then for this slim moment she emerges in full. One might expect the throw-away *you know nothing lasts for me!* to sound like a regret or, better yet, a lament. But here it sounds like a point of pride, like a prayer. It is as if the very end of a life, any extension in time continuous enough to be called a life, or for that matter a thing, is when she's most alive, for "nothing," which is to say no thing, shall last. The end: the life to seek.

You know nothing lasts for me! could be the motto of this chapter, which is about something I find as jolting as the joke itself: the power in endings, the power in suspending the stubbornly sticky hope that a movement like the League's should steadily persist. We could start by observing that Baker disassembles the platitude that "nothing lasts" into a dictum where nothing lasts "for me." In her allusion to handily touchable things and why they cannot be "for me," she reminds us of *last*'s seedier side, its utilitarianism. The *Oxford English Dictionary* puts this powerfully. To "last" also means "to operate without impairment, deterioration, or loss of effectiveness," to remain like a clock in good working condition, "useable," "serviceable." By refusing to be serviceable, co-optable, used, the ephemerality of a movement serves the movement's makers. She reminds us, as well, of the original meaning of "last" from the Old German "to follow." With larger implications for Baker's philosophy of leadership, this is the definition that in her zest—in the difficulty one finds in locating her now (Hayden's and Thrasher's awkward chuckle, the pull I feel to keep rewriting this scene) and in her departure from the interview's line of questions—Baker cites by twice negating, underscores by x-ing out.

Her joke is nothing less than a forced fugitivity, and with that let's pan out a bit. It is a penchant to take leave that also cites and underscores the convergence point between this grain of movement making and the broader tradition of Black expressive culture. Interested in charting a series of leave takings, this is a culture of life etched on the edge, "the very edge [of oneself and which is one and the same thing] of semantic availability."[2] As Nathaniel Mackey argues regarding its jazz and blues, it is a culture in "pursuit of another voice, an alternate voice."[3] He describes Billie Holiday's, for instance, as "evacuated, cracks where / accents fell," conjuring up escape routes and abandoned fields.[4] *You know nothing lasts for me* (including "me") recalls that in the context of African American history, "last" as "to follow" and to be followed in return bears an etymology with *blood on the leaves, blood at the root,* in the full sense of the line.

Baker and Schuyler met in the late 1920s. In 1927 Baker arrived in New York from North Carolina, where she grew up. She had just graduated from Shaw University, summa cum laude, and soon met this nationally renowned "iconoclast," as she described Schuyler, at the Harlem YMCA. To slake her appetite "for debate," she immediately started attending his regular soirees, late night tête-à-têtes about whatever political issues felt pressing at the time. Bespeaking an interregnum between old and new forms of capitalist domination, these soirees were, more often than not, gatherings by twilight. Soon to be League headquarters, their location was swank, Schuyler's 321 Edgecombe Avenue apartment with hardwood parquetry floors.[5] Apartment 321 was perched in a part of Harlem thought to be so sweet for Blacks that people called it Sugar Hill. To give a feel for the weight of these twilight talks, they were also attended by labor unionist A. Philip Randolph, founder of the Brotherhood of Sleeping Car Porters, editor of the socialist magazine the *Messenger* for which Schuyler wrote from 1923 to 1928, and Schuyler's inspiration. Communist journalist Marvel Cooke was often there as well. Cooke and Baker co-wrote one of the most cited essays in Black feminism and the urban experience, "The Bronx Slave Market" (1935). Baker did not meet her until after the parties ended, so it seems the future really was in the room, tomorrow in the air. To this point, when Baker and Cook went undercover to expose "the stench" of "the auction block" in female domestic labor, Baker and Schuyler, another devious duo, had long been working to clear the general stench of capital.

In temperament and style, the League's two founders were ironically leagues apart. If Schuyler fashioned himself as the people's superintendent and wrote with the air of a man awfully underestimated (perhaps part of what gave such torque to his prose), then Baker fashioned herself as the people's support and wrote with the grace of a woman who knew their power to the bone. Yet this unlikely pair, volleying ideas often into the morning behind caramel brick, decided to unite to jar loose a dream: "the day," as Baker wrote, "when the soil and all its resources will be reclaimed by its rightful owners—the working masses of the world."[6] They would also reclaim (and which reclamation was the more daring I do not know) the boons of movement-brevity, of forced impermanence in a movement's making. Why? These boons were outside choices to continuous, cumulative time, what Althusser calls "ordinary time," and its tricky universalisms, lateral history, and lateral leadership. All the boons, all the choices, boiled down to one: the hard recognition, from the viewpoint of its holders, that we have what we need to have what we want. That's what "cooperative" meant: knowing despite the strain that the dream of reclamation is here, right here, in the brutal present.

In racial and critical theory, the universalisms of lateral leadership and lateral history have been particularly tricky, easily reproduced in their moment of erasure. They hide in an ethics that feels as necessary as breath. The ethics of persistence, of "standing through time," or as my father used to say, "to keep on keeping on," alongside my mother's promise that "nothing lasts forever."[7] Residing in the realm of nothing-lasts-forever, the League's big lesson is that the ethics of persistence, of standing through time, and the hierarchies of the social are made of the same essentialist stuff. Both depend for their survival on structures of permanence, and structures of permanence on universality. The League's big question is what does it matter if we displace the fiction of historical progress and the regulative power of top-down planning only to reinstitute their ontological conditions? As M. NourbeSe Philip asks, "What if Black life is not so much about persistence? . . . What if persistence is but a tiny part of something else . . . something that cannot be trapped . . . something other, over there, can't you see it . . . splitting time?"[8] If persistence is a standing (signifying in law, the right to seek redress, *locus standi*; and in the history of empire, "a place of settlement," a standing on land), then what might it mean to live standing out, to live without standing, as out-standing?[9] Part of what it means is sketched by the way those two outstanders, Baker and Schuyler, made cooperatives possible. They ended the movement they made not once but repeatedly so that both could have proclaimed with almost giddy guffaw, *you know nothing lasts for me!* What follows is a look into the ways they split time. Into their actions as large as a League's "formation." Into their gestures as large as an offhand joke.

Dangerous Slips

Today's reflections on social movements have hardly been a joking matter. Assessments of movements past have become a kind of mourning. Along this vein, Frederic Jameson notes that the concept of revolution has been facing tough times. "There have been," he claims, "few moments in modern social history in which people in general have felt more powerless."[10] The late Toni Morrison takes a similar temperature of the day. "Time seems to have no future," she writes. "In the late twentieth century (unlike in earlier ones) it seems to have no future that can accommodate the species that organizes, employs, and meditates on it." Indeed, everyone from Deborah Gould to David Scott has been eyeing a growing "sense of a stalled present," "a tragic out-of-jointness," "a political despair," a sense that Marxist progressive time has failed so often to deliver those times—especially at the times they felt closer than ever—that teleology writ-large has become obsolete.[11] It appears time itself has tapered to an end, where only the past remains.

But there is a lament lurking beneath this, far less recognized yet often charging it. Unlike the Marxist movements of yesteryears, roughly prior to 1968, today's not only fail to deliver. They fail to last. As political theorists Nick Srnicek and Alex Williams put it, "whereas that period saw mass mobilisation, general strikes, militant labour and radical women's organisations all achieving real and lasting successes, today is defined by their absence," the absence, that is, of "lasting successes."[12]

Following a preeminent queue, Williams and Srnicek take weary note that activists of the global north evince a growing "preference" for the "transient" and the "small scale," at the expense of those two words—"lasting" and "success," so commonly thought together one might think they were synonymous.[13] I am interested in the League for the doors it opens to the questions, what social movements come into view when longevity and success are not made synonymous, and when success does not depend on schemas of duration? What kind of social? What kind of movement? And if political transience charges a collective mourning, what kind of affects?

I am also interested in stirring up some calcified views of Baker and Schuyler, the second of whom is more often rued for his "race to the right" from the 1940s onwards than freshly observed for his rumblings on the left during his early years.[14] As for Baker, it is now a commonplace to see her as a model of "egalitarian" leadership and, in Barbara Ransby's words, as an "architect" of enduring democratic spaces.[15] Part of what I'm up to in portraying a slightly more contentious Baker, someone who challenged the virtues of making a movement last, is to show how this Baker might have learned to last differently for her egalitarianism to last at all. The two techniques were codependent. A bright forgetting at the horizon's edge, this is the Baker I see as I depart from the way she has been predominantly spatialized, the tendency to see her primarily in spatial terms and in a rather fixed space at that.

This mirrors the tendency in social movement theory to prioritize movement spaces that constitutively recur: boycotts, vigils, rallies, mass meetings, occupied buildings, strikes, and so on. In a watershed intervention on the field of sociology, the late Charles Tilly identifies certain protest strategies that curiously reemerge across time and distance, from eighteenth-century Britain to twentieth-century Mississippi: "the collective-action repertoire."[16] Describing a shift from riots to strikes among predominant movement tactics, Tilly writes, "some time in the nineteenth century, the people of most western countries shed the collective-action repertoire they had been using for two centuries or so, and adopted the repertoire they still use today." Limited in variety and "embedded in material routines of daily life," repertoires emerge according to a particular configuration of social, ideological, and material relations (to use Tilly's example, in the premodern period mass marches were unthinkable but grain seizures were not). As a sustained, stable, and legible set of actions upon which actors might choose to improvise, and thus as acts that accrete over time, they operate rather similarly to literary genres. Tilly's collaborator, Sidney Tarrow, also considers these "repeated public displays" a defining feature of movement formation.[17] I highlight these arguments not to contest them in some superficial exercise, nor out of a wish to again make sociology the proverbial strawman, but because these arguments reflect a common sense that pervades neighboring and distant disciplines. My sole point is that the categories assumed by these arguments obscure, even undermine, the kind of social movement that artists like Baker and Schuyler helped to spur. For starters, Baker was as much an "architect" of movement spaces, but less extravagant, less legible, and less sustained, as she was of movement time. She and her bandmate invite us to delve a different genre of performance.

There are still, I think, broader implications in pausing at the slippage, the metonymic slide, between a movement's endurance and its success. The slip may betray another. The notion that anyone devoted to the tradition of Black insurgency would want to undermine their own insurgent practice, as part of the practice, seems to stand against good sense. But it may be fruitful to ponder where this common sense comes from or at least what it involves. I wonder if the insistence on sturdy movement organizations, on sturdy social movements, and the allergy to the opposite involves a certain slippage in the way we conceive freedom, conceive the very axis on which much of Black studies turns. Here the slippage I am thinking about occurs between the constancy of the fight, "the beautiful struggle," and the length of its iterations.[18] A slip of this nature puts a dangerous pressure on the stories we hear, let alone tell. For the problem with this slip is that it is not horizontal. It is a kind of fall, a logical descent (from the iterations to the struggle) that reflects and reinforces a hierarchy of value.

Voicing the perspective of African American conservatism, a gospel of self-reliance, after making it clear that this is not his perspective, that his generation hungers for a different form of activism, Ta-Nehisi Coates writes, "The civil rights generation is exiting the American stage—not in a haze of nostalgia but in a cloud of gloom troubled by the persistence of racism, the apparent weaknesses of the generation following in its wake, and the seeming indifference of much of the country to black America's fate."[19] This is a "fate," the logic goes, that might have been avoided. This is a "cloud" that the old troupe might not have had to enter, had they, had the movement, somehow stuck around. The biggest problems are surely the "persistence" of racial violence and the "indifference" of the country, but the central problem is the persistence of the fight, its ebbing disappearance, its "apparent weaknesses." Placed exactly at the center of the sentence, the phrase "apparent weaknesses" significantly occupies in form and thought the center of gravity. To keep to his argument, Coates would have to explain this equation between strength and staying power as merely another feature of the behavioral thesis of racial disadvantage (straighten up and die right), but the equation may have deeper and more politically pervasive roots.

Two registers appear merged: the constancy of resistance as a structural, fundamental, or paraontological condition within Blackness at large and the performance of resistance as a personal, intentional, or epiphenomenal condition within Black lives. "Freedom is a constant," writes Elizabeth Povinelli, glossing the old Foucauldian principle that if the pressure is constant so too must be the resistance.[20] Explaining Foucault's preference for the term *gay freedom* over *gay liberation*, Povinelli reads freedom as the beginning of all potential (potentiation) and reads liberation as the beginning of the end (an achievement). Such freedom is "a set of ongoing reflexive practices that the subject undergoes in relation to a given formation of power." But there's a problem with this freedom, as Povinelli explains.

Because its ongoing-ness is entwined with and thereby determined by structures of power, going on may keep those same powers going.

Positing an excess of Black persistence over persistent white supremacy, Brent Edwards asserts with arresting eloquence the inevitable adjacency within Black culture of "dispossession and invention, perdition and predication, catastrophe and chance." Similarly, Fred Moten claims that "Black studies' concern with what it is to own one's dispossession . . . makes it more possible to embrace the underprivilege of being sentenced to the gift of constant escape."[21] Both these postulations suggest the stuff we are made of is doomed to fly. Whether at rest or at battle, the flight never stops.

But what of the battles within the battles? What of the lives they contain, the lives within this life? Is there not a difference between the stuff we are made of and the stuff we make? I see Ransby, for example, substituting one for the other, blurring this difference in her quick reversal (ultimately, a back-and-forth) of who she claims Baker was. Ransby remarks that "inherent in Baker's philosophy . . . was the recognition that no organization should last forever," that organizations should fall. But only pages later she notes that the founding of the Student Nonviolent Coordinating Committee (SNCC) in 1960, Baker's most famous act, was "the accumulation of Baker's efforts over spring and summer to help build a permanent organization." Seemingly aware of what looks like contradiction, she writes, "Baker realized that the radical pulse she had detected needed to be sustained, cultivated, and propagated."[22] The pulse is all, not the program. One might say this resolves matters. With the help of the word "detected," "pulse" implies that what constitutes a movement is less fixed and less visible, and not any deeper, than what constitutes its structures. The notion that a movement is not simply a pulse, but a detection of a pulse, not the pulse itself, but the transfer of its feeling, implies that a movement is made up of resonances—personal, conceptual, and material resonances.

But then why use "pulse" at all? What is this draw to a bodily metaphor in order to imagine something radically out of body, radical by its refusal to be bound in *any*body? In other words, if this "pulse" must be "detected" then it must also be uncertain, essentially so: of questionable length, presence, and ontological status. It must be here and not here. Otherwise, there'd be no need to lay it bare. By Ransby's own words, it is this somewhere-else-ness that "needed to be sustained." On some level, Ransby herself seems to detect an impermanence that carries over to the very thing that on first sight seems imperative to carry out. And it seems to me this imperative partakes in a conflation, quick and slippery, between the facts of Blackness at the level of a resonance and the acts of Black life at the level of a "pulse." I do not mean to suggest the registers of Blackness are actually separable. They are not. But as fraught adjacencies, they are also not coterminous or reducible to each other. I simply think we need to be critically aware when we speak of one under the sign of the other, Blackness as Black life. For in the end this awareness reminds us of something we can't bear to forget. In the words of Erica Edwards, it reminds us of Cedric Robinson's "deceptively simple creed that oppression is only one of our realities," that the "pulse" beats to more than the rhythms of abstraction written to override it. That's a tough spade of optimism for some uniquely tough times.

Something out Somewhere Else

I'd now like to give a brief biography of the League. A straightforward recital of this organization hardly does justice to all its enigmatic breaks and ambiguous life forms, but I offer one here for the sake of orientation. In October 1930, Schuyler released a call from his "Views and Reviews" column for what would become the League. He had been talking about cooperatives since 1923 in what can only be called a prolonged fever, but it was from his post as staff writer for the *Pittsburgh Courier* that the organization started taking shape on the national stage. Auguring the first and last words in their name, "young" and "league," Schuyler wrote, "I would like very much to organize a corps of 5000 militant Negroes, men and women, ranging in age from 15 to 30." By calling for a "corps" of "militant[s]" no older than thirty he was asking for nothing less than a group of co-conspirators willing to risk their lives. Their motivation? As "a spearhead of Negro advancement," they might very well save Blacks "from degradation and pauperism." They might also save themselves. For "corps" alluded to corpse, and the allusion implied Black life was becoming a kind of lack-life, but that this very lack (corpse) could body forth a new vitality, produce by entanglement a new body of strength ("corps"). Such was the principle, anyway, of cooperative life: bound and emboldened by common need, "shockproof[ed]" as Schuyler claimed, by a formidable sociality.[23]

Naturally enough, this message of mutual aid for mutual relief attracted more Blacks to cooperatives during the Great Depression than in any other decade over the course of the century. But it attracted few to Schuyler's call, replies barely trickling in over the next two months. Nor was he appreciably helped by the *Courier*'s ascent to Black America's most popular press. Not until a twenty-six-year-old Ella "Jo" Baker, who as the *Crisis* reported "credits her education" less to Shaw University than to the "'courses'" of "domestic service, factory work, and other freelance laborers," agreed to assist "the most recognizable name in black [American] journalism" did this "movement," as they'd christen it, burst into bloom. Why? Schuyler's grand leadership needed a ground leadership. In testimony after testimony, the primary pull of cooperatives was their avoidance of messianism and the totalizing ideologies in which it tended to be caped. As the president of the League's Columbus, Ohio, council, William Henderson would attest, "It is not communism, capitalism, syndicalism or Republicanism—it is consumers' cooperation." Baker echoed this ethos when she spoke for the latter at the Harlem Economic Forum in 1933 as part of the symposium "Communism, Garveyism, Consumers' Cooperation." The latter is that which lacks coherence of an "ism" or totality, that which refused to rhyme. And when Schuyler appeared to counter the very horizontal leadership he helped to construct, Floyd J. Calvin, a popular Black radio talk show host in New York City, scoffed. "Let George Do It," ran his op-ed in the *Philadelphia Tribune*. The immediate target was Schuyler's presumption of the League's historical singularity in one of his columns, but the real issue was Schuyler's ego. "George has criticized all the efforts and movements of Negroes. Now he is going to do this job himself. That is what we call a man. . . . Go to it George, we hope you will succeed."[24] By calling out his chauvinism and emphatically calling him George, the op-ed gave the damning impression that in the school of Black insurgency he had yet to grow up.

I should say before I go on that I hardly mean to imply Baker was a sort of catalyst. While I do mean to contest the lopsided credit Schuyler is given for the League (his most recent biographer does not even mention Baker's name), I do not intend to dispute what in other spaces might have been true, that Schuyler was "her mentor," as her biographer Barbara Ransby claims. In this space, models of development like that of mentor-mentee prove more convenient than clarifying. The issue I face in divulging Baker's contribution is far more elemental than any contestation over relative influence. It is an issue about how to tell a story at all about someone who undoes the basic unit of a story, a discernible protagonist with a point of view, whose metaphysical consistency gives character to character. Baker did not receive misrecognition. She invited, even courted it, only to reject it later, taking the call to cut the line.

I was struck, for instance, when she said in an unpublished essay written sometime around 1940 that the League "was organized by George

Schuyler." From the organization she described as "the first" and most important "spring" for the "increased interest in consumers cooperation" among Blacks during the 1930s, she astonishingly withdrew her name. This may remind you of the dialogue with which I opened this chapter where Baker does the reverse. "*We* called" for the League's "formation," she says (emphasis mine). It reminds me of the part I did not quote, where just seconds earlier she states their collaboration then suddenly recants it. Speaking of the Cooperative League of America and its offices in the city, she says, "and we had opened—when I say we, George, among the other things, had written about the virtues of blacks having cooperatives."[25] When I first heard that I thought, but what did they open? "We had opened" what? Their office, presumably. Or maybe what they really opened, what the "we" opened, is exactly what follows, the hardest thing to see because it's actually there: the negation itself, the negation of itself. She negates the "we," her "we," which is to say her own articulation of basic common ground: "when I say we, George." Six years before she left this life, she said on tape with heavy eyes and a voice thin as a thread, "my ego wasn't at stake at any point." How does one tell a story that has no ego in it at any point, where the ego is negated at every point, a story that may feel like no story at all?

Baker's hidden influence on the most momentous civil rights movement organizations (SNCC, the NAACP, the Mississippi Freedom Democratic Party, and so on) is everywhere being reappraised and applauded, from *Nation Magazine*'s spat with MLK-monomania, "It's time we celebrate Ella Baker Day," to Cornel West's encomium, "Yeah, Ella, she's one of the greatest." Perhaps it's unavoidable, but the problem with this premise is that it turns her into the same figure she worked deftly to avoid, the figurehead, the foreground, so towering she's calendrical, one of the greatest. It obscures the profundity in her gesture of denial, a gesture that recalls the political move Gayatri Spivak terms "the first right," asserting the right to refuse that which has been refused.[26] In this case, recognition. But Baker's move seems different. It is less a declarative act than an interplay, a partial acceptance for a total cancellation, taking the call to cut the line. It is a sneaky yes-no, akin to the vexed relationship cooperatives by necessity maintain with capital. Baker's move, less dashing to an elsewhere than dashing it, is additionally different by virtue of its sequence. If the first right is a negation of a negation, then Baker's right is the negation of herself, or more precisely, of a self. What kind of story, what lexis, what frame, can illuminate a freedom produced and preserved by a willful disappearance?

Colored Co-operative Store at Buffalo, New York

"Colored Co-operative Store at Buffalo, New York." *Crisis* (January 1932).

Maybe a story that questions the certainty that the League fell at all. It may come as no surprise that given Baker's approach, given her "group-centered leadership" to use her phrase, she was "unanimously" voted the League's national director in 1931.[27] Membership soared. Verticality vamoosed. Within the first year, membership increased "400 percent," as Baker cheered, from forty-two members to two hundred and one. Exactly a year since Schuyler's call for a "corps," they hosted their first national conference. And this national conference made their fledgling group a national sensation. At the YMCA in downtown Pittsburgh, Baker and Schuyler welcomed an overflow crowd of more than six hundred. By year two, they had four hundred members, had started buying clubs, a milk distribution service out of Harlem's Dunbar Apartments, a cooperative newsstand in Philadelphia (their most popular enterprise), a grocery store in Omaha, Nebraska, and another in Buffalo, New York, named Citizens' Co-Operative Society, which earned and redistributed a weekly net profit of $850. Rehabilitated multiple times under slightly different names, and holding on until 1961, Citizens' would be one of the longest running cooperatives in twentieth-century Black history. On the preceeding page is a picture taken of the store's proprietors. When I look at it, I'm struck by the two women in the middle. For all the store's profits and persistent success, unbroken fatigue looks memorized in their bodies. Unbroken success does not.

The years 1930 to 1932 were a swell of activity. For a year the League ran a cooperative farm in Doylstown, Pennsylvania.[28] They established and connected twenty-four "councils," local enclaves of cooperative study, planning, and organizing in twenty-two cities and twenty states, including California, New York, Maryland, Ohio, Louisiana, South Carolina, Virginia, Arizona, Pennsylvania, Washington, and Tennessee. This proliferation of councils expressed a hostility to a parliamentary or party system of governance. A party system functioned through representative assemblies. And it was the problem of indirect representation that gave rise to the League in the first place. The council system, alternately, harkened back in recent history to the soviets of the Russian Revolution and the secret societies of Black cooperative organizations, like the chapters of the National Colored Farmers Alliance. As organs of self-representative action, councils in the hands of Blacks and particularly Black women were designed to protect the influence of the people on public life and expose the fiction of the divide between the private and the public sphere, a fiction that concealed the state's cooptation of reproductive labor. Schuyler also traveled to England to develop ties with other cooperatives running on the same premise of direct democracy, and by publishing through a Barbadian press he tried to develop similar ties across the West Indies.

No vision this broad could unfurl without contention. In 1929 Black union organizer Frank Crosswaith headlined that he glimpsed a "New Era of Cooperation Replacing Individualism."[29] The editors of the paper in which his article appeared, the *Philadelphia Tribune*, did not want that era to look anything like the League. In their mind the League drew far too hard a line in the sand against capitalist enterprise, a line tantamount to a "malicious stab" against Black businesses. The editors were responding to the resolution by the Pittsburgh conference goers that the "fundamental difference" between the YNCL, the National Negro Business League, and the Colored Merchants Association (CMA) be "duly recognized," as Baker wrote in a newsletter, and as Schuyler repeated in his own columns. Intimating her own interest in the self-transformation a social movement can bring, she explained that "the latter [organizations] are interested in the BUYING POWER of the consumer; while the former is interested in the CONSUMER HIMSELF."[30]

But it was Schuyler the editors of the *Tribune* reprimanded for having gone "out of his way to do harm to a potentially great Negro organization in its infancy," the CMA.[31] That this was actually a cooperative of Black grocers underscored how distinct the League would be from other novelties in this "New Era of Cooperation." At the other end of the political spectrum, a writer in the communist journal the *Liberator* went so far as to title his article "Introducing a Traitor." Unlike the *Tribune* editors, he charged that the line in the sand was not drawn hard enough. "Under a capitalist dictatorship, cooperatives offered as a solution for economic ills are merely a means of drawing the masses away from the class struggle. Under a workers' dictatorship, the question of cooperation assumes an entirely different aspect."[32] Clearly the League's percussive ambitions rang through the Black press in various keys.

And still they wanted more than this, co-ops. Like Du Bois's Guild, the League wanted, as Schuyler saw it, a "cooperative commonwealth," transnational and diasporic.[33] The term *cooperative commonwealth* was introduced by late nineteenth-century labor Republicans to name "a condition in which all workers exercised joint ownership and control over industrial enterprises."[34] Some economists define the term today as "a system of cooperatives" necessarily designed to "replace" a capitalist market.[35] As I mentioned in the previous chapter, this transnational coalition was first popularized, with unfortunate implication, by Laurence Gronlund's *The Cooperative Commonwealth in Its Outlines: An Exposition of Modern Socialism* (1884). By traducing Marx's dialectic into a gradual, evolutionary process without class antagonism, Gronlund helped assure cooperatives the bad reputation of disinterest in the class struggle. The idea that capitalists and laborers would peacefully unite in a self-governing association of producers and consumers appealed to heightened sensitivities during the 1930s toward the fascist rule that was flowering in Europe. Norman Thomas, six-time Socialist Party presidential candidate, wrote in 1934 that "the only effective answer to the totalitarian state of fascism is the cooperative commonwealth."[36] For Blacks of the 1930s, however, the commonwealth meant "battle," to use Baker's word. And the common of the commonwealth had an additional meaning, that increasingly irresistible idea of a "Black metropolis."[37] In early 1931 Schuyler traveled to England to expand the League's alliance and study firsthand famed cooperatives there with special attention to their business practices. He visited cooperatives in Liverpool, Manchester, and London and took a picture of himself before the publicity department of Cooperative Wholesale Ltd.[38] By this point,

George Schuyler with Mr. Massey outside the offices of the Co-operative Wholesale Society of Great Britain, in Manchester, England. February 5, 1931. Schuyler Family Photograph Collection, Photographs and Prints Division, Schomburg Center for Research in Black Culture, New York Public Library.

the wholesale had absorbed his main inspiration, commonly known then as the first successful modern consumers' cooperative, the Rochdale Society of Equitable Pioneers. Rochdale was a general store and lending library, born primarily among weavers after a failed strike in 1844.

Schuyler, for his part, turned to *Economic Outlook*, the Barbadian magazine I mentioned above, to drum up home support for an "international cooperative exchange."[39] As the dispossessed, he argued, await the historical break of "world revolution," this exchange, "in the mean time," would provide an entirely different break, something one League member called simply "relief."[40] As a new social arrangement across the Black diaspora, "Negro farmers" would "co-operate with Negro urban workers . . . in the United States and the West Indies"—"for the first time." If Schuyler sent the dream, Baker hauled it to the light, or hauled her light to the dream, for it seemed the dream was already awake. As director of branches for the NAACP in the mid-1940s, she corresponded with D. A. Cooper, secretary of West India Co-Operative Bank. Inspired by Jamaica's new constitution "for self-government," the bank was a credit union that in anticolonial resistance of what they called "Free Enterprisers" built one hundred and eight branches throughout the island to "meet the requirements of the man-in-the-street."[41] Little record remains, unfortunately, of exactly the kind of solicited "help and advice" Baker gave, if any, on establishing a "trade relation" across the wordless seas.[42]

In her mind, each of these efforts "was a small thing."[43] By comparison to the League's goals, it is easy to see why: 5,000 charter members to start; 5,000 general members within a year. A "cooperative wholesale in each state" by year three, a "cooperative bank in each community" by year four, "producing many of the necessities we consume such as food, clothing, and shelter" by year five, a "cooperative housing department," and a "cooperative university" sometime in the future.[44] But on September 1, 1932, due to desiccated funds at the bottom of the Depression, when the average Black unemployment rate was over 50 percent, they had to "close" their central office. "Office," Schuyler specified, as if to reiterate that they did not close their doors.[45] Some councils and offshoots were very much still operative. Citizens' survived until 1961.[46] Lewis Anthony, chair of the Philadelphia council, received a grant from the Federal Emergency Relief Association in 1933 to start a cooperative farm in Georgetown, Pennsylvania. By 1936 it boasted "residence quarters," and for five families "on relief" it "allotted" each "a plot for its own use."[47] So when Baker wrote that "they functioned as a national body from 1930 through 1932," "national" and "body" are the keywords. As if destined by its original lure of decentralized leadership, the Young Negroes' Cooperative League by 1933 dissolved as a centralized body, dispersed as a national unit. Who then could call it dead?

Perhaps this is why, to Thrasher and Hayden, Baker was a little cryptic about the League's life and death. Referring to the entire range of their activities, from buying clubs to buying land, and how these activities did not last, referring then as well to their life and death, "they were," she said, "just part of the drive."[48] Then trying to recall what she also could not forget, another League "experiment," she said with a touch of strain, "there was something out somewhere else."[49] Let's pause for a moment on the phrase "something out." It signifies two things: a termination and an ambiguous presence.[50] Something out in the terminal sense evokes a light, as in *out like a light*. In the ambiguously present sense it evokes a ghost, as in *the ghosts are out tonight*. A fair image for a ghost might be a shadow. A ghost, like a shadow, is always here and not here, around but also gone, "somewhere else," as Baker says. All this is to say, the phrase "something out somewhere else" evokes a play of shadows and light. A paradox of shadow-light. It is uncanny, but I see this play in a photograph of Baker from 1964 speaking in Hattiesburg, Mississippi. She appears to be conducting, summoning, the shadows—or is it the light?

We might call this shadow play, in the words of David Toop, "the mystico-political undercurrent of black American thought."[51] C. L. R. James might call it "the future in the present," the "affirmation that is contained in every negation," except here James, the chief defender of dialectical negativity, is not negative enough.[52] The "drive" Baker speaks of, the full force of the movement, was to extinguish something that it both encounters and creates, put "out" what it puts "out." As "something out somewhere else," the movement, in terms of time, was both fugitive and foreclosed. As hard as it is to imagine, the movement's temporal structure is something akin to an indefinite sempiternity, an eternity with a definite beginning but an indefinite end. I say an indefinite end because its definite ones are many. It's not that the movement has no endpoint, but that it has too many for any one to be definitive.[53] In terms of space, the League's cooperative movement is both rooted and shifty. Spatially, it is certainly somewhere, and certainly somewhere else, a paradox that has less to do with a relationship of distance, as in the common contrast between local and global, than with one of perception. From whose perspective does the movement actually take shape? Baker adopts the vantage of one participant and many at the same time, less pinpoint than pan-point, a truly "group-centered" view that bucks the notion

Ella Baker addresses a group from the podium in Hattiesburg, Mississippi, 1964. Behind her sits Charles Evers, brother of Medgar Evers. Photograph by George Ballis. Courtesy of TakeStock/Top Foto.

of a center and of a single shape. So to answer the question, a movement takes shape from a perspective paradoxically "group-centered," which means it takes shape to the extent it does not.

The movement's resistance to immediate visibility dovetails with Baker's repeated remarks that the grand shows of mobilization have been over-emphasized at the expense of the less visible and more diffuse dynamics of organization. In 1968, she told journalist John Britton, "I have questions about the long-term effectiveness of big demonstrations and what you get from them." Speaking of the Southern Christian Leadership Conference (SCLC) she said, "to be honest, in terms of historical facts, their mobilization was usually predicated upon some effort at organizing by someone else." From Karen Sack's concept of "centerwomen" to Belinda Robnett's concept of "bridge leaders," the work of organization has been powerfully interpreted as embedded within the work of interpersonal bonds, developed mainly by women, beneath the threshold of visibility, through monumental, hourly labor.[54]

What Baker suggests in her group-centered emphasis on organization is not that this work should suddenly become visible, but that invisibility should suddenly become integral to any interpretive frame of movement activity, with ramifications for how this frame frames time. Movements are more frequently equated to a "wave-like form," something visible and familiar that out of the right context rises and falls.[55] Sociologist Kevin Gillan usefully notes that this perception of time has a number of weaknesses. It foreshortens the movement. It visually elevates the extravagance of mobilization over the quiet of organization by assuming the sequence of "mobilization, interaction, and demobilization." But most of all, it misses the time beneath the wave. Focusing on the Alter-Globalization, Anti-War, and Occupy movements, Gillan adapts from physics the term *vector* to discuss cross-vectors in a "timescape." Vectors allow him to consider the way time fluctuates in speed ("velocity"), affect ("intensity," "salience"), and direction. Modes of time may "diffuse" even as they repeat.[56] It is this diffusion that I see Baker addressing to the effect of interrogating our reliance on the vertical in the production of sight. To think here of movement formation is not to think of emergence, but maybe of fractures in a political context, where the movement itself are the gaps left behind, spaces for something new, something like "revolution," as Schuyler would call it.

The apperception of a movement from the vantage of a singular pluralism, from the one-many not the many-one, from what Cedric Robinson calls "collective being," no longer sees the masses as binary and discrete, but as dispersive and uncountable. Resistant to sociological representations in which society takes a determinant form, the masses are neither one being nor many. Because "group-centered" does not name, as we might be tempted to think, a unified or central experience, neither can the experience of it be central or unified. Gone is the binary between leader and base, along with, one must hope, the concomitant binaries among gender and sexual difference. As the Germanist Paul North has said about the meaning of "a mass" in "a mass movement," an account of a movement from a pan-point perspective makes it impossible to break it down into individual positions or to sum it up into a collective will.[57] This results in much more than the advantage of resistance to cooptation. By painting the movement and the masses that comprise it, in one tentative gesture, as a nondenumerable dispersion, a shadow play, Baker calls us to rethink how one participates in such a thing. What mode of participation corresponds to this altered and thoroughly qualitative mode of perception? For starters, a visibly hidden one, as Baker's own involvement in movements suggests, and as the photograph opposite uncannily captures.

Jacques Derrida defines "messianicity," a word he coins to distinguish it from the overdetermined nature of messianism, as "a waiting without expectation." We might define Baker's "group-centered" view as an expectation without waiting, for what it anticipates is already "out somewhere." Her view does not foreclose the future so long as one believes, to again evoke Povinelli, that there are many futures, many futures to come as soon as certain ones are closed. Nor does it extend Derrida's flirtation with political disengagement, the dangerous consequence of the effort to hold onto an improvisational openness, a capacious receptivity, or in his terms an "active preparation," with zero plan or direction. There is, however, something affectively similar between Baker's mindfulness of the masses and Derrida's "waiting without expectation." Both excite an "amalgam of desire and anguish, affirmation and fear, promise and threat." What is the feeling, after all, of "something out somewhere else" if not also threatening to whatever degree it is promising, if not also ominous however much it is desired? From Baker's point of view (if I may be so bold to say), the Black cooperative movement is like an offscreen sound, "something out somewhere else." It is a movement that arrives before it is seen.

May Things Fall Apart

We have missed Baker's shadow play and the strangeness of the League because like most leftist movements across the twentieth century, the movement the League began has been invariably told as a story of unfortunate failure. This is a tragic tale where the tragically blind has been indubitably Schuyler, and where Baker's exemption is also her erasure, an "absented presence," in Katherine McKittrick's term.[58] Avoiding this historical judgment (it is a declension narrative that from its point of retrospection unwittingly assumes a longer narrative of ascent), I'd like to venture a counterintuitive reading of the archive. On the one hand, the record lends itself to tart exasperations like the idea the League fell due to Schuyler's "naivety concerning the plight of the Black working class." Following Schuyler's admission of mismanaging funds, the record lends itself to quips like "one might expect an organization led by a professional satirist to come to this."[59] On the other hand, the same documents that support the reception that the League was "a qualified failure" are sites to reinterpret why the act of disentangling Blackness from property is necessarily bizarre, and why this need is still unintelligible in the predominant frames of political rationality.

Flyer for joining the Young Negroes' Cooperative League. George Schuyler, "An Appeal to Young Negroes," 1930, box 2, folder 3, page 6, Ella Baker Papers, Schomburg Center for Research in Black Culture, New York Public Library.

Perhaps nothing was more bizarre than the movement's founding document, a sixteen-page four-by-six booklet with an imprint of lucky clovers framing the cover and a deceptively quiet title: "An Appeal to Young Negroes."[60] Authored by Schuyler in the fall of 1930 it was distributed to prospective members as a kind of manifesto. One can divide it into three sections: a preamble (a fiery list of grievances and a rallying cry), pragmatics ("tentative program," "co-operative principles," "by-laws"), and a roll-call of the founders. In sum, the "Appeal" announced the five-year plan I listed above, a plan of economic autonomy that to them spelled protection against all racial assaults, from arbitrary incarceration to gender and sexual violence. In addition, Schuyler wrote that in this "ultra-democratic" group Black women "stand on equal footing with men." And while gender parity was unusual for a political organization, it was not bizarre.

The bizarreness began in a strikingly topsy-turvy leadership structure. For a participatory democracy, "complete power resides in the hands of the rank and file who can remove any official at any time, even the National Director." If you were to read this slim booklet to the end of the roll call, you'd find two conflicting sections printed side by side on adjacent pages: "The Founder" (Schuyler) and "A Partial List of Y. N. C. L. Organizers" (twenty-eight in all, Baker hidden in the middle). Not only is it unclear how the organizers here are different from the founder, but in the second and last edition of the "Appeal" he made it even less so. In bigger font, Schuyler renamed its second section, "Associate Founders and Organizers." He effectively brought the two camps closer even as he kept, or by way of keeping, them apart. He dramatized a face-off between high and low leadership, and the tension would persist with explosive effects.

It was a bold plan, all this instability, but one plan was even bolder. From the letters that recipients of the flyer sent to Schuyler's office at the *Pittsburgh Courier*, the boldest part of the manifesto concerned the term *young*. The part of the "Appeal" that elicited the greatest surprise was, no kidding, "the much-discussed age limit," as Schuyler described it.[61] It was not the incredible projected size of the cooperative commonwealth itself but the bizarrely impractical membership requirement that brought the most controversy. "If you have reached your 16th but not your 36th Birthday, you are eligible to join," Schuyler wrote and emphatically placed at the very end of the preamble. "We do not want those who have grown weary and disillusioned," he continued. "We want those who are energetic, intelligent and believe in the power of their own organized effort." With the prospect of ageing out, this is also the power to disorganize the "organized."

Mandating not only an age limit but also a maximum age was tantamount to instating a date of expiry, a moment when one's membership would come to a prescribed end. To make matters more surprising, Schuyler himself would already be thirty-five in 1931; Baker, twenty-seven. But she was on no firmer grounds. Remember Schuyler specified the masses could remove "even the National Director." The organization was set to lose its "president" and could easily lose it cofounder just as it disembarked, giving its leadership and organizational coherence about the same permanence as an etching on water. This method of liquidation was stated twice in the "Appeal." "No person under sixteen or over thirty-five years of age shall be accepted for membership, except by two-thirds vote."[62] The two-thirds vote meant they did allow exceptions, seemingly loosening the mandate. But if only a supermajority could vote to exempt a member, then the same law that loosened up the age restriction equally doubled down on it.

One reporter inquired about the situation. But Baker did not so much explain as reiterate. "The officers now serving are only nominal and these include Mr. Schuyler himself," his leadership being "temporarily assumed."[63] Retention, Baker emphasized, was not the point. One comical byline in Schuyler's own paper could scarcely repress its bafflement: "Founder of Y. N. C. L. Plans to Retire as Soon as Program Is Definitely Launched."[64] One Herbert Robinson read Schuyler's essay of promotion with its no-frills title "The Young Negroes' Cooperative League," and he still wrote to the *Crisis*, triggered by the word "young," "You see I had taken the headline as a joke and I was going to read it and get a laugh," but "being young myself" he decided to read on.[65] Members and observers were wrestling with the question, how did the age limit define the duration of the League as a whole and the larger commonwealth Schuyler and Baker intended to plot?

This question of stability in the machinery of governance was grounded in a deeper question about the movement's integrity. The age-limit bylaw, Schuyler's wholesale fulmination against Black representatives, and the choice of federated councils over centralized parties were all ways of addressing an inescapable dilemma. One their movement shared with the dilemma of revolution: how to maintain the powers of the people from which the movement springs in the institutional life slated to survive it. Hannah Arendt famously frames this as the problem of preserving "the revolutionary spirit" once the revolution has come to pass. Because the revolutionary spirit is the spirit to start anew, the issue, Arendt notes, that revolutionaries face is how to start a new order that does not rob from posterity the freedom they enjoyed: the freedom to start anew. In the context of the League, this "perplexity" applies as much to the time after the movement as it does to the time during it. Arendt applies the "perplexity" strictly to the aftermath because for her revolution is bound on one end by violence and on the other by "the establishment of a new form of government." But lacking a discrete period of violent overthrow, and calling into question who gets to say what does and does not constitute violence, the League's cooperative movement also lacked a discernible end. The point here is that the most radical part of the League was not all the things that didn't happen but the foundation that did.

Referring to the founders of the American Revolution, Arendt claims that this dilemma of sustaining the revolutionary spirit seemed worse than unavoidable. "It seemed unsolvable. If foundation was the aim and the end of revolution, then the revolutionary spirit was not merely the spirit of beginning something new but of starting something permanent and enduring; a lasting institution, embodying this spirit and encouraging it to new achievements, would be self-defeating. From which it unfortunately seems to follow that nothing threatens the very achievements of revolution more dangerously and more acutely than the spirit which has brought them about. Should freedom in its most exalted sense as freedom to act be the price to be paid for foundation?"[66]

The difficulty of generating in the process of generation the process of degeneration, of rooting the riot, grounding the swarm (recalling Hartman's retort to the conventional opposition between form and formlessness), is simply Byzantine. The scale of the difficulty may help explain why Schuyler likened the famed bylaw to a form of magic. With the number three symbolizing magical force, he restated the age limit as the magically third bylaw in a set of sixteen. The bylaw was magical because it alone gave shape, lasting shape, to the freedom not to last. It maintained, to quote Arendt, the "original sources" of the people's power.

I am interested less in whether the League resolved the trouble of beginnings than I am in exploring the more fruitful question of what philosophy of activism the bylaw betrays. To proffer an answer, I deploy a concept I call *planned failure*, the performative codification of strategic anarchy. Planned failure designates the intended demise of the original plan. It assumes that to maintain the structure of a movement's organization, which is made up of not only social arrangements but also the constitution of its political subjects, it is necessarily to reinforce the very problems one sought to escape: the distribution of the surplus, from revenue to respect, according to hierarchies of class, race, and gender. In the context of cooperatives, planned failure begins with the insight that, as Karl Marx wrote, "the cooperative factories run by workers themselves are, within the old form, the first examples of the emergence of a new form, even though they naturally reproduce in all cases, in their present organization, all the defects of the existing system, and must reproduce them."[67] This alternative political practice does not seek to transcend these defects so much as disassemble them until they cease to cohere. In planned failure, freedom and its foils, possibilities and their hindrances, are tensed, present tensed, into a seriality of ecstatic, choreographed, gestures. The importance of Baker's and Schuyler's activism being largely gestural, incomplete, and inconspicuous, cannot be overstated. Action requires context. Because it was always their context that conscripted their action, they had to negate both—context and action—to allow them to act at all, beginning with gestures. This shift from action to gestures mirrors what I call later a shift from tragic to comic time because following Henri Bergson's famous apercu in his essay on laughter, *Le Rire*, action not gesture is the domain of tragedy; only action can ever be tragic.[68]

As an echolalia of subtleties, planned failure is too gestural to be regarded as a public display, open dialogue, organized chaos, or a commitment to contingent action, the last still defining the veritable lodestar of democratic politics and radical socialist strategy.[69] Nor should it be conflated with the capitalist imperative of planned obsolescence and reinvention. Its plunge into the present not only rebuffs the "re" in the idea of reinvention. It rebuffs invention. If anything, its aim is to hear out and sound out the very mother of invention: necessity. Consider it the necessity of countering an always exclusive progressive line of history, the necessity of jumping the fence. Consider it the wild undercurrent of Baker's "group-centered leadership," or what Patrice Cullors, cofounder of Black Lives Matter, hails as "leader-full" not leaderless movements.[70] Planned failure belongs to a horizontality of social arrangements still practiced by a long series of Black and Brown insurgencies, from the autonomous movements in Argentina, which to the shock of many but the evasion of the National Guard, practiced "desorganización" (meaning "disorganization" as well as "unorganization") after the 2001 recession, to the Movement for Black Lives after the death of Michael Brown.[71]

Planned failure inverts the perspective of policymakers ventriloquized by Fred Moten and Stefano Harney in *The Undercommons*. Policymakers, they say, are fixed on being fixed, yet always in "need [of] hope," capital's cynosure. These policycrats "keep making plans and plans fail as a matter of policy. Plans must fail because planners must fail."[72] Those who devise the failure of their own plans inhabit that failure. Sure, this desire for institutional collapse, for a serial construction and deconstruction, for splintered and rhizomic forms of power over constituted and centralized ones, for the always-irregular, makes for an odd activism. But its affects are ecstasies. In 1933, Olga Cassels, League member in the Ohio council, suggested Blacks needed something more than hope not only to join a movement. To move at all. As though prodding a slouching body, she beseeched Blacks to "get going" on the League's "consumers' cooperation plan," for "quite a few of us are more than hopeless."[73]

Planned failure is an ecstatic makeup (and breakup), a mode of being out of body while never more in it. Ecstatic is the sort of pleasure Schuyler referred to when he wrote in the "Appeal," "All officers serve only during the pleasure of the electorate." If *ec-static* means to literally be outside oneself, beside oneself, by way of some passionate feeling, then, to echo Judith Butler, it can also mean a people living utterly "beside themselves." Beside themselves with "rage," "grief," and, let us add, glee.[74] To be *beside oneself* renders planned failure too counterintuitive for the recent reappraisals of social movement failure. Deeper than a readiness to alter one's plans according to an evolving historical landscape, planned failure is a frenzy, being out of one's wits with fear and delight. Planned failure is preset self-negation, an ungovernable generativity encoded in and against the initial form. On its deepest level, planned failure names the synchronized operation, the co-operation, of two affective drives: a love for the world and thus a desire for its preservation, and the sense that the world must come to an end for the world to have a chance, for property to be dismantled and for shared freedom to be secured.

The security of freedom was, in more ways than one, a matter of time.

In the preamble of the manifesto, Schuyler was thinking a lot about time through an engagement with Yeats's "The Second Coming." Yeats's twenty-two-line, two-stanza masterpiece on the ruptures of modernity was the flint against which Schuyler's prose took their light. "The Fourth Decade of the Twentieth Century is at hand," Schuyler wrote as the beginning of the fourth paragraph. In luminously loud, capitalized words, he reminded his readers of the poem's observation that when "Things fall apart" and "the center cannot hold" and "Mere anarchy is loosed upon the world," then "Surely some revelation is at hand / Surely the Second Coming is at hand / The Second Coming!" Schuyler's second coming was time itself. As a matter of fact, by putting his statement on "The Fourth Decade" at the start of the fourth paragraph, in the same way the "Second Coming" starts Yeats's second stanza, Schuyler makes the whole document, indeed the whole League, a matter of time, in both senses of the phrase. He completely combines the subject of time with its written expression, a combination so complete as to be gestalt.

The League's biggest problem was not finally "emancipating the Negro masses from subserviency, insecurity, insult, debauchery, crime, disease and death," as Schuyler sonorously wrote in the previous paragraph. Their big problem was actually not the dubious and potentially disastrous logics that hold in those categories, but the material basis that gives them hold in the first place. Their big problem was, quite literally, the composition of time, how to express and enjoy a wholly new time. Yeats began writing "The Second Coming" in January 1919 during the fallout of the Great War, the Russian Revolution, and Ireland's unrest, right on the eve of the Irish War of Independence. The poem addressed the time *of* modernity. Schuyler's manifesto addressed the time *for* it. The phrase "The Fourth Decade of the Twentieth Century" refashions Yeats's "The Second Coming" into words about time pure and simple, capitalized nouns for capital-T time. Yeats expressed "the feeling that the old rules no longer apply and there's nothing to replace them."[75] Schuyler wondered less what might replace the "old rules" than if anything should.

What gives this wonderment, this form of political engagement, the salience progress has lost in cultural studies today is that it actively escapes the erroneous opposition between optimism and pessimism, between believing in some possibility of redress (from reparation to relief) or inhabiting the melancholy of its permanent loss.[76] A lifeline of scholars ever more mindful of an "abiding negativity" in minoritized lives, mindful, too, of our slave ships and our fugitivities, of "the ways the hold cannot and does not hold even as the hold remains," has been asking a tart question: how do we live and plan for a day that will never come?[77] Schuyler and Baker ask another: how do we live and plan for a day that must not, a day opposed to and unforeseeable by that same life and plan? This is a day incompatible with the affective structures of hope or despair.

For above all, planned failure is a metacritical commentary on the study of Black activism, whose outcomes have led many of us down Escher-stairs of despair. By reversing the terms through which we have come to understand Black social movements as failed plans, planned failure unsettles prevailing conceptions of what it means to succeed at anticapitalist resistance and the metrics of measurements commonly deployed to assess that success. Planned failure characterizes a broad logic of comic—even ecstatic—political activism in a set of poetics on the page and the pavement. That logic in a nutshell? May things fall apart for their tendency to hold.

Schuyler Was an Anarchist, Baker Was Close

The League was launched not on the usual plank, the articulation of desires, but on the rearticulation of successful resistance. To continue the cooperative project of unraveling Blackness from property, Schuyler suggested that redefining failure was even more important than clarifying what they wanted and how, the point and the principles of cooperative economics. The manifesto began as an indictment of the Black public sphere at large. "Young Negroes! . . . The old Negroes have failed! . . . The old Negroes have failed!" Schuyler exclaimed, over and over to a total of nine times in the span of two pages. "The Negro's past and present leadership is a failure! It is a failure." By "old" he meant both an age and a stature, those who have reached a certain lifespan and political prominence, like "Drs. Du Bois and Monroe Trotter."[78] He shot a litany of attacks on a panorama of Black leaders, attacks blunted or edged, depending on your angle, by his heavy humor. Every sentence of this fusillade, in characteristic style, was a cunning combination of fury and funny. "They have meekly protested when they should have fought; . . . talked Heaven while catching Hell."

His words for the ways "the old Negroes" acted were no more endearing, every word an evocation of empty talk, destitute of direction. They "prated," "fiddled," "mouthed," "cadged," and "gabbled"—when they weren't "begging." The "old" leaders operated with an alarming level of passivity, comparable perhaps only to Yeats's "rough beast." Closer to a maimed monster than a beast, it "slouches toward Bethlehem to be born." In the same way one would expect prominent leaders to take action, not take action away, one would expect a beast to plod, stomp, trounce, trample—pretty much anything other than slouch. The implications are severe. As Nick Tabor remarks, "plodding is a conscious activity; slouching is not. We can't even tell whether the beast has a will of its own."[79] How, Schuyler asked, can one expect Black leaders to marshal the collective will when one is hard pressed to find a will of their own? For Schuyler, who describes the entire project of resisting premature death as the entire arc of the Black public sphere, then condemns both as a passive failure, no "rough beast" was going to lead this second coming.

His readers might well have wondered, If every luminary from Du Bois to Trotter has managed to falter, is success impossible or the possibility to seek? Schuyler charged the "oldsters" with capitulating to capitalism, but if all the "past and present leadership," which by implication must include himself, has failed at creating the conditions for emancipation, has "mouthed cooperation and practiced destructive individualism," was Schuyler suggesting that the leadership should have viewed failure as inevitable? In this line of logic, the problem for these leaders was not that failure occurred, but that they sought to avoid it. Given the form of Schuyler's manifesto, a call not only to the young but to failure itself, a call to the young by recourse to failure, given the fact that the phrase "the old Negroes have failed" is so intense and incantatory it threatens to materialize off the page, failure emerges not as something to sidestep or surpass but to celebrate and embody.

There were, to be sure, at least two kinds of failure. Baker told League members that "We bring a NEW ECONOMIC PROGRAM to Aframerica. We

CANNOT AFFORD to fail." This sort of failure was terminal and had all the marks of quantitative time to say so. It was a failure measurable in monetary units, big, visible ones, as evinced in Baker's capitalized words, and thus given over like race to the fixity of sight. Literary theorist Lindon Barret partially attributed the production of racial value to the "condemnatory efficacy of sight," the dominance of the ocular over every other sense. This dominance, which Baker's majuscules visually represented, was indeed a failure the League could not afford. The failure they could, the failure they embodied, was not terminal but recurrent. It moved across senses in a synesthetic saturation, capable of overthrowing the reduction of the human to the object of a gaze.[80]

The avowal of planned failure and the refusal of longevity is most emphatically signified by "young" in the League's name. Schuyler wrote to Baker in 1930 that he interprets the age limit as more symbol than fact: "it is deemed advisable to stretch a point for unusually worthy individuals and to interpret the 'Young' as referring as much to intellect and militancy as to longevity. There are unquestionably individuals over 35 who will be of tremendous assistance to the League and should be members." No record remains of Baker's reply, but she clearly favored the figurative sense of age. Preparing for total collapse, Baker writes to all the members, "It is our hope that in the near future, the National Office will be able to prove its worth. But if it fails to do this, the responsibility rests upon all of us who have declared ourselves to be militant and progressive young Negroes. This is our job shall we do it well."[81] Youth was a discursive construction (to be "declared"). It designated a "job," a professional title about assuming the "responsibility" of failure. The main question here is what defines the "worth" of the National Office? What would "prove" it? Whatever it is, it is bound up with Baker herself, since she was, after all, the "national director." Was the worth of the central administration measured by how many local councils it inaugurated throughout the country? That would be one kind of worth they unquestionably fulfilled. But another form of the office's worth, and by extension its extension—Baker herself—appears to be measured by how easily it could self-dissolve. Only a collapse would leave the "young," the membership, to do, as Baker implores, "our job," decentralize cooperation. The hesitance in employing older members was an anarchic suspicion of centralized planning.

Schuyler made his own suspicions clarion clear, but his readers were likely prepared for them by the moniker "Young Negroes." The category of Young Negro conflicted with the popular concept of the New Negro, which straddled the political gamut. The New Negro ranged from Alain Locke's cosmopolitan unsullied by mass protest to Garvey's émigré to A. Phillip Randolph's personification of class consciousness. Whether dressed in boots or wing tips, the New Negro was usually a he and he was always new. Because his newness meant progress and renewal, the figure of the *"Young* Negro" meant the renewal of renewals. To call her "young" was to resist a genealogy of patrifocal political thought. But the resistance was oblique, not direct, hence the word "young" instead of "new." The resistance moved not from the bottom to the top, thus creating another structure of sovereignty, of general causation, but from the inside to the outskirts.

Planning for the collapse of the governing body was tantamount to remaking the body of the Black public sphere, turning a community defined by identities of equivalence and parachuting leaders who never actually land into collectivities defined by gender critique and the frictions of affiliation. The move from the language of direct to oblique opposition, from antinomies to adjacencies, is the move from a comparative model of the social to a relational one, from the new to the young. It is to think of the "social" in "social movement" as made up of linkages and common problems, not of equivalences and a common identity. The focus on encounters and motion over unity and positions open up an analytic better able to address not only the intersections but also the incommensurability of gender and racial violence. If "Schuyler's skill as a cultural provocateur surpassed his ability to run an actual organization," it is because the organization was designed to outrun him.[82]

The moniker "young" signified generativity. Schuyler no doubt stretched the term to embarrassing proportions when he linked it to "virility," but it still remained shorthand for the general principle of a cooperative life: "supply yourselves with everything you consume," as Schuyler stated in the "Appeal." While Kathi Weeks and other political theorists have denounced such an edict as promoting "Left asceticism," austerity to our peril, it becomes through Schuyler and Baker an attempt to establish a different relationship to subjecthood.[83] In the socialist phase of the association of producers, or in the league's economy of productive consumers, the borders between people and their products blur. Blurred are the lines separating consumption from production, so that at no point can the production processes and their engineers be differentiated.

Consider this circular statement, a kind of verbal eddy: "You cannot," asserted Schuyler, "get this economic power except through the co-operation as consumers," but he continued, "you cannot get anywhere if you are always on the buying side of the counter!" Consumers operate by negating themselves as consumers via the objects they buy. This nonprogressive negation renders consumption a failure; it renders the consumed into objects that failed. Schuyler and Baker were concerned with, in Baker's words, "the increasingly more important role of the consumer," for the fact that "all work is but a means to the ends of meeting consumer demands."[84] This focus on consumption may look like a mere historical description of evolving economic "demands," but I see Baker's formulation of work as a "means to the ends"—work as a meeting of ends—almost in line with Schuyler's eddy: both may be a codified ambivalence between subjecthood and objecthood, between the worker and the thing she works on. And the ambivalence spins beyond the starting point into something unexpected. Thinking the collective without recourse to self-possessed individuals might be thinking subjecthood without recourse to subjects: the refusal to divide us from our things, to the extent that things are objects that fail.[85]

So much for the tag "young," what about the "league," a mutual pledge against a common enemy, a common complex of problems? This question brings us to the issue of anarchy. Strands of anarchy were central to Schuyler's activism, and to some extent Baker's. Peter Kropotkin might have been the most well-known anarchist at the time, and "The Appeal to Young Negroes" was an allusion to his best-known editorial, "An Appeal to the Young." In her capacity as assistant project supervisor for the Consumer Education Division of the Workers Education Project, Baker flirted with anarchy when in 1937 she made Kropotkin's book *Mutual Aid* mandatory reading for her course "The Consumer: His Problems and Their Remedies."[86] She mostly held these lectures at the Uptown Bronx branch of the YWCA, and sometimes at the Rand School of Social Science where she related African American cooperatives, before a left-leaning crowd, to cooperatives across the Atlantic, focusing on the "movement here and abroad."[87]

But wherever she lectured, she reaffirmed what Cedric Robinson considers the foremost lesson of anarchism, "that political freedom is only prior to political organization and experience, never following out of it." Along this vein, Baker wrote in the margins of an unpublished speech from the 1960s, "Why Negroes Should Vote" that "Every increase in actual enfranchisement spells an increase in potential self-government. Every gain in potential self-government . . . decrease[s] . . . injustices suffered."[88] The aim of voting was not liberal inclusion, but radical reconstruction: a new governance directly charged by the electorate; and with its hyphenated detachment, a new government distinct yet following from the social "self." This brief marginalia questions the reduction of the movement-subject to the citizen-subject, of the political actor to the abstract citizen. Keeping her anarchic leanings in mind is important not least because of how they reframe the prevailing definition of a social movement today. A movement for Baker was much more than the effort by the disenfranchised to end their exclusions from civil society. "We are going to have to learn to think in radical terms," Baker said in 1969. "I use the term radical in its original meaning— getting down to and understanding the root cause."[89] A movement meant potentially tearing the political infrastructure out from its roots.

Designating a space "without rulers or authorities" that interrogates the legitimacy of the state, anarchy and cooperative economics had been long bedfellows. Whether one chooses to trace their romance back to Pierre-Joseph Proudhon, the first self-declared anarchist who announced in 1840 that "Property is theft!" and tried to create an interest-free bank for French farmers, or whether one begins that history with fugitive maroon societies in the Caribbean and the U.S. or as Cedric Robinson has done with African stateless societies, whose refusal of the sovereign state and its hobbling forms of recognition constitute a classic anarchic principle, by the 1930s Schuyler was trumpeting the notion that mutualism and anarchy are not only bedfellows, they're symbionts. "The co-operative movement is anarchism in action," he said in 1932 from the platform of his "Views and Reviews" column in the *Pittsburgh Courier*.[90]

Anarchy for Schuyler was as much antiauthoritarianism as the negation of the state. As Robinson remarks, "In the West, anarchism developed as a specific negation to the evolution of political authority—the State—which served to orchestrate and to some degree mystify the structure of economic relations."[91] Thus working from the inside, "within the shell of capitalism," as Schuyler refrained, he hoped that cooperation as the practice of reciprocal service would displace proprietorial relations and that its social freedoms and metaphysical fulfillments would make it irresistible. To plan anarchically— to be young, gifted, and ecstatic—is to think of planning in Moten and Harney's terms as "self-sufficiency at the social level."[92] Planning, they assert, "reproduces in its experiment not just what it needs, life, but what it wants, life in difference, in the play of general antagonism."[93] No social movement exists without plans, as Gould reminds us, but for Schuyler and Baker, top-down planning was a limitation to overcome. The neglect of the largest Black movement of their day to do so, in fact the largest in world history— Garvey's United Negro Improvement Association, which despite corralling over six million members toppled like a deck of cards after Garvey's capture and subsequent deportation in 1927—buttressed their resolve to launch their plans against plans.

Unlike the European anarchists who inspired Schuyler most, Kropotkin and Mikhail Bakunin, he saw no contradiction in government-sanctioned anarchy. Not only were the League and its satellite cooperatives legally incorporated, but Schuyler (and Baker to some extent) believed that anticapitalist resistance had to double-deal with the state to catch it unawares. In Schuyler's mind, the demise of the U.S. Communist Party came down to its use of direct confrontation. Two months before the League was born, Schuyler extolled a battle through class consciousness that would prepare the way for "world revolution," an approach Antonio Gramsci might call a war of position.[94] "Whereas the Socialists hope to usher in such a Utopian society through the ballot and the Communists hope to turn the trick with the bullet, the co-operator (who is really an Anarchist since the triumph of this society will do away with the state in its present form—and I am an Anarchist) is slowly and methodically doing so through legal, intelligent economic co-operation or mutual aid (of which Prince Kropotkin, the Anarchist, spoke)."[95] As the anarchic plans of cooperatives become the "methodical" policies of the government, failure corresponds with the eventual inability to govern. Schuyler's plan? Incapacitate governance through sly indirection: "He [the African American] has learned to use the tactics of attrition and infiltration rather than headlong mass attack. The more educated he becomes, the more developed his technique; the more civilized the whites become, the more they weaken in the face of his advance."[96]

And Baker's plan? Be similarly indirect. She carried around in her teaching materials an essay by Samuel Cartmell, inconspicuously titled "Consumers Cooperation." "Cooperation is REVOLUTIONARY," Cartmell stated, "for its ultimate aim is to create a better social structure by making unnecessary the present form of government which is operated by and for a privileged class." If this argument is any indication, taken together with Baker's provocations of militancy, like when she reminded League members that "we are of the opinion that the building of a strong Cooperative Movement among our people is equivalent to a battle," then we can safely say that Baker, for a time, perhaps a long time, cunningly fought for the overthrow of any government prone to instrumentalize social life.[97]

She knew the dangers. They both did. Schuyler alluded in his "Appeal" not only to Kropotkin but also to the most radical antislavery document of the nineteenth century: David Walker's *Appeal to the Colored Citizens of the World* (1829), a stirring pamphlet whose secret dissemination along the East

Coast (as an owner of a clothing store, Walker actually stitched it into the pockets of the pea coats he sold to Black sailors) incited the most punitive antiliteracy laws from Carolina to Georgia. Plus Baker and Schuyler bore witness to the "reign of terror" that befell the Southern Tenant Farmers' Union, an interracial cooperative organization marauded by landowners and the National Guard in 1934.[98]

So Schuyler was forcibly duplicitous about his anarchic plans, never letting us forget that such duplicity has stuck to Black cooperatives like a shadow. No clearer example exists of Schuyler's double-dealing than his letters to government officials requesting federal funds. Here he appears to undermine Black social life by casting economic cooperation as congruent with American capitalism.[99] Importantly, these contrary appeals—to Blackness and to whiteness—were issued at the same time. It is through this subterfuge that we must read Schuyler's emphasis on consumer cooperation and partly extend it to Baker. Against Marxist reason and in concert with the new literature on cooperation at the time, Baker and Schuyler deemed it more pressing to corral the economic power of buyers than of producers (their social base made up of Blacks who recently migrated to the city). Under the benign banner of cooperation, they were simultaneously exploiting President Franklin D. Roosevelt's unprecedented valorization of the "consuming public." Over the course of the 1930s, this hold-all term, *consuming public*, would become idiomatic. For the first time in American history, Roosevelt included official representatives of the consuming public alongside business and labor through his keystone New Deal program, the National Industrial Recovery Act. As the labor historian Lizabeth Cohen notes, "Empowering the consumer seemed to many New Dealers a way to enhance the public's stake in society and the economy while still preserving the free enterprise system."[100] Under federal sanction, planned failure constitutes a duplicitous form of social consent, or as Schuyler would salvo, "the most *insidiously* disruptive force ever loosed against the government racket" (emphasis mine).[101]

A Space for Living

Like the Black nationalisms evolving around it, the dream of a commonwealth was really the dream of home. But unlike Black nationalism, the League sought a home unconfined by the lineaments of the nation-state. In its resistance to be placed, its evasiveness, and in its corresponding efforts, sometimes successful, to oppose versions of home that sustain allegiance to the seductions of the father, the League joins the other cooperatives I explore throughout this book in proffering home as much more than a place: a perspective, a place in perspective. We may remember Hortense Spillers's claim in "Interstices: A Small Drama of Words" that the alterability of domination depends first and foremost on the "return of the gaze," on harnessing the power of a gendered double-consciousness.[102] "It is this return of the gaze that negotiates at every point a space for living." And it is "this space for living" by way of a certain gaze that Baker, above all, considered a home, a "counter-power," a "counter-mythology." Home was as much what she searched for as a particular way of searching: renegade.

The League was one such example of Baker's vision of home, her home-vision. Soul City, one of the most incredible experiments in Black home-making, was another. Baker's involvement with this intentional community was by all indications minimal (perhaps why it has been entirely forgotten), yet no less significant for what it says about her commitment to the reclamation of land and her approach to the construction of a Black metropolis. Located on the upper edge of North Carolina, Soul City was a town formally proposed in 1969 to the federal government by Floyd McKissick, attorney and former national director of the Congress of Racial Equality. With resounding similarities to the League's ambitions, except of course its capitalist frame, the proposal included "sufficient employment opportunities to upgrade the economic level of the entire population," "good housing for all residents," "commercial," "social," and "public facilities," "the establishment of a community college," "parks, playgrounds and open space, both developed and wild."[103] All for an ultimately affective end that would then ripple out to ends of the earth: "pride and encouragement for Black America and for all depressed people everywhere."

Its welcome sign would outsize the billboard on the county line stating "Klan Country," where two-thirds of the population was Black and Indigenous, and one-third was white. "There will be a tower or tall building . . . with a beacon of light on top . . . to welcome all people," declared McKissick, "a beacon of light to let the world know it's there and a place man can develop himself to what he wants to be."[104] Its initial organizers expressed to local newspapers that they considered this city something akin to the end of history, which to them was akin to an aftermath that wouldn't quit: "Soul City will be an attempt to move into the future, a future where Black people welcome white people as equals." Note the inversion, a reversal of racial power. On these terms, integration, which McKissick thought they should try because "no one has really tried it yet," would stop the stammer of history and allow Blacks to move as equals into the free market for the first time.[105] But McKissick repeatedly flirted with the very enclosures, the totalities, they were breaking from. He envisioned this "model," though Black owned and managed, as a "a total town," "a total community."[106]

Soliciting Baker's help, McKissick sent her the proposal that summer. Its casual inclusion of the patrifocal "imperative that young Black men be found who can develop the expertise necessary to lead such a project" embodied the spirit of casual disregard that eventually made Baker take a step back.[107] In a "conference" to discuss her potential role, McKissick asked her to move to the town, less than thirty miles, incidentally, from where she grew up. For $600 a month she would advise its development and "undertake a civic survey of Warren, Halifax and Vance Counties," focusing on the "lack of human resources in the communities." Partly because of a disagreement over her pay (to Baker's mind this was almost a bait-and-switch), partly because of McKissick's sexism (without her consent he assigned her to the job of "Coordinator for community and civic affairs"), Baker agreed to do the survey and only the survey, which "may be regarded," she wrote, "as an exploratory basis for determining any future working relationships." After citing his patriarchy in a ferociously clear, numbered complaint, she supplied McKissick the right words to describe her by pretending he already had them in ample supply. "Since you first elicited my interest last Summer, by giving me a copy of the proposal, it has been clear that you regarded my organizational and human relation experiences as having significant potential benefit for your program. I appreciate your evaluation, and agree that the years of experience and knowledge of the area is a combination not easily duplicated; but is not an indispensable one. Furthermore, I know my tendencies to become totally involved with a challenging program, and am mindful of recent health problems. Hence, I do not see myself in a key role, at this time."[108] She acknowledges with a phrase there is no record of McKissick using, "*key* role," that access to sanctuary depends on Black women like her. She then extends the point in that conspicuous sentence, more like part-sentence: "but is not an indispensable one." Why does she omit or withhold the sentence's subject (i.e., the "combination" of "experience and knowledge")? Perhaps to disidentify from this "indispensable" "combination," from her "experience and knowledge," or, more precisely, from the categories of experience and knowledge. When you look again, you see that she performs this same detachment twice. Where one expects her to say *my* "experience" and so on, she says "the" in an act of self-withdrawal. If sentences tend to turn on a verb, this one turns on an absence, a double absence. Her personal history and her present self. Implying that her history and her self cannot be reduced to familiar categories of experience and knowledge, she unsettles the intimacy McKissick had assumed.

If that's her first point, her second one is bigger. By pivoting on an absence, the sentence partially breaks from her preceding point of view (her you-and-I voice), and this break seems to say a couple of things. I am not the only Black woman equipped to do the job; and, furthermore, don't you see, don't you see at least in part, that ironically the job may very well dispense with all my "years of experience"? And this less because of what you didn't ask for as because of what you did. You're asking me to occupy a normative point of view, one equipped to "undertake," "survey," surveil. It is this double-bind of having to refuse what's traditionally involved in playing a "role," the imposition of a normative, locatable self, while refusing its denial, all in order to play any role whatsoever—it is this double-bind between involvement and withdrawal, bestowal and deprivation, that I see in Baker's hesitance, as Baker's hesitance, her decision to do the work on "an exploratory basis for determining any future working relationships." Baker's response was a revisionary discourse that, to return to Spillers, refused to "extend" the authority it revised.[109] But more: it discontinued it.

We do not know what happened to Baker's relationship to the project. We know that among the pines, oaks, star-shaped violets, and muddy roads that flourished in the region, Soul City was built, "multi-racial" but "Black built" in 1973. By strategically giving his support to Nixon, McKissick secured a $14 million loan from the federal government's Model Cities Program. The following year its first residents, from Richmond, Newark, and Atlanta, arrived to enjoy their new houses, a health clinic, a water systems plant, a day care converted from the "Big House" of the old Satterwhite Plantation, and the Soultech 1 industrial and business center. Janice Crump of Atlanta said she and her husband saw "more than the fields and the dirt roads and the mud." She saw "a promise of what it could be," if not what it already was.[110] Everyone who came drove off the highway down Soul City Boulevard, passed the "Soul City marquee," a rectangular concrete monument with the city's name, rolling like the hills, in red, gleefully round sans serif. Quite a welcome. The marquee was not "a beacon," as McKissick had hoped, but it was closer to a beacon than a marquee.

Despite all its lost light, historian Christopher Strain was able to see that "the scope of Soul City as a 1970s-utopia is without parallel." Strain made this estimation even after reviewing the valiance of its predecessors. In the antebellum era: Black self-help communities like Brooklyn, Illinois; Nashoba

Community in Tennessee; and the Port Royal Experiment on South Carolina Sea Islands. Following Reconstruction: "exodusters" who settled in Nicodemus, Kansas; Mississippi's Mound Bayou; Promiseland, South Carolina; and Boley, Oklahoma. And a year before Soul City was conceived: the Republic of New Afrika, a Black nationalist organization that demanded $400 billion in reparations from the federal government that would "liberate" land in Georgia, Alabama, Mississippi, Louisiana, and South Carolina for a separate Black state. In 1971 New Afrika's headquarters in Jackson, Mississippi, were raided by the FBI and local police, who arrested and convicted ten members on sedition charges, and another on a murder charge for the death of one of the officers. Yet all eleven continued to organize while incarcerated. This was, in broad strokes, Soul City's history, as well as its future: continued organization under extreme constraints.

The oil crisis of 1974 drove up the price of plastics and asphalt, and a federal audit demanded by segregationist senator Jesse Helms drove construction to a standstill. In a startling fog of logic, the kind of logic that becomes a kind of captivity, the U.S. Housing Department pulled its funding in 1979 because of "severe criticism that the project wasn't progressing." In the following year, they auctioned the city away. Result? Almost allegorical. Soul City was absorbed by the city of Manson. Soultech became the county jail. The Soultech complex now serves as a factory manned by prison labor for the production of soap. Yet another story about the price of inclusion, the tax on their investment in developmental progress precalculated to judge them as "wasn't progressing" (the "projected 20 year population is 18,000," McKissick wrote, "virtually doubling the population of the county"—50,000 by century's end).[111] But to people like Janice Crump and others like Elvira Kirkland, who staked their lives and livelihoods to move to this place, its future was a different story. When a local paper concluded that the city had "all but faded away," Kirkland wrote to the editors in 1988 to remind them of the preschool, the volunteer fire station, the health clinic, and assisted living center. How, she asked, "can a community that has acquired so many assets be fading away?"

A *Guardian* reporter visited the grounds in 2016 and noted that "portions of it resemble a ghost town, rotting." To go back to Baker's exchange with McKissick, one wonders if her reference to "health problems" in the same moment she mentions her "tendencies" toward a "challenging program" had anything to do with the health of the grounds on which the challenge began and ended. One wonders if the health of Soul City—to some a late-rot, to residents a persistence, to all undone—is one of those awful blessings, the license to begin again on healthier grounds. One wonders what might have happened if McKissick had accounted for the sexism he expressed at the heart of his "dream." Perhaps he might have seen Baker's agreement to do the "survey" and only the survey of the "lack of human resources in the community" as already, in a way, partly done. Perhaps he might have been forced to give up, as Jared Sexton writes on the impulse to afro-pessimism, the "emancipatory pretense of access to, and perhaps investment in, civil society and its accoutrements, including, one must hope, hetero-patriarchal gender and sexual discipline."[112] Baker's renegade reply to McKissick's invitation forces us at least to ask, with no easy answers, how does one make a home, a place of one's own, that unmakes the logic of patriarchal domination? How does one build up a place like a Soul City or a cooperative commonwealth that doesn't also build up standards of modern progress? The very notion of such a place with all its verticality appears to depend on those very standards. Whatever the answers, Baker's reply suggests political inconsequence may itself be a critique of the available political options, whose gendered contradictions one could not or would not want to resolve. Better to disengage them on an "exploratory basis."[113]

In 1961, Baker wrote a marvelous docu-essay, "Tent City: Freedom's Front Line." Shortly after the New Year, she visited Somerville, Tennessee, and reported on an outcrop of tenant farmers evicted from their homes for registering to vote. Through sheer descriptive force, through specificity and scale, she expresses her outrage. She was outraged that these exiles were living in squalor, that they were forced to form a cooperative economy in squalor, and that the media did not care. The essay is a critique of their available political options with the passion of life or death. To the extent that she must mourn what has not even begun—planned alternatives—it is also a mourning cry. She begins by marking a conflict in perspectives about the meaning of home. The outcrop was named "Tent City" by officials, she says; "Freedom Village" by its dwellers. This conflict between two ways of giving the name and its potentially deadly fallout is already staged in the essay's title. "Freedom's front line" is both the horizon of freedom and those sacrificed for it. Then moving from high to low, for the rest of the essay she draws our eyes to the mud.

She appends to the essay a picture of the scene. The village kneels on mud that has become so thick and wide, offset only by some wheat grass and two bare saplings, that the mud is now more than a physical hindrance. It's a rhetorical one, seeping into and slowing down Baker's description itself. She goes almost a paragraph before using a single verb. Here's the lumbered start of paragraph three: "The olive-drab tents without floors, surrounded by inches of mud and mire; the darkness within these tents that are lighted by kerosene lamp and heated by wood stoves; the not-too-well-clad children crowded into the tents or squashing around in the mud, and the hungry shivering dogs wondering about: all of this painted a picture of anything but hope for the new year." With the smoke kerosene flames easily emit in the slightest adjustment of air, a smoke rivaled only by that of a woodstove, even the light within the tents seems awash in the mud.

After cataloguing the yearly profits some of the farmers collected, ranging from $125 to $180, which landowners claimed as debt, Baker exclaims, "floors have to be put in tents, land has to be drained and packed to offset the mud . . . and electric lights and windows secured." Given their inability to move from this place, it is as if the mud both expresses and extends the debt, figures and corporealizes it. Baker's disbelief of their casual suspension in some sort of space between home and homelessness, toggles between the fact that they feel this is better, that "their mud-floored tents were more comfortable than the shacks they formerly called home," and the fact that this stasis spells the conditions on which their freedom is felt at all.[114] That's the toggle her title performs between the blithely idiomatic "Tent City" and the transfigured "Freedom Village." It is a toggle of time. If the city is futural in its accumulation of speed, the village is present in its delay. With symbolic implications for messy but necessary political entanglements with the capitalist state, "Freedom Village" exemplifies a muddy temporality that thickens and sprawls.

Their freedom is "mire[d]," but still a respite from the logics and logistics of accommodation, the impositions of personhood (always regulated by a patriarchal code), and the linearity of ends or "final outcomes," "which," Baker says, "the demands of the moment leave little time to think." In short, their freedom is embroiled but unengulfed. The mud is the visual analogue to a wayward temporality that muddles the transparency assumed by the sovereign subject. If the city is the domain of the sovereigns and the village of its subordinates, then the city possesses temporality and the village is possessed by it, since the village is seen as empty space. In this schema of sovereign-time and subordinate-space (which is really Denise Ferreira da Silva's, as I'll discuss later), the "city" is temporal; "tent city," terra nullius. Unsettling this schema without recourse to sovereignty, the troubled freedom of the village is arguably germinal. It inspires their idea, with dilating detail, for a new social arrangement in an old form, cooperatives. "Despite this yeoman task" of making a home in homelessness, "there is talk in Fayette County about buying land for group or cooperative farming." Baker curbs the temptation to extol hope here. That these conditions have afforded greater "comfort" is "the real tragedy," she says, "anything but hope." So if not hope, then what? Her relentless description of mud and the excesses of mud displace hope with something more akin to a felt entanglement, a new sensitivity to material constraints. What all this amounts to is a vexed and vexing vulnerability. In eight years time Baker would call this vulnerability, with deceptive ease, creating a space for living "on an exploratory basis," where "exploratory" means disruptively open.

Over the course of her life, she would occupy the edges of centralized power as the principal spaces from which to disrupt it. It is no coincidence that after being pushed out of the SCLC office, the main office of SNCC was initially located along a string of edgelands. First "the little room in back of what was the SCLC offices," as Baker explains. Then "a little cubbyhole across the street." Baker is painting an iconography of place consonant with that fact that she ran SCLC out of a phonebooth and her pocketbook (her metaphors), that she and Schuyler supported a council over a party system, and that she advised League members in 1931 to embrace spatial extremities in the cooperative economy. "We are advising all councils," she wrote in one of the newsletters, "to guard against the more pretentious type of business. To devote attention to the more simple lines—such as buying clubs, newspaper stands, and distributing agencies—will be of more value to the growth of the movement and the success of the enterprise. For not only is the risk so much less, but ample opportunity will be given to the training which is valuable in the larger fields."[115]

These "simple lines" describe the very edges of metropolitan power, of "the larger fields," and they give pause to the critique most famously made by Rosa Luxemburg in 1899 that cooperatives lose their power to the extent they lose their place in the centers of production. Pit against "the larger fields," "simple lines" are short and, as Baker recommends, decidedly shortened. Baker is not composing another liturgy on the liminal. As has been often noted, liminality reduces the complexity that excites it to a conceptual order only it can understand. Baker's composition is *without* "pretentio[n]." Nor is she invoking with "simple lines" "the limit-experience of the Other," the enjoyment of which Foucault once recognized as reinforcing his position of power, and which would only make sense from a position of whiteness.[116]

Cooperatives as "simple lines," viewed through Spillers's lens, are precisely not this experience. They are not "interstices," in which the Black female is "the principal point of passage between the human and the non-human world" and is thereby both hyper- and de-sexualized. Cooperatives are the location from which to expose and undercut the heteropatriarchal, sexuating logic of interstitiality. In the context of accounting for anticapitalist organizations and in evaluating the movements they foment, this logic assumes the form of endowing spatial prominence and extensive temporal length with the privileged markings of economic success, let alone of radicality, notability, and power. To follow Ella Baker in her Black feminist practice is to live like an edgelander on the borders of built space, prefer the margins to the main as our spaces for living. With as much rage as grief, Baker conducts a practice of thinking with, in, and for the world "without separability, determinacy, and sequentiality," to quote Ferreira da Silva, a constellatory thinking where there are no ends, only tangents and traces, remains and remainders—where nothing adds up, in the double sense.[117]

Baker's Odd Moments

At an unknown date but most likely, given the style and the topic, during the end of her Shaw years, Baker wrote an essay in which she coined her own concept of time. She titled the essay "Personal Thrift," and I think it bears separate consideration precisely for how the temporality she sketches differs from planned failure but lays its foundation, and for how in a single paragraph the essay brings together—or more like gnarls—all the stakes of this book: political time, the various momentums of Black cooperation, and aesthetics. I say "gnarls" because what she ultimately shows is that the agency of the subaltern is inescapably bound to its scenes of subjection. And what I want to show is that there's something revolutionary in this bind.

In a style characteristic of her university work in the mid-1920s—at once methodical and inquisitive, impassioned and austere, and, as ever, beguiling—she explored the benefits of exercising thrift in almost all areas of life, "earnings," savings, consumption, expenditures of energy, and time. Thrift emerges as a stuttered restraint, a pedal-pump of desire, in which "self-sacrifice" now spells indulgence later. Thrift, she says, "does not mean no pleasures, it means more and better ones at regular intervals." This is an essay based on an old book about Black self-help, thrift its hero, and all manner of respect (financial, civic, cultural, personal) its reward. In this sense it is an essay about Black cooperation at large, whose guiding philosophy, basically its namesake, has historically been the philosophy of self-help, or as

Baker refers to it in the essay, dovetailing a different nineteenth-century American tradition, "self-reliance."

In terms of thought and political ramifications, the essay is kaleidoscopically complex. First, it is complex just finding Baker beneath an argument that sounds like strange capitulation to the authorities of her school. The university prohibited a range of fun activities, "dancing, card playing, and the use of tobacco," for instance, and Baker appears to justify these prohibitions, by asking, "what is the sacrifice of a few indulgences—say a bottle of beer, a cigar, or a box of candy, if such a denial puts one beyond the need of sacrifices in the future?" The troubling thing about these interdictions is the echo they carry of the freedmen's manuals.[118] As Hartman shows, these nineteenth-century primers on navigating the transition from slavery to freedom grafted on the freedmen's back for arriving in the world with "sumptuary excess" "standards of productivity, sobriety, rationality, prudence, cleanliness, responsibility, and so on."[119]

Exemplified by Clinton Fisk's *Plain Counsels for Freedmen in Sixteen Brief Lectures* (1865), these standards were imposed "through education, religious instruction, and, when necessary, compulsion." Short of the third method, Baker appears to adopt the first and second, exercising them with exasperation and statistics. "A few years ago there were fifteen billion cigarettes, one hundred thirty two million pounds of snuff, eight and a half million cigars, and one million packages of chewing gum sold. Who were the consumers of such extravagances? I dare say over 75% of such luxuries was consumed by working people." Baker's vocabulary closely and uncomfortably resembles Clinton Fisk's. "It may cost you a struggle," Fisk says of thrift, "but stick to it resolutely and you will be able to purchase not only the necessaries but the luxuries of life."[120] (Clinton Fisk, by the way, worked for the Freedmen's Bureau and donated the first endowment for another historically Black school, the eponymously named Fisk University.) While Fisk targets appearances, "a new hat," a "breastpin," and a "fine dress," Baker targets something deeper, an interiority clear down to one's breath ("cigarettes" and "cigars").

None of this so far sounds like Baker then—or at any time since. We know that she resisted the respectability politics of respectable dress, among some other moral sanctions, and that despite her academic record she was to university officials unruly. And yet her endorsement of this code of punishing behavior is the lesser surprise. The entire argument is sold as counsel on how "working people" and "the poor" can acquire, like Andrew Carnegie, Benjamin Franklin, Abraham Lincoln (Fisk's exemplar), like others of "the world's greatest," and, I kid you not, like "the great street car systems": "honor, glory, and fame." Unlike the freedmen's counsels, she does not use the word "freedom" as if to suggest it is not on offer; what is, is limited to external determinations ("honor, glory, and fame"). Inside meets out: thrift for oneself becomes thrift for others. At any rate, when I put her words like this, condense them in this fashion, the argument probably sounds more like parody than promotion of upward mobility tales. To some extent it is. But I do not mean to rescue a pure or unharmed revolutionary politics. That would falsely represent the thick sincerity of her tone and it would undermine precisely what makes this essay compelling. The mess. The political entanglements of the philosophy of self-help with the specters of capital. There are no imagined solutions to real-world problems here: only smudges and complications.

Only part of the essay remains, a total of seven loose-leaf cursive pages in fine-point arabesque. It is beautiful to read. And without a single error, a single uncrossed "t," with her even, unhurried hand, one can see the care Baker took with her approach. Thrift was her message as well as her means. On the last remaining page, Baker dilates her scope across a single paragraph and it is this dilation that interests me here. She turns from thrift as a discipline to thrift as a temporality. She describes something she calls "thrift of time." To be thrifty with one's time is to fill a motley of "odd moments," cracks in the workday, with transformational study.

> "Time is gold," says Franklin. Reasonably then we can infer that there can be thrift of time. If we review the lives of the world's greatest, we find that most of them have not been men of leisure. Benjamin Franklin, perhaps one of our best examples of personal thrift, only spent about one year in school. He saved his meager earnings and bought his first book, Bunyan's "Pilgrim's Progress." After reading and rereading this, he sold it to buy another. By such a system he so economized his time in study that soon he was a well prepared young man. David Livingstone, the beginner of the missionary activities in the interior of Africa, owes his educational foundation to the use of odd moments. While working at the cotton factory, though quite a small boy, he would place his Latin grammar on the spinning jenny and learn sentence after sentence as he passed by. Lincoln, after a hard day's work, instead of lounging around with the "gang," would walk for several miles to get a book to read. By employing his odd moments in reading and study, he was prepared to meet the larger demands which acted as mediums to honor, glory, and fame.

I know, again, "honor, glory, and fame"—at this point it is tipping if not into parody, then into something less comfortable. (To mark what may be the sharpest point of contrast to the Baker we know, we may remember when she lamented that the American labor movement "succumbed . . . to the failures of what I call the American weakness of being recognized and of having arrived and taking on the characteristics and the values even, of the foe.")[121] This discomfort, however, is where things get interesting. By introducing the phrase, really the refrain "odd moments," the essay turns from an endorsement of political conservativism to a reflection on it, to a reflection as well on the lines that don't abide, the odd ones in, as the saying goes. One could say that Baker is reflecting on whiteness or more exactly on "self-reliance" as an instrument of whiteness. The odd ones in, then, are the ways the instrument breaks, refuses to cooperate. This noncooperation then signifies something else, something that in the context of cooperative economics is, well, "odd."

There's a complication, however, about the people in this essay. Reminiscent in our times of the late Toni Morrison's "Recitatif," a short story that "tried," as Morrison said of another work, "to carve out a world both culturally specific and race free," the essay never once uses a racial moniker to situate the people it purports to advise, "the working people." But we never once get the sense that these people are anyone but subalterns, racialized subalterns. If her "poor" were white, were not stigmatically racialized, it would be needless to commend thrift as a path to protected citizenship. It would be needless to say, "Since the worth of a State, in the long run, is the worth of the individuals comprising it, personal thrift extends beyond the acquisition of self-reliance . . . it is of paramount value to the nation. Just as no jewel can be any better than the metal of which it is made, so no state can be any greater than its included citizens."[122] Aside from the double-speak that affirms the nation-state, national belonging, and assimilation, while reducing all three to little more than an ornament, vulnerable and constructed, Baker reminds us of the non-"included." Their exclusion in this equation *is* their protection, blessed to not belong. She reminds us of the absent referent, the racial subaltern, who, as always, haunts her erasure. It is here where the odd ones in, the deviant acts of the dominant (Lincoln, Livingstone, Franklin), momentarily meet the odd ones out, the deviance of the erased.

So these "odd moments," what are they, other than time seized for study? You'll note that each one of them occurs in transit, and that they are semi-escapes from assigned labor (supervised learning, factory obligations, and hard day-work that literally hardens the day). In short, then, they are a certain kind of transitory and entangled escape. Through the cliché "loung-ing around," Baker suggests that the discipline of productivity extends into leisure hours by way of a certain kind of rest, a clichéd, which is to say a prescribed rest (Fisk calls it "enforced leisure"[123]), a socially imposed dull-ing of the senses. This recalls an old argument about the unexpected links between rest and labor going back to Frederick Douglass's first slave narra-tive of 1845. The point, though, is that no matter the time, "odd moments" are moments of what one could call distraction. Livingstone is distracted from his "spinning jenny," Franklin from "school," and Lincoln from any destination whatsoever (he walked to get a book to read, but where did he or the reading go from there?). These moments are what happen "after" a concentration that is also a confinement. We tend to think of distraction as either pro- or passively capitalist and, in the main, not just nonrevolutionary—antirevolutionary. Distraction brings to mind pricey entertainment and the opiate of the masses, mental weakness and moral slack, the way we suc-ceed at being consumers and another way we fail at being good workers, students, writers, thinkers, and so on.

Here's a different take. As moments of distraction, odd moments undo the discipline one typically ascribes to thrift, and by extension to capitalist labor, the discipline of application, discrimination, and efficiency, all being virtues of unencumbered attentiveness. One could say it is through the vir-tue of attention that the subject, who is always sovereign or always seeking to be so, bears its capacity for coherence. If this is true, then so long as Bak-er's subjects are essentially distracted, they are not technically subjects. They are pulled away from their work, and, more profoundly, its productiv-ity. Livingstone is "reading" a language long dead. Lincoln's "reading and study" are, yes, "employed" but "employed" for their own sake, thus ironiz-ing the word. This is why Baker's protagonists are momentarily odd. In the context of their legacies, lives geared toward magnificent ends, they at least for a moment barely resemble the people bearing their names. We could go further. As defined by distraction not attendance, her subjects are as much the sovereigns she refers to as the subalterns she does not. Her subalterns are diversionists. This was a word coined in the 1930s to vilify conspirators, saboteurs, or "wreckers" of Stalinist government, and I use it loosely here to reference a general resistance toward oppressive governance. Against a capacity for coherence, her subaltern bears a capacity for diversion.

A capacity for diversion is nothing if not an openness so it is certainly hard to pair with a focus on closures, the closures of sovereignty and his-torical time ("honor, glory, and fame"). But we can begin by observing that the first disturbance of sovereignty and its formalist grammar surfaces, of course, in the word "odd." "Odd" vacillates in meaning between deformed and unformed, and it is this vacillation, the total inability to reckon with the thing as merely badly formed or lacking form, that makes *odd things*, and here "odd moments," extraordinarily strange. The oddity of the moment weds well with the possibility that at stake in Baker's advice is not only how one attends to the issues of sovereignty, but how one may get powerfully distracted from it. Paul North has written a brilliant book on distraction among Western canonical thinkers. Through works like Heidegger's *Being and Time* and Benjamin's notes to Adorno titled "Theory of Distraction," North argues (and I'm simplifying a bit) that distraction means a stoppage of thought and being that is sometimes beautiful, sometimes devastating. This is not how I'm using the word "distraction." In Baker's examples, distraction is obviously a deviation less from thought than from thought rigidly formed. She recommends a kind of thinking that is either piecemeal and partial ("sentence after sentence") or recursive and revisionary ("reading and rereading"). These qualities evince a thinking necessarily subject to radical change, a thinking that is revocable, vulnerable, and risky. That the odd moment, the distraction, became a "medium for honor, glory, and fame," is both beside the point and essential to it, "beside" because the moment could have been otherwise or it would not have been "odd," "essential" because the desire for exaltation is simply one of the risks. Distraction, it turns out, is the way into their "study" as well as the way to conduct it, both medium and method, portal and port. It yields no guarantee where one will end up when its moment has passed.

In terms of situating distraction in Baker's larger project of Black cooperation, North does remind us of something key. That attention is a possessive faculty. Etymologically, it is a hand stretching out (*adtendere*) to take hold, to watch over, to apply oneself to, or to otherwise possess its object. Distraction is the opposite, associated with the flights and dangers of daydreams, thus "tending . . . toward fantasy, literature, and art."[124] Attention is exclusive, barring other objects from view (why "divided attention" feels like both a moral failing and an impossibility); distraction surrenders, as North notes, "gives itself away" (why "divided distraction" feels flatly redundant). For Baker distraction is partial and recursive, lacking forward direction, progress, and foresight. It wavers and wonders to the extent that one could say it lacks all direction, period (all consistency and predictability of movement). In fact, by definition, as soon as one directs it it is no longer distraction. This is what makes distraction so "hard to catch," so discordant for Baker; "as a tendency toward the limit of what is, distraction is nearest when it escapes notice and most remote when attended to."[125] In terms of time, one can safely deduce that if attention is signified by "honor, glory, and fame," an attention both given and received, then attention is linear, progressively so. Distraction, we could say, is errantly splintered: is adventure. It bends back or away, remembers or chances, revisits or deviates, or all, all at once. Distraction is the line of time, frayed. So I have come to think of distraction, of Baker's "odd moments," as a splintered time: openings that never wholly escape their closures.

Within the limits Baker sets, I have come to see distraction as the meeting of two poles: subjecthood and subjection. In the argot of the essay, these would be, respectively, "self-reliance" and reliance (the implied opposition). Nothing has been more important in helping me understand this convergence point, as well as its possibilities, than Ferreira da Silva's "transparency thesis," an exceptionally powerful frame from her groundbreaking book *Toward a Global Idea of Race*. Her thesis holds that Western philosophy and science has produced as its main tool of racialization the fantasy of an all-knowing subject, a figure she names the "transparent I." (That's the first breakthrough. The second is: how this tool is exercised by even its staunchest critics.) The "transparent I" is so called because it renders itself and the world perfectly observable to itself alone, because it independently gives transparency to its objects and to itself. It is maddeningly tautological. Picture, if you will, the "transparent I" as a cul-de-sac at the end of a private street and you start to get a picture of this ontological dead-end, barring outside entry, this "formal entity" that encapsulates the figures of Man and the subject.

The "transparent I" assumes all sorts of guises. In art criticism, for instance, it plays the role of the critic who relies on interpretive formulas in fear of the flights, which is also to say the falls, of his own imagination, in fear of "surrendering" to the mess of the art, the "mayhem," the "errant and unbounded," all of which amplify the bounds of his body ("scent," the senses). This kind of criticism "offer[s] no entry point for a reflection on artwork that is not immediately taken as an expression of it."[126] To read in this way presumes that the artwork is autonomous from history and social influence, which is really a presumption about oneself. (Although little recognized, artistic autonomy was what Schuyler, at bottom, was contesting in his most famous essay "Negro-Art Hokum" (1926), when he notoriously wrote with an, albeit, unfortunate turn of phrase, "the Aframerican is merely a lampblacked Anglosaxon." Beneath his integrationist rhetoric, he was contesting the possibility of cultural isolation, the idea that Black American art is "fundamentally different" from white American art, that any art, in short, is autonomous.) Contravening an old debate about the differences between such presumptive and immersive reading—or in Eve Sedgwick's terms, between the "paranoid" and "reparative"; in Stephen Best's, between one's "first" and "second thought"; or simply in Baker's, between "reading and rereading"—Ferreira da Silva contends that to critique in a self-solidifying fashion instead of to "appreciate" is to execute a formula, to fix not unfold, to succeed at one's plans instead of, we could say, planning their failure. Not limited to human forms, the fantastical fiction of individual autonomy that such partial reading presumes states that the apex of life is to be relatively undetermined by external conditions and principally determined by oneself. The touchstones of this fiction are universality and self-determination (or "honor, glory, and fame" combined with "self-reliance"). Here's the crux of the point. The "transparent I" divides up the globe into fictions like itself and to fictions who can only be affected by it. Hence Ferreira da Silva names its opposition the "affectable I," or the reliant one.

The "transparent I" presents itself as the sole proprietor of temporality and universal reason, as opposed to the "affectable I," the racial other with no reason to speak of and no ability to move, fixed in space. Because only the subject, who expresses in Husserl's terms the "ideal of humanity," can enjoy and transcend necessity, he is, to speak loosely, the only person in the world gifted with time, the only person who can feel and oversee it unfold. Everyone else is out of it, out of time and out of time, since presumably already caught or stranded in space. The subject can make decisions about its future. The subaltern has no future to make decisions about. As Zakiyyah Iman Jackson notes in her perceptive summary of the *transparency thesis*, the racialized other lacks "capacities of interiority" that "enable one to decide his essence and existence." Jackson may remind us of Baker's allusion to this preference for the internal over the externalized, her reference not to dress but to "cigarettes" and "cigars," to the push and pull of the breath, and, with resonance to today, this in turn may remind us of those who can breathe and those who can't. The figure for the ones who can "is underwritten," Jackson continues, by "fantasies of 'self-determination' as self-sufficiency, 'the will' as self-discipline, and rationality as 'self-regulation.'" Upon hearing these fantasies, it is not hard to see how the gospel of self-help underwriting cooperation may partake in their enjoyment. It is hard to see how it might not.

At the beginning of this section I said that Baker referred to self-help through the word "self-reliance." That was only half true. I should have said she also uses interchangeably the word "self-dependence." By doing so, she marks a difference between these two notions, which taken together essentially spell independence, not self-help. Self-help is precisely not independent. It is susceptible and collective, risky and open handed, hence the "help." "Self-reliance" as "self-dependence," and vice versa, is sealed and autonomous. There's a reason self-reliance evokes in the American imaginary a lone cabin in the woods. I also said distraction bears the capacity for diversion. I could have equally said, the capacity for self-help. At bottom, distraction is the crossroad of transparency and affectability, a risky endeavor that fails to be either by, for a moment, being both.

As the crossroad, distraction yields the potential for being otherwise, for going somewhere else that is always right here. Baker's "odd moments" remind us how easily one can tip into conformity with the liberal humanist subject, into its central fictions of autonomy and consent, and how important it is to face it, the mess, without fantasies of escape. In the end, this immersive orientation is at best a saving grief, but it is also, to cite Brent Edwards, "the necessary coexistence of dispossession and invention, perdition and predication, catastrophe and chance."[127] One could say the same of planned failure's enabling conditions: where extremes meet they tend to fall apart, and the detritus is redemption. The difference between self-help and self-reliance, and likewise between distraction and attention, a splintered and progressive time, is the difference between a normative reading and an odd one: between reading how Baker outplays her plans and purely reading how she plays them out.

I'll close by showing how in the context of her later work on Black cooperation, one can see how she does both, plays out her plan of "personal thrift" and outplays it. Again this awkward blend has everything to do with time. When she wrote in the essay, a "penny may seem very worthless, but if it is saved and others are added to it, it will prove to be quite valuable," she wrote the rough outline of what would become her first major fundraising campaign for consumers cooperation, the "Penny-a-Day Plan" launched in 1940. Over the course of three months beginning in January, the drive, as she wrote in her "synopsis," was designed to extend "self-help concepts" like the "Double Duty Dollar" (buying goods and buying Black: patronizing Black business). She wanted "to reach a minimum of 500 to 10,000 persons who will contribute or raise at least $1 over a period of 90 days." And she hinted in "Personal Thrift" when she said the "first requisite is 'Begin'" that the temporality of her "self-help concept" was sharply present, and sharper still than merely beginning: making manifest. In broad strokes this later form of self-help broke its ties with gradualism to render an extended instancy, a long-form nowness. For instance, when Lawrence Campbell, assistant secretary of the Cooperative League USA, from whom she solicited support, advised her to wait, she politely responded, "I agree with you that it would be more desirable to be granted at least six months in which to do some of the basic and preliminary educational work before attempting to raise funds. . . . But I am convinced that, even if launched 'Cold,' such a campaign, built around some novel phrasing of the self-help philosophy, can be made to pay its way."[128]

It's interesting, isn't it, that success depends on "some novel phrasing," as though to suggest *not* some novel idea. The "novel phrasing" of "penny-a-day" ultimately doubles down, by way of historical contrast, on the importance for self-help to don the temporal structure of self-help-now, of a menial immediacy. Baker seems to be aware, at least on some level, of a long and neighboring history of practical sedition that went by close but different names. The "penny-a-month" club, for example, in early nineteenth-century England. Started in 1816 near the city of Rochdale, the club was made up of weavers who bought and distributed seditious newspapers and periodicals, gathering at "hush-shops," inns, bookstores, and private houses for public readings in the evening. The papers were too expensive for any one person to buy, so buying them collectively was itself a form of sedition against what was scorned as "taxes on knowledge." Baker also brings to mind, from the same period of time, the "penny-a-week" schools run by English factory workers and coal miners for children who couldn't afford standard institutions.[129] This lineage of English cooperatives to Baker's campaign may seems like a stretch, but we should remember the inspiration for both parties was largely drawn from the same fount: the work of the Welsh socialist Robert Owen, whose fight for free education and just labor conditions inspired the establishment of the League's stated predecessor, the Rochdale Society of Equitable Pioneers in 1844.

Regardless of whether Baker was looking across the pond, what distinguishes her campaign in this cooperative tradition, what gives historical novelty to her "phrasing," was that she made "self-help" ever more present. Her unit of time was not "a week" or "a month"—it was "a day." All these compositions, the English associations, Baker's fundraising campaign, "Personal Thrift," all were spaces of radical learning, where working hours were deployed to contrary ends. Through schools with low walls or, as Baker would have it, with none, they disseminated insurgent literacies. This brings us right back to the League and its grammar of comic time.

Comic Time

During a long speaking tour on economic cooperation, Schuyler got himself embroiled in a scandal. In a 1932 essay on the Scottsboro Case (1931–76), he encouraged the communist supporters to reconsider their method of legal defense: "I am tired of the . . . lack of humor of most of the radicals, especially the extreme radicals. . . . I am tired of these so-called radicals' assumption of omniscience. Indeed, I have about to come to the conclusion that most of them are not radicals at all, but are maladjusted sentimentalists."[130] This essay was one of many smug pasquinades Schuyler delivered against the International Labor Defense, the legal arm of the U.S. Communist Party, and specifically Joseph Brody, its chief attorney, for assuming that they knew what was best for the nine Scottsboro defendants falsely accused of rape, even over the counsel of the NAACP. By 1934 Schuyler's attacks were "read with horror" by twenty-four prominent intellectuals, including Langston Hughes, Gwendolyn Bennett, Aaron Douglas, and Channing Tobias, all of whom signed a letter to Schuyler demanding he immediately retract his dangerous "treachery."[131]

The controversy hinted at the life-and-death stakes in adopting one narrative frame over another to interpret racial violence, especially when that violence is reproduced by the law. By excoriating the assumed "omniscience" of the agencies fighting to represent the men, and by calling for more humor with less sentimentality, Schuyler all but said outright that the attitude of public support was marked by a tragic pathos. As tragic characters try to be effectively omniscient, their blindness excites the audience's pity and terror. Thus Schuyler implied the real tragedians were not the defendants but the "radicals," "mal"-sentimentalists who *would* not see what they *could* not see: how their feelings for the defendants displaced the defendants, a trap reminiscent of the sentimentalist novel epitomized by *Uncle Tom's Cabin*. Schuyler's lampoon flagged the hegemonic hold that narratives of tragedy have had on those trying to understand and redirect revolutionary action. We might think of Hannah Arendt's *On Revolution* (1963), Raymond Williams's *Modern Tragedy* (1966), Karl Jaspers's *Tragedy Is Not Enough* (1953), George Steiner's *The Death of Tragedy* (1961), David Scott's *Conscripts of Modernity* (2004), Jeremy Matthew Glick's *The Black Radical Tragic: Performance, Aesthetics, and the Unfinished Haitian Revolution* (2016)—we could all extend the list, for the dominance of the tragic frame has been almost remarkable. Planned failure is what comes into view when we see the political actor and ourselves as not tragic but comic.

Ironically, a tragic frame still underwrites some of the most far-reaching efforts to get beyond it. Take, for example, Jack Halberstam's *The Queer Art of Failure*, a perspicacious and playful study on how, facing the grin of capitalist success, queerness has modeled failure as a way of life. Baker and Schuyler would likely agree with Halberstam that success is but a ruse, a preemptive "set of standards" to "ensure that all future radical ventures will be measured as cost-ineffective." Bringing to mind Schuyler's distress call to humor, Halberstam favors the word "revel" to describe queer encounters with capital's grin: "revel in the detours," "revel in innovation," "revel in the glory of invention," "in the sheer animality of our precariousness and survival"—"let us instead revel and cleave to our own inevitable fantastic failures." In the end, however, Halberstam does more to glorify the tragic plot points of this revelry than to adopt a new plot altogether. His heroes, after all, enact a life-way, or life-wreck, "predicated upon awkwardness, clumsiness, disorientation, bewilderment, ignorance, disappointment, disenchantment . . . immobility," and no surprise, "despair"—they enact, in short, the ending, the dead-ending, of every good tragedy. Schuyler, for his part, helps us navigate the comic field of political action, helps us think what it means to feel beneath the despair of "immobility," defeat as de-feet. Rinsing our vision, he allows us to see that tragedy has become so discursively pervasive it is terribly hard to see anything else, even when that's the point.[132]

The conventional idea of comedy is that the comic actor seeks transcendence and escape through her acceptance of contingency. For instance, Søren Kierkegaard remarked that "the tragic and the comic are the same, in so far as both are based on contradiction; but the *tragic is suffering contradiction, the comical, the painless contradiction*. . . . The comic apprehension evokes the contradiction or makes it manifest by having in mind the way out."[133] *Bosh!* Baker and Schuyler might have replied. Far from tragedy's binary opposite, far from the idea that comedy is falling and getting back up over and over (and over), comedy in Schuyler's fiction and his activism alongside Baker constitutes an immersion in the breaks. Comedy was their envelopment in historical contingencies and human finitudes. Their comedy, a form of writing and activism, a mode and a modus vivendi, foreshadowed the aperçu by Alenka Zupančič that comedy is "a nonrelation that lasts."[134] Comedy is "a paradoxical continuity that builds, constructs (almost exclusively) with discontinuity; discontinuity . . . is the very stuff of comic continuity."[135]

This may be the right place to note that Baker's partial adoption of planned failure does not in any way contradict her general efforts to build sustainable coalitions, even when their sustainability meant waiting to begin. In 1941 she wrote to NAACP *Crisis* editor Roy Wilkins, "Because of a combination of pressure for action and a lack of patience to wait and save slowly over an extended period of time, many cooperatives were launched with insufficient capital and/or insufficient business experience."[136] Working with Schuyler on their experimental maneuvers did mean, however, that she operated on at least two registers: on a high and a low pragmatism. Planned failure operates on the lowest, a messy political engagement that can only be mistakenly split from the philosophical, the imaginary, or the dream.[137] To imagine is not to see a better world; it's to see the world better.[138]

Baker's ability to move between these registers was nowhere more evident than when she said, in that same summary letter to Wilkins: the "mortality rate [of Black cooperatives] is still rather high," but "enough projects have survived to prove that the technique of consumers' cooperation can be successfully employed by Negro groups."[139] Perhaps the absurdity of this statement was too obvious for Wilkins to note, perhaps intentionally so, given the conventions of a bureaucratic memo, let alone one for institutional support. How does one explain the incongruity (thinking of Zupančič) between a "high mortality rate" and surviving "enough"? Does anyone really survive a high mortality rate even if they go on living? Probably not, and this is the contradiction evinced in the irony of surviving *enough,* in the notion that *"enough . . . have survived."* I cite this letter to show that while Baker might not have embraced planned failure as wholeheartedly as Schuyler, she continued to tread in its comic undercurrent. Baker is not usually appreciated for her humor (Ransby contends "she took everything seriously").[140] Yet one rare biopic while she was alive twinned her tenacity with her ability to laugh. "She's been struggling. . . . Struggling to make it, and making it still, though the white world tries to keep her down. No, it's neither sadness nor resignation you see. It's intelligence, wit, humor."[141] And Baker herself thought of humor as even more elemental than a source of strength: a source of sight, the very ability to see at all. In 1931 she wrote to the editors of the *Courier,* responding to a column outraged by Schuyler's satirical novel *Black No More* (as a masterpiece of speculative fiction and a satire on the plasticity of race, it is still to this day his most famous work). "It is evident," Baker wrote, "that Mr. Newman is a Garveyite and that in itself would disqualify him from seeing or appreciating humor and satire such as one finds in *Black No More*."[142]

Baker was never laughing. Baker was always laughing.

Schuyler unfurled his own comic vision of the Black cooperative movement soon after their League collapsed. In sixty-two weekly installments between November 1936 and April 1938, Schuyler wrote his novel *Black Empire*, part speculative pulp, part revenge fantasy against imperial conquest. The 1930s were a heyday for empire across the globe. Japan occupied Mongolia, Nazi Germany ballooned, Spain witnessed a civil war, but worst of all for Schuyler in 1935 Italy invaded Ethiopia. The invasion, Schuyler wrote, portended "a major catastrophe for the darker peoples of the world."[143] African American concerns about the impact of an Italian victory over Ethiopia, the oldest independent African state and the preeminent destination of freedom in African American folklore, ran as deep as they did wide. One Chicago reader wrote to the *Courier* assuming (wishing?) that the novel was true. "I want to understand about this Dr. Henry Belsidus. Is his conquest going on now, at the present time, in Africa?"[144]

I laughed with a twinge when I first read that. I was instantly reminded of how difficult it has been for both critics and historians to laugh at the novel in any way whatsoever. With a few exceptions,[145] it is most often read straight as utopian romance,[146] or as predominantly melodrama.[147] This despite Schuyler stating that he intended it to be funny, laugh-out-loud funny. "I have been greatly amused by the public enthusiasm for 'The Black Internationale' [the title of its first half], which is hokum and hack work of the purest vein. I deliberately set out to crowd as much race chauvinism and sheer improbability into it as my fertile imagination could conjure."[148] Coming to terms with the novel's humor also means coming to see it through his work with the League. Let's begin by noting that it ends with the founding of a cooperative commonwealth, where Schuyler pretty much quotes word for word his early ode to cooperatives from 1930. If the ode is the call, the novel's end is the response. The ode: "Co-operative democracy means a social order in which the mills, mines, railroads, farms, markets, houses, shops and all the other necessary means of production, distribution and exchange are owned cooperatively by those who produce, operate and use them."[149] The end: "We are going to build roads . . . factories, operate giant collective farms, ranches, mines, mills, become self-sufficient . . . toward a cooperative civilization."[150]

The novel is a satire of how wrong such a commonwealth can go (the leader of the empire, Belsidus, the sultan, is totally totalitarian, colonizes Africa, kills at will, etc.), how detached it can be from the actual commonwealth Schuyler and Baker imagined when, we could say, its failure is not planned. The first line of dialogue in this bewilderingly long story is the sultan telling his conscripts, "'So you have failed. I cannot tolerate failure.'"[151] Then in the next installment, the sultan praises "the great schemes" of the "Communists, Fascists, and Nazis" and says "in a plan such as this there can be no talk of right or wrong. Right is success. Wrong is failure. . . . I do not intend to fail."[152] I pair the League with this novel because it elucidates the comic attitude Baker and Schuyler enlarged into a critical practice. Furthermore, just like the League, the novel helps us think about possible interruptions to the temporality of empire. As evinced in the seriality of the work, its indefinite extension into the future, and the fact that at the very end Belsidus absconds from view, and his empire advances on its own, the temporality of empire works to purloin not only the present, not only the past, but the future itself.[153] This is a novel about the trespasses of progressive time and the means of interrupting them.

Toward this point, let's consider how the novel starts. Belsidus kidnaps our narrator Slater in a car, serving him a drink to quell his resistance. Slater then enjoys a wild hallucination. Here we might think of Sigmund Freud's contention that hallucinations are promiscuous minglings of jokes and dreams. Jokes seek pleasure; dreams the "avoidance of unpleasure" by the "detour of hallucination."[154] This promiscuity is precisely what Slater remembers when he says, "I could feel, see, experience, but what I saw was strange, uncanny, unthinkable, utterly mad. I felt as if my head had been turned by 180 degrees . . . my feet turned into spirals and scrolls. . . . Suddenly, to my surprise I found that I had no head but in its place a sheet of ground-glass like a camera-screen."[155]

After allegorizing the reflexivity of the creative process ("my head . . . turned by 180 degrees"), Schuyler then construes this self-reading as comic: Slater's head is "discontinuous," to again use Zupančič's word. It's a sequence of disjunctures ("ground-glass"). Likewise, his body, both a dialectical time ("spiral") and linear time ("scroll"), represents time out-of-joint. Comedy is not configured as historical contingency against historical progress (dialectical or linear) but as the very disconnection between these two orientations toward the future. All these fractures in Slater's body depict the basic fact that, just like planned failure, comedies love to strut out in one direction and then completely change course as if nothing had happened.[156]

By configuring Slater as the reader of his own narration in the story's very first chapter, Schuyler encourages readers not only to read themselves in their own time but also to notice the gaps in the seemingly smooth ("like a camera-screen") and thus seemingly invincible technocratic logic of global empire, the League's principal point of negation. When we combine the de-imperial introspection modeled by Slater with Schuyler's citation of his earlier ode to cooperatives, it is hard not to read the form of the League beside that of *Black Empire*. Both exemplify the Marxist dictum that the conditions of capital are also those of its ruin, a dictum backlit by Slater's searing hallucination.[157] Slater is disassembled into an "utterly mad" state of being by a drink whose malevolence is also emboldening. It is arguably this moment of attempted subdual that then emboldens Slater to tell the story in the first place.[158]

As Slater shows, to live in comic time is not to identify a disjunction in order to reach greater insight, as in Kenneth Burke's famous definition of a comic attitude toward history, a "perspective by incongruity."[159] To live in, enliven, comic time is to identify insight as itself disjunction, as itself the break in the legacies of slavery between the now and the not-yet. In the break, as Moten notes, "mourning turns so that the looker is in danger of slipping, not away, but into something less comfortable than horror—aesthetic judgment, denial, laughter."[160] Moten's fall into laughter recalls a similar fall in Freud's definition of the joke, the "plunge": any "thought" exerting the "intention of constructing a joke . . . plunges into the unconscious," "seeking there for the ancient dwelling-place of its former play with words."[161] To laugh is to plunge into the present.

What else can we say about the psychic economy of comic time? In *Black Empire* Schuyler repeatedly describes the experience of disjuncture as a psychological blankness, an instance of Slater's mind going "blank." These instances call the reader to literally forestall any assumptions about the emotional texture of the character's experience. When Slater wakes up the next day following the kidnapping, "I remembered the . . . strange, unbelievable phantasmagoria that had whirled through my brain before everything went blank."[162] Blankness is the classic symbol of epistemic aporia, indicating not emptiness or vacancy but the failure of reason, the total inability to make sense of a situation. It is in this blank space that the psychic negotiation of Baker's and Schuyler's cooperative economics resides.

Explaining their field studies of various worker cooperatives in Argentina, political theorists Ken Byrne and Stephen Healy end up trying to explain a gap. They contend that cooperatives operate by traversing the gap between knowing how to proceed and knowing how not to, a gap that manifests itself as a sustained conflict among the cooperative members. But since these members never imagine that a utopia awaits and that intragroup tensions should or ever will be completely solved, they maintain an "openness to contingency." This attitude can be described as looking lightly on deep tension since those tensions never become paralyzing. Byrne and Healy position economic cooperation as contrary to the romantic attempt to build "*an ideal economy*, an economy in which needs *would be* met, desires *would be* satisfied, proper human and social development *would be* achieved, *if only . . .*" capitalism could be overturned.[163] This romance is waged under the straightjacket logic that if there are no cracks in the system, if its domination is complete, then every reaction to it must necessarily be an extension of its rule, and, likewise, its subversion requires a level of omnipotence on par with a figure like Belsidus. We can see how the idea that capital penetrates every facet of life attracts either a tragic narrative, in which even the mightiest hero is necessarily inadequate to the task, or a romantic narrative, like *Black Empire*'s, in which the hero quite magically triumphs. By contrast to these two approaches, the cooperative attitude Byrne and Healy extrapolate, though they never say so, could be called comic.

Schuyler's correction to the double-binding assumption of total violence, of complete reification, is to inspire a comic set of economic desires among those weary about the project of capitalism. Like Du Bois and other forerunners of the Black cooperative movement, Schuyler configures an economic crisis as a crisis of desire, a configuration evident in his use of the term *phantasmagoria*. Its meaning makes Slater's real world inseparable from his fantasies. This intimation that fantasies and real life are intimately close if not indistinguishable resonates with Schuyler's wish that his fiction become a sort of cognitive instrument, instructing his readers on how to adopt a certain critical life practice: "Readers want to be entertained and instructed, and I know how to do it," he wrote to Ira Lewis, general editor at the *Pittsburgh Courier*.[164]

Similarly, Byrne and Healy's psychoanalytic reading of any "subject who desires nonexploitation" suggests that the struggle to subvert or transcend capitalism writ large resembles a longing for a lost Lacanian wholeness; such resistance is therefore motivated by a fantasy of unity, certainty, and consensus that would alleviate the pain of the lack or "the gap." My point is that "the gap" Byrne and Healy observe cooperative members traversing rather than trying to alleviate is represented by the psychic "blank" Slater experiences right after he drinks the hallucinatory cocktail. Schuyler's sets the "phantasmagoria" of blankness against a fantasy of wholeness, a fantasy that is itself a symptom of psychic lack since it is also the obstacle to ever recovering a wholeness. The perception and apperception of comic time are more than an "openness to contingency." They are its literal embodiment. After all, Slater's curled and seated body distinctly resembles the shape of a question mark, or what Erica Edwards calls an "alternative *punctuation*" to antiracist political strategies, where "the privileging of the question mark over the exclamation point leaves the reader space to imagine a new relation to leadership, to politics, to history itself."[165] As suggested by the ebullience, the curious glee, that Slater maintains in the face of terror (a reaction that reminds me of Toni Morrison's Sixo, the character in *Beloved* who laughs with defiance as schoolteacher attempts to burn him alive; when you're already composed of fire, it's hard to fear it), the psychic economy of comic time entails the assumption of deep uncertainty. Surprising as it is, the novel proffers deep uncertainty, the social poiesis of bodies as much in motion as in disjuncture, as one way to counter the sheer emotional drain of anti-Black negativity.

When we examine how Schuyler and Baker organized the second national conference for the League, we can see them attempting to fashion a similar traversal of disjuncture for the attendees. Meeting at the Twelfth Street YMCA in Washington, D.C., in April 1932, Schuyler and Baker designed a program that "courageously" invited and dangerously revealed crucial points of potential conflict among the conference goers and the twenty delegates present.[166] So contentious was the program that one literary critic described it as "plagued" by problems.[167] The discussion topics included "Getting the Members to Pay Dues to the National Office," "Should There Be a 'Depression' Joining Fee?," "Does Discussion of Religion & Politics Make for or Against Harmony Within the Council?," and "How Has Impatience and Intolerance Led to Disharmony Between Officers & Members?"[168] I can't help but notice the rhetorical tone of these questions. They smack of a certain obviousness. Alongside the irony in asking about "a 'Depression' joining fee," there is something comic, something quite redundant, in investigating how "impatience and intolerance" has led to "disharmony." The circularity of this procedure made the discussion as much about understanding the stated topic as about staging conflict itself.

The issue broached by such sensitive concerns at this 1932 gathering, concerns such as religion and personal character ("impatience," "intolerance"), was the importance of staging issue as such, which is to say the practical imperative to generate new issues. After all, the greater issue in all the discussions was how the participants might allow issues to emerge. Schuyler and Baker were creating less a problem than a problematic. A problematic is a praxis that is precisely not a particular position, doctrine, or creed but an "allegiance to a specific complex of problems, whose formulations are always in movement and in historic rearrangement and restructuration, along with their object of study" (here cooperation).[169] Baker's main complaint about the NAACP was that its leaders silenced dissent. Baker and Schuyler were putting into practice the meaning of cooperation as a dual operation, as the notion that the only point of ever proffering a "we" is to discover who *we* are not.[170]

I hear in their conference a question Jared Sexton asked in 2016. Reflecting on the social of the Black Lives Matter movement, he said, "Perhaps we should speak, then, simply of a bunch, or even a gathering of those whose *gathering* is what matters, like the gathering of momentum or the gathering of a storm." Likewise, Baker and Schuyler put into play a political community of false correspondence, of connection by miscue. Theirs was a unity of something greater than difference—of disaffiliation. Theirs was a "gathering," a mash-up, at best "a bunch," challenging the supposition that constructing a movement requires common interests, when really it may need no more than common issues, a problematic.[171] The displacement of a problematic for a univocal idea of a people was not only Baker's grievance. It was also Schuyler's, specifically addressed to the collectivism in the U.S. Communist Party. Six years after the conference, while writing the final serial of *Black Empire*, Schuyler would make plain his philosophy of leadership. As if he had a premonition of Henry Williams's remark, Schuyler declaimed in his address at the 1938 national NAACP conference that "the business of a branch is not to avoid trouble *like the plague* but to hunt for it" (emphasis added).[172]

The 1938 audience that heard these remarks might have remembered his testy speech at the last NAACP conference when he said, "If we had as many co-operative banks as we have branches [of the NAACP], we would be one of the great financial factors in the country."[173] The more conciliatory tone he struck in his second address made one thing clear: that although he remained concerned about the NAACP's decision to downplay consumer cooperatives, he saw sharing a philosophy of horizontal leadership paramount to walking the same path of political emancipation. He explained that the principle of welcoming "trouble" in and beyond the group ultimately justifies itself in the expansion of the social base: "If the colored citizens of the community feel that the branch is carrying on an effective fight on *all* fronts for the improvement of their social and economic status, they will properly support it."[174] Schuyler charged that effective leadership is "uncouth": propelled by the willingness to be led not just by the people but by the people's problems and their personalized solutions. "An uncouth, uneducated fighting branch leader is preferable to a pacifist Ph.D., for culture and knowledge may be acquired but courage is inherent."[175] He subordinates knowledge, whether partial or full, to the willingness to act and be acted on.

With the League behind her toward the end of the 1930s, Baker reengaged what her biographer Barbara Ransby beautifully calls "the carryover": learned political strategies from yesteryears, which in this case was a comic approach to activism consonant with Schuyler's. As though to underscore this consonance, Baker used that very same word "uncouth" to signify her very similar war of position, punsition. In her new role of assistant field secretary for the NAACP, she expanded the organization's base. She wrote to then assistant secretary Roy Wilkins that she wanted "to place the NAACP and its program on the lips of all the people."[176] Then, with mockery: "the uncouth MASSES included." Focusing, as she did in the League, on consumer sites of social reproduction and discussing the dissemination of the *Crisis* magazine, she conveyed to Wilkins "her ideas for 'increasing the *Crisis* circulation and bolstering my campaign efforts [by visiting] some of the pool-rooms, boot black parlors, bars, and grilles,' with the aim of 'having a *Crisis* made available to regular patrons of the business.'" This is Ransby quoting Baker and Ransby's arrangement of Baker's words—the sites of social reproduction "having a *Crisis*"—perfectly intimates another crisis (in fact, crises) that Baker hoped to convey. This was the crisis of gender norms created by her trespass of hypermasculine habitats, "boot black parlors, bars, and grilles" (do you hear her poetics?), and the crisis of the NAACP's centralized power, here being redistributed to its local extremities, from "boot black parlors, bars, and grilles" to—as Baker mentioned in an earlier report on her membership drive in Baltimore—"mass-supported beer gardens, night clubs, etc."[177]

What if *Crisis* magazine was merely a prop, a barely veiled allusion to a crisis as such? Then crisis with a capital C would be like the word "uncouth" with Baker's mockery, both deployed figuratively. The uncouth would be a figure for class chauvinism, the *Crisis* for all chauvinism and all coherence of the self. Capital C *crisis* would be more than the staging of crisis itself, even more than "'having a *Crisis* made available to regular patrons,'" as we saw at the League's conference and just heard Baker say, splay: it would be the crisis of the person, since *Crisis* is crisis personified. Instigating such a crisis, of a *Crisis*, takes some nerve, which is exactly what Baker took to the central office when she wrote, "We must have the 'nerve' to take the Association to the people wherever they are,"[178] and, now we could add, wherever they will fail to be.

All this tarrying in crisis, heavy handed in Schuyler, openhanded in Baker, was presaged in the very structure of the 1932 YNCL conference. The schedule reflects this duo's leadership philosophies, especially in its contrast to the typical program of the more popular NAACP conferences. The latter usually ended with celebrity lectures, followed by an "Election of Committee on *Resolutions*" (emphasis mine).[179] To be sure, the League's gathering drew to an end with authoritative talks by the historian Carter G. Woodson, the literary scholar Benjamin Brawley, and the economist Abram Harris, but it closed with a mass meeting open to the public. If these renowned guests had been placed last on the schedule, their lectures would have formally reconciled the day's conflicts, like a denouement. But the closure with a last hurrah of the masses, along with the fact that participants traversed tensions for the majority of the day, invited a more ecumenical power dynamic between the audience and the penultimate speakers, transforming the traditional dyad between passive listeners and ministerial orators into a horizontal structure of an audience participating actively in an extended debate. Given that a self-declared literary artist had a heavy hand in designing the conference, these matters of form and sequence, of emplotment, attain a significance that they otherwise might not have. The YNCL conference goers practiced and performed a radical polyphony, the planned failure of a resolution, necessarily free of an enlightenment objective and its teleological time.[180]

Failure Is Ecstatic When History Is What Hurts

There was ecstasy in them, the League's activities and discourse, just as there was in Slater's hallucination. Ecstatic is what it feels like to form a cooperative and plan its failure. The ecstatics have long had a privileged place in Black radical thought for their inbuilt disobedience to the logics of property. In Black studies, ecstasy has long been viewed as a transformative force inherently related to political desire, flagrantly expressing the sensuality of labor.[181] For starters, there's Du Bois's portrait of emancipation in *Black Reconstruction* as a "frenzy," a "howling and dancing" "in many a wild orgy."[182] There's the "ecstatic screams and yells" rippling out from *Black Empire*'s "Temple of Love."[183] Recently, there's Saidiya Hartman's recounting of the English aristocrat and rave of Harlem, Lady Olivia Wyndham who, besotted with a nurse, knifed herself on the forehead and flung herself down the steps just to be attended by this nurse (cunning label, then, "Lady"). There's Hartman's recounting of the soigné sex parties thrown by the daughter of

Madame C. J. Walker, A'lelia Walker, at 80 Edgecombe Avenue, a short walk from the League's headquarters on the same street. There's Hartman's recounting. "Edgecombe": how fortuitously named, "combe" being another name for "coastline," the line where boundaries dissolve. It was on Edgecombe where people, according to Hartman, experienced that "sharp edge of pleasure," where men and women were "unmade," social divisions "effaced," personal boundaries "shattered," as though edging the edge of a combe.

The work of the League broadens the archive of what Aliyyah Abdur-Rahman has named "the Black ecstatic." She defines the ecstatic as a "mode of pleasurable reckoning with everyday ruin in contemporary Black lives," the "joy" and the "disaster" of unspeakable intimacies.[184] Her version of the ecstatic is both a reply and a supplement to José Muñoz's *Cruising Utopia*, which for a while occupied the last word on the subject.[185] While Muñoz rightly rejected the way "gay pragmatic political strategies . . . tell us not to dream of other spatial/temporal coordinates but instead to dwell in a broken-down present," Abdur-Rahman does not so much disagree as reconsider what it may mean to dream in an expanded present, what dreaming becomes when our sense of the present becomes more acute. In a commemorative address to Muñoz, she writes, "A post–civil rights expressive practice, the Black aesthetic eschews the heroism of Black pasts *and* the promise of liberated Black futures in order to register and revere rapturous joy in the broken-down present."[186] The present for Muñoz functions as an "impasse" or, at best, as an object of historical materialist critique.[187] While being mindful of the way enjoyment in the present can invoke a complacency, the equation of joy with accomplishment or triumph, Abdur-Rahman explores what we might have missed about radical things, queer and otherwise, going on right now.

Her exploration brings to mind some of the contradictions of the ecstatics as they appear in Muñoz's work, particularly in his concepts of "queer relational bliss" and "ecstatic time." These arrangements, derangements of progressively "straight time," express a longing for a "better world," a freer future, while they also, "more immediately," draw that future closer, or in Muñoz's preferred parlance, "glimpse" it. "Queer relational bliss" signifies "better relations in the social that include better sex and more pleasure," but why, I wonder, aren't these relations in the present? The present seems to carry potential only to the extent that it borrows it from the future: the present is habitable only at the very point it no longer exists. Muñoz's ecstatic describes an orientation that, despite his insistence on "doing, performing," ends up becoming a waiting to do, to fully do and perform. It is a waiting for the future, our "destination," to arrive.[188] Muñoz asks us to dwell on a beach of time, where "queerness is not yet here but it approaches like a crashing wave of potentiality. And we must," he says, "give in to its propulsion, its status as a destination." To follow Abdur-Rahman's excavation of the present is to see a problem in this metaphor, the very problem satirized in Schuyler's *Black Empire*: since the wave, the future, hasn't shown up, Muñoz's beach feels ironically like an entrapment, a place to make a dwelling out of a dwelling, a home out of a stasis, promise out of a delay. If the present is a beach lapped by the future and beat by the past, then Abdur-Rahman looks to find the hidden clamors for life.

It is not only the imagery that gives this waiting a stubbornly static feel; it is also and more deeply, the concept of time that Muñoz imports from Heidegger. While he otherwise stretches Heideggerian thought into an actively political life, he unwittingly undercuts this hard-fought and complex elasticity by carrying over Heidegger's basic logic of time. Extending a genealogy that had cumulated in Bergson's *Time and Free Will* (1889), Heidegger separates time from space and holds the first as primary. "The future is a spatial and temporal destination," says Muñoz. "It is also another place, if we believe Heidegger, who argued that the temporal is prior to the spatial."[189] The problem I see with this primacy of time is that if the future is another place only after being another time, then we have no place to go until that time shows up.

All the work that Muñoz does to undo Heidegger's separation of the human from political activity, by first retranslating Heidegger's "Dasein" as not only "being-open" but "being-open-*with*," is itself undone here. Reconstructing a Heideggerian word, Muñoz claims that to "dwell" in this openness is to be both active and to activate "hope," "the emotional modality that permits us to access futurity, par excellence." To dwell is, in essence, to begin a social movement—"to denaturalize the way we dwell (move) in the world is to denaturalize the world itself in favor of a utopian performativity."[190] But so long as time remains primary to space, older and unintended senses of the word "dwelling" start to rear their heads. While today we are most likely to hear "dwelling" in the sense of "remaining" or "lasting," as in "dwelling suspicions," or in the sense of "lingering over," "fixing one's attention on," not too long ago we would have encountered it as "tarrying," "delaying," "desisting from action." Dwelling starts to sound less like movement than sourly like desisting. Simply put, Muñoz effectively, under the aegis of hope, concedes the present to the dominance of "straight time" and in so doing unwittingly empowers it.

As a kind of corrective to the implicit teleology, even linearity, of positing a "a better world" as a better-yet, Abdur-Rahman contends that "the critical and political task at hand . . . is to imagine a beyond that is not temporal—that is, not future directed—but that reaches in and reckons with the ruinous now as the site of regenerative capacity and of renewed political agency."[191] In friction with the notion that the past and future are all, that Muñoz's "*then* and *there*" redemptively displace the here and now, Abdur-Rahman's Black ecstatic is a shuttling between the "*here* and not *here*," with an emphasis on the *here*. Her notion of the ecstatic is less a recovery of the past, and still less one of the future, than a recovery of the present. The ecstatic elucidates "modes of endurance in our broken but ongoing present." For Baker and Schuyler, however, it was as though the only way to keep the present "going" was to keep it from going on. Planning such failure was the oddly generative gesture that Schuyler's satire urges us to describe.[192] As if to make the urgency clear as a chalk line, Schuyler hastened a planned failure sixty-two times over twenty-four serial months. And as if to forefend the suspicion that what he hastened cannot be done, he first modeled this activism with Baker and with haste.

I'd like to amplify how Abdur-Rahman scales our present in yet another way: observing ecstasy's synesthesia. Hartman depicts this synesthesia as an "inhabitation" of "breath, touch, and taste," a field of senses displacing the primacy of sight in the process of racialization.[193] Configuring it as the very feeling of fugitivity, Moten paints this pun of collective senses as "chromatic saturation," as "the illicit commerce between the language of music and the language of vision," a Black market, we could say, of sight and song.[194] This social synesthesia, a kind of fleshy wake work, before, in, and beyond the body, has an urgent role to play in the way we confront the changes to capitalism felt as new in the 1930s, but taken as given today.[195] The League's attention to the tilt in the national economy from producer to consumer-based modes of profit-making, conjoined with the "ecstatic" anticipation of global empire in *Black Empire*, renders planned failure an anticipation of the post-Fordist focus on affective labors, like optimism, self-esteem, happiness, good cheer, et patati et patata.[196] If these affects are harnessed to render communication between sellers and buyers effective and expedient, then, in the spirit of Lady Wyndham, the figure of Lady Ecstatica was their fall.

Hurtling down the steps, Wyndham enacted an indestructibility by way of a self-destruction, and she thus recalls Schuyler and Baker's nickname for the cooperative members: "shock troops."[197] The name captured the ability "to render themselves shockproof" while paradoxically shocking themselves and the capitalist system.[198] But the "shock troops" were also an excess: not shock free, shock itself. They were the failure of the self that exceeds the self. A glance at Schuyler's organizational work proves that Ecstatica jived from the page to the pavement, inhered in the margins and the street. Schuyler notes that "from July 18th to August 18th, the writer, with money from the Elmhurst Fund, visited all except two of the councils and affiliated groups, in an effort to stir the members to greater efforts."[199] The meaning of his labors came down to the word "stir": from the German, "to disturb," and in Schuyler's day, "to poke" at coals or other "solid bodies" so as "to promote combustion." To stir their members was to promote their combustion. It is as though the League were jiving syllable to syllable on Moten's line of flight when he says, "I believe in the world and want to be in it. I want to be in it all the way to the end of it because I believe in another world and I want to be in that."[200] What could have been more comic than this? Again, Zupančič: "If humans were 'only human(s)' if the human equation indeed added up so neatly and with no remainder, *there would be no comedy*," for in comedy "finitude is always-already a failed finitude."[201] On the high seas of planned failure, we are not born in order to die, we die in order to begin.

To think of activism through the structure of the ecstatics is not to deny or displace the day-to-day slog of organizing a social movement. That would overlook the YNCL's meticulous balance sheets, the weekly printing and dissemination of "nearly 25,000 pieces" of educational documents, graphs, and statistics of total Black capital, the news releases "to some fifty Negro . . . newspapers"; it would overlook Schuyler's and Baker's lecture tours in "about fifteen cities," the research to compose the "bibliographies" sent to members and to figure out where in each of the "twenty" member states and "nine" council cities they could "purchase books on the subject"; it would overlook the preparation and arrangement of meetings, forums, and conferences, not to mention the decisions of where and when to spend the marginal monies; but it would also overlook that there's an ecstatics here, too.[202] An ecstatic movement of the social in its quotidian slog compels us to reevaluate a common explanation for social movement failure: burnout, exhaustion. This was one of the primary suspects Du Bois had pointed to in his 1907 study *Economic Co-operation among American Negroes*. Likewise, Beatrice Potter's renowned *Co-operative Movement in Great Britain* (1893), which was listed on the first reading list dispensed to League members, claimed that "physical nausea and mental exhaustion" is caused by cutthroat materialist greed and justifies making abstemiousness, restraint, ironically "compulsory," not self-willed.[203] If thrift were not mandated, Potter argued, movement builders would remain too attached to their consumer fantasies and in the process lose the energy to continue building the movement. Baker and Schuyler unsettled this assumption by finding ecstasy in the slog.

Across the humanities and social sciences, the prevailing interpretation of political action has been that the players are tragic, that tragedy best elucidates the nature of their demise. Baker and Schuyler invite a reconsideration of how we assign grades, let alone legibility, to social movement formations and their development. "History is what hurts," writes Fredric Jameson, because it "refuses desire."[204] It is the scar people show to recall their "determinate failure," which leaves, he claims, only the future as the gauze. We would succeed, suggests Jameson, but for the "'ruses' [that] turn into grisly and ironic reversals of their overt intention."[205] But not when you intend them, not when you want them. In the quotidian zones of forced error, "this loophole between hope and resignation," this rupture in being and historical time is always already our revolutionary habitat.[206] Schuyler's and Baker's cooperative practice compels a shift of perspective from unfulfilled demands to unexpected satisfactions. Now whatever happens is not only what was never anticipated, but is ever more than that: "Not only do we (or the comic characters) not get what we asked for, *on top of it* (and not instead of it) we get something we haven't even asked for at all."[207] In the hole of a perpetual hold, the point is not to feel better but to get better at feeling. Soon, Baker would be racing further to the left; Schuyler, to the right, one failure he did not plan and would never explain. But for a time, we can say, all the planned failures of the cooperative movement, all twenty-five thousand graphs and statistical summations of existing Black capital, which metaphorically compiled Black buying power in a single place, all the ecstasies, were so many ways to visualize that the future is already here.

3 Pluripresence

Fannie Lou Hamer's Freedom Farm

• •

There must not be a woman's place for us
We must be everywhere our people are
Or might be—

—Bernice Johnson Reagon, "My Black Mothers and Sisters"

As
though what we wanted
was to be everywhere at
once,
an altered life lived on an
ideal
coast we'd lay washed up
on, instancy and elsewhere
endlessly
entwined.

—Nathaniel Mackey, *Splay Anthem*

Nowhere to Go

Civil rights icon Fannie Lou Townsend Hamer is most widely known for her electoral politics and her legal battles against desegregation. Hamer joined the civil rights movement in 1962, retiring her life as a sharecropper to work as a field agent for the Student Nonviolent Coordinating Commission. In April 1964 she co-founded, as vice chairman, the Mississippi Freedom Democratic Party, which in 1967 campaigned for more than a hundred Black candidates for political office and helped twenty-two of them win, including Robert Clark, the first Black state legislator since the end of Reconstruction. Her notoriety was launched when she spoke in August 1964 at the Democratic National Convention in Atlantic City. There, before prime-time cameras zoomed into her face with Bergmanesque proximity she described in a voice soft as lifting rain Mississippi's refusal to seat Black delegates and the repercussions Blacks faced, literally faced, for trying to vote. Her most fabled achievement: opening up a space to transform electoral politics by integrating (though the better word would be transforming) the Mississippi Democratic Party.

On the back of all these feats and as now a renowned orator, Hamer ran twice for Mississippi state senate (unfortunately lost), she won two of three law suits against local voter fraud and school segregation, she became a founding member in 1971 of the still-thriving National Women's Political Caucus, she even started a singing troupe dubbed the Hamerettes, with whom she serenaded crowds from 1968 into the '70s all over the state. This after touring all over the country, protest to protest, with the gospel choir Freedom Singers, mainly as a soloist, a thundery mezzo-soprano sometimes soft as lifting rain—to call her an icon feels a lot like pinning a medal on the moon.[1] What is less known and still less understood is the project that occupied the final decade of her life, her Freedom Farm cooperative.

In the summer of 1971, Fannie Lou Hamer, together with her board, proudly announced to potential funders, "Freedom Farms has purchased three existing houses in Ruleville, which they provide free of charge to families displaced by natural disaster or acts of man and have no where to go."[2]

It's a strange thing to have nowhere to go, to have to go to a nowhere. Hamer's Freedom Farm has been most widely critiqued for failing to provide a somewhere strong enough to fend off the nowhereness, the oblivion, the despair, or in the words of its primary objective, the collective physical "hunger."[3] Even when its influence is judged in the aggregate as extending the myriad cooperative ventures that stormed the South throughout the 1960s, from the Poor People's Corporation of 1965, which opened sixteen worker-owned crafts and clothing stores in Jackson and New York City, to Hamer's neighboring North Bolivar County Farm Cooperative, which by 1968 was the largest in Mississippi, even then the prevailing judgment remains that Freedom Farm "barely made a dent in the problems of Black unemployment and poverty."[4] That image of a dent is telling. It returns to the insistence on creating even the smallest somewhere to go, a crook in a flat nowhereness, as the mark, naturally enough, of impact and success.

But what if Hamer's greatest impact, as it were, was in refusing the logic of impact altogether, in refusing to try to excavate a somewhere to go? As we in Black studies envision the possibilities of Black radicality on the flatlands of confinement, a confinement so sprawling it mocks the word, we've become deft at descrying sites of movement in sites of stasis. Joy James, for instance, describes the condition of the "captive maternal" in what Saidiya

Hartman calls the "loophole of retreat," quoting Harriet Jacobs. Exemplified by Jacobs, as much as by Hamer, the captive maternal embodies the contradiction of being the celebratory caretaker of U.S. democracy, whose very stabilization destabilizes her. The captive maternal is the figure for whom one's means of survival means a new captivity. Thus Jacobs's "retreat" from the plantation, hiding in a crawlspace of her grandma's attic, worked on her body with its own set of terrors, her "hole" to escape doubling as a "loop." As Jacobs conducted the work of the mind, reading and sewing, which is to say de- and-recomposing what she read, she "could not turn" on her hip "without hitting the roof," and her inability to turn spelled escape from the very life in which she could, in which "she was never so beaten and bruised that she could not turn from side to side."[5]

I'd like to explore Hamer's exploitation of this bind. I'd like to offer a history of Hamer's Freedom Farm as a reclamation of nowhere, not an escape from it, not even a marginal escape from it, when all one has, as they said, is "no where to go." Freedom Farm found ways to let its members embody with a frightening degree of presence the extremes of nowhereness, securing nowhere houses for Hamer's fellow nowheres. I hope to show how, out of this presence, Hamer forged a social movement as a mode of stillness, a movement entirely based on ceasing to move. Because Freedom Farm was a zone in which a social movement was lived and imagined, because it was the vision and materialization of a "movement" (Hamer's word) toward a better future, nothing for me has been more extraordinary than the fact that its futurity depended on time seizing up.[6] It practically preordained that time stop moving.

I have come to these conclusions, which at this point I imagine sound prodigiously abstract and a little outlandish, based on the fact that the makers of the Farm, and Hamer especially, courted, even exaggerated, the contradictions of poverty that they proposed to resolve. They exaggerated these contradictions as they deployed opposing forms of property rights, and this exaggeration became a kind of resolution with dramatic effects on the nature of time. The Farm is the longest lasting cooperative in this history I have sketched, but it might be said, in one way, to have never occurred at all. One could say that for all its operations, from providing "medical care" to of course providing food, Freedom Farm, on the one hand, lived ten times its nine years of age from 1968 to 1977, but on the other, never once came alive.[7] The Farm happened in the sense that we say *whatever happened to them?* or *stranger things have happened.* We use these expressions to talk about the random, seemingly baseless nature of an event, which, to boot, might or might not have made a measurable difference. The Farm happened in this sense but it did not occur.

There was simply too much tension to brook any forward flow, any movement whatsoever. There was tension in the property rights regarding the assets, the designation of ownership, sometimes the members, sometimes the Farm itself, not only undecided but forever opposed. There was consequently tension in the names the Farm was given (should it be called a cooperative, a corporation, a nonprofit, or, as Alice Walker suggested with a portmanteau, a "collective," a question never settled throughout its whole existence?), tension in its membership criteria, in its membership numbers, in its overall plans, in, most strangely, the subjectivity of its leader, Hamer herself, who claimed to exist in antonymous places at once, in the North and the South while in one human body, as though she were a light that could stretch across the sky—there was scarcely a document in any file I pulled pertaining to the Farm that did not appear enjoined in some scheme of divided direction. Every image, every speech, every memo, every letter, nearly everything I found conspired to produce such an intractable tautness that I often wondered how Hamer and the closest nowhere in her flock, Joseph "Joe" Harris, held the Farm together as long as they did.

Hamer's Concept of Progress

What I am saying, see I'm saying as I write this, is that the documents flashed up out of their tensions. They released a kind of light, which I found I could trace only after the light went out. I found this to be the same orientation to history adopted by Hamer and her collaborators. No doubt, this describes a common relationship to Black archives, the feeling that we can only approximate documents that themselves only approximate the life and the lives that made them. But with Hamer this more or less common experience feels deliberate. All I'm saying is what I felt was not only the common fever of sifting through mysterious files. With Hamer, it was more than that. The tensions in turn produced a sense that the meaning the documents hold always emerges suddenly. The meaning emerges so suddenly that the meaning itself registers only as loss. I have tried to seize hold of this history. What I've learned to hold is loss.

I've learned that the only way to understand Hamer's production of time is to position oneself as she did: in the entryway of time. There the possibilities of the tensions they worked so tirelessly to make, which worked tirelessly on them, have a chance to emerge. In sum, these possibilities were ways of having private property that didn't reopen the scars of that having, which, as Hamer joked, was also called "halving" among her fellow share-croppers, half for the owner and half . . . for the owner.[8] All Hamer wanted was a new mode of having. To let its possibility arise was to stand firm in a threshold, an entryway. It was to desist from inserting whatever arose into a preexisting, let alone a linear, meaning. Living in the entryways allows new meaning, the surplus surprise, to live with us, too.

When we fall in love, our beloved takes us by surprise, giving us more than we hoped for not because they exceed our expectations; they could of course fall short of them. They give us more than we hoped for simply because it wasn't what we hoped for at all. They give us more because they give us something different. Lovestruck. You might say the sense of being lovestruck is what I felt while encountering these archival up-flares, encountering Hamer encounter herself. The only way I knew how to glimpse this story of temporal stasis, liberal logics of property, historical progress, co-operatives, and plantation culture, all under the name of Fannie Lou Townsend Hamer, was to actually glimpse it. I glimpsed the fact that Hamer deployed the law to protect what the law itself could not legitimate. She used bylaws for by-ends. She protected personal privacy without private property and a commons without ownership. Personal privacy was of course what a Black woman with little means in a Mississippi burb needed to protect most. Hamer expressed what I'll talk about later as a *pluripres-ence*, the production and traversal of mutually exclusive property rights. For now, my only point is that the closest I could get to her innovations of activism was to try from various angles, over and over, a kind of trial by foul, hence all the small sections or, better, the entries.

The notion that it is only the feeling of loss itself that gives us any sense of what we have lost, that it is ongoing grief alone that allows us to go on, might as well be the mantra of Walter Benjamin's lifeworks. Benjamin writes that our revolutionary moment will always emerge suddenly "in a flash" and must be seized in a flash. But the issue here is that "the rescue carried out by these means—and only by these—can operate solely for the sake of what in the next moment is already irretrievably lost."[9] Susan Buck-Morss interprets this sentence to mean a sort of waiting for Godot.[10] As Buck-Morss sees it, what results from this attempt to seize the now is an endless waiting because the now is always the "next moment" and the next moment is always "already irretrievably lost." In our context, the revolutionary moment was Hamer's seizure of unused land the moment she saw how to seize it.

I interpret Benjamin's elusive passage differently. I interpret "the irretrievably lost" as meaning that what one seizes is loss itself, literally the "flash" of the image, which isn't really anything. Seizing the now is like standing in a room and trying to describe the clipped shimmer that lingers when the light goes out, trying to describe something that happens but fails to occur. The point is to seize the emptiness. One can interpret the power of this seizure as the creativity inspired from empty spaces, which is to say the refusal of closure. One can interpret the power as the reminder that there must be things that remain if there are things that are lost. So let's turn to what remains.[11] But we cannot forget that all of these apprehensions of loss would fail to apprehend anything if we ever surrendered our feeling of loss—to optimism, pessimism, or most of all hope. Loss and revolution are tessellated, mutually implicated. They're one-in-two.

It is in Benjamin's notes that I find the words I need to talk about Hamer's movement in stasis, find two words above all: "dialectical image." In *The Arcades Project*, Benjamin proffers the notion of an historical dialectic that comes in the shape of a tangible image. Yes, oxymoronic to say the least. We have a dialectic, a potentially deadly ricochet to better tomorrows. We have, in short, the dominant narrative about the civil rights movement, usually told as a series of takeovers, from a Woolworth's lunch counter to an Alabama bridge.[12] Then we have an image, something static, lacking nothing if not dialectical speed. The reason the dialectic is frozen in an image is that the image is pushed to the limit with tensions.

It is difficult for me to probe a movement that was all about bringing time to a standstill without using Benjamin's idea of a "dialectics at a standstill," his sobriquet for "the dialectical image."[13] I have found it easier to explain the way I see the experiment that unfurled from Ruleville, Mississippi, to Chicago all the way to Wisconsin and beyond by keeping in mind that a dialectics at a standstill is the place "where thinking comes to a standstill in a constellation saturated with tensions—there the dialectical image appears. It is the caesura in the movement of thought. Its position is naturally not an arbitrary one. It is to be found, in a word, where the tension between dialectical opposites is greatest."[14] Benjamin has a specific tension in mind. He's referring to the tension between the apparent newness, the promise, of a commodity and the hellish return of a historical disaster. Thus the best dialectical images, images in which the "tension" was "greatest," were broken and discarded items, like a lost button or a worn-out shoe. The apprehension of these commodities in our hands and minds is in itself revolutionary. Why? Because what one apprehends is that their broken nature and devaluation record the events that left or tried to leave certain populations equally broken and devalued. What one apprehends is that such commodities are not just symbols. They're symptoms. And to apprehend that is to clear the fog of historical forgetting. To bring this way of seeing a misfit commodity, a dialectical image, to Hamer's oeuvre is to suddenly see her traversing the tension between open and closed (collective and private) forms of property. The tension is itself the image, discarded like a worn-out shoe. We see that these forms of property initially promised pure possibility, a world full of nothing but surface and sky. And when we trace how Hamer brought opposing kinds of ownership to a head, to a hammer, shall we say (reprising a joke from a song she loved to sing, "If I Had a Hammer"), we finally see the Farm.

Taking hold of opposing forms of ownership, all to hold a new logic of property, was to make an interruption in "elapsing time."[15] Interruption, interference with elapsing time, was for Hamer, as for Benjamin, the only meaning of progress. Listen to how Benjamin's words resonate with Hamer's. Benjamin writes, "the concept of progress must be grounded in the idea of catastrophe," that "hell is not something that awaits us, but this life here and now."[16] "This is a shame," said Hamer in 1967. "Today, all over the state . . . we're going [back] into the second phase of Reconstruction."[17] Four years later, she streamlined her point, speaking of the shape and state of Mississippi: "it's been a disaster area fifty-three years. . . . I know people older than me said it's been a disaster area before then."[18]

Benjamin took particular issue with the rectilinear treatment of time, the same issue Hamer raised in her discussion of disaster. Sitting in a villa in Spain during the summer of 1916, Benjamin told the mystic philosopher Gershom Scholem that the shape of time isn't orthogonal. If anything, it's "a cycloid or something else, which has no direction at many points. (Where there are *no* tangents.)"[19] Whereas what crystallizes from this cycloid is a momentary constellation, as bright as it is brief, Hamer's temporality is as much a passing light as it is a constant darkness. The darkness is key, for it reframes what often felt to appraisers of the Farm as a people lost, a managerial staff without direction, slapdash and haphazard, when in fact they were operating in a different order of time: a dark time in dark times.

If time no matter which way it points, backways or sideways, is always moving in some direction on the account of philosophers and our diurnal clocks alike ("we cannot even represent time without . . . *drawing* a straight line," says Kant), if time may be regarded as a nighttime urban sprawl with streamers and swirls of crimson light, conveyed at variegated speeds by freeways and roundabouts, back alleys and bridges, illumining every arterial pathway and junction like contrast dye, then Freedom Farm was like a blackout and the collective coming to a stop.[20] What went dark as I slouched through the files of Freedom Farm is time as I had known it, time with duration, measurable time, comparable by degrees to times hitherto. It is from this perspective that I submit that Freedom Farm was, in the full meaning of the phrase, entirely exo-tempo. It happened but never occurred.[21]

In her transcribed autobiography, Hamer had this to say: "What I really feel is necessary is that the Black people in this country will have to upset this applecart."[22] Later she defines this "upset" as systematic destruction, which recalls the anarchy of Schuyler and of Hamer's close friend Ella Jo Baker. "The land of the free and the home of the brave is all on paper. . . . The only way we can make this thing a reality in America is to do all we can to destroy this system and bring this thing out to the light."[23] She herself brings out the light through this critique, and if we read this dazzling move in line with her description of historical stasis, in line with the stasis she is very much in, then we should say she remakes what it means "to destroy." To destroy is to progress. It is not to negate the dark against the dark, or against the light. It's to avow that the darkness is bright, so bright.[24]

A Tale of Two Farms

I'd like to talk straightway about these tensions in the darkness as they pertain to property, but for the sake of orientation, I should first give you an arc of what the Farm was and why it came to be. It was formally incorporated in 1969, but it really began the previous year with what they called "the Pig Bank," or in the official, internally circulated documents, the "cooperative livestock program."[25] This was a dissemination of badly needed food financially supported and initially organized by the National Council of Negro Women. Coordinated by Hamer and "supervised" by farmer Myles Foster, the Pig Bank bore one of the major marks of a conventional cooperative: beneath the smoke cloud of "transnational corporate concentration and expansion," it facilitated community participation in an equitable distribution of gathered resources.[26] The returns or the "interest," as the thirty thousand pounds of pork were called, were distributed in direct proportion to need and involvement, rather than to investment and the ownership of stocks, as is the case in the corporate model.[27] This was a program of "poke," to summon Hamer's word, and the program became a nearly fabled piggery. The poke program was inspired by how Hamer responded to the use of hunger as a political weapon. Despite the advance of state-imposed starvation by way

(*Top*) Hamer on the Farm, VA04.04.07.001.T2. (*Bottom*) Hamer in her home, VA04.04.07.001.C24, single contact sheet frame, Louis H. Draper Artist Archives (VA-04). All images from this collection were taken in July 1971 and acquired from the Louis H. Draper Preservation Trust with the Arthur and Margaret Glasgow Endowment Fund, VMFA Archives, Richmond, VA. © Louis H. Draper Preservation Trust. Unless otherwise noted, they are digital positives of a single negative frame.

Man and boy posing before Freedom Farm headquarters. (*Top*) VA04.04.07.001.T6.
(*Bottom*) VA04.04.07.001.T18, Louis H. Draper Artist Archives.

(*Top*) Girl looking at camera on Freedom Farm, VA04.04.07.001.T11.
(*Bottom*) Three girls stand before a food sign and repurposed kitchen
equipment, VA04.04.07.001.T15, Louis H. Draper Artist Archives.

(*Top*) Workers on Farm, VA04.04.07.001.T2. (*Bottom*) Children holding up crop inventory sign, VA04.04.07.001.T9, Louis H. Draper Artist Archives.

of denied food stamps or retracted surplus food for anyone daring to vote or daring to protest against the inability to vote, "[Hamer] was able to maintain independence because she always kept [as she said] a pig and a garden."[28]

The Pig Bank started with fifty female gilts and five male boars, growing by 1975 to a total of two thousand. The families who joined this program signed a contract that stipulated that for each litter raised, two female pigs must be returned to the pig bank to then be distributed to more families, which amounted to at least eight hundred and sixty-five.[29] The only existing record of the contract is a recording of National Council of Negro Women member Eloise Moreland reading a draft in a founding meeting. In upright orderly words that matched the sobriety of the contract's contents, Moreland articulated the eighth and last stipulation to preserve the pigs as a commons: "I agree not to sell, trade, or borrow on any pig received from this program, but to use the pig to feed my family and other families of the community."[30]

Although most accounts of the Pig Bank end there, usually with applause for its comparative success to what the Freedom Farm would become, there was also, even at this early stage, a coy critique of liberal property and its life in the afterlives of the slave plantation. The formality of contract and the extraction of monied value from human labor were collectively pinned to one enormous bullseye of a joke. Not only was the bank labeled the diminishing term "the Pig Bank" (National Council president Dorothy Height's coinage), ironic, too, since as a commons it could not be further from a bank, but as though to ensure the parody would not be missed, the commons in turn was labeled the "Oink-Oink Project."[31] As to the contract, it was discussed as precisely that in the official documents, but its actual and only name for its signatories was the "Pig Agreement." When Hamer later explained the name "Pig Agreement" in a tone whose sprightliness invited her audience to chuckle, she then reminded them, through a sort of set up for an upset, how nefarious contracts have been for African Americans: "And you know, each family had to sign a pig agreement. This sounds funny to you but you don't believe we really live it," really live, the joke goes, contracts designed to reduce us to animalia.[32] Given how tartly funny Hamer found the whole affair, most of the titular parodies were probably hers.[33]

The playful titles bring to mind something else, as well: in a report by the National Council of Negro Women, the color of the pigs was given rather gratuitously (while this report was certainly not authored by Hamer, her words so suffuse the page that its author seemed to have considered scare quotes superfluous). The female pigs, outnumbered, remember, ten to one, are brush stroked "white," the males "burnt-brown," the bipolar racial undertones visible as day.[34] Whether these colorful allusions are meant to mock or mark the myth of Black male licentiousness is hard to tell, but they certainly are of a piece with the titles of the program in that they too unsettle the logic of the plantation, racial myth mocked or marked here as another way to segregate and forbid property rights. Hamer for her own part scratched at the myth that the Pig Bank on its own alluded to, scratching at its gendered surface in what sounds like a dithering: "We had the *first* fifty pigs!" Hamer beamed in 1976, addressing a Wisconsin crowd. "Five females—I mean, five males. It was hard on 'em, you know." Surely the audience is chortling at the joke's red face, not at her seemingly accidental flip of the scale, flip of gender roles, not her suggestion that the historical kitsch of these racial myths cover over Black women's reproductive labor.

It is almost unaccountable that three years prior Hamer was telling this exact joke while roving from house to house of the Pig Bank beneficiaries, and her friend, Sallie Carther, made the same exact mistake. She flipped the genders. "They was talking about them five males," says Carther about to slip. "They wanted to get how many males to what? They thought first they was gone get five, f-f-fifty males," she stammers, "to go along with the—" "Naw," says Hamer interceding, "that would have been too many 'cause honey I'd a died."[35] Perhaps sent from some cultural unconscious, it's as though the joke had picked up legs and walked out on its own. All in all, the jokes, allusions, and the titles combine to generally upend the sanctity of contract and its promise to bestow freedom, status, and self-possession. The titles alone imply that contractual relations were never meant to be solemnly and seriously performed, never meant outside the space between role play ("Oink-Oink") and real play (the "Pig Agreement"). Here was Hamer quite literally hamming it up.

The dishevelment of contract had to be, like everything else, in service of their first aim: to attack a starvation that very much like kudzu was devouring the South. The problem of this chronic hunger was commonly described as an "epidemic" (a "malnutrition epidemic," news reports often read), but Hamer made plain it was far worse than that. Because of its sweep and longevity, its historical protraction, and most of all, as she famously said, its deployment as a "weapon" for voting or marching, a better description for the nature of the malnutrition and the hunger might be *endemic*.[36] It was endemic to a state structure of subsidized deprivation, that racial regime, as Hamer would reiterate, where the largest farmers would receive financial benefits for letting crops go to waste. Hamer told one reporter, "Where a couple of years ago white people where shooting at Negroes trying to register, now they say, 'go ahead and register—then you'll starve.'"[37] It was partly its endemicity that pushed Hamer to say, "if black communities are going to move economically and politically, they must have non-federal support."[38] At one of the founding meetings for the cooperative livestock program, a local pediatrician by the name of Aaron Shirley remarked in a dim baritone, "I see it, and it hurts": children are getting "smaller," their bodies are declining, their bodies are preparing to die. It's "winter," he said, and their feet are "cold."[39]

It was thus met with relief that if in 1968 they had their pigs, in less than a year they finally had their garden, an historically proverbial garden in a sum total of forty acres. That dream of a dashed forty acres and a mule had long been a traveling companion for Fannie Lou Hamer, a fact made plain in her co-authored 1968 program proposal for the Mississippi Freedom Democratic Party. The document distilled their many promises (a guaranteed basic income, the transfer to a public good of unused private property, and so on) down to a single stated effort to "seek redemption" for that one broken, Reconstruction promise of forty acres and a mule.[40] So following behind Myles Foster, a bustling sea of "close to 300 men, women, and children" churned the tough, scabby soil, row upon row, into a lush aerial view of green upon green: string beans, butterbeans, okra and corn, tomatoes and turnips, snap beans and soybeans, cucumbers and kale, mustards and wheat, purple hulls, June peas, "all distributed as needed," 10 percent given to those who could not work the land "for reasons of health or age," the remaining 90 to those who could.[41] "We fed 1,500 people from this forty acres of land," Hamer later announced.[42] This collective involvement in a shared production of surplus easily befits the cooperative title, but future operations, in which participation waned and reciprocity was relaxed, just as easily grate against it, half-picked vegetables left for dead on the vine.[43]

That future ironically began when Foster, Myles Foster, stepped into the fullness of his name. With financial support from singer Harry Belafonte and a small Wisconsin charity Measure for Measure, with Hamer as assistant director beside director Joseph Harris, farm manager Myles Foster worked double time with thirteen laborers to turn exactly a square mile into another lush sprawl of edible green.[44] But this time it jostled, in one-to-one ratio, against a cash crop of cotton. In 1969, with a modestly estimated total of six hundred eighty acres, the enterprise (if we can call it an enterprise, in the sense of a productive activity) was chartered as a "corporation" (if we can call it a corporation) through the legal counsel of Pascal Townsend. Once Hamer's foe, Townsend was now oddly her ally.[45] Around fifteen hundred families were less fed than unstarved in northwestern Mississippi: Sunflower County, dead center in the Delta.

I now feel the need to get my geographic bearings. So I pull down a biography on Hamer by Chris Asch to look at his hugely clarifying state map. I see a jutting forehead with a witch's chin. Sunflower is its eye, the Delta its dark surround, the Farm, if it were there, no more than a glimmer.

The map immediately brings to mind the image on the cover of the journal *Freedomways* from 1965. An interview with Hamer appeared as their star first story between pages 231 and 242. There she raised a perfectly pat and frank question that she could not have possibly known she would answer, years later, so defiantly: "Where are those people going?" she asked, "Where will they go?" referring to Chicago's Urban Renewal program or, she quipped, "Urban *Removal*" program. They will go to the Farm, she would effectively reply. But the image, that image—the whole reason this chain of recollections emerges for me is that Freedom Farm seems mysteriously captured on the journal's cover through their image of Mississippi. It then seems to resurface as an eerier incarnation on the frontispiece of Asch's book. Like Freedom Farm itself, the journal's three-dimensional rendering looks literally thrown into the middle of nowhere. All surface and sky.[46]

In Freedom Farm's best years (1971 and –2 and –3), it acquired three homes for the poorest to live in "free of charge" (Hamer seemed to consider this a sort of reparation, making good on her gravamen, "America owes us a debt").[47] By December 1972, they bought seventy "prefabricated" houses then personally "bricked" them, bought lots for seventy-five more, started a sewing factory and an African garment store, a day care center, offered high school and college scholarships, not even to mention the miles of food, which at one point reached Chicago as humanitarian aid.[48] Hamer reported a total acquisition of sixty-eight houses by 1972, largely funded by loans for mortgage funds from the Farmers Home Administration. Freedom Farm created the Delta Housing Development Corporation with Hamer on the board of directors and they ultimately helped seventy-three families attain housing across ninety-two newly purchased housing lots.[49] Continuing her report, "80 percent of the families who needed shelter could not afford the required $200 to $300 dollars down payments," so "with revenue from the crops, coupled with small loans from the local banks, more

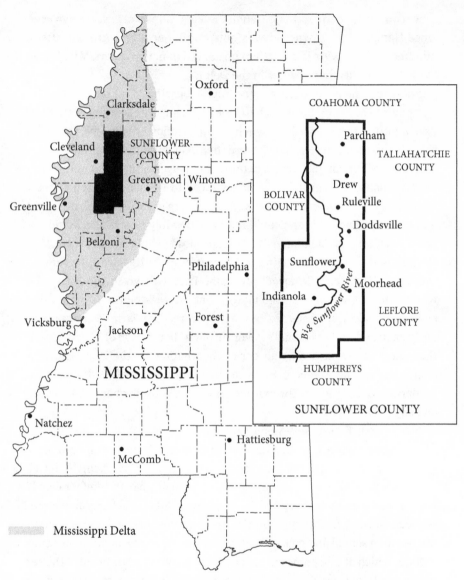

Map of Sunflower County. Courtesy of the University of North Carolina Press.

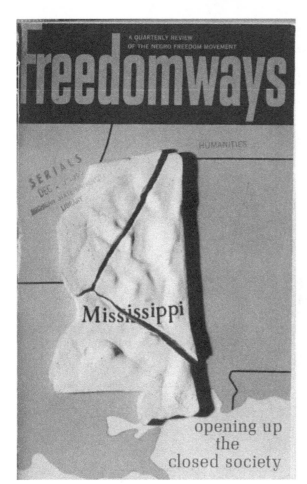

Map of Mississippi, *Freedomways* 5, no. 2 (1965). Courtesy of Michigan State University Libraries.

than 35 families received money for down payments"—all this from what she liked to dub with slight tongue and cheek, "the little co-op."[50]

But in the Farm's decline (1974 and –5 and –6 and –7) all manner of "weeds" devastated the land, lacking money "to keep [them] down," and their principal fundraiser advanced her career in setbacks.[51] In January 1974, they lost all but their first forty acres to creditors, a diminishment that reflected Hamer's new state of mind.[52] Directly after the loss, she was delivered to her local hospital for what her friends called a "nervous breakdown," the exigencies of orating, fundraising, traveling, leadership, diabetes, and hypertension having taxed her nerves beyond what they could bear.[53] For the next three years even after all this, even after Harris's heart decided

Fannie Lou Hamer Daycare Center welcome sign, VA04.04.07.001.T16, digital positive of a single negative frame, Louis H. Draper Artist Archives (VA-04).

that August 1974 to permanently disengage, Hamer vehemently insisted on holding the Farm together despite the constant strain, as if the things that give the most to us must take in equal measure. Beneath a blindingly blue sky on a Sunday afternoon, the twentieth of March 1977, the members of the Farm buried their frayed leader among an overflow of grievers. Soon after the funeral, the Farm's directors were forced to sell their last forty acres to the state for a dollar. For the token of a dollar, the state forgave their loans. By decade's end, the Farm was reduced to the size of a burial plot. The only thing left of Freedom Farm was and would remain the plot Hamer was buried in. Suffice to say, Hamer's "little co-op" might have been less than freedom, but it was always more than a farm.

Cooperatives versus Nonprofits

I first observed that Hamer was enacting contradictions of property holding in a fact frequently mentioned by scholars but just as quickly dismissed:
the fact that Hamer chartered the Farm as a nonprofit (alongside cofound-
ers Foster, Harris, George Jordan, and Juanita Harvey) but then described
it as a cooperative. It is true that legally they had to incorporate it this way,
for Mississippi still restricts cooperative businesses to only one of two types,
aquatic and agricultural. It is also true that cooperatives and nonprofits have
historically been conflated by the very people who establish them since both
belong to a "sector that uniquely mobilizes private initiative for the common
good."[54] There is, besides, nothing all that unusual about a cooperative being incorporated in a state as a nonprofit.[55] For instance, twenty miles down
the road from Hamer's cooperative farm stood the headquarters for the Sunflower County Cooperative League, which was chartered as a nonprofit. It
was Hamer's awareness of the tension between the two forms of business
and her discursive reenactment that make it worthy of note (we will see by
the end the material effects). Take her 1972 interview with the historian Neil
McMillen: "How many acres do you have all together now?" McMillen asks.
"640 and 40, 680. . . . It's in the 700s I imagine—but that's not ours, now," she
says coolly. She's almost in song. Then adds, "But we *bought* it . . . Freedom
Farms did *buy* it."[56] The tangle of property rights is so difficult to state plainly
that she stumbles over her words. Freedom Farms is theirs and it is not theirs,
bought by everyone and no one, at the same time.

While both nonprofits and cooperatives provide to members benefits
that are sometimes monetary, the two could not be further apart in terms
of property rights. When it comes to the birthmark distinctions between
a nonprofit and a cooperative, few legal scholars have been more quoted
than Henry Hansmann, who writes, "Although cooperatives are sometimes
loosely said to be 'nonprofit,' nonprofit corporations are conceptually quite
distinct from cooperatives. The defining characteristic of a nonprofit organization is that the persons who control the organization—its members, directors, and officers—are forbidden from receiving the organization's net
earnings. This does not mean that a nonprofit organization is barred from
earning profits; rather, it is the *distribution* of the profits to controlling persons that is forbidden. Thus by definition, a nonprofit organization cannot
have owners."[57] The opposite situation holds true for cooperatives, which
are mutually owned by all members, all of whom receive dividends. Hamer
and the three-hundred-plus families that belonged to the co-op, along with

its fifteen hundred beneficiaries, were straddling a paradox: land that was at once all-owned and unowned, owned by everyone and owned by none.

The paradoxical ownership was forthrightly manifested in the toggling membership criteria: at once open and closed. According to the bylaws, members had to pay three dollars to join, but in practice anyone could join, making the bylaws by-ends. This membership fee was no random number. Hamer appeared to gladly withdraw this one demand in particular as a gestural dismissal of the poor being forced to pay at least three dollars, which they didn't have, to receive food stamps. Consider the documentary *Hunger: Starvation in Affluent U.S.*, aired nationwide at 10:00 P.M. in the cold winter of 1968. Through a screen redolent with that VHS-haze, I watched Hamer say, as though suddenly tasting something sour, "how can a man have dignity if he can't scrape together the three dollars necessary to buy stamps this month?"[58]

Nonetheless, the bylaws promised to be strictly enforced: "the dues of all of members shall be a sum of Three Dollars ($3.00) payable annually on the tenth day of July in each year. Any member in default of payment of dues shall be ipso facto suspended from all privileges of membership, and if, after notice, such default be not cured within a period of ninety days, the membership of such members shall automatically cease and terminate."[59] Hamer formally contradicted this. In answering a question on a funding application about the "description of membership (Ethnic or racial composition, number, age range, social, education and economic background)," Hamer said, "the membership is composed of one racial group. The total membership cannot be determined because there are no card carrying members. Those who identify themselves are members. Educational background is between 6th to 8th grades."[60] The standard of inclusion into the Farm was hereby transfigured from a normative yardstick to a idiosyncratic measurement scheme.

The indetermination of the total membership did not reflect an inability to precisely count the people. It reflected a principle of openness. After all, as they proved on an application submitted around the same time in 1973, they indeed could have given a population estimate: "FFC serves approximately 650 families each year," they said. On this application (submitted either by Joseph Harris or then secretary Nora Campbell), they even indicate the average age of forty-five. In another application for funding that same year, they were acutely precise with their numbers, indicating "969 families" were served, 45 white, 924 Black, through 4 seasonal farm laborers, 2 members of staff, 11 Board of Directors, "fifty three part time employees," all with a total membership of "756."[61] Might the point have been that Hamer and her team wanted to model a way of imagining inclusion into a polity that did not reinforce patriarchal frames of personhood or identitarian means of exclusion? An open-closed membership—a membership resolutely at odds with itself—mirrored the broader conflict between the wish that a social movement organization would deliver national inclusion and the lie that for Black women this would be possible.

In her extremely perspicacious book *Vexy Thing*, Imani Perry makes the point that "the politics of inclusion overwhelm our struggles." She contends that U.S. legal recognition has depended not only on property holding, but on wielding that property as a patriarch over others, such that the capacity to dominate took precedence in the courts over the property's market value. Put another way, property's domination over nonpersons became for the court its real market value.[62] "Incorporation has its merits, whether registered in our history as same-sex marriage, interracial marriage, or integrated schools, because it corrects the logic of personhood as one that is exclusive along the lines of identity. But these merits are insufficient for the larger purpose of seeking gender liberation because they ultimately sustain the logic of personhood as an exclusionary structure . . . predicated on patriarchy." Hamer's revolving door of membership, stipulating exclusions while refusing to exclude, appears to be a way to turn this patriarchal structure in on itself. Is that not what's happening when she says, "Freedom Farms Co-op is continually seeking new ways to serve its members, both paying and non-paying."[63] Is this not a way of saying, you can belong to this organization without having to buy into it?

The Local and the Global

When we place Hamer's membership criteria in historical context, her decision to reverse the criteria grows even more powerful.[64] In Derek Jones's historical survey of producer cooperatives from 1790 to the 1870s, he concludes, "In most cases the dominant practice has been to restrict initial membership to (though not require it of) the current workforce."[65] This restriction is a good thing to Jones. Restricted membership makes for a more genuine cooperative, as if this were a personality trait bequeathed to it at birth: "It seems that the necessary features for an ideal PC include requirements that: (a) membership be restricted to all the current active work force; (b) all control and management be vested in the work force on the basis of one member, one vote; and (c) the surplus be distributed to members as workers (rather than as capital suppliers)."[66] Dovetailed in the membership restriction is an assumed homogeneity in the member demographics, which is subordinated in importance to the issue of longevity. What makes the organization last makes the organization and that is the ability to self-reproduce: "In order to survive, all organizations must develop the internal mechanisms for self-reproduction. Educational and training programs to shape 'participatory consciousness' . . . perhaps the most important."[67]

In line with Jones's vision of a sort of immaculate conception, one survey by the United Nations from 1954 insists on the association between cooperatives and cultural homogeneity. Attempting to explain the failure of Black cooperatives in the American South to last scarcely longer than three years, the committee wrote, "the prospective members of the collectives were not sentimentally attached to particular plots of available lands, nor were they in cohesive social groups, despite the economic adversity they suffered. They lacked the 'cooperative spirit.'"[68] As we can see from the pat manner of this last sentence, axiomatically short as if restating commonsense, the word "cooperative" had become a mask for nativism, the margin in the margins. These studies give a glimpse of how violent the glorification of local culture could be. They reveal that cooperatives were extensions of a liberalist machinery, disciplining diversity into insignificance: to be incorporated into global markets was to obey the dictate that they remain small and local. Historian Greta de Jong provides the example that by funding the Southwest Alabama Farmers Cooperative Association, the Office of Economic Opportunity "aimed to test the cooperative model as a tool for fighting poverty and stemming out-migration from the rural South."[69]

Combining the concept of the small cooperative model with that of the large nonprofit—a containable population in the first, an uncontainable one in the second—rebuffs this localism, this defensive retreat into the places one can see and touch. Stuart Hall's classic lecture, "The Local and the Global," helps place Hamer's resistance to localism in the context of social movements. Hall proposes a rubric for thinking about globalization as the construction, affirmation, and absorption of local difference. He aligns 1960s U.S. social movements with this form of globalization that does not try to constitute a unitary world, as many predicting the totalization of capital had expected, but is "constantly teasing itself with the pleasures of the transgressive other."[70] There is therefore an odd complicity between globalization (an exoticizing "global post-modern" as Hall puts it) and the demands in social movements for particular representation. "You could not discover, or try to discuss, the Black movements, the civil rights movements, the movements of Black cultural politics in the modern world, without the notion of the rediscovery of where people came from, the return to some kind of roots, the speaking of a past which previously had no language."[71] By marginalizing minoritization, Hamer's membership stipulation refused to let Freedom Farm calcify into cultural fundamentalism, an "exclusivist and defensive enclave."[72] The inclusion issue was a small manifestation of her larger transnationalism, namely, her unwavering critique of the U.S.-backed corporate takeover of Angola and Liberia, her support of the Black Panthers as they made alliances with decolonial struggles in Ghana, and her effort to raise "seed money" for "the development of cooperatives in African countries [in] support of African liberation movements."[73]

At the time, cooperatives, like Hamer's, deprioritized the equal rights discourses that defined the civil rights movement, hence today's bigger, elbowing term Black Freedom Movement. Instead, cooperatives prioritized the broader struggle against colonial conquest and imperial expansion. It was partly this subordination that Hamer expressed when she said, "Equality is something I wouldn't even use to dust off my shoes."[74] Hamer's transnational vision of cooperative antagonism reflected, for example, Amiri Baraka's Congress of African Peoples. The Ideological Statement of this Pan-African group, apparently written by Baraka in 1970 but signed by all the delegates, offered a cooperatist definition of "self-sufficiency: to provide all the basic necessities for sustenance and growth and survival of our people, i.e., food, shelter, clothing, etc., based on the principle of UJAMAA (cooperative economics)."[75] It has become commonplace to note that the evidentiary basis for making equal rights claims in civil rights litigations was the provision of proof that instances of discrimination occurred. The court tacitly assumed that these instances were aberrations to institutional norms, an assumption that indirectly reinforced structural inequities on a global scale.[76] By using her cooperative to disrupt not the intent to discriminate but genealogies of dispossession, not personal prejudice but systemic wrongs, she was able to fight harder against the prevailing social and economic order than her legal cases on public desegregation and electoral disenfranchisement would ever allow.

Hamer's Poor Reception

Despite all the ramifications of just one of the manifestations of fusing nonownership with all-ownership, scholars uniformly have called the Farm a cooperative. They have done this without pause, without query, even when they also acknowledge its counter-structure of incorporation. After pointing out that the Farm was "never chartered as a cooperative of any kind," Nembhard swiftly states with finality that "it was run as a cooperative."[77] What hammering down the enterprise does is erase the possibility that Hamer was enacting, perhaps inventing, an unusual system of value, one inassimilable into either enterprise form. It is breathtaking that despite the stakes in choosing one mode of property holding over another that scholars have dismissed this as an oversight, an accident, or an illiteracy, as in Nembhard's closing reflections: "Freedom Farm's difficulties and ultimate demise . . . were in great part a result of lack of coordination of resources and not enough education and training about joint ownership."[78] The Farm has not fared well in recent historical assessments: said to have been anywhere from woefully ineffective to pathologically inefficient (operating with a "plantation mentality," affirms biographer Kay Mills), frequently judged for its poor managerial operations, its overambition, its collapse into insolvency and insurmountable debt, its hesitance to accept government loans and aid, its refusal to impose reciprocal relations between the members receiving the food and the farmers providing it, its near indifference to stability, longevity.[79]

Etcetera.

One of the reasons for these scribbles in red ink is the standard of success presumed to be propelling the Farm: significant change to existing institutions, from welfare agencies to public schools, and economic power for its members that would assume some permanence. A closer read of Hamer's work on the ground and the page, as it were, a read of her verbal fretwork in conjunction with some of her more surprising decisions, like choosing to invest in small-scale cotton production while admittedly knowing it would generate few if any returns, suggests that the Hamer widely remembered for her resolute commitment to linear, commonsensical progress was not at play in this arena.[80]

Primarily since it was better managed, the neighboring Bolivar Cooperative is frequently compared to Hamer's "little co-op" as the more successful of the two. The assessments often have the feel of comparing a darling child to its prodigal sibling. "The two cooperatives were very different," begins Nembhard. "North Bolivar was a farmers' cooperative started by experienced, landowning farmers and managed professionally. Its managers had abundant experience in running a farm; some came from three generations of farmers. They handled their assets better—kept their equipment in proper sheds, for example—and operated with an effective business plan."[81]

Historian Chris Asch uses a similar yardstick of capitalist achievement: "from a lack of accounting to poor long-term planning, the farm suffered from its leaders' inability to run an efficient operation."[82] Henri Lefebvre offers a tart reminder that the very thing celebrated most today about cooperatives and, without fail, about Hamer—the practice of self-management—necessitates the leveling of organizational hierarchies, "even infringing on managerial functions." Direct democracy in an open "system," a word that Lefebvre contends must always be put in quotes since its referenced contours are "continuously renewed," must continuously remake its structural and formal consistencies.[83]

The interpretive infelicities in question here point to the longest through-thread among the reception of Hamer's speeches: that she really did, as she said, "tell it like it is," as if her speeches "just are," devoid of dissemblance.[84] By considering Hamer an artist, I am challenging the portraits that have all but bowdlerized and traduced her into a gendered cliché of transparency and intuition. A notable scholar of her oratory brands her "sense of justice" as "intuitive," a likely complement to an oft-repeated, backhanded compliment. The compliment goes that she was "perhaps one of the most unlikely persons to reach and participate in the summit of U.S. political life, Hamer, a poor, *barely educated* woman lived the life of Black tenancy in the Mississippi Delta for forty-four years."[85] Meagan Brooks (together with Davis Houck) has done more to make Hamer's orations available than anyone, yet she still simplifies things by contending that Hamer's "superior perspective and, hence, the credibility necessary to address authoritatively both local and national audiences" derived from "Hamer's training in the school of the soul." This comes from an article on Hamer's vernacular titled "Oppositional Ethos" rather than, say, "oppositional thought," the usual pairing.[86]

The problem with placing Hamer in the vernacular is not the vernacular but how she's been placed. Her vernacular expression is too often discussed as a natural byproduct or derivative excrescence of a community's parole, an extension and replication without artifice or technique. If the vernacular is bedrock, Hamer's speech is outgrowth, a logic that pulls the vernacular's meaning of "home grown" into farce. Her "means of communication" was "accessible to all," "'commonplace'" and commonplaced, a speech so ready to hand as to be desexed.[87] Refusing to see Hamer as a sophisticated thinker is like looking through a telescope and refusing to see stars. Too many scholars have been looking at this star through the wrong end of the scope.

Without a smidge of irony, Asch titled his comparative history of James Eastland and Hamer *The Senator and the Sharecropper*. Asch depicts Hamer

as a shamanic figure who could clear in one stroke as much thistle as necessary between herself and the annoyances of moral ambiguity. "Like Eastland, Hamer saw her struggle as a battle between good and evil where there
could be no in-between. . . . Hamer considered anyone, white or black,
who did not identify with the MFDP and support its agenda either racist,
ignorant, or a sellout."[88] On some level these studies puppeteer her power.
On some level I hear how she was made in her lifetime through strange
rhythms of abstraction into an absolute pronoun, a pronoun without perim-
eter: someone, who could be anyone. To go back to her day, even the extremely discerning Paule Marshall said after they met, "she's 'Hatt' Tubman
with a gun hidden in her basket. . . . There's the same short muscular build,
in fact, as well as the same daring and determination. She's the indefati-
gable nineteenth-century abolitionist Sojourner Truth. . . . She's Zhinga"
of Portugal, and so on, a dreamy luftmensch of words that traipse through
the church doors all the way into the eulogies above her white, lacquered
casket: "*We* are Fannie Lou Hamer," howled Stokely Carmichael, again and
again, standing somewhere between awe and a daze.[89]

I've had to wonder why the name "sharecropper" trails Hamer like a mos-
quito long after having retired from that post. I've had to remember that
Brittney Cooper also felt the need to recently say, "It seems to escape notice, that we have not engaged with the content of what black women intellectuals actually said, even as we celebrate all that they did."[90] Toward this
end, I've worked where I could from Hamer's live recordings (rarely cited),
in addition to their transcriptions, which are sometimes machine-made with
the expected machine mistakes that compile beneath her cadence. Following her sound has helped me to better parse the manner and means through
which she conveys her thinking and manipulates the vernacular as a ver-
nacularist. It's her sound that works to rinse my vision.

The Little Co-op

Following the Farm's reception, I expected my observation that Hamer
seemed to be staging opposing treatments of property to be contested by
records that escaped my notice. Not quite. Even observers at the time encountered this complication, trying in vain to resolve it once and for all. In
1970, Hamer was interviewed in her home by the photojournalist Franklynn
Peterson. Judging from the pictures he took on tour of the Farm and from
the on-the-job pictures taken of him in uniform, years later, I imagine him
padding the grounds that February in 1970 in a heavily pocketed, brown

explorer's vest and a matching outback hat, missing only the binoculars, a clip compass, and a safety kit, the dry road to the cooperative houses narrowing behind him into the narrowing light. He could have used those binoculars to understand what Hamer told him when he returned for his second visit following this one: "we decided to organize everybody who lived in a shack, which was most of us, and teach them how to take advantage of low-cost FHA and farm mortgages. Once we got started, we found so many people wanted to take part that we didn't have time to give the organization a name. We just sort of call it the Co-op."[91] They sort of called it, sort of named it—the name was never meant to settle down. What's in a name? Property. No name, no property. Given the impetus behind a cooperative toward collective ownership, as opposed to that of a nonprofit, we might read "take part" as more than a glib remark. Across its vector of double meaning, we might read the full participation indicated by "take part" as partial possession. Hamer's description of this sort of co-op, this business that can only be called one thing if we call the calling vague, explains why they might have wanted to achieve nonprofit status, aside from the easiest answer of tax exemption, which in fact they did not receive for the majority of their existence, if they ever did at all.[92] Perhaps the fact that so many people wanted to take part signals that it would be too pricey to have so many stakeholders with equal voting powers and minimal hierarchical management. This issue of "asymmetrical information" often begets the need for a nonprofit status.

But more was going on here. The title of Peterson's article from 1970 with the picture of the Farm foreshadowed Hamer's "sort of call" by foregrounding the deception of official names: "Sunflowers Don't Grow in Sunflower County," Peterson punned. Peterson goes on to wrestle with the terms that would appropriately name the redistribution of property. And it is odd because he opens the paragraph in which this struggle begins by lashing out with a sudden refutation. It is as if, for a heartbeat, he is no longer addressing his readers, but a ghost only he can see. "You can't call Freedom Farms that much cliched 'Black Capitalism' because nobody is out to make a profit. It's a cooperative, yes, and more than that. 'Black Socialism' might be an appropriate term if it weren't so disreputable at the moment."[93] He scarcely abandons his losing skiamachy, his shadow-boxing of names, when he goes on to reiterate with striking frequency, considering the brevity of the article, that the members enjoyed full property rights over their houses and the land on which their houses sat. He even searches for creative ways to emphasize this ownership. In a stilted fashion, suggestive of an inability to discern the precise relation between the people and the land, he calls the members "the earth folk" and, them in turn, the "Delta earth people," recalling, in counterpoise, Du Bois's term for the laborers spread across the swamp in his novel *Quest of the Silver Fleece*: "earth-spirits." He then describes their agricultural labors not as acts of tilling or of preparing the earth, as one might expect, but as "caressing their plot of ground with plows and hoes. Their plot of ground," he repeats with the obvious stress on "their." It undermines his point that he fails to name a single member among the hundreds of earth folk, ironically rendering them the farm's terra incognita (and it is curious how few names have made their way onto paper). Such poor turns of phrase seem to be driven by more than the normal myopias of racial stereotypes, bizarre equivalences between Blacks and the soil, so many configurations of the eponym "black belt," its most popular broker.

These verbal maladjustments seem to reflect a more than metaphorical fundamental instability. Most telling, for instance, when Peterson uses the phrase "plot of ground" in the quote above, he is working to keep with Hamer's nomenclature when she said to him, "You can give a man some food and he'll eat it. Then he'll be hungry again. But you give a man some *ground* and he'll never be hungry no more." Granted, Peterson quotes Hamer in another article as saying "ground of his own," an inconsistency that suggests he was cognizant on some level of the difference. If he had stayed closer to her terms as quoted in "Sunflowers Don't Grow," he would have retained the barely ambiguous meaning of "giving . . . ground" as giving protection, giving space or platform, rather than ownership or, his word, "plot." But by emphasizing the plots as individualized parcels, Peterson implied a distinction between this more-than-cooperative and community land trusts, in which the nonprofit business own the land while their people own the house on which it sits. He underscores this distinction: "Each of the Delta earth people will own their own land and their own house." He repeats, "It [the house] will be in their name. . . . They'll be in charge." I have not been able to track down the title of the deeds at the Sunflower County Record's Office, but even if they existed they would do little to clarify the demarcations between the claims of the corporation and the claims of its members. Furthermore, I know that although Peterson heard "For most, it will be the first time monthly payments have been anything other than rent or car installments," for many no monthly payments were mandated until the end.

It was not just Peterson who wrestled with the flux in property rights, who tried to hush its coloratura of names. Poet June Jordan wrote the first biography of Hamer. It was a children's book. Naturally, she tried to depict the property rights clear enough for a child to comprehend yet dramatic enough to evince the difficulty she was having. Through fictional scenes contrived to simplify the complicated reality of any attempt to ascribe a title of ownership and describe relations of contract, Jordan says, referring to Hamer, "on the contract beside the word *Owner*, she wrote: *The Freedom Farm Cooperative*. This means that the farm belongs to everyone who works on it."[94] To confuse matters further, in Alice Walker's laudatory review of Jordan's biography, Walker jettisons the nomenclature in preference of her own: "Freedom Farm Collective."

This tug of proper names invites the question of what a cooperative meant to the people laboring beneath it. One way of approaching an answer is to think about the distinction people were making between "cooperative" and "co-op." The cooperative that neighbored Freedom Farm and was the one other venture in Mississippi, Measure for Measure worked to fund vocally avoided the name "co-op." An extension of the low-cost medical facility, the Tufts-Delta Health Center, the North Bolivar Cooperative Farm began as a way to improve the diets and provide health care for poor malnourished Mississippians. It began in 1967 by the fatefully named John Hatch whose colleagues were shrewdly sensitive to business nomenclature. His fellow physician Jack Greiger saw that they were setting off alarms to red bait potential funders and powerful local whites by simply stating their wish to establish a cooperative at all. As historian Thomas Ward reports, "Much of the opposition centered on the very idea of a co-op, and Greiger noted that in order to deflect some of the opposition for the farm cooperative, 'which sounds suspiciously communistic in the Mississippi environment,' he made sure to refer to it instead as a 'nutrition demonstration project' rather than a co-op, especially when asking for funding."[95] Cooperative and co-op appear in Ward's account on a sliding scale of communistic to fully communistic. Co-op, the surname that Hamer favored and insisted on, piped an extremely leftist ring in the inner ear of Mississippi. In this light, when Hamer qualified the co-op's dimensions as "little," she extended the Black feminist tradition of "dissemblance," doing more to emphasize the clandestine threat than doing anything to allay fears.[96]

The Freedom and the Farm

So much for the name "co-op"—what about Freedom Farm, my sobriquet of choice? The moniker signposts an understanding of agriculture as the historical nexus of personhood and progress. It signals an awareness of the deep reasons that the USDA loans issued by the Farm Service Administration prioritized agricultural cooperatives, and it offers another explanation for why Hamer would want to resist such government support despite knowing, as John Dittmer remarks, that "even in the early days of the cooperative movement, when enthusiasm was running high, movement activists realized that Black poverty was so endemic that only the federal government had sufficient resources to combat the problem."[97] It was not until I put the designation Freedom Farm in context with the historical value of not only land owning but also of land honing that it began to make sense. I often wondered why Hamer would nickname the many operations the cooperative undertook as the "Farms." Why was "Farms" and its evocation of "he or she farms" the prism through which to illuminate her antipoverty movement?

Historian Richard Drayton notes that the meaning of improvement was first applied to the "improvement of agriculture" and the subsequent "expansion of the frontier of private farming and grazing." In fact, "the verb 'to improve,' which we use in the sense 'to ameliorate' or 'to perfect,' originally meant to put to a profit, and in particular to enclose 'waste' or common land."[98] And as Alyosha Goldstein argues, proving agricultural prowess was a strategy of power, agriculture being a crucible for assimilation into a patriarchal order. African Americans and Native peoples were reorganized "in conformity with Euro-American conceptions about proper approaches to agriculture as a means of colonization and control."[99] Goldstein summarizes a siege of legal policies: the 1862 Homestead Act, which gifted federal farmland to settlers to encourage westward expansion, the 1888 Allotment Act, which divided Indigenous land into allotments and put them into trusts "until allottees were deemed 'competent,'" and the USDA's resettlement of Black farmers in the 1930s, to name a few.[100] Against this sinister backdrop, Goldstein observes that "imperial economies of scale and scope" are "underwritten by long-standing affective settler attachments to an imagined agrarian republic and the heteropatriarchal 'family farm.'"[101] Stemming from the agricultural revolution in England between the sixteenth and eighteenth centuries, showing your keeps meant keeping up the land.

The symbolic apotheosis of agri-power was Thomas Jefferson's promotion of an agrarian democracy. This cut a particular sore spot for generations of Blacks less because he deemed them, unlike Indigenous peoples, inherently inadequate for its manufacture, but moreso because this outlandish slight (beyond the pale of parody) bore material echoes from the nineteenth century through to Hamer's day. Jefferson's plans for a "gradual emancipation" of enslaved Blacks by way of shipping them back to Africa or to the Caribbean resonated with the juggernaut deprecations of Blacks in nineteenth-century utopian communes. "The function of [these] communities, in brief, was to train the negro for complete freedom."[102] In places like the North Hampton Association of Education and Industry in Florence, Massachusetts, where Sojourner Truth lived for two years until she finally abjured the realm in disgust, or in Tennessee's Nashoba Commune where women's suffragist Francis Wright bought slaves and trained them for freedom by dividing their time between manual labor and study (freedom, that is, in Haiti, where they were shipped by original plan to avoid a slave insurrection!). In arcadias like these Blacks could "learn to be free, learn how to earn their way in a free American society, and learn the virtues and the morals as well as the customs and mores of American society."[103] Being trained for the promise of freedom was like being dunked under water for the promise of breath. Hamer's play on the word "Farms" was a recognition that terracultural tutelage had long been a tactic for territorial conquest, and these had long been birthmarks on cooperative experiments.

Hamer and her entourage engaged nothing less than the effort to rearrange an abiding relationship among personhood, progress, and property. By dubbing the operation the "Farms," Hamer basically accepts the traditional Jeffersonian postulate that freedom is the activity of reshaping the land toward human needs, but pries from this the liberal individualism at its spine. She achieves their separation stretched to their limit, and eventually a ways beyond it, not by sublating the individual into a transcendental collective or communitarian subject, but by eschewing all reference to transcendence in the first place. Whether looking for its geographic or its demographic referent, one cannot see the "farms" without prying apart the whole from its parts and keeping them at odds. One cannot see the "farms" without thinking, to put the word in a sentence, "she farms" or "he farms" together but apart, never as a whole. When we say the full appellation with its forename, Freedom Farms, we see that it is freedom that does the farming: freedom can free float in polymorphous relation to all figurations of the human. Hamer and her circle viewed a certain attitude toward agriculture as the siphon through which imperialism was expanded overseas, manifest destiny over Indigenous sovereignties was legitimated at home, legal personhood was enshrined if not defined in the South, and progress was drained of meaning.

Freedom Farm Cooperative housing development, Ruleville, Mississippi.
Photograph by Franklynn Peterson, held in his personal papers.

Far from Disorganized

Freedom Farms was a meeting of climactic extremes. The clash of property belonged to a clash in material conditions, the day-to-day texture of their working lives. In the first two years, every image, every budget, every delay in production all bore a testament to the extremely dry conditions, which some workers called drought, some onlookers negligence. One C. V. McTeer followed Foster throughout the Farm in July 1971 and observed that "due to serious lack of irrigation, much of the crop is being burned to waste by the sun."[104] When I look at that picture of the cotton crop, taken before McTeer or any cotton had arrived, a gray patina of dust layered on all the leaves, as though the smallest gust of wind would whip up a dust cloud as far as the eye could see, I wonder how anything grew at all. Foster strides ahead of the camera, thigh-high in the papery foliation of this "first crop of cotton." Through Peterson's underexposed Kodachrome technique, the camera captures him almost two dimensionally. Foster appears to have lost his legs, to be hovering lightly as the dust, just above the leaves, and, like the dust, to be disappearing, en mass, into a vast, shadowy sinter of tiny remains.[105]

In the other sunny picture, a line of the cooperative houses ascends out of frame and, on the bank of the road before them, a child stands barefoot, his feet slightly sunken into the dirt. The dirt is so dry and glassy beneath

"Miles Foster checks on first crop of cotton," photograph by Franklynn Peterson, *Sepia* Magazine Photography and Prints Collection, African American Museum of Dallas, Texas.

the heat that it seems one could kneel down and scoop it up like beach sand in the palm of one's hand.

When the two years of aridity receded, it was followed by two years of unusual rain ("it just keeps raining," reported donor Martha Smith).[106] At one point, twenty-thousand dollars' worth of cotton and soybean crops were reduced to total "rot" by all the rain, marking the members' initiation into "saturated" conditions. When Joseph Harris reported in the "Certification of Losses Caused by Major or Natural Disaster" that "we have not had a normal year, we have only been farming for three years," he was speaking with restraint.[107]

I look again at Foster. Something about the strangeness of that photo, him fast nearing a point of total dissipation, seemingly nearing it fast enough that had the photographer waited another second to release his shutter Foster might have been gone—this general unreality makes me notice something else maybe stranger yet. Roland Barthes might call this "that expected flash," the part of the picture that "breaks" free from continuity by being "motionless" and "without future." But this part of the picture breaks from continuity by simply moving in more directions than one.[108] Foster could not be dressed more incongruously with the backdrop, appareled, top to bottom, in a perfectly placed fedora, its rim descending as smoothly as an aircraft above the diamond in his right ear, and then his collared shirt, buttoned tightly at the wrist, is tidily tucked into his belted trousers. The only aberration to his finely tuned attire is a recently used handkerchief, white, mottled, and clamoring out of his back pocket. If on the one hand he seems to be vanishing into the dust, on the other he seems to be fighting mightily against it. He has clearly stopped at nothing to express the dignity of his office. In fact, as stoically serene as his voice always sounds on tape, it seems this dignity and the shell of his clothes may be the only things left keeping him together. It is impossible for me to look at this picture and not recall the remark made a year after it was taken that Freedom Farms had entered a zone of disenchantment: "they are very disenchanted about growing vegetables because of the problems they have run into," said Martha Smith flatly.[109] One is inclined to say, against the accusations of a haphazardness and managerial informality, that if not for their decorum in the face of their troubles they would have dissolved into nothing no sooner than they began.

The Reinvention of Ownership

It was on September 27, 1971, that Hamer made clear for those who weren't yet sure that property rights would be the one recurring node on the Farm's grid of maximum contradictions. Standing before an audience in her childhood hometown of Ruleville, she explained, if that's the word, that appropriating property in the form of land and houses was, beyond all other activities and achievements, essential to their survival. Running for a seat in the Mississippi State Senate, her main message was that such appropriation was not merely a promise but something Freedom Farm had already undertaken. There is no record of how the audience understood the address, but anyone among them looking for clear and direct guidance where it was purportedly needed most—how to go about attaining property—would have been disappointed.

Hamer made it almost impossible to conceive, let alone to visualize, the primary means of having any means. Compounding the strangeness that the central source of their survival was what Benjamin would call a "caesura in the movement of thought" was the fact that Hamer drew all the other forms of subsistence and resistance with such a fine brush. She extolled "guns" to deck racism when governments fail, handy measures of defense against disenfranchisements. She extolled "local self-government" with "everyone participating to the maximum degree possible," a concept that echoed the central principle and highly popular motto behind President Johnson's war on poverty: "maximum feasible participation" of the poor in the drafting and rolling out of the interventions that affect them. She extolled the hugely controversial 1969 "Black Manifesto," which she had co-signed, requesting "reparations" for slavery from the white and Jewish religious establishments toward debt relief and "seed money."

All these side ventures, so to speak, could not have been more pragmatic and recognizable—they could not have been any easier to see, a map of bunkers and escarpments for a life under siege, but when it came to the main lifeline, for which one would expect the greatest clarity and pragmatism, it looked like a hole in the middle of the picture. "I have taken steps of acquiring land through cooperative ownership. In this manner, no individual has title to, or complete use of, the land. The concept of *total individual ownership* of huge acreages of land, by individuals, is at the base of our struggle for survival. In order for any people or nation to survive, land is necessary. However, individual ownership of land should not exceed the amount necessary to make a living."[110] What a vexed oxymoron to build an activism on. Geographer Priscilla McCutcheon reads "total individual ownership" as something Hamer commends. But how could she commend it while phrasing it so pejoratively? McCutcheon's gloss serves my point that while it is not something Hamer wants it is neither something she negates, hence the easy confusion.[111] What we have here are two opposing forms of holding property referred to each other as if they were the same, "cooperative ownership" and "individual ownership," the defense of one swiftly sliding into a defense of the other, yet both coming to head in the ownership of land. A pragmatic activism, the kind that comes to mind when we think of Black protest during this civil rights period, was indefinitely discontinued.

The more one probes the difference between individual and cooperative ownership, the more pronounced one hears their clash. Cooperatives, no matter the type, in Hamer's day and ours, are not owned by individuals in the most familiar sense of ownership, in the sense that one owns shares that can be transferred or sold, as one would stocks in a company. By definition, cooperatives restrict such transferability, so the concept of having individual property in the firm, especially over a parcel of land, clicks into sense here only if the individual is itself the aggregate, the person a fiction for the broader collective. But Hamer is not saying that the person represents the broader collective. She is contrasting individual ownership, which sounds a lot like unchecked private accumulation, against cooperative ownership, or what property experts often call collective ownership, to demarcate against private property, the kind of property the collective holds.

Collective property is the predominant form of property held in a cooperative. Collective property is any resource available for use by any member of a community according to mutually agreed rules. What is interesting then is that this is not what she ends up defending in her speech. She defends a type of private property with the difference being that the one held by the Farm's members is that theirs is checked, limited to their basic needs. But the problem remains that even this socialist asceticism is far from assimilable into cooperative ownership. Making matters more confounding, when I read her statement that no individual has title to the land, I have to ask, what then in the land does the individual own?

The land can only be said to be owned if it can also be said to be unowned, leaving us with the puzzle that the possibility of ownership is its impossibility. The conclusion I draw is that the only form of possession sustainable beneath this conceptual lever is a possession of possession itself. If that conjures up Marx's celebrated salvo for the dawn of communism or collectivism, then that salvo to a degree applies here as well: "the knell of capitalist private property sounds. The expropriators are expropriated."[112] Again we are dealing with an affirmative not a negative response to the general conditions of material theft, to any individual's "complete use of . . . the land." As Etienne Balibar remarks on Marx's salvo, "the negation has been reversed into an affirmation, the dispossession into a new possession or appropriation."[113] In a bewitchingly brilliant flight of the pen, Balibar speculates that "the expropriation of the expropriators is an 'appropriation' by society and the individuals in it of the very means and forms or conditions of appropriation—an 'appropriation of appropriation.' In this sense it appears as eminent 'self-ownership' or *subjective* property, where the *individualized individual* (i.e., the 'desocialized individual') gives way to the 'socialized individuals.' The true 'society of individuals' can consist only in the actual socialization of individuals. Individuals are 'proprietors of themselves' (or 'their own Person') only if they reappropriate their labor power and its complete use, and thus labor itself. But the only 'subject' of this process is the collective social relationship."[114] As to Hamer's oration, there may be some evocation of a broader "collective" lurking behind her defense of limited "individual ownership," but again I do not see it, despite her reference to cooperative labor. Her thinking is not so cathartically aligned with Marx's usurpation of private property. Survival depended on the exertion of a pull to the greatest possible extent in opposite directions from multiple points of property.

What I see is an austere individual ownership against a "total" one, an againstism that at base is still individual ownership against itself, as though the real point is to perpetuate internal tensions. It is in this perpetuation, without having to go another step, that Hamer's words interact with a Marxist logic of appropriation. When I look again at Hamer's phrasing and pare it down to its bones—"individual ownership . . . by individuals"—I see its passive construction suggesting ownership itself has displaced its owners.

Perhaps you're asking, as I was, who on earth is doing this? Where are the agents? Balibar, for his part, locates the power of usurpation in actual people, a multitude, so as not to lapse one presumes into pure poststructuralist discursivity. The plain answer for us is that the agents are the traversers of the tensions. The hard answer, however, is that they are nowhere, nowheres, and, making things even harder, that a nowhere is never nothing. Let's look at how peculiarly passive Hamer's description remains. She gives us two additional passive constructions: a "concept . . . at the base of our struggle for survival," and, most addling, "to survive, land is necessary." The passivity envelops the traversers in a nowhere, forcing us to account for how they survive while existing nowhere. Yet this makes sense since the possession of possession would also produce a nowhereness.

To the extent that disabling the capacity to possess comprises or causes an event in its own right, to the extent that interpretive method and actual circumstance have shaded into each other without reducing the world to words, to the extent, put another way, that the material base and the cultural superstructure are entangled, co-determined, then this disablement would be enough to bring time to a stop. As Benjamin might say, it would take the "era" of Freedom Farm and "blast [it] out" like a flare from the "homogenous course of history."[115] It would inaugurate "a Messianic cessation of happening, or put differently a revolutionary chance in the fight for the oppressed past."[116] It would lead us to believe that stranger things are yet to come.

We Never Did Get Back Up Again

It is difficult to imagine owning anything in the ravaged setting Hamer paints in that campaign speech. Everything is ailing including the light.

Hamer depicts her people as an economically "crippled" Black community, standing there in Ruleville on everything but its feet. A dwarfed capacity to walk is the dominant thematic and given the associations it conjures with marching, with the walks for hunger that considerably funded the Farm, and with Hamer's increased aversion to sit-ins as support for the militancy of the Black power movement, this thematic was cleverly chosen. As she speaks, one can see the motif of flatness gradually plaster not only the landscape, but more and more Black bodies, until it seems that these bodies symbolize, en masse, progress itself laying with its eyes open toward the sky. Hamer begins by remembering Jo-Etha Collier "shot down as she stood looking at her diploma," leveled no sooner than she "completed the *first step* toward the American way of 'survival.'"[117]

When I first listened to Hamer here, I was reminded of her memoirs where she describes what happened after her father finally saved enough to climb out of debt: a white man killed their cows by stirring the chemical Paris Green into the feed. "That poisoning," Hamer said, "knocked us right back down flat. We never did get back up again."[118] A few minutes later I came back to the speech, and heard her state with emphatic finality: "We must put the black man on his feet." It was then I suddenly heard an earlier statement she made in the address, "step by step he will achieve many victories," as steps are the victories he will achieve. Will but hasn't yet, because he's flat on his back. From so much horizontal imagery, one might think her audience, together with the town, are all but waiting to be carted away.

Not so. Really, she suggested that in the leveling conditions of poverty, even inside it not in a promissory world beyond it, the poor persist, as though the conditions themselves are less resisted than rearranged. This rearrangement resembles Du Bois's second sight by being an accursed gift. There are indeed moments when someone is able to put one foot in front of the other. Unsurprisingly, the first of them happens on the grounds of Freedom Farm, the hallmark of her campaign. Remember, in the property passage, she says, "I have taken steps of acquiring land." We could add, given the complex of property, that these steps leap toward the very edge of time, where there's effectively nothing and nowhere beneath one's toes. Given the property-complex, the farm most ironically is a terra incognita. The farm is a caesura in thought that doubles as one in being.

Is it not, at this point, positively bizarre to find such iconography in a campaign speech, something usually replete with promises and sunlight, recollected scenes of heroic overcoming? Yet Hamer's drawings above the rostrum sounded more like a survivor's guide for the end of times. Is it not then remarkable how radical her vision could be despite remaining coupled to a drastically diminished, almost chocked, amount of hope? Perhaps her radicalism comes from this coupling. Yes, Hamer called for "total freedom" and "complete progress," but political optimism was far from the dominant key. No wonder the speech was given the rather wry title, "If the Name of the Game Is Survive, Survive."

Surviving a crisis gone rogue, "where the violence is not an exception," to quote Saidiya Hartman, "but defines the horizon of her existence," describes the innermost principle of Hamer's activism and reflects the statement that had become her mantra: "America . . . is sick," she'd say quite slowly, as if dragging the country inch by inch onto a stage, "and man is on the critical list."[119] These three nouns, "America," "man," and "list" are not randomly strung together but placed to suggest that the crisis drips down from the level of the nation to the concept of "man." Outside of this concept, stands someone placing it on, which is to say reducing it, to a list. To find the kind of person who could be external and perceptive enough to put "man" on a list is to return us to Hamer's discussion of property. When we look again we see this concept of man portrayed as "individuals" doubled over on themselves. We see an image as horrid as the phrasing is weird: "the concept of *total individual ownership* of huge acreages of land, by individuals, is at the base of our struggle for survival." We witness these people unhinged by a pair of commas, sleights of hand that avert the impression of accidental redundancy (I should add that this is the only speech on record Hamer read off the page). Freedom Farm does not so much reject these figures (or, figments) of the human as create the kind of person who will bury and build upon them as the conditions, as the "base of our struggle for survival."

Pluripresence

For this section my main aim is to usher in the kind of person who traverses the tensions of Hamer's property-complex. Would you believe that the answer Hamer gives is pluripresent, that the kind of person who walks the line of these tensions is an otherworldly pluripresence? Hamer liked to portray herself as dwelling like a climate in two places at once. This poly-portrait of sorts would eventually debase the reception of Black cooperatives as local entities fighting in a binary-bout against obliteration by globalized markets, particularly international flows of finance capital.[120] She makes us reconsider even more broadly the dichotomy imposed on social movement spaces between the local and the global, to recall Stuart Hall. Although it cumulated in a Freedom Farm fundraising speech, her otherworldly presence first made itself felt, as far as I can find, on the third of November 1963, while speaking at a civil rights rally in Greenwood, Mississippi.

I hear her tell the crowd how a maraud of vigilantes tried to end her life one night for voting the day before, a scene she returns to as if by compulsion over and over and over. I am struck by how her voice maintains a sort of cruising altitude but dips now and again into a baritone, as though a sign of things to come: "I have walked through the shadows of death because it was on the tenth of September in '62 when they shot sixteen times in a house and it wasn't a foot over the bed where my head was. But that night I wasn't there—don't you see what God can do?"[121] Indeed, I do. I see a dues ex machina. I see two miracles, actually: the shots miss her through the window "where [her] head was" and she misses the shots because her head "wasn't there," was also elsewhere. What makes this scene additionally powerful is that she is separated from death by a few hours and a room: space is configured as a metonym for time and vice versa, so that her simultaneity layers locations, which otherwise comprise a one-dimensional plane.

I see this again in Hamer's most widely known speech, whose title would be carved out on her tombstone: "I'm Sick and Tired of Being Sick and Tired," delivered a year and a month later to a small audience in Harlem. She begins, as she began so often, with this one startling statement: "My name is Fannie Lou Hamer and I exist at 626 East Lafayette Street in Ruleville, Mississippi."[122] What a curious way to introduce oneself, and, on top of that, to introduce the way one inhabits one's address. Reduced to its lowest common denominator, the postal address is but a site of existence, attaching her location in Mississippi with the same marks as her location in Harlem: the absolutely present tense in the category of the I-Exist. Now in Harlem, now in Mississippi, "I exist" at a place here and not here, a one-in-twoness, she explains, required by the conditions of normalized violence against the Black body, assailing its ability to don a liberal persona and be singularly self-possessed. "The reason I say 'exist' [is] because we're excluded from everything in Mississippi but the tombs and the graves. . . . Instead of the 'land of the free and the home of the brave,' it's called in Mississippi 'the land of the tree and the home of the grave.'" The quip is hard to hear. It amplifies the difference between living and existing with the latter being far more basic. But the ability to quip also demonstrates Katherine McKittrick's claim that "racial-sexual geographies," especially those "of domination," are "alterable sites of struggle," that just like time, "space is socially produced and alterable."[123] And in the specific context of domestic- ity, a geography of small rooms, to exist instead of live, and to exist across distances as a pluripresence, is to refuse the right to private property, to a private room, that has been refused. She was after something less and more than that.

It is the category of the I-Exist that rearticulates what anthropologist Arjun Appadurai passionately refers to as "bare citizenship." "If you cannot be sure about the walls (however thin)," he says, "that mark off your intimate sphere from the wider world and the roof above your head as a shelter from the elements, then the physical basis for citizenship as a series of spa- tial activities is highly circumscribed."[124] Never does Hamer let us under- estimate the volatility of lacking in Appadurai's terms a "secure and legible social map," but neither does she let us forget the volatility of having it, for in neither case did she receive the most basic civic provisions, sewage sani- tation and water (to my point, she even had to enjoy the absurdity of pay- ing a bill for an excessive use of water she never received). Four months before moving into her home on East Lafayette Street, she was evicted from her lifelong house on W. D. Marlow's sharecropping plantation, at which point, by her own account, she felt the "most free," "'cause they couldn't do nothing to me no more."[125] It's as if, in preparing for "the future of the co-op," which remained "uncertain," as director of North Bolivar Cooperative L. C. Dorsey said, she metamorphosed the instability of shel- ter into a malleability of space and time.[126]

All roads lead to this: January 1971, the University of Wisconsin, with a voice as full as the lecture hall was packed, she says, "I was born fifty-three years ago in Montgomery County. Now Mississippi," she says, then inter- rupts herself, flitting to another subject, "you heard about this twister the other week. But it was *already* a disaster area before the twister!" The way she says "already" makes the audience laugh, swinging the word open with a theatrical glee as if to mock and lament the open stretch of time the dev- astation has occupied. The remarkable thing is how quickly she closes the door and floods us again in darkness: As you might recall from a few pages ago, she says, "it's been a disaster area fifty-three years. . . . I know people older than me said it's been a disaster area before then."[127] The scene (really, scenelet) lasts for a blink of an eye, a flash. A flash is the same speed with which she alights all her other ravaged scenes. This shrunken temporality seems to best express the boundlessness of the disaster, as though it is the longest catastrophes that appear most evanescent (maybe the real message of a dialectics at a standstill).

The colonial terror extends farther than Hamer's own eyes can see. Precisely because of its indefinite extension, the terror might also, paradoxically, have just begun. My point is that her pluripresence testifies to the fact that in states of lasting emergency time loses all scale. Trinh T. Minh-ha discusses today's U.S. imperialism as a "serialized destruction" in "replay."[128] Hamer seems to experience a serialized disaster in déjà vu: the long, long ago that could also be yesterday, today, or to come. At the level of the sentence, she traverses these seemingly ineradicable conditions by not so much dashing from subject to subject in a desultory fashion, as reappearing across distances, flash by flash, now in Wisconsin, now in Mississippi, just as figures in dreams emerge in our heads at night: on two, disparate landscapes at once. Hamer suggests that only in a now-time, a here-and-there, a here-and-here, can one inhabit such a landscape of detritus, and live on.

Freedom City

Hamer's surreal approach to social movement development had a broader context. The temporality she performed had been promulgated and practiced by the people of an ambitious project to which Freedom Farms was indebted both in lesson and in name: a four-hundred-acre site of Washington County less than fifty miles from Hamer's home that in 1966 was christened "Freedom City."[129] Like Freedom Farms, Freedom City was an effort, as one report held, to "break the economic ties that bind the movement to the system."[130] It was carved out at first as a refuge for fifteen farming families who had been evicted from their homes. For simply requesting a higher wage, they were worse than put out. They were put outdoors. This micro-metropolis built for and by the Black poor was, as though heralding Freedom Farms, an effort "to design whole new cities on formerly unoccupied land." The broader experiment to which it belonged was known as "New Community." New Community was described in a report by the Delta Ministry and it is this description that I see Hamer quoting gesture-for-gesture when she portrays herself as pluripresent at the start of her speeches and elsewhere: "[New Community] represents not geography (not one specific locality) but a movement in a new direction or emphasis." The gestural "not one," subtle as the announcements of Hamer's multiple addresses, intimates its counterpart: more than one.

The crafters of Freedom City went through great pains to get across the message that by stating it did not occupy "one specific locality" but a multivalent "movement," they did not mean to abstract the physical place of

the new land

(*Top*) Freedom City Housing. (*Bottom*) Freedom City Soil. Both images from box 59, folder 4221, Delta Ministry—Pamphlets, Brochures, and Reports, Wilson Special Collections Library, University of North Carolina at Chapel Hill.

the city into a purely conceptual one. They meant to blend them. They reiterated its total acreage in disseminated flyers and underlined this numerical concretization with photographs of the land. They deployed a number of photographs, from aerial views of the enormous hectare-like plot with outcrops of white barns and matching bungalows to foot-level views of bare, defenseless furrows rolling into the horizon. The city's designers, however, equally underscored, sometimes with suspenseful pause, that "Freedom City is . . . an idea, not a single geographic site."[131] Freedom City's crafters were not saying that the land is ideographic over and above its geographic content. They were conjoining the two realities. As implied in the quote by that exaggerated ellipses and in the flyers by the multilevel views of the ground, Freedom City undercut the notion of a calculable geography and expanded the physical ground a single person could cover at once. Hamer suggested much the same when she distinctly echoed Freedom City's flyer by repeating that her Farm was also an "idea."[132] Hamer inherited and inhabited a meaning of social movement that signified the capacity to be here and elsewhere, to be simultaneous, "not one" but more, in opposing places.

Individual Ownership by Individuals

Pluripresence relates to property in the most precise manner conceivable. It appears to emerge out of Hamer's critique of John Locke. Let us return to that property passage from her campaign speech, in which she partially critiques Lockean theories of property. These were the theories to which she and the Black poor, especially poor Black farmers in the South, were predominantly exposed (no other word will do). The awkward contortion envisaged in the phrase "individual ownership . . . by individuals," which is essentially "individuals by individuals," constitutes an allusion if ever there was one to the ideal proprietors in John Locke's theory of property. Nearly to the exclusion of every other kind of worker, Locke's ideal was the farmer, who was rather unideally, and perhaps unknown to Locke, doubled over on himself.

Intended to justify the personal possession of common property so long as the person adds more value to the material through his labor, Locke's theory, published in 1689 as a brief section of *The Second Treatise on Government*, was used more than any other to dispossess Indigenous people from their presumably "waste[d]" land and to keep Blacks from owning any whatsoever (Freedom Farm was designed to equally support both groups).[133]

I do not wish to leave the impression that Hamer and her executive board thumbed through the *Second Treatise* at any point for any reason, but rather that Locke's ideas have so pervaded the American colonial consciousness from laws to clichés that his philosophy would be hard to avoid for Freedom Farm members. I do wish to bypass, however, the more overt ramifications of Locke's labor theory, like the laws Locke helped to pen in 1674 for the establishment of Carolina, whose gargantuan size, covering half the South, enveloped Hamer's Mississippi. For in the beginning this crisis of theft was no bigger than a sentence, Locke's most famous sentence: "every man has a property in his own person. This," he continued, "no body has any right to but himself." Change all these pronouns to "individuals" and you basically get "individual ownership . . . by individuals." It was this picture of the proprietor that spread out like an inkblot into a broader defense of colonial power. For if Locke's free individual is supposed to be unobjectified, never to be enslaved, yet at the same time has the natural right to objectify himself, then all he needs to do to justify owning others is consider those others an extension of himself.

Balibar traces how this single conundrum ripples out into the work of Rousseau, Marx, and Derrida, suggesting, in other words, the magnitude of its significance and its conceptual slipperiness. "The difficulty," writes Balibar, staring at that famed sentence, "lies in considering the same thing, or the same person, as simultaneously alienable and inalienable, separable and inseparable."[134] You see, in addition to defending appropriation to the extent that it "improves, cultivates," the land, Locke's *Treatise* was also a defense of democratic self-governance against monarchic rule (here Locke was usurping the rival theory at the time that backed the right of "first occupancy," the right to own the land by the mere fact of living on it).[135] Thus even without Locke's syntactic stammer, the notion of carving property out of the common lot already posed a problem to his defense of self-management. Balibar notes that Marx and Kant interpreted Locke's attempt to overcome the quandary as slipping into a confusion between people and things, "since only 'things' can be appropriated."[136]

Balibar's intervention is to argue that Locke's subject isn't split between himself and his property (or what is etymologically—and racially—the same, his properties).[137] Locke's subject is actually equivalent to—is himself—the process of appropriation. The reason is that the rest of Locke's sentence is all about the fact that the "mix" of one's labor is, in Balibar's words, the "'origin' of every property": "The labour of his body, and the work of his hands, we may say," writes Locke, "are properly his. Whatsoever then he removes out of the state that nature hath provided, and left it in, he hath *mixed his labour with,* and joined to it something that is his own, and thereby makes it his property."[138] Balibar extrapolates his point that property itself makes the Lockean individual, not the other way around, from (without saying it) Locke's image of liquid labor, labor as a "mix" or a fluidity. Locke's self-possessed "body forms an indestructible whole" that is "not split or broken," so long as we understand, as offered elsewhere in Locke's corpus, that "labor in general is the process where the places of the subject, the *self* and the *own,* are continuously exchanged," in stark resemblance to a liquid. Balibar rephrases his interpretation and boats us back through many bends in the river to Hamer's passive construction, "individual ownership . . . by individuals." "To put it another way," Balibar writes, "what is my own/my ownership can always become alienated if *I myself* remain my *own* self," as if that self is itself the labor of appropriation.[139] Balibar is saying the same thing that Hamer says with no more than the word "by" and a couple of commas: in the colonial imagination, the capacity to own has displaced the discrete inalienable individual.

Balibar's most salient point for us actually unfolds in the background of his argument. Locke's theory singularly helped to spawn the concept at the brainstem of the liberal subject, the concept C. B. Macpherson named "possessive individualism." Balibar suggests that to be a possessive individual is not to have the special skill of crossing the line between me and mine. It's to fuse these spheres of being and having, so that ownership and selfhood are subridently the same, closing the last crevasse of alienation. What Balibar doesn't say is that the figure who erases the line between human and thing is also the enslaved or the Black, that lodged in this liberal imagination of liberty is the abstraction of Blackness known as the Black, one who is "simultaneously object of ownership and subject (who can be held liable for crimes)."[140]

In what can only be called a reparative reading, Balibar asserts that for Locke the acquisition of property belonged to a single teleology, extended along one duration. If possession for Locke is indeed a clean and tidy ascendance, then by Locke's own account this ascendance is brief: those *"things really useful . . . are* generally things of *short duration;* such as, if they are not consumed by use, will decay and perish of themselves."[141] I'm citing this simply to underscore that every relation to property is a relation to time. For Locke this time was linear, which helps explain why it was so important for a new property logic to bring time to a standstill. Hamer's embodiment of a pluripresent property holder, who traverses the tension between a self-alienated subject and a self-coherent subject, without, that is, ever becoming either, formed an alternative property-holding subjectivity. Her pluripresence encapsulates the conflict between the split-self and the same-self, each of which respectively manifests the conflict between private and collective property.

Why go through such lengths, why not merely negate these pestilent forms of ownership toward their absolute extinction, hassle-free? For the simple fact that (say it) only a kind of private or "individual" property could safeguard the Black woman's body; that, as Claudia of Lorrain in *The Bluest Eye* observes, just as Hamer of Ruleville will remark in 1973, "outdoors, we knew, was the real terror of life." No matter how much it spelled freedom, dwelling on a farm is nowhere if not outdoors. So when Hamer was asked by a journalist how Blacks are responding to "self-help programs" like the Farm, I wasn't surprised to hear her refer to the weather: "The one kind of remark which really means the most to me is one that I hear frequently outside on really cold mornings. . . . You'll see two men walking out their front doors. One will kind of stop, look around and say, 'Phew! I didn't realize how cold it was outside!' . . . Every place they ever lived in before, it was always just as cold inside as it was outside."[142] Her anecdote is oblique. She could have chosen one that more directly celebrated owning a new house. The elision wasn't lost on her listener, who felt the need to detail as if filling in an absence that Hamer walks "to the window . . . [to] look out of her own new house." The obliqueness suggests that Freedom Farm was less about becoming home owners, adopting what Lisa Lowe perceptively calls "the property and privileged signifier of the liberal person," than about changing how Blacks experience weather, weather the outdoors.[143]

As the direction of Hamer's eyes imply, it was the outdoors that Freedom Farm was about surviving, a space that, as Claudia sees, is "the end of something, an irrevocable, physical fact, defining and complementing our metaphysical condition," from which and in which "there is no place to go."[144] Of course "it bred a hunger for property, for ownership." McCutcheon points out that "Hamer sought to map a Black agrarian space that was prosperous and free from the physical violence that Black women were often subjected to on agrarian land," those "particularly lawless spaces."[145] The pluripresent subject was one answer to the question of how it could be possible to own oneself without enlivening the logic that legitimates ownership of another person: How to have total privacy without "total individual owner-ship," to have self-protection irreducible to private property.

The Comic Horror of Sharecropping

I just can't get over it, the comic horror of a scene in which Hamer makes visible—quite literally visible—the necessity for property against an omni-invasion of personal space. I'm looking again at Hamer's 1971 twister speech, where here what is being twisted to salvos of laughter is the relationship between the sharecropper and the land she sharecrops, between subject and object. The lines between subject and object are so smudged that Hamer's original transcribers mistook her saying "sharecropping is out of sight" for "sharecroppers is out of sight." In any case, this is perhaps her funniest parody of debt peonage on record.

With ironic zeal, Hamer exclaims, "Now sharecroppin' is really something—it's out of sight! Number one, what I found, since I been old enough, it always had," here stamping out each syllable one by one, "too many . . . 'its' in it. Number one, you had to plow *it*. Number two, you had to break *it* up," speaking in staccato as though to say, *like this.* "Number three, you had to chop *it*. Number four, you had to pick *it*. And the last, number five," which Hamer says swiftly as though snatching the words back, "the landowner took it. . . . This left us with nowhere to go. It left us hungry."[146]

That's a lot of "its," and a lot of equivalences between the activity of share-cropping, the object of one's labor, the sharecroppers themselves, and, if that weren't enough, the words. The sharecroppers and the words are the "its" in the phrase "too many 'its' in it." But by referring to each and all of these as an "it," couched in an absurdist verbal play, any one thing could be any other. Prompted by her sort of optic onomatopoeia, I see a field in which so many tentacular shoots of vegetation look like so many charades of the word "it," thronging and thronging into the horizon, "its" quite literally "out of sight."

The plot is comic because of the masquerade and horrific because the masquerade is also supernatural, producing an ongoing disorientation be-tween whoever "you" are (the "you" could be the audience, the workers, us) and whatever the objects "you" shape are. Produced is a profound confusion around one's actual identity and its proliferating distortions that seem to walk out on their own and threaten to take over: a runaway objectification simply from their being "too many 'its' in it." An objectification that begets objec-tification, sharecropping turns its laborers into things eerily indistinguishable from the things they sharecrop. And this proliferating panoramic disorientation of things rests entirely on the suggestion that the plantation for Blacks means a basic loss of boundaries, the fact of there being "too many 'its' in it." The loss is of such magnitude that it creates a boundlessness which itself pervades everything, all, from language to action to things.

So how might one hold property in oneself without again becoming property's hold? Disassemble the invader. And who is that? She answers numerically, seriatim. We might expect him to be the landowner but she places him "last," emphatically "number five." The odd one out, the landowner is the very "last" one to act. No concrete person, the invader is a certain relationship between the creation, distribution, and regulation of property. He is the elastic structure that creates ("plows"), distributes ("picks," "chops," "breaks it up"), and regulates ("takes") property rights. What is surprising about this structure of otherwise familiar components of capital is their equivalence in Locke, which Hamer, by her enumeration and by what she proposes her cooperative to do, parses and stretches into opposing directions. Here's Locke drawing a chain of virtually interchangeable synonyms: "As much land as a man tills, plants, improves, cultivates, and can use the product of, so much is his property."[147] This renowned sentence exemplifies that Locke is never clear in his *Second Treatise* whether improvement comes before usefulness or if usefulness is itself improvement, an ambiguity that gives one the impression that the creation, distribution, and regulation of property are synonymous: it's out of sight.

When Hamer closes her speech, it becomes apparent that this opening scene of occult-like comic horror is the setting her cooperative movement occupies and reclaims. "So now what we plan to do is to grow our own vegetables, is to grow our own cattle, and to grow our own pork and have a hundred houses in that area. Now it's no way on earth that we can gain any kind of political power unless we have some kind of economic power." No arbitrary list, this: a tension between ways of property, between creation and distribution, that climaxes in a paradox, the paradox of growing pork. How do you grow pork? Here creation and distribution are extremes that meet. This joco-horrorscape resembles Benjamin's dialectical image by being "essentially static" in conception, even while being "historically fleeting": all signs of movement are cut short into serial nouns, "to grow," "to grow," "to grow."[148] And with her mantra of nows ("now . . . now") she envisions a collective that comes, as the saying goes, out of nowhere. Now here, now there, "we," she effectively says, are pluripresent.

Pluripresence Meets Social Movement Theory

Pluripresence: no other word sufficiently evokes the kind of simultaneity through which Hamer's cooperative movement emerged. As a formation and a navigation of time at a standstill, it challenges the directionality a social movement is often said to have. However movements are defined, they typically must *go* somewhere, especially under the aegis of their most common definition among social scientists as a "contention" with state institutions toward "making claims in national politics."[149] As construed by Donatella della Porta and Mario Diani, movements require much more than demands or a declarations of grief: goals.[150] As political scientist Rodrigo Nunes observers, "the word [movement] inevitably suggests some degree of cohesion or community regarding goals, identity, practices and self-awareness."[151] To unveil a different historical reality, Nunes prefers the terms "network-system" and "network-movement" because they denote the plurality of movements that people participate in (a network of movements), as well as the ability for people to be part of a movement without consciously saying so. "'Network-system' thus allows us to look beyond explicitly or self-identified political expressions, as well as any suggestions of shared goals, practices, etc., and to picture a broader 'moving' of social relations."[152]

As I espy a broader "moving" in Hamer, I am somewhat in line with Nunes's notion of many movements in one viewed from below, from the lower frequencies, so to speak. The difference is that the performances I trace of Hamer's cooperative movement are particular forms of simultaneity, pluripresences. These anticipate across race and custom what some sociologists, who today are contesting their discipline's dominant frames, have dubbed "new age movements." These fresh purveyors are couraging new theories to make sense of emergences like Argentina's autonomous movement spawned by the 2001 crisis, emergences that are decidedly anti-institutional in all respects ("Horizontalidad!" they shout, promulgating from a Solano fish farm all the way to Spain, Greece, and Occupy in the U.S. the practice of direct democracy across a flat surface, a style of self-organizing without definitive answers to what the future should look like), or Spain's 15M, which "has begun to refer to itself as a *clima*, that is, a climate or way of being," uncannily reminiscent of Hamer's habitation.[153] Plurispresences are modes of being simultaneous, modes that exceed the limits of social relations based either on accumulations of property or on their abolition. Pluripresence troubles not only progressive or regressive historical trajectories, but all directionality. It's a kind of all-at-once-ness. As an analytic category for social movement formation, pluripresence pictures a timescape of dual and mutually exclusive emergences, across great distances, flash by flash.

I'm replaying that interview Hamer had with Neil McMillen, sitting somewhere in her home at 721 James Street. "What are you doing today in the civil rights movement?" he asks, his tone tight with formality. "Are you still active in the civil rights movement in a formal sense?"

"I still—well, I move around speaking and working with the little co-op here."[154]

After some time, he returns to these questions. "The civil rights movement . . . I hear it's dead, is that right?"

"I don't think that you would say it is dead, but every so many years things change and go into something else. Now, you might never see demonstrations. I'm tired of that. I won't demonstrate no more. But I try to put that same energy, what I wish I had, I try to put that into politics, too. You see, if you notice, a lot of these people that was out there marching is congressmen now: Andrew J. Young, Ivanhoe Dennison is not a politician, and he was one of the—oh, he was a great civil rights person. But, if Ivanhoe Dennison moved into a place and stayed right there on the job, they don't lose that election. So, it means that even though it's not just called civil rights, it's still on the move to change. And it's just this phase of it has faded out and now we're pushing for something else."

Needing clarification, McMillen asks, "so direct action has given way to political action?"

"Yes, that's what it is!"

I stop the recording to recap. Having heard Hamer mention electoral politics as one "something else" that she continues to engage, I see—am seeing as I write this—no way of reading that "something else" as not also the cooperative movement she decisively mentioned first. The cooperative movement is a phase in a bigger movement to change, but the questions are, Change how? A movement to change what? It'd be wrong to forget the big changes she had in mind, but risky to overlook how change remains unspecified, unverifiable. To evoke Hartman on the "stubborn desire for an elsewhere and an otherwise yet to emerge clearly," this was less the future "you wanted but couldn't name" than the present she had but wouldn't name.[155] A movement toward an unspecified change intimates a movement without direction, a movement that is, in the fullness of the word, a "phase." The nature of the change is not only a change to indirection, but to a "fad[ing] out," the only image Hamer offers. Each phase, a fade, always fading out.

Hamer the Timekeeper

Hamer liked to tell a story about time and a pea. It all began with an awfully morbid contraption she assumed her listener could visualize at least in outline: a primitive cotton scale that looked like the letter j flicked onto its back, head down and feet up as though waiting to be carted away. Reminiscent of an instrument of constriction or torture, this cast-iron device was typically the color of unevenly dried lava, years of slow decay, a bumpy sooty-black pocked with spots of molten red. Exactly at its waist, it was held up by a chain of the same dappled hues. Directly beneath this hung by hook an oval, metal basket, like an enlarged gravy bowl, often bubbling over with rounds of speckled cotton. From the base of its neck hung that small, deceptively heavy, cylindrical weight known as the pea.

All the power over a worker's wages, whether one were robbed or remunerated, lay with this pea, and from the trusted age of six Hamer's official job was to guard and adjust it, sliding it along tiny numbered serrations until it counterbalanced the basket distended with the day's labor. "I would take my pea to the field," said Hamer to interviewer Robert Wright in 1968, "and use mine until I would see him coming because his was loaded. . . . I know he was beating people like that."[156] She was referring to some ominously unnamed man and she explained that for eighteen years she exercised this particular act of rebellion against him and his system of seizure: "All I could do is rebel in the only way I could rebel, like when they will have our people out picking cotton and the man would have the pea loaded. Well I kept mine with all the weights." The weight of the pea determined the value of the worker's time. Since Hamer retained her pea with all of the weight, she retained all of the value. "A timekeeper?" asked Wright. "Yes, I was a timekeeper."

Hamer manipulated the value of labor time by bringing her own pea, a form of property that very much like the formal structure of the Farm was owned by everyone and by none. On the one hand, it was all-owned since directly tied to everyone's labor, hence her surprising pluralization of "weights" ("I kept mine with all of the weights"). On the other hand, it was unowned since tied to an average labor time, hence her abstract and generalized designation of "all." The pea is not a symbol of time. It's a symbol of the reclamation of time, plantation time, to be exact, which in another interview, years later, she portrayed as a landscape, a flatland. "Working the field left an impression. . . . They [her fellow croppers] just worked from one season to the other. . . . There wasn't no such thing as a period where they had a lapse between there. They just chopped cotton, chopped cotton, over and over." These sentiments were similar to what Hamer heard a fellow organizer describe as their common working day, sitting beside her in a National Council of Negro Women meeting: "we don't work nine to five. . . . We work nine to nine to nine to nine."[157] They reclaimed this total conflation between solar and labor time, this borderless "impression." It is a time that remains flat and indiscernible, without "period" or "lapse," punctuation or pause, a time that's now theirs.

Talking to Robert Wright, Hamer swayed, by association, from her story about the pea to her genesis of activism, whose origins she also discussed in terms of time. She recollects that mass meeting held by the Student Nonviolent Coordinating Committee in 1962. She remembers acutely the sermon preached that Monday night in a "little church" with a "green top on it": "the 12th chapter of St. Luke and the 54th verse, 'Discerning the Signs of Time.'" The scripture is typically titled "the Signs of the Times," so she's again presenting her craftiness. "He talked," she says in less speech than *recitative*, "about how a man could look out and see a cloud and predict it's going to rain, and it would become so, but still he couldn't know in a sense; he couldn't tell what was happening right around him. He looking at a cloud and he didn't know right then 'What was happening the next door to him.'"

By refashioning "Signs of the Times" into "Signs of Time," Hamer refashions a lesson on historical contingency into one on temporality writ large. She does not replace the one with the other. She draws an implicit analogy between the ability to see time as such and the ability to see local time emerging in the present. Although this parable is usually interpreted as a cautionary tale about the dangers of going blind to your immediate surroundings, Hamer recasts it as a generative problem of mixing the here with the there. If we imagine "the times" in the parable's normal name as a scarred human body facing the sun (I know, just go with it), a body that bears all the contingencies produced by "the times," then "time" in Hamer's appellation is the shadow the sun casts, time in potentially endless regress. Hamer's initiation into activism was a practice of not only double but of redoubled sight. From timekeeper to timekeeper, she commandeered an art (let's call this pluripresence) of visualizing not only the now and the not yet—but the not yet as the now: the shadow as the body, the embodiment of the shadow.

What Happens to a Deed Deferred?

It was a night nowhere near where
We were.

—Nathaniel Mackey, *Splay Anthem*

Tonight, as I bring these entries to a close, is the 15th of July 2019, 9:28 P.M. On this very day, in this very hour, forty-one years ago, Hamer's experiment with property relations unraveled to its own close, entering its final days into what can only be considered the shell of the Farm. It was the penultimate meeting on record, gathering together that evening from 7:45 until a little after 10:00 the Farm's remaining board with some of the remaining members to make a plenary total of seventeen. Out of this bunch sprang the confession from one distressed member that she "was tired of the way things was going and . . . would like to see some action or changes made immediately."[158] For one member in particular, however, one Hattie McGrover, this reunion marked the end of life as she knew it.

Twenty-two days before this night, fast becoming a nighttime wringing-of-hands, Secretary Bobby Bounds relayed to McGrover the board's felt desperation in the face of encroaching creditors, the board's need "to pay tax and to secure insurance."[159] Bounds had informed Hattie McGrover that she must start paying rent in order to keep her home, which Hamer had provided, as Hamer publicly said on more than one occasion, "free of charge." Yet it was in that July pow-wow that the officers of the Farm ruled it all but a crime to July the days away. A few minutes before the clock hit 10:00 P.M., the then recording secretary Nora Campbell jotted down that "Mrs. Hamer had told her [McGrover] she could live in the house as long as she lived," and that "when she received the letters she did not know what was going on. . . . This [meeting] was a chance for her to learn what was happening."[160] That last sentence is presumably President Charles McLaurin's words transcribed secondhand and it reveals unequivocally that with the walls closing in on him, and on them, McLaurin felt the need to close in on the weakest joints.

In June the year prior President McLaurin and Secretary Bounds had dispatched a number of letters to the other denizens of the Farm ("denizens" because where was their home now?). After Hamer had dislodged them from debt, each letter assailed them with new commands nigh impossible to meet. To Hamer's sister, Sarah Mae Ratliff, McLaurin wrote, "[O]ur records [of the assets] shows that Freedom Farm owns the property on which you live." Then lower down: "since there is no records of the type of agreement you had with the prior Board of Directors, or the administrators of the Corporation . . . I request a meeting with you for the purpose of rectifying the situation. . . . If I have not heard from you by Friday, June 3, 1977, I will consider your refusal to call a request to visit." The letter was dated Wednesday, June 1. In the best conditions of the U.S. postal service, unless he dropped off his letter personally, Ratliff would have had less than a day to respond.[161] Yet conditions were arguably worse for Hattie McGrover, who had less than a month to find thirty dollars for the newly stipulated rent when she couldn't even afford the three-dollar member fee. The letter she received in May, three months before the meeting, proclaimed, "the board has made a decision that all tenants living on property belonging to Freedom Farm Corporation will begin paying rent June 1, 1978."[162]

I should note that McGrover "had received three (3) letters" requesting payment by that point, this probably the third, but in truth that placed her in about the same limits she was given at the end of that two-hour-plus meeting, exactly "five minutes" for which "the floor was . . . now open" for "talks and discussions." Could I be reading the notes wrong? McGrover's "statement" was typed beneath the header of "talks and discussions" and it was followed by a motion that the meeting be "adjourned."[163] But could I be wrong that the order of the notes, that the notes themselves, reflect what occurred in the meeting, when something else took place? I honestly hope so. Either way, Bounds's gaffe at the end of his letter to McGrover said enough: "thank you for your corporation" (no misprint), a gaffe missing only a comma and an eviction of an 'r' to be complete: *thank you for you, corporation.* Sure, this company surname, "corporation," was written on the charter, but at no point in a decade did Hamer refer in letter, in dialogue, or in public speech to the Farm as a corporate firm. Since there was no record of the agreement between McGrover and Hamer, ambassador Bobby Bounds expressed more flexibility about the timeline he and the Board erected, signing his epistle, "please pay promptly."[164]

As soon as Freedom Farm's poorest inhabitants were placed somewhere, legibly designated as "tenants" to be disciplined by a board and by its deadlines, the freedom they likely felt in comparison to this new circumference must have vamoosed. The board's response to Farm members recalled, if not reflected, international trends, when cooperatives having crested after World War II rapidly waned during the 1970s. Following the 1975 global recession and the expansion of neoliberal government policies, almost all types of cooperatives, particularly agricultural, faced either "rapid" closures or demutualization, as in became investor rather than member-owned (one exception: with mass unemployment, U.S. worker cooperatives actually peaked in 1979).[165] The extreme contradictions between private and collective property sustained on the Farm, day in, day out, as if for dear life, had finally to snap, a pressure I myself felt daily, as I tried from entry to entry to lay bare what I saw as the traversal of these tensions, Hamer's pluripresence. I tried to understand her pluripresent activism as a crossing of linkages between temporal stasis, liberal logics of property, historical progress, cooperatives, and plantation culture. I tried, in short, to tell a new story about Black protest and Fannie Lou Townsend Hamer. Tonight I find it hard to say this, but it's hard to find it false: it was dangerous to make a nowhere one's existence; it was death not to. It is true that "by the early 1970s cooperative farming was in decline."[166] But if this is what it meant to decline obedience to the logic of liberalism and its solutions to poverty, then when it came to Freedom Farm its highest point was its lowest.

Conclusion

Trouble in the Water

. . . .

. . . but some dreams
hang in the air like smoke
touching everything.

—Lucille Clifton, "Breaklight"

Building voice upon voice until they found it, and when they did it was a wave
of sound wide enough to sound deep water and knock the pods off chestnut
trees. It broke over Sethe and she trembled like the baptized in its wash.

—Toni Morrison, *Beloved*

This has been a story about a people in peril living in the present without
saviors, without triumph, without progress or peace, and, what's more, without the need for them. Chapter after chapter, box after box, I have been
amazed by how an imperiled people bejeweled the ruins trying to ruin
them, amazed at the way they eked out a living against all odds and how
bright this living was. I was never surprised by the fact of its brightness.
The fact of its brightness is "the tradition," as Jericho Brown has said ("My
God, we leave / things green"), a beauty bestiality has never managed to
degrade.[1] What surprised me were the whys. I have tried to understand not
if but why the quality of Black life so routinely outstrips the circumstances
of it, to parrot Toni Morrison, why cooperatives were the zones in which
that beauty raged, and why so many Blacks found in cooperatives economies of abundance, temporal, social, material, and otherwise.[2] That this
abundance was clearest to them exactly at the moment deprivation was
most extreme, the Great Depression, that abundance and deprivation are
often within cooperatives locked like an ampersand, only amplifies the urgency of my questions. At no time in my own life has a certain deprivation
felt greater than it does today, knowing that every morning I hug my son
goodbye he or I, by more than chance, might not return.

So perhaps it's the conditions under which I write this, the on-and-on-
and-on of a prescriptive disappearance, Black, Brown, queer, and Indigenous

lives incrementally disappearing, that make the answer I have found to my string of whys, if "answer" and "found" are really the words, both odd and oddly refreshing. From the habits and habitats of four artists, and the word is certainly "artists," I have proposed that cooperation offered a kind of break, a respite and release from hard lines of progress etched deeply into the cultural imaginary, as deep as the old saws *keep on keeping on* and *joy comes with the morning.* When I say "lines of progress" I mean their liberal, technological connotations as much as I do their classically Marxist ones. In both, as Frederic Jameson notes, history moves only in one direction, forward, never swerving back.[3] The inborn teleology of historical materialism states conditions may "certainly decay or fall apart, cease to be what they were," but "there is an inevitable increase in complexity and productivity at work which cannot be reversed."[4] It was clear to me early on that while cooperatives have been mainstays of socialist party projects, Du Bois, Baker, Schuyler, and Hamer all expressly pried them away from Marxist historical reason on which this socialism was often based. It is not that they gave up or dispensed with the promise of dialectical overcoming, along with its touchstone of historical materialism. It is that in this zone, they felt free to act differently, free to try out and try on, levy and live, different orientations to political time. Historically, cooperatives have been most attractive to Blacks less for the future they promised than for the present they availed, less for what they promised than for what they presented. The luminaries I followed throughout these pages took this logic of presencing to its upmost limit, and I could equally say, took me to mine.

This journey has been tough, but refreshing for the simple fact that what I've learned about time has fundamentally made it a little easier to breathe. It may be no coincidence that present-day cooperatives for marginalized folks often describe their temporality through metaphors of breath. Kali Akuno, who cofounded Cooperation Jackson in 2014, the year "I can't breathe" surfaced as a slogan through which to wrest one's breath back, describes with respiratory nouns the way this bustling cooperative exploits the contradiction of uneven capitalist development. "The weak and relatively sparse concentration of capital in Mississippi creates a degree of 'breathing room' on the margins and within the cracks of the capitalist system that a project like ours can maneuver and experiment within in the quest to build a viable anti-capitalist alternative."[5] Capturing an innate tendency in cooperative life, Akuno's statement suggests the convergence of respiration and expiration, finding breath on the fringes, in the "cracks" between what is and what will be: a beautifully unabsorbable, broken time.

With a different present-tense, but one still evinced in an ability to breathe, arrives the Earthseed Land Collective, a forty-eight-acre agricultural "land cooperative," in Durham, North Carolina. One visitor to this refuge, "where people of color can come and get free and feel safe," expressed the ability "to hold a conversation without the impulse to hold my breath. To move my body without arrows directing my path."[6] By invoking this synonymy (to move without a mandate is to breathe without a hold), she expressed, in other words, that her felt respiration came from an openness, a planfulness without a plan, to how, among other things, they can produce food sovereignty, facilitate "collective healing" from setter colonialism, and protect Indigenous rights on ironically bought, "stolen land." Another exemplary contact zone between cooperative economics and artistic practices, Earthseed was founded in 2012 by seven Black and Latinx farmers, food justice organizers, and copoeira practitioners, all inspired by Octavia Butler's novel series *Parable of the Sower* and *Parable of the Talents*. Butler imagines Earthseed as a set of evolving beliefs for living and thriving on "new earths" through new relationships with nonhumans. The cooperative took this name because their principal desire is to rub thin the perimeters and prestige of a human life reinforced by capital. Creating such a collaborative space has meant creating, like Baker, a constellatory time: more pattern than progress. Evoking a long and a now time, a now time as a long time, cofounder Corre Robinson said, "We're moving along one plant at a time." Referring to the sociality that Butler's Black protagonist Lauren Olamina helped to sow on the wreckage of empire, cofounder Justin Robinson said, "even if nothing about that future comes true, this [cooperative] is still necessary."

For both Earthseed and Cooperation Jackson, just as it was for their predecessors, the present proves to be more than an instant, oceanic, because the remains on which we live after inestimable loss prove to be just that: that which remains. Even in death, says the lesson, to quote Danez Smith, "please, don't call us dead."[7] For all the variations played on this theme of lasting, lasting precisely in the refusal to last, the theme comes down to this: "a gesture or a step . . . toward that which will have only ever been that which will have remained."[8] Those words are Nahum Chandler's, and everything I've had to say about the life and times of the Black cooperative movement are captured writ small there. Taken from his astonishingly deft study of Du Bois, I quote Chandler's sentence, one, because of its devastating beauty, the elegance in how it refuses to progress, how it doesn't let a sentence become another sentence. And, two, because the way he turns a phrase returns me to the questions with which I began. What does it mean to make a social movement that could not nor would not depend on a better tomorrow? What does progress look like without the vector of progression, progress that tolls like a busted bell? It means and looks like "a gesture or a step . . . toward that which will have only ever been that which will have remained."

Chandler arrives at this sentence, this respiration, after a somewhat stuttered breath. He has been meditating at once on the lifeworks of Du Bois and on what he calls "the massive violence of the *disaster* that was in Los Angeles," otherwise known as the LA riots of 1992.[9] Rodney King was beaten in March the previous year. That same month Latasha Harlins was cut down by store owner Soon Ja Du over a box of juice. Du thought she was stealing it. She was clutching the money to pay. She was fifteen years old. A small fine for the store owner, an acquittal for the cops, and blossoming rage for LA, midspring, '92. This "disaster," this "ditto-ditto" of devastation, as Christina Sharpe has called it, brings Chandler to the loss of Du Bois's son. Lost to diphtheria then to segregation, he was nineteen months. "In the face of such," Chandler says, unable to name exactly what he's facing, "we cannot speak," a speechlessness that finally stutters his breath. "I propose we undertake, in turn, as a form of our own responsibility, even as we remain without measure, of success, across this millennial passage, a gesture or step, at least a turn, toward a desedimentation of dissimulation—of an epoch of war—and toward that which will have only ever been that which will have remained."[10] I find it remarkable that just as he stutters, maybe in the stutter, he finds a way to breathe.

Chandler's sentence not only performs the coincidence, at the heart of this book, of respair and breathlessness, confinement and expanse, that is also at the heart of Black politics and performance. His sentence, moreover, questions the meaning of success, and not just questions it, almost rids the word of meaning altogether. Because we could liken what Chandler proposes to a general insurgency, to a mass movement (what else do you call the living that remains regardless of the "war"?), we could say it's the meaning of movement success that's thrown into crisis. Look at how Chandler's sentence lurches and reels, heaving with commas, seething with ofs, until we (and maybe he) no longer know *of what*? "Success" of what? The "form" we took? Or the "measure" we refused to take? The point is that these questions beg potentiating ones. What is success that can't be measured? Something other than success. Maybe disaster, maybe the reclamation of disaster as failure in ecstatic proportions, as I explored in chapter 2. And where does success as a label fit, a label for something "favorably ended," on what might be ongoing and certainly never took coherent shape? Maybe Nowhere. Maybe, in this sense, it fits only a no where, an "inwardly elsewhere" (Nathaniel Mackey), as I explored in chapter 3, but implicitly throughout.

The aesthetics of these cooperative elsewheres and (elsewhens) put me in mind of Theodore Ward's play *Our Lan'*. Ward is better known for starting the New York–based Negro Playwrights' Company with Langston Hughes, Richard Wright, and Paul Robeson in 1940, and for restaging with the Company his first and most famous play *Big White Fog* than he is for his stern, hyperkinetic *Our Lan'*.[11] Here he dramatized the fallout of one of the most momentous events in African American history: General Sherman's Field Order No. 15, which at the behest of twenty African American religious leaders granted to former slaves 400,000 acres of ex-Confederate land on January 16, 1865. With news of this order the play begins, and it crescendos to the creation of a cooperative society anchored in a farm off the coast of Georgia. Self-governing, self-sustaining, this is a society as much in-becoming as it is in-"bloom," to use its own descriptor.[12] It boasts a school, a playground, daycare for the children, housing, industry, food, and kin. Such bloom inspires an "unsuppressable joy."[13] This is the joy in the "realization that they have in their hands now, complete and undeniable, the economic means which can guarantee their new life." Johnson their leader is as plucky as the prose itself. Standing before the white man who will, as he promises, plunder Johnson's body with "canon fire" by the end, Johnson rifles back, "neither yuh nor all de rest of de planters put together goin' ever kill da thing wes after."[14]

The "joy" is "unsuppressable"; the "thing" they're "after" unsuppressed. And with these two facts, the play imparts a message that upsets the reception of it as a tragedy. I've tried to do the same to much of the legacy of Black cooperative life. When the play premiered in 1947, it boldly suggested to the audience that the "thing" the characters are after isn't after at all. It's here. Despite the dispossessions, they have what they need, the "economic means" to do much more than seek inclusion in the new nation-state: to root a "new life" on "our lan,'" "now": now in 1865, now in 1947, and for that matter now in 2022. What I find most rousing, however, is the double meaning of "after." The people are still "after" the "thing" that can't be "kill[ed]" as much because this thing's not yet as because they're "after" more. The remuneration of forty acres and a mule to every former slave in 1865 might have been the most radical idea in American Reconstruction that ever happened, then didn't. As the play recounts, the many Blacks (40,000 in fact) who settled on the coastal land by June of that year were forced through President Johnson to vamoose by fall. Yet forty acres and a mule hardly circumscribes the span of radical desire expressed in the play. Ward's biggest message may be that the radical aesthetic practices of Black cooperation suggest cooperatives bloom in the dark on haunted terrain, a haunt that lies between the now and the not-yet, devastation and repair, and it is this haunt that provides the conditions on which to bloom.

Really what I want to leave you with though, aside from this precis, is the idea that, at bottom, the movements I have been talking about may just as easily go by a different name. In deference to the argot used by my authors, I have kept the term, grappled with it, but in essence these movements may also be called riots. A riot leads Chandler to an "historical movement . . . not restricted to art."[15] A movement for him, as it emphatically was for Baker, is "the most general disruption of boundaries," a disruption that "dissipates any simple notion of inside and outside, of above and below." A movement is itself the opening to difference, and in this way the Black cooperative movement reminds me of a riot. Just like rioters, the cooperatists of this book lived without reserves and so, too, without the promises of institutional improvement, let alone reform, and redistributive politics, let alone rights. And by breaking "the index between one's labor input and one's access to necessities," this riot of cooperatists contested the socialist creed that workers must command production and distribution.[16] When Schuyler and Baker asserted the primacy of the Black consumer, they not only refuted the adage that capital is most vulnerable at the point of production: They broke the equation between what one can give in a narrow sense and what one can get in a narrower one.

As Amy Dru Stanley observes, there is a growing range of voices turning to cooperatives as practical solutions to the tensions between relations of dependence and the formal rights of citizenship, between wage labor and popular sovereignty.[17] But resolution for the figures that people this book was hardly the point. Hamer's efforts to reclaim lost land, to reclaim loss (and land), Du Bois's narrativization of this reclamation, Schuyler's and Baker's own land sovereignty projects—none of these, despite appearances, was an attempt to reclaim level ground and the spirit of equality, of equivalence, but unsteady ground and the spirit of trouble: burial grounds. I read Chandler's word "desidementation" as signifying this macabre reclamation. This is not a remembrance of the buried, who in real and weird ways may live among us, if we are to believe a few cooperatists. It is not a remembrance of the dead, but of their false burial, their "dissimulation." In short, there's something powerful, riotous even, in living with loss.

In *Riot. Strike. Riot: The New Era of Uprisings*, Joshua Clover argues that since the seventies the riot has overtaken the strike as the "leading tactic" in social movement repertoires.[18] Yet he also suggests that riots have been unfurling beneath the surface of every explicitly chosen movement tactic. He states that "a riot is itself the experience of surplus," not the experience of dearth or deprivation, as commonly thought, but of "surplus danger," "surplus emotion," surplus ungovernability, exceeding the capacity to be policed. As soon as the police are pitched into a crisis, a riot has bloomed. We could add that when a riot looks like a surplus that cannot be governed it also looks like a swarm that has lost its hive. Both populations are doomed to fly and internally differentiated to infinite regress. We could go further. A riot is the spirit of remaining on remains, to return to Chandler, the spirit of felicitous ruin. The Black cooperative movement has taught me that every movement of minoritized lives, precisely since their lives are always already judged as criminal acts, may be a riot in the open even in disguise, in "desedimentation of dissimulation."

In a virtual talk on Black studies in September 2020, Fred Moten gives this beautiful read of an epigraph by Édouard Glissant, which appears in Patrick Chamoiseau's magnificent novel *Texaco*. The epigraph reads, "Because historical time was stabilized in a void, the writer must contribute to restoring its tormented chronology."[19] Against the impression that restoration here means a sort of equilibrium, and that the restored would be a whole and stable home, the antithesis of "a void," Moten interprets the passage as encouraging a recovery of the void itself. "Part of what it is that a transplanted people are trying to recover," Moten says, "is not necessarily stability, but rather instability. And I think that this desire to recover instability can be seen and associated with this sense of time as a kind of general uprising . . . to recover the general uprising."[20] His comments remind me of the difference between being a bridge over troubled waters, to cite that gorgeous song, and being the trouble in the water, to return to my epigraph from Morrison's *Beloved*. The difference between renewal by stillness whether in the water or at the mountain top and renewal by trembling is the difference between linear and rippling time, between a movement as progress and movement as resonance. It's the difference, in sum, between cooperation as a single operation and co-operation as a double operation that doubles, and doubles (and doubles), because, and here again is Chandler now evoking Du Bois's double-consciousness, "the double is never only double, proliferating its marks without end."[21] Thus to discuss cooperation as mutual aid is to assert the mutuality, the reciprocal but uneven co-constitution, rather than the opposition, of a set of operations that proliferate without end, be they disaster and creativity, waking and dreaming, progress and nonprogress, or remains and remains.

Afterword

This Bridge Called the System:
An Interview with Stephanie Morningstar

• •

I mentioned in my conclusion the resurgent turn today toward cooperative economies. Here's a phenomenal example of one such turn, from an interview I conducted on January 21, 2021, with Stephanie Morningstar, co-director of Northeast Farmers of Color Land Trust (NEFOC). I offer it because its ongoing grounded knowledge bears unmistakable resonance with the conditions of cooperation I explored in the book, with their entanglements and temporalities. As Morningstar discussed the remarkable ways she conceives the present on great-great-great Black, Brown, and Indigenous backs, she left me with the thought that all radical politics are fundamentally encounters with radical loss.

Morningstar is unassuming and speaks with a stillness, a warm resolve, pitched in a deep sense of service and of history. Phoning me from her small farm in Canada, she told me when I asked how to pronounce NEFOC that "We made a conscious choice to pronounce it *nee-foke*."[1] They wanted to signal whom they're working for, the folk, the Black and Brown people on whom this nation was built, and with the loss of the "l" how they're reimagining what the folk, and their relation to this nation, can be. "We're not turning back the clock trying to reverse time to go back to some imagined past. We're trying to create something completely new."

NEFOC began in 2019 as a collective to address unimaginable loss and the health disparities that accrue in its wake. By the dawn of the twentieth century, ex-slaves and their descendants owned 14 million acres of land; by the dawn of the twenty-first, they lost 90 percent of it. For Indigenous people land loss was, of course, even greater, but just as swift. Between the founding of America in 1776 and the Dawes Act of 1887, through which the federal government forced Indigenous nations to sell their "surplus" land and put the rest in a trust controlled by the state, Indigenous people lost more than half the entire country, 1.5 billion acres. Morningstar has aptly named the fallout of this cumulative theft "eco-grief," a loss of futures in ecological proportions. Yet unimaginable as it is, she and her collaborators, seven board directors and two other full-time staff, Çaca Yvaire and Dr. Gabriela Pereyra, are working to imagine how to suture the wound. They are working the law to reclaim the land.

There are two kinds of land trust, "title holding" and "conservation." The first allows owners to anonymously maintain all rights over the property. The second requires them to relinquish some rights over land use and development for the protection of wildlife and cultural sites. Conservation trusts are therefore mostly used for statues and buildings. "We're using both," Morningstar explained, "doing everything from purchasing conservation easements to helping create 501c(2) title-holding organizations," corporations made with the sole intent of holding property titles and turning over all profits to a designated party. "What I like about the cultural respect easements is that there's this understanding that reclaiming the land is about reclaiming our responsibilities to it"—not, in other words, laying claim on the land itself. Part of what distinguishes NEFOC from other trusts is their hybrid model, a two-pronged approach designed to provide "permanent and secure land tenure," a trust and stewardship in perpetuity.

Working closely with other New York–based collectives—Soul Fire Farm, Black Farmer Fund, Corbin Hill Food Project, and Farm School NYC—NEFOC's aim is to steward over 2,000 acres in the next five years through purchase, land return, donation, and rematriation. Inspired by such lodestars as Fannie Lou Hamer's 680-acre Freedom Farm Cooperative in Mississippi and Shirley Sherrod's 5,700-acre New Communities Land Trust in Georgia (both founded in the same year, 1969) NEFOC is also building "a flagship community with incubator farms, commons for production, childcare, health care, and integrated ecosystem restoration." As a member of the New York State Climate Action Council, Morningstar, in conjunction with NEFOC, advances environmental policies that demand the deep and meaningful inclusion of and consultation with Indigenous communities. Centering land access for BIPOC, she hopes to soon see and support legislation that upholds the Rights of Nature, the complicated legal process of granting personhood to land.

With these ambitions and achievements NEFOC joins a growing wave of land sovereignty and cooperative projects sweeping across the country. Cooperation Jackson and its urban Freedom Farm (named after Hamer's) again come to mind, for their aim, like NEFOC's, is to fashion "a regenerative economy, one that not only restores and replenishes the resources it extracts from the earth, but aids in the actual restoration of our earth's ecosystems."[2] Old earths, new earths. One might also think of the Black-owned multistakeholder cooperative Georgia Freedom Initiative. Founded in 2020 by nineteen Black families on 502 acres of hills, valleys, and loblolly pines. It's "just outside Toomsboro," they say again and again, as though to register their mission of "healing from racial trauma" in an agricultural, recreational, and cultural "haven"—in "a new city"—for Blacks across the diaspora.[3] This is all a part of a proliferating effort among the Black, Brown, and Indigenous to puzzle out new timescapes from/within the bonds of ownership.

This is tricky work, using a form of property holding to disrupt property's hold. But Morningstar bears no illusions. Recalling Audre Lorde's 1979 groundbreaking essay "The Master's Tools Will Never Dismantle the Master's House" from the 1981 volume *This Bridge Called My Back*, which very much like NEFOC gathered an ongoing dialogue on radical feminism between Black and Indigenous women, Morningstar told me, "Nobody is saying that you're going to dismantle the system with these colonial tools. They are meant to only be used to a certain extent, but we're trying to use them as much as we can to bend the system on its back."[4] What they're bending is ownership toward the goal of stewardship.

"Seeing land go back to First Nations is one big goal of ours, right? So we're not looking to be somebody who owns all or holds title to all of these pieces of land across the Northeast. That's not our goal. That would be like hoarding wealth. We're not about hoarding wealth or resources. We're ensuring that we have a proper channel." This means being careful about everything clear down to the words she uses, about everything from the proper law to the proper verb. For instance, she never says she or any one of her affiliates seeks to own land, but seeks to understand "how land is to come into our care." Even the word "give" she uses with caution. Instead of "given," she said, "when this land is put in front of us, the first thing we do is check in with the respective nation to say we have this land, it's potentially going to be donated. What would you like us to do with it? Would you like us to pass this on to you? Would you like this? Would you like us to facilitate this in any way?" It is clear from talking to Morningstar, with her carefully honed words in a carefully honed calm, that any use of language is thoroughly tethered to any disuse of property.

Another piece of their novelty is the very way in which they're bringing people together to displace a language that in every way keeps people apart. Theirs is a solidarity based not on the unity of similar cultures, but on the adjacencies of cultural difference, not on assumed agreement but on ongoing conversation. This conversation, she told me, "includes Black folks.

It includes Brown folks. It includes migrant folks—it includes all these different people who are now here. They have these different covenants that come from other lands and their ancestors come from other lands, but all our values align. And that's what connects us as a board and as our staff. We all have these varied expressions and varied facets of a relationship with the land, and with each other, and we're living into this vision together."

The Place You Will Not Come Out Of

I asked Morningstar to share with me where her own vision comes from, what brought her to this work. She shared a genealogy that exemplifies a common bind for minoritized lives: between having to resist in order to survive in one way and having to assimilate in order to survive at all, between the preservation of one's spirit and preservation of one's self. In the broadest strokes, her work at NEFOC is to refuse this sour choice, to choose a different premise on which to live on.

"I have an interesting intersection of ancestry that put me into this interesting frame of mind around land and land-based wealth, redistribution and justice and healing." Then with a slightly heavier breath, she quickened her pace, clipping the ends of her words, as though encountering her story again for the first time. "My grandfather is/was a residential school survivor, and my grandmother and he moved to Buffalo, New York, in the late forties to sort of evade the ramping up of the Sixties Scoop, which was the morphing of the adaptive mechanism of racism from the residential school system into another way to abduct Indigenous children and assimilate them out. . . . Whether it was just the assimilation that taught him, my grandfather, that his ways and his languages and his customs were backward, or if there was a more imminent physical threat, which there often was—whatever happened when he left that place, he never spoke of it, and he never participated in Longhouse again, and he really didn't allow us to do that either. My grandmother kept a connection to the reserve, and that was sort of my soul."

Her grandparents had Haudenosaunee citizenship, also known as Six Nations, which through the Jay Treaty allowed them to move freely between Buffalo and Canada. "My way of connecting was through my grandmother, but we didn't have the same linkages that we would have had had we lived on the reserve, or if we had gone back and forth more and traveled like many other folks in Buffalo. . . . My father," she continued, "is of Western European descent mostly, and my mom is Mohawk and Oneida. I think they especially wanted to make what they considered a better life for their kids, so they moved to the suburbs of western New York." How is making a life, I wondered, different from making it better? To go off Morningstar's example, perhaps the question is moot, the difference nonexistent, perhaps to make a life is itself to make it better.

"I went to an all white school and was brought up in this very white way: to just sort of blend in. Don't tell people you're natives, just be safe and pass. And that's really, I think in the back of my mind, what I was attempting. But by being visibly Indigenous, I didn't fool anybody. So there was taunting, ostracization—all those things when I was young. It wasn't until I was in my late teens, early twenties, that I started really going back to my culture and I went back to Six Nations for the first time on my own. That's where we started doing a lot of genealogy." There, she made a discovery that foreshadowed her pre-NEFOC work as a photojournalist and then as an archivist at the Deyohahá:ge (Two Roads) repository of Six Nations Polytechnic—"We found all these photos of our great-great-grandfather. We're not really sure who he was or where he came from, but what we could see was that he was visibly Black-identifying." Yet "my aunties," she said, even in the teeth of all the evidence, "actually denied that he was Black. It didn't make sense to me, that they could be native, full blood Mohawk women, and anti-Black. . . . Racialized trauma is complex, manifests in so many ways."

One of those manifestations was especially hard to hear, but for Morningstar it was germinal. Regarding how she came to rethink the work of health care, she talked about her mother, and brought home the meaning, as well as the urgency, of rematriation. "My mother was deeply afraid to go to the hospital or the doctor's and had something called 'white coat syndrome.' I remember fighting with her to get her to go get health care. She said she would disown us, me and my sisters, if we pushed her any further. We were watching her deteriorate with health issues we couldn't pinpoint. We'd sneak her to the doctor's, but every time she would go, she would end up in the emergency room. Her blood pressure would skyrocket because of the anxiety."

"Adding injury to injury," I sighed.

"Yeah, it was let's-make-sure-you-don't-have-a-stroke versus let's-get-your-pap-done. She could never do basic preventative care, could never get past an acute situation." Prevention holds no meaning when a crisis persists.

"I remember hearing somebody in my family say, if you go to the hospital, you're only coming out in a pine box. That was the general consensus, the family narrative. It wasn't until I was helping set up the Indigenous Archive at Six Nations, that—." There she cut off the rest of her sentence as though suddenly stumbling on a trapdoor. When she returned, she said the meaning and the weight of what her mother carried, "where it all came together for me," came down to a single word. She was translating family and historical documents, a whole collection from the Smithsonian, and she realized there wasn't a word for "hospital" in any of the languages of the Six Nations. "The closest was a word that meant, and it really hit me hard, 'you will never come out of that place.' The translation for hospital is 'the place you will not come out of alive,' or 'the place you go to die.'"

"My mom ended up getting really sick with what she thought was pneumonia. It turned out to be stage four ovarian cancer. And she was gone within a week. It was this moment of my mom needlessly dying because of intergenerational trauma that informed not just her life, but all of our lives, that catalyzed me to want to make a change." From then on, she said, "I wanted to figure out, How do I help? How do I honor all of those things in me?" Morningstar convinced me that those things in her, in us, in "our lives," are a knot between two pulls: grief and possibility, dispossession and chance. And she navigates this knot with grace and gratitude.

The Trust of the Trust

Morningstar's heritage of love and loss has taught her the importance of cultivating trust, a term in NEFOC's name that signifies another way they're bending the law on its back. The term is at the end of their name for a reason: it is the end toward which all their actions bend. And there, at the end, is where they begin. "Being a land trust, what we're working on right now isn't so much the land but the trust."

They have started an Indigenous Consultation and Partnerships Program, through which they create new forms of solidarity, of alongsidedness, with Indigenous nations. But the name of the program, as Morningstar suggested, is a bit of a misnomer. "We need to have achieved not just consultation with Indigenous people, but actual partnerships and relationships, deep, deep relationships and reciprocal agreements with the Indigenous nations of these territories." Her co-directors are key in this endeavor. Çaca Yvaire, director of the Community Conservation Program, conducts a "BIPOC land access convergence," a space for community to gather and collaboratively look at their legal tools, learning how to "manipulate" for everyone's specific needs. Dr. Gabriela Pereyra is the Land Network Weaver. She facilitates lease and purchase agreements, supplies resources to education and financing, and generally ensures everyone has the tools they need to thrive on the land. Together they are facilitating up to fifty leases for farmers of color over the next five years, as well as providing fellowships for farmers to join them. For the past two years "what we've [been] doing is just setting up the organization and the governance of the organization." They've been working with Harvard Law, as well as Suffolk Law's Human Rights and Indigenous People's Clinic, because governance and organization "are the most important parts to understanding how this multicultural, intergenerational collective will work together."

It became clearer to me as she spoke that what makes creating trust particularly hard work is as much pragmatic as it is existential. Given their structural relationship to coloniality, it is an issue not only of demonstrating good faith but of finding ways to make good on it. "The bodies and the labor and the land of our peoples undergird the system—they haven't created it but they have given it the strength it needs." As they work to undermine extractive and transactional relationships among themselves, they must all do the same in their relationship to ongoing colonial terror. Reminiscent, like Hamer, of Joy James's "Captive Maternal," a figure for whom the work of survival unavoidably sustains the system she survives, NEFOC's question is the following: How do we exercise our strength without strengthening the system under which we labor?[5] Keenly aware of the conceptual, on-the-ground difficulty of this conundrum, Morningstar avoids definitive solutions to it. She partakes in the much harder work of "holding" it, "holding all that," while "knowing we will have to create the mechanisms as we go." The magic of holding, Morningstar seemed to say, is that the more one holds the less it holds you.

Morningstar's mother bore the last name of "Schuler," and she dreamt of a village she called Schuylerville. "She lived in a house that was really dilapidated and honestly unsafe for anybody to live in. And she had this fantasy of buying a big piece of land that she could put a house on, that I could put a house on, and my aunties and our friends and everyone could have a place to live . . . drumming and singing and dancing and celebrating culture, multiple cultures." For Morningstar, NEFOC's flagship community, though not yet established, has already begun as her mother's Schuylerville, a place where the trust meets the trust, where all the dimensions of their vision gains ground, "a place to live."

Living into the Present

The expression you're most likely to hear in discussions on time for lives in peril is "living into the future." Living into the future is usually expressed as what's at stake. Morningstar proposes a "living into . . . the present." She was stating the imperative of "not just picking up our ancestors' ways of being, doing, and knowing from the past, but really living into them in the present." In truth, I couldn't make sense of the phrase at first, "living into the present." All I knew is that it struck me as something more than "not linear," which is how she described the way she sees the world. It is altogether different from "living into the future." The second suggests succession and continuity, a horizon we approach but never quite touch; the first, surplus and simultaneity, a horizon we touch because it's always touching us. If one is anticipation, the other is surprise.

When she hung up the phone, I thought, how do you live "into" something you can't live without? How do you live into what's always right here? Unless, of course, it's not. Then I thought about the word "into," that it also means "in to," as in toward something else. So what fascinates me now about the idea—really, the practice—is that in it the present is constantly becoming new, when we usually give that boast to the future. What fascinates me, too, is that the idea suggests a gap between the time we're living in and the time we're living into. How else can we think of "living into the present"? How can we even picture it without a certain gap between the living and the present that the living ever fills and perhaps, by degrees, even overflows? The living, the present—each unfolds like a dream, internally differentiated to infinite regress. I thought of a school of birds pooling and pooling into the sky.

It seems, doesn't it, like there's more openness to difference with a living into the present (cultural difference, personal difference, a whole proliferation of difference) than there is with the common call to live another day, to keep on keeping on. If living into the future assumes an essentially enduring self, a self identical to itself on which the living is carried, then living into the present assumes an endlessly ending self. This, I thought with a touch of glee, is what radical selflessness is; this, the expanse I felt talking to Morningstar: a self that proliferates with oceanic complexity in order to meet a present just as large. To live into the present is to forget about progress, the hero's quest for brighter days, and to think instead of excavating what's here, on this land, in this place, now, losing ground, yes, but gaining it back, too.

The Forethought of Grief

At the end of the interview, I asked her how she deals with the pessimism growing around radical political projects today. I asked her if she thinks about the prospect of failure, the historical precedent of boobytraps and supremacist backlash. She did not answer the question directly, so for days I thought I botched it. But reflecting on her practice of what might be called presencing, not to be confused with the complacency of presentism, I realized that my question makes no sense in her sense of time. I realized that, maybe, the power of living with and on remains is just that: they remain.

Perhaps it is the fact that *every* thing we do remains, that we the underprivileged are doomed to fly, perhaps it is the fact that the hereafter is here so if we are the heres we are also the afters—perhaps it is this that brought Morningstar to joy. Beginning almost in midsentence, as though it had been spinning in the back of her mind the entire time we spoke, she said (as I'll quote again), "but then there's also just watching the joyful, celebratory brilliance of global Indigenous knowledge and resituating that stewardship, in these territories in ways that are not just picking up our ancestral ways of being, doing, and knowing from the past, but really living into them in the present." A loss that remains is also not a loss. It is a loss and yet it is not, a fact with staggering effects on one's relation to time.

"The biggest hurdle," she expounded, on living this kind of time, is a superficial impatience. She names this impatience "white supremacy culture," which hides, she said, in temporalities of accumulation. Recalling sociologist Avery Gordon's idea of "urgent patience,"[6] of having no time to waste but having to take our time, Morningstar asked, "How do we constantly keep this need for production in check, this pace setting, this urgency? . . . 'Where's the land? Where's the money? Where is all this, and why hasn't it happened yet?' My attitude is to say let's pump the brakes for a minute. It took hundreds of years to get to this place. It's not going [to] take us two to get it back. And we're not turning back the dial either." To boot, she said, "we're trying to create something completely new."

In case I'd misinterpret this newness as an endlessness, an old and uncomplicated immortality, Morningstar told me of another register in which this timeliness operates: planned obsolescence, with and against its capitalist frame. "I remember writing a grant a while ago, when we first started, and wrote that the goal for the land trust is to basically work itself into obsolescence, not to exist anymore, because we've changed the landscape so much. The person who was giving the feedback on the grant said, 'But land trusts are supposed to be forever.' And while I agree with that, its current form, in this current day and age, in this current political environment, in this system we have right now, the goal is to become obsolete because we have catalyzed together, with other collective forces, so much change that this current system no longer exists." I was struck by how a definitive embeddedness (notice how many times she used the word "in," notice her preference for "with") forms the way to initiate a definitive end. Trust and trust, remains and remains, grief and possibility—ends, extremes, literally meet in NEFOC, whose greatest message may be, why not live into them? Living into the present is where liberation may lie.

We ended the interview where we began, which made a lucky contrast to Morningstar's practice of beginning where we end. I had heard her recite a poem from environmentalist Wendell Berry, "The Peace of Wild Things," in a keynote she gave in 2019 at the North American Biodynamic Conference. The poem is about how we grieve what hasn't even happened yet. I read her these lines and asked her what she thought.

> I come into the peace of wild things
> who do not tax their lives with the forethought
> of grief . . .

"Forethought of grief," I said, "it's a beautiful phrase, right?" "Yes," she said, "but sometimes that forethought can mire us in the past." It was then that I heard something click-click into sense. My question about possible failure, about possibly avoiding it, made no sense in Morningstar's sense of time because to anticipate what hasn't happened yet can only be to anticipate exactly what has, the reinstitution of a narrowly defined past under the guise of an even narrower future. Then she said something else. She thinks of grief as something not to avoid but to be grateful for. "If we're going to have the grief, what is it there to fuel?" So she starts each day "from a place of gratitude," grateful for the chance "to use our grief so that others don't have to."

Acknowledgments

Written with halting progress across many years, this book owes a million debts to my colleagues at the University of Illinois, who nurtured my work and gave me an intellectual home without which this book surely would not have surfaced. Candice Jenkins was a crucial mentor, who early on helped me entirely rethink the second half of the book. Chris Freeburg posed transformative questions that helped me clarify the overarching stakes. Siobhan Somerville helped me frame much of the project and gave me generous comments on multiple versions of the chapters. Patricia Loughran offered crucial feedback at crucial junctures. And Susan Koshy was a stalwart support and rigorous reader throughout. The Americanist Workshop organized by Derrick Spires helped me hone the bigger historical picture, and Derrick provided line by line edits on early drafts of my second chapter, twice. For their encouragement and an unwavering support, I also thank Vicki Mahaffey, Bob Parker, Bob Markley, and Ron Bailey. Michael Rothberg helped me shape my book proposal. Elizabeth Hoiem and the other members of the First Book Writing Group, its senior faculty readers Carol Symes and Craig Kosoflsky, and its intellectual and organizational lodestar Maria Gillombardo helped me write my fellowship applications and meet my biggest deadlines.

For helpful comments on early drafts, I thank Jennifer Doyle, the Marxism for Artists reading group, Erica Edwards, and Evie Shockley. For nourishing the book with vibrant conversation and intellectual fellowship, I'd like to thank Jean-Christophe Cloutier, Jarvis McInnis, Julius Fleming, David Lloyd, Ronald Williams, Kinohi Nishikawa, Clare Callahan, Joseph Entin, Ben Lerner, and Tyehimba Jess.

This book leans against a stack of inestimable influence. No scholar has left a greater imprint on my approach to archival research and to close reading than Brent Edwards. The way he funnels out a small turn of phrase into big turns in the diaspora, the depth and spread of his perspective—whatever rigor I have I owe to him. Brent pointed me to indispensable books that changed the course of the project for the better. Six years later he helped me think through my title.

Then there are books I never mention, but whose style gave me new ways of seeing and being in the historical record. There are really too many to name, but some mark inception points to the way I wrote and thought through my chapters. I could not have even started this project without the language and methodology of Hartman's *Scenes*. Dellilo's *Underworld*, Pynchon's *Gravity's Rainbow*, Girmay's *Kingdom Animalia* and *The Black Maria*, Sebald's *Emigrants*, and Faulkner's *Light in August* all at pivotal moments stretched my imagination and helped me keep the writing going by bringing fun to the page. I couldn't have born even a fraction of the weight of what my actors were up to, let alone the weight of what I was trying to think, without the play and perspective these books provided.

I could not have completed this book without the support of fellowships and grants. My greatest gratitude goes to the UNCF Mellon Foundation and the entire Mellon community. Cheryl Wall's Postdoctoral program at Rutgers not only brought me into her incredible mentorship, but also into the colloquium series at the Center for Race and Ethnicity led by Mia Bay. All provided feedback on early drafts and forums in which to discuss them with the larger Rutgers community. I thank the Woodrow Wilson Fellowship Foundation who afforded me the leave I needed to finish much of the project. I thank the research board for their Multiracial Democracy Manuscript Workshop Award, through which I was able to workshop the complete draft of the book with Fred Moten and Roderick Ferguson. Fred and Rod offered a treasure trove of insights that centrally guided the revision process. Equally central has been the way their work inspires me and stretches my imagination.

An early version of chapter 2 appeared as "Planned Failure: George Schuyler and the Young Negroes Cooperative Guild," *American Quarterly* 72, no. 4 (2020): 853–79. I thank Mari Yoshihara for her kindness and cool, and I especially thank Paula Dragosh for her impressively sensitive editorial skills. I thank Sara Clugage and her editorial team at *Dilettante Army* for bringing out a version of "This Bridge Called the System" in their Winter 2021 issue. A section of chapter 1 appeared as "Necromance: A Commentary," *American Literary History* 31, no. 4 (2019): 829–39.

A special word of thanks goes to Lucas Church at UNC Press, and to Ron Williams for making the introduction. Lucas not only championed the manuscript from beginning to end but also helped me hone its language from his huge satchel of technical craft. More than that, Lucas has been a friend I could call at any time. For their generosity and care during the production process, I'd also like to thank Dylan White, Kim Bryant, Jamie McKee, and Kirsten Elmer. Thanks to Jessica Ryan for proofreading and to Paula Durbin-Westby for the index.

I am grateful to the archivists and librarians who helped me procure a wealth of documents, pointed me to other repositories, and overall provided a sense of community. Special thanks goes to Cheryl Beredo at the Schomburg Center, the all-star lineup at the Louis Round Wilson Special Collections Library at UNC, Susan Krueger at the Wisconsin Historical Society, Lisa Moore at the Amistad Research Center at Tulane, Howell Perkins at the Virginia Museum of Fine Art for the last-minute rush, and Monica White for helping me secure copyrights in the final hour.

Deepest debt of all, though, goes to Anna Hunt.

Notes

List of Manuscripts

Amistad Research Center, Tulane University, New Orleans, LA
    Fannie Lou Hamer Papers, 1966–78
    Free Southern Theater Records, 1963–78
Harvard University Archives, Student Folder, Graduate School of Education
Library of Congress, Washington, DC
    National Association for the Advancement of Colored People Papers
Martin Luther King Jr. Center for Nonviolent Social Change, Archives
    Department, Atlanta, GA
    SNCC Papers
Mississippi Department of Archives and History, Jackson, MS
    Fannie Lou Hamer Funeral (videotape)
    Fannie Lou Hamer Vertical File
    Patti Carr Black Film Collection
Moorland-Spingarn Research Center, Manuscript Division, Howard University,
    Washington, DC
National Archives for Black Women's History, Landover, MD
    Fannie Lou Hamer File
    National Council of Negro Women, Inc. Records, Audio Recordings and
    Transcriptions
Schomburg Center for Research in Black Culture, New York Public Library
    Ella Baker Papers, 1926–86
    Interreligious Foundation for Community Organization Records, 1966–84
    Jean Blackwell Hutson Research and Reference Division
    Ralph Bunche Papers, 1922–88
    Schuyler Family Photograph Collection, Photographs and Prints Division
Smithsonian Institution, Archive Center of the National, Museum of American
    History, Washington, DC
    Moses Moon Civil Rights Movement Audio Collection
Stanford University, Department of Special Collections and University Archives
    KZSU Project South interviews
Syracuse University, New York, Special Collections Research Center
    George Schuyler Papers, 1895–1977
University of California at Los Angeles, Special Collections
    Special Collection on Civil Rights Struggle and Black Movement in the
    United States 1950s to the present

University of Massachusetts Amherst Libraries, Special Collections and
University Archives
W. E. B. Du Bois Papers, 1877–1963
University of Southern Mississippi, Center for Oral History and
Cultural Heritage
Fannie Lou Hamer Files
WGBH Media Library and Archives, Brighton, MA
Hunger: Starvation in Affluent US (videotape)
The Wilson Library, University of North Carolina, Chapel Hill, NC
Delta Health Center Records, 1956–92
Floyd B. McKissick Papers, 1940–80
Jack Greiger Collection
John Hatch Collection
The Southern Historical Collection
Wisconsin Historical Society Archives, Madison, WI
Eric Smith Papers
Madison Measure for Measure Records, 1965–77
Sweet Family Papers, 1970–77

Introduction

1. "Co-operation Seen as Best Way Out," *Pittsburgh Courier*, August 1, 1931; George Schuyler, "Consumers' Co-operative Movement Gains in Support in This Country," *Atlanta Daily World*, February 3, 1948; Frank Crosswaith, "New Era of Cooperation Replacing Individualism," *Philadelphia Tribune*, July 11, 1929.

2. George Schuyler, "The Economic Outlook of the Negro," *Forum Quarterly*, December, 1932, 19–20, Schuyler Papers, box 6, Special Collections Research Center, Syracuse University.

3. Ben Fowlkes, *Cooperation: The Solution of the So-Called Negro Problem* (Birmingham, AL: Novelty Book Concern, 1907), 86.

4. Lester Spence, "Ella Baker and the Challenge of Black Rule," *Contemporary Political Theory* 19, no. 4 (2020): 551–72.

5. Brittney Cooper, *Beyond Respectability: The Intellectual Thought of Race Women* (Chicago: University of Illinois Press, 2017), 10.

6. It is still the basis for the definition of cooperatives offered by the International Cooperative Alliance.

7. Rochdale Equitable Pioneers' Society, *Rules of the Rochdale Equitable Pioneers' Society: Adopted at Special Meetings Called for That Purpose, Jan. 8th, Jan. 22nd, and Feb. 5th, 1877* (Rochdale: 1877), https://archive.org/details/rulesof rochdalee648roch/page/n3/mode/2up.

8. The typology of consumer, worker, or producer-owned cooperatives originated with Charles Ryle Fay, *Co-operation at Home and Abroad*, 3d ed. (London: P. S. King & Son, 1925).

9. Darlene Clark Hine, William C. Hine, and Stanley Harrold, *The African-American Odyssey*, 6th ed. (Upper Saddle River, NJ: Pearson Education, 2014), 126.

10. Bruce J. Reynolds, "Black Farmers in America, 1865–2000: The Pursuit of Independent Farming and the Role of Cooperatives," *United States Department of Agriculture* (2002), 6.

11. Denise Ferreira da Silva, *Toward a Global Idea of Race* (Minneapolis: University of Minnesota Press, 2007).

12. Barbara Ransby, *Ella Baker and the Black Freedom Movement: A Radical Democratic Vision* (Chapel Hill: University of North Carolina Press, 2003), 270.

13. Antonio Gramsci, *The Gramsci Reader: Selected Writings, 1916–1935*, trans. David Forgacs (New York: New York University Press, 2000), 333–34.

14. Gramsci, 334; Cedric J. Robinson, *The Terms of Order: Political Science and the Myth of Leadership*, ed. Erica R. Edwards (Chapel Hill: University of North Carolina Press, 2016), 203.

15. "The Voice of Protest: Ella Baker, Legend of the Rights Movement," Baker interview with Jacqueline Trescott, *Washington Post*, December 14, 1978, C23.

16. Patrizia Battilani and Harm G. Schröter, *The Cooperative Business Movement, 1950 to the Present* (New York: Cambridge University Press, 2012), 176; Omar H. Ali, *In the Lion's Mouth: Black Populism in the New South, 1886–1900* (Jackson: University Press of Mississippi, 2010).

17. Ali, *In the Lion's Mouth*, 76.

18. Elizabeth Hyde Botume, *First Days amongst the Contrabands* (Boston: Lee and Shepard, 1893), 17.

19. Roland Edgar Wolseley, *The Black Press, U.S.A*, 2nd ed. (Ames: Iowa State University Press, 1990), 86.

20. Steve Leiken argues that cooperatives were places to practice and model citizenship, combining a blend of "Christian triumphalism" and labor republicanism, which essentially means an "abiding faith in reason, natural law, and self-help" in *Practical Utopians: American Workers and the Cooperative Movement in the Gilded Age* (Detroit, MI: Wayne State University Press, 2005), 50; Ransby, *Black Freedom Movement*, 88.

21. Rosa Luxemburg, *Reform or Revolution and Other Writings* (Mineola, NY: Dover Publications, 2006), 47.

22. Charles Tilly, "From Interactions to Outcomes in Social Movements," in *How Social Movements Matter*, ed. Marco Giugni, Doug McAdam, and Charles Tilly (Minneapolis: University of Minnesota Press, 1999); Hagar Kotef, *Movement and the Ordering of Freedom: On Liberal Governances of Mobility* (Durham, NC: Duke University Press, 2015), 131.

23. Kotef, *Movement and the Ordering of Freedom*.

24. Mary Helen Washington, *The Other Blacklist: The African American Literary and Cultural Left of the 1950s* (New York: Columbia University Press, 2014); William J. Maxwell, *New Negro, Old Left: African-American Writing and Communism Between the Wars* (New York: Columbia University Press, 1999); Bill Mullen, *Popular Fronts: Chicago and African-American Cultural Politics, 1935–46* (Urbana: University of Illinois Press, 1999); Anthony Dawahare, *Nationalism, Marxism, and African American Literature between the Wars: A New Pandora's Box* (Jackson: University Press of Mississippi, 2003); James Edward Smethurst, *The New Red*

Negro: The Literary Left and African American Poetry, 1930–1946 (New York: Oxford University Press, 1999).

25. "Editorial," *Crisis* 17, no. 3 (January 1, 1919): 111.

26. Ali, *In the Lion's Mouth,* 51.

27. Lizabeth Cohen, *A Consumer's Republic: The Politics of Mass Consumption in Postwar America* (New York: Knopf, 2003).

28. Fannie Lou Hamer, "First," in *The Speeches of Fannie Lou Hamer: To Tell It Like It Is*, ed. Maegan Brook and Davis Houck (Jackson: University of Mississippi Press, 2011), 127; "New": W. E. B. Du Bois, "Next Steps," May 13, 1933, W. E. B. Du Bois Papers, MS 312, Special Collections and University Archives, University of Massachusetts Amherst Libraries, 9–10; "I want very much to start with him [W. C. Matney] as a nucleus[,] a movement for co-operation among American Negroes": W. E. B. Du Bois to James P. Warbasse, August 22, 1929, W. E. B. Du Bois Papers, MS 312, Special Collections and University Archives, University of Massachusetts Amherst Libraries.

29. Jeff Goodwin and James Jasper, "Editor's Introduction," in *The Social Movements Reader: Cases and Concepts* (Chichester, England: John Wiley and Sons, 2003), 4.

30. Belinda Robnett, *How Long? How Long? African American Women in the Struggle for Civil Rights* (New York: Oxford University Press, 1997).

31. Doug McAdam, *Political Process and the Development of Black Insurgency, 1930–1970*, 2nd ed. (Chicago: University of Chicago Press, 1999).

32. Aldon D. Morris, *The Origins of the Civil Rights Movement: Black Communities Organizing for Change* (New York: Free Press; Collier Macmillan, 1984), 81.

33. Deborah Gould, "Rock the Boat, Don't Rock the Boat, Baby: Ambivalence and the Emergence of Militant AIDS Activism," in *Passionate Politics: Emotions and Social Movements* (Chicago: University of Chicago Press, 2001), 135.

34. Robnett, *How Long? How Long?*, 10.

35. See Roderick A. Ferguson, *The Reorder of Things: The University and Its Pedagogies of Minority Difference* (Minneapolis: University of Minnesota Press, 2012), Kindle.

36. Myra Jehlen, "History before the Fact; Or, Captain John Smith's Unfinished Symphony," *Critical Inquiry* 19, no. 4 (1993): 690.

37. Zakiyyah Iman Jackson, *Becoming Human: Matter and Meaning in an Antiblack World* (New York: New York University Press, 2020), 212.

38. James to Martin Glaberman, "Letters on Organization," December 17, 1962, in *Marxism for Our Times: C. L. R. James on Revolutionary Organization*, ed. Martin Glaberman (Jackson: University Press of Mississippi, 1999), 77.

39. Robin D. G. Kelley, *Freedom Dreams: The Black Radical Imagination* (Boston: Beacon Press, 2002), 162.

40. Jacquelyn Dowd Hall, "The Long Civil Rights Movement and the Political Uses of the Past," *Journal of American History* 91, no. 4 (2005): 1233–63.

41. Charles Payne, *I've Got the Light of Freedom: The Organizing Tradition and the Mississippi Freedom Struggle* (Berkeley: University of California Press, 2007), 174.

42. Jessica Gordon Nembhard, *Collective Courage: A History of African American Cooperative Economic Thought and Practice* (University Park: Pennsylvania State University Press, 2014), 1.

43. Pierre Nora, "Between Memory and History: Les Lieux de Memoire," *Representations*, no. 26 (Spring 1989): 7–24, 7, 17.

44. David Scott, *Omens of Adversity: Tragedy, Time, Memory, Justice* (Durham, NC: Duke University Press, 2014), 6.

45. Elisa Gabbert, "The Unreality of Time," *Paris Review*, August 11, 2020, https://www.theparisreview.org/blog/2020/08/11/the-unreality-of-time/.

46. Carl Boggs, "Marxism, Prefigurative Communism, and the Problem of Workers Control," *Radical America* 6 (Winter 1977–78): 100.

47. Tina Campt, *Listening to Images* (Durham, NC: Duke University Press, 2017), 22.

48. Kara Keeling, *Queer Times, Black Futures* (New York: New York University Press, 2019), 89.

49. Joshua Chambers-Letson, "The Body Is Never Given, nor Do We Actually See It," in *Race and Performance after Repetition*, ed. Soyica Diggs Colbert, Douglas A. Jones, and Shane Vogel (Durham, NC: Duke University Press, 2020), 350. Kindle.

50. Keeling, *Queer Times, Black Futures*, 63.

51. Stephen Best, *None Like Us: Blackness, Belonging, Aesthetic Life* (Durham, NC: Duke University Press, 2018), 10; Jericho Brown, *The Tradition* (Port Townsend, WA: Copper Canyon Press, 2019).

Chapter 1

1. W. E. B. Du Bois to John B. Jefferson, April 16, 1918, W. E. B. Du Bois Papers, MS 312, Special Collections and University Archives, University of Massachusetts Amherst Libraries.

2. Formalized in 1919 following the Russian Revolution, the Bolshevik concept of "World Revolution" held that the success of socialism depended on the ability among workers of colonies and the first world to mutually and simultaneously assist national liberation struggles. See Bill Mullen, *Un-American: W. E. B. Du Bois and the Century of World Revolution* (Philadelphia: Temple University Press, 2015); Eric Porter, *The Problem of the Future World: W. E. B. Du Bois and the Race Concept at Midcentury* (Durham, NC: Duke University Press, 2010); Manning Marable, *W. E. B. Du Bois: The Black Radical Democrat* (Boulder: Paradigm Publishers, 2005).

3. Vaughn Rasberry, *Race and the Totalitarian Century: Geopolitics in the Black Literary Imagination* (Cambridge, MA: Harvard University Press, 2016), 205.

4. Slovoj Žižek, "How to Begin from the Beginning," in *The Idea of Communism*, ed. Costas Douzinas and Slavaj Žižek (London: Verso, 2010), 210.

5. Elton Glaser, "This Is Your," in *Winter Amnesties: Poems* (Carbondale: Southern Illinois University Press, 2000), 54.

6. Du Bois considered cooperative economics "the gateway to the colored millions of the West Indies, Central and South America. Here is the straight path to Africa, the Indies, China, and the South Seas." W. E. B. Du Bois, "The Winds of

Time," *Chicago Defender*, November 23 (1946), 15. "Gateway" rings of Frederick Douglass's famous phrase, "the blood-stained gates into slavery." It therefore rings of grief as well as opportunity, an opportunity to transvalue grief.

7. William Holmes, "The Leflore Massacre and the Demise of the Colored Farmers' Alliance," *Phylon* 34, no. 3 (1973): 267–74. Given the number of deaths (estimated by some reports as over a hundred) and the attack's rippling impact on the Alliance writ large, the Black press called this the "LeFlore Massacre," the white press downplayed it as a quelled "race war." As Holmes shows, the shootings, hangings, knifings, and so on by white vigilantes against LeFlore's Alliance leaders inspired other white planters in neighboring counties to stop the distribution of the *Colored Farmers Alliance Advocate*, along with the selling of goods or loaning of money by white merchants and lenders to Alliance members.

8. Ida B. Wells, "Malicious and Untruthful White Press," in *The Light of Truth: Writings of an Anti-Lynching Crusader*, ed. Mia Bay (New York: Penguin, 2014), 75. In the introduction to the edition, Mia Bay observes the offense of the lynched proprietors (president, manager, clerk, and others) "seems to have been the success of the store, which competed directly with a white-owned store across the street" (xxiv). That this lynching was the first to occur in Memphis highlights the particularly potent threat cooperatives posed to racial capital.

The People's Grocery was incorporated as an employee-owned, joint-stock company. Some economists consider this arrangement, the ability of the founding members to sell their membership shares to future members, a solution to the problem of under-investment. The founding members have an incentive to invest because they can leave with some future returns on the investment. I mention this because over and above competition, under-investment is frequently blamed for the ephemerality of cooperatives, but the hypothesis is increasingly being debunked. See Saul Estrin and Derek Jones, "The Determinants of Investment in Employee-Owned Firms: Evidence from France," *Economic Analysis* 1, no. 1 (1998): 17–28; Fathi Fakhfakh, Virginie Perotin, and Monica Gagao, "Productivity, Capital and Labor in Labor-Managed and Conventional Firms," *Industrial and Labor Relations Review* 65, no. 4 (2012): 847–79.

9. W. E. B. Du Bois, ed., *Economic Cooperation among Negro Americans* (Atlanta: Atlanta University Press, 1907), 105.

10. W. E. B. Du Bois, "Cooperation," *Crisis* 19, no. 4 (February 1920): 171.

11. W. E. B. Du Bois to John Hope, qtd. in David Levering Lewis, *W. E. B. Du Bois: A Biography* (New York: Holt Paperbacks, 2009), 312.

12. Sylvia Lyons Render, "Afro-American Women: The Outstanding and the Obscure," *Quarterly Journal of the Library of Congress* 32, no. 4 (October 1975): 306–21, 315.

13. W. E. B. Du Bois, "A New Creed for American Negroes," ca. October 5, 1935, W. E. B. Du Bois Papers, MS 312, Special Collections and University Archives, University of Massachusetts Amherst Libraries. Committee on Cooperation; Proposed scheme of co-operation among American Negroes, ca. 1918, W. E. B. Du Bois Papers, MS 312, Special Collections and University Archives, University of Massachusetts Amherst Libraries; W. E. B. Du Bois to Julius Rosenwald Fund, February 27,

1936, W. E. B. Du Bois Papers, MS 312 Special Collections and University Archives, University of Massachusetts Amherst Libraries.

14. "Editorial," *Crisis* (September 23, 1918).

15. W. E. B. Du Bois to R. R. Wright Jr., August 24, 1918, W. E. B. Du Bois Papers, MS 312, Special Collections and University Archives, University of Massachusetts Amherst Libraries.

16. Cooperative League of America to W. E. B. Du Bois, August 22, 1918, W. E. B. Du Bois Papers, MS 312, Special Collections and University Archives, University of Massachusetts Amherst Libraries.

17. C. W. Banton to W. E. B. Du Bois, September 11, 1918, W. E. B. Du Bois Papers, MS 312, Special Collections and University Archives, University of Massachusetts Amherst Libraries; Lee J. Martin to Negro Co-operative Guild, October 12, 1918, W. E. B. Du Bois Papers, MS 312, Special Collections and University Archives, University of Massachusetts Amherst Libraries. Here Du Bois mentioned with urgency, "people had been writing in to find out more."

18. George W. Mitchell to W. E. B. Du Bois, October 19, 1918, W. E. B. Du Bois Papers, MS 312, Special Collections and University Archives, University of Massachusetts Amherst Libraries.

Charles E. Lane, Letter from Charles E. Lane to W. E. B. Du Bois, October 21, 1918, W. E. B. Du Bois Papers, MS 312, Special Collections and University Archives, University of Massachusetts Amherst Libraries.

19. Amenia Conference Leaflet, August 1925: "We all believed in thrift, we all wanted the negro to vote, we all wanted the laws enforced." W. E. B. Du Bois, *Dusk of Dawn: An Essay Toward an Autobiography of a Race Concept* (London: Oxford University Press, 2014), 243: "All shades of opinion." In the report for what would become the NAACP, Chairman William Hates Ward wrote, "From the outset this committee was composed of white and colored people alike, and represented the most varied opinions; all agreed only in the feeling that no one of the great efforts now being made by the Negroes or by whites in their behalf of all of them put together fully responded to the needs of the situation." "Preface," *Proceedings from the National Negro Conference* (New York: National Negro Conference, 1909). Du Bois corroborates this account in *Dusk of Dawn*, 223–25.

20. W. E. B. Du Bois, "Opinion of W. E. B. Du Bois," *Crisis* 17, no. 1 (November 1918): 10.

21. C. W. Banton to W. E. B. Du Bois, September 11, 1918, W. E. B. Du Bois Papers, MS 312, Special Collections and University Archives, University of Massachusetts Amherst Libraries. W. E. B. Du Bois to C. W. Banton, September 25, 1918, W. E. B. Du Bois Papers, MS 312, Special Collections and University Archives, University of Massachusetts Amherst Libraries.

22. Du Bois, "Opinion of W. E. B. Du Bois," 10.

23. Richard Sims to W. E. B. Du Bois, October 26, 1918, W. E. B. Du Bois Papers, MS 312, Special Collections and University Archives, University of Massachusetts Amherst Libraries.

24. Richard Sims to W. E. B. Du Bois, January 6, 1919, W. E. B. Du Bois Papers, MS 312, Special Collections and University Archives, University of Massachusetts

Amherst Libraries; for more on Jones Scott and these clubs, see *History of Education in West Virginia*, prepared under the direction of the State Superintendent of Schools (Charleston: Tribune Printing Company, 1907), 267.

25. For all the elitism that leached his vision, Du Bois was trying in this sector to see more clearly. In his study of German socialists at the University of Berlin (1896), he had noted a portable lesson: "curiously and yet naturally, the greatest foe of this socialistic state is the Social-Democratic Party of today, and this for the sole reason that Germany today in spite of reform, remains at bottom paternalistic and aristocratic." W. E. B. Du Bois, "The Socialism of German Socialists," ca. 1896, W. E. B. Du Bois Papers, MS 312, Special Collections and University Archives, University of Massachusetts Amherst Libraries, 26.

26. Jones Scott, "The Progress of the Huntington Negro," YMCA Speech, February 26, 1911, 10, 3. Speech in possession of author and Fain Cicero. Reprinted with permission.

27. John H. Pilgrim to W. E. B. Du Bois, August 19, 1918, W. E. B. Du Bois Papers, MS 312, Special Collections and University Archives, University of Massachusetts Amherst Libraries.

28. W. E. B. Du Bois to John H. Pilgrim, October 7, 1918, W. E. B. Du Bois Papers, MS 312, Special Collections and University Archives, University of Massachusetts Amherst Libraries.

29. W. E. B. Du Bois to Twentieth Century Fund, February 13, 1941, W. E. B. Du Bois Papers, MS 312, Special Collections and University Archives, University of Massachusetts Amherst Libraries.

30. Bert M. Roddy to W. E. B. Du Bois, July 17, 1918, W. E. B. Du Bois Papers, MS 312, Special Collections and University Archives, University of Massachusetts Amherst Libraries.

31. Jessica Gordon Nembhard, *Collective Courage: A History of African American Cooperative Economic Thought and Practice* (University Park: Pennsylvania State University Press, 2014), 88.

32. W. E. B. Du Bois, "Roddy's Citizens' Co-operative Stores," *Crisis* 19, no. 2 (December 1919): 48–49.

33. Bert M. Roddy, "The Roddy Chain of Grocery Stores" (speech), *Report of the Twentieth Annual Convention of National Negro Business League*, St. Louis, MO (August 1919), University Publications of America, microfilm, 122.

34. Fred Moten, "Uplift and Criminality," in *Next to the Color Line: Gender, Sexuality, and W. E. B. Du Bois*, ed. Susan Gillman and Alys Weinbaum (Minneapolis: University of Minnesota Press, 2007), 336, 337.

35. Moten, 338.

36. W. E. B. Du Bois to Ira Latimer, February 26, 1932, W. E. B. Du Bois Papers, MS 312, Special Collections and University Archives, University of Massachusetts Amherst Libraries; Nembhard, *Collective Courage*, 128.

37. My description is inspired by Naomi Rosenthal and Michael Schwartz's use of the term "federal movement organization," a pluripresent structure that "coordinates activity in more than one locale, from a headquarters that is not proximate to all of the local activities. It usually has a constitution (or the equivalent), a defined

purpose, a hierarchy of governance, and a routinized method of acquiring resources necessary for survival—in short, all the attributes of a formal organization." Naomi Rosenthal and Michael Schwartz, "Spontaneity and Democracy in Social Movements," in *International Social Movement Research, Vol. 2* (JAI Press, 1989), 33–59, 44.

38. Burt M. Roddy, "A Bank Fails for a Million: In Memphis 'Down in Dixie,'" ca. 1928, W. E. B. Du Bois Papers, MS 312, Special Collections and University Archives, University of Massachusetts Amherst Libraries, 9.

39. Samuel Keiser, "Unsubdued," *Illinois Central Magazine* 1, no. 1 (July 1912): 86.

40. Keiser, 123.

41. For a discussion on provisions against demutualization, see Virginie Perotin, "The Performance of Worker Cooperatives," in *The Cooperative Business Movement, 1950 to the Present*, ed. Patrizia Battilani and Harm Schroeter (Cambridge: Cambridge University Press, 2012), 195–221.

42. Roddy, "The Roddy Chain of Grocery Stores," 123.

43. Carlo Borzaga and Ermanno Tortia, "Cooperation as Co-ordination Mechanism: A New Approach to the Economics of Cooperative Enterprise," in *The Oxford Handbook of Mutual, Co-operative, and Co-owned Business*, ed. Jonathan Michie, Joseph R. Blasi, and Carlo Borzaga (Oxford: Oxford University Press, 2017), 68.

44. W. E. B. Du Bois to Burt M. Roddy, March 6, 1918, W. E. B. Du Bois Papers, MS 312, Special Collections and University Archives, University of Massachusetts Amherst Libraries. Elsewhere Du Bois emphasized this axiom over accepting the discomfort of being "particularly disgruntled because the stores do not carry the particular brand of goods he likes, or because the clerk is not quite [as] polite as he might be, or someone is served before him or out of turn . . . or even possibly in some cases paying higher prices." W. E. B. Du Bois, "Forum of Fact and Opinion," *Pittsburgh Courier*, August 28, 1935, 11. That is quite a barrage of inconveniences, which underscores the meta-metaphysical or para-ontological import of the store.

45. Du Bois to Roddy, March 6, 1918.

46. Roddy, "The Roddy Chain of Grocery Stores," 123.

47. Andre Gorz, *The Critique of Economic Reason* (London: Verso, 1989), 111.

48. R. P. Sims, "Cooperation," *Crisis* 20, no. 4 (August 1920): 167; Du Bois, *Dusk of Dawn*, 280.

49. Du Bois, *Dusk of Dawn,* 280.

50. W. E. B. Du Bois to Twentieth Century Fund, February 24, 1941, W. E. B. Du Bois Papers, MS 312, Special Collections and University Archives, University of Massachusetts Amherst Libraries.

51. Carl Boggs, "Marxism, Prefigurative Communism, and the Problem of Workers Control," *Radical America* 6 (Winter 1977–78): 100.

52. Nick Srnicek, *Inventing the Future: Postcapitalism and a World Without Work* (Verso Books, 2016), Kindle.

53. Luke Yates, "Rethinking Prefiguration: Alternatives, Micropolitics and Goals in Social Movements," *Social Movement Studies* 14, no. 1 (2015): 3.

54. Achille Mbembe, *On the Postcolony* (Berkeley: University of California Press, 2001), 16.

55. Stefano Harney and Fred Moten, *The Undercommons: Fugitive Planning and Black Study* (New York: Minor Compositions, 2013), 98.

56. Michael Hardt and Antonio Negri, *Assembly* (Oxford: Oxford University Press, 2017), 16, Kindle.

57. Hardt and Negri, 285–86.

58. Hardt and Negri, 69.

59. Rosenthal and Schwartz, "Spontaneity and Democracy in Social Movements," 33–59, 34.

60. Diana Coole and Samantha Frost, eds., *New Materialisms* (Durham, NC: Duke University Press, 2010), 87, Kindle.

61. Du Bois, *Dusk of Dawn*, 140.

62. William C. Matney, "Comments on the Work of W. C. Matney," February 3, 1928, W. E. B. Du Bois Papers, MS 312, Special Collections and University Archives, University of Massachusetts Amherst Libraries.

63. Roderick Ferguson, *The Reorder of Things: The University and Its Pedagogies of Minority Difference* (Minneapolis: University of Minnesota Press, 2012).

64. Harvard University Graduate School of Education, Student folders (graduate), Student folder of William Clarence Mattney: UAV 350.284, box 431, Harvard University Archives.

65. Du Bois, *Dusk of Dawn*, 140. For more on the state's reaction, see Charles McGehee and Frank Wilson, *Bluefield State College: A Centennial History (1895–1995)* (Bluefield, WV: Bluefield State College Press, 1995), 54.

66. W. E. B. Du Bois to W. C. Matney, August 22, 1929, W. E. B. Du Bois Papers, MS 312, Special Collections and University Archives, University of Massachusetts Amherst Libraries.

67. Wilfred Bion, *Experiences in Groups and Other Papers* (New York: Basic Books, 1961), 151.

68. Du Bois, *Negro in Business* (Atlanta: AMS Press, 1971), 15.

69. Bion, *Experiences in Groups and Other Papers*, 151.

70. W. C. Matney to W. E. B. Du Bois, February 24, 1930, W. E. B. Du Bois Papers, MS 312, Special Collections and University Archives, University of Massachusetts Amherst Libraries.

71. James P. Warbasse to W. E. B. Du Bois, March 17, 1930, W. E. B. Du Bois Papers, MS 312, Special Collections and University Archives, University of Massachusetts Amherst Libraries.

72. John Brown Jefferson to W. E. B. Du Bois, October 7, 1941, W. E. B. Du Bois Papers, MS 312, Special Collections and University Archives, University of Massachusetts Amherst Libraries. "Solve the problems" from John Brown Jefferson to W. E. B. Du Bois, December 12, 1941, W. E. B. Du Bois Papers, MS 312, Special Collections and University Archives, University of Massachusetts Amherst Libraries. The remaining quotes in this paragraph are from this archive.

73. Saidiya Hartman, "The End of White Supremacy, An American Romance," *BOMB*, June 5, 2020, https://bombmagazine.org/articles/the-end-of-white-supremacy-an-american-romance/.

74. W. G. Sebald, "A Comet in the Heavens: On Johann Peter Hebel," in *A Place in the Country*, trans. Jo Catling (New York: Random House, 2013).

75. W. E. B. Du Bois, *Darkwater: Voices from within the Veil* (New York: Harcourt, 1920), 269.

76. Du Bois, 270.

77. Hartman, "End of White Supremacy."

78. I am referring to Mbembe: "a current that carries individuals and societies from a background to a foreground, with the future emerging necessarily from the past and following that past, itself irreversible." Mbembe, *On the Postcolony*, 16.

79. A new creed for American Negroes, ca. October 5, 1935, W. E. B. Du Bois Papers, MS 312, Special Collections and University Archives, University of Massachusetts Amherst Libraries.

80. Coole and Frost, eds., *New Materialisms*, 71, Kindle.

81. Jacques Derrida, *Specters of Marx: The State of the Debt, the Work of Mourning, and the New International*, trans. Peggy Kamuf (New York: Routledge, 2006), 20, 249n11.

82. Laurence Gronlund, *The Cooperative Commonwealth* (Cambridge, MA: Harvard University Press, [1884] 1965), 245.

83. Adolph Reed, *W. E. B. Du Bois and American Political Thought: Fabianism and the Color Line* (Oxford: Oxford University Press, 1997), 54; Manning Marable, *W. E. B. Du Bois: Black Radical Democrat* (Boston: Twayne, 1986), 109. The challenges to this progressivist gloss have been numerous, sometimes numinous. See Charles Lemert, "The Race of Time: Du Bois and Reconstruction," *boundary 2* 27, no. 3 (2000): 215–48. Lemert's notation on a painfully recursive time that "races by only to revert, reverse, and revise itself" is no doubt the less than half-light in which much of Du Bois stands, from his suspensions of Marxist historical time in *Black Reconstruction* to his calligram the "present-past," the past that returns abruptly in the present, in *Souls of Black Folk*. In both these texts the breach of slavery is lived as a split infinitive, a now cut from a not yet, dangling in a dream.

84. Du Bois, *Dusk of Dawn*, 783.

85. Du Bois, 761.

86. Du Bois, "Nation within a Nation," in *W. E. B. Du Bois: A Reader*, ed. David Levering Lewis (New York: Henry Holt, 1995), 568, 569.

87. Du Bois, *Dusk of Dawn,* 706.

88. Du Bois, *Negro in Business*, 15.

89. Du Bois, "The Negro College," *Crisis* 40, no. 8 (August 1933): 175–77.

90. Du Bois, "Separation and Self-Respect," *Crisis* (March 1934): 85.

91. Du Bois, "Negro College."

92. Frederic Jameson, *The Seeds of Time* (New York: Columbia University Press, 1994), 60.

93. Kathi Weeks, *The Problem with Work: Feminism, Marxism, Antiwork Politics, and Postwork Imaginaries* (Durham, NC: Duke University Press, 2011), 202.

94. Du Bois, "Atlanta Creed, 7th Edition," ca. October 5, 1935, W. E. B. Du Bois Papers, MS 312, Special Collections and University Archives, University of Massachusetts

Amherst Libraries; Hardt and Negri, *Assembly* (New York: Oxford University Press, 2017); Mark W. Van Wienen, *American Socialist Triptych* (Ann Arbor: University of Michigan Press, 2014), 155.

95. W. E. B. Du Bois, *W. E. B. Du Bois on Asia: Crossing the World Color Line*, ed. Bill Mullen and Cathryn Watson (Jackson: University Press of Mississippi, 2005), 67.

96. Bill Mullen, *Un-American: W. E. B. Du Bois and the Century of World Revolution* (Philadelphia: Temple University Press, 2015), Kindle; Van Wienen, *American Socialist Triptych*, 158.

97. Jacques Derrida, "As If It Were Possible, 'Within Such Limits,'" in *Negotiations: Interventions and Interviews, 1971–2001*, ed. and trans. Elizabeth Rottenberg (Stanford: Stanford University Press, 2002), 361.

98. Nick Srnicek, *Inventing the Future.*

99. bell hooks, *All about Love: New Visions* (New York: Harper, 2000), 193, 192.

100. Jennifer Nash, *Black Feminism Reimagined: After Intersectionality* (Durham, NC: Duke University Press, 2019), Kindle.

101. Michael Hardt and Antonio Negri, *Commonwealth* (Cambridge, MA: Harvard University Press, 2009), 189; Alain Badiou with Nicholas Truong, *In Praise of Love*, trans. Peter Bush (New York: New Press, 2012), 27.

102. Baruch Spinoza, *Ethics*, trans. Michael Silverthorne and Matthew Kisner (New York: Cambridge University Press, 2018), 190.

103. Lewis Coser, *"Greedy Institutions": Patterns of Undivided Commitment* (New York: Free Press, 1974), 1. See Jeff Goodwin, "The Libidinal Constitution of a High-Risk Social Movement: Affectual Ties and Solidarity in the Huk Rebellion, 1946 to 1954," *American Sociological Review* 62, no. 1 (1997): 55. Sigmund Freud, *Group Psychology and the Analysis of the Ego* (La Vergne: Acheron Press, 2012), 22, Kindle.

104. Slavoj Žižek, *Incontinence of the Void: Economico-Philosophical Spandrels* (Cambridge, MA: MIT Press, 2017), 348.

105. Achille Mbembe, "Necropolitics," trans. Libby Meintjes, *Public Culture* 15, no. 1 (Winter 2003): 14, 40.

106. Mbembe, "Necropolitics," 36.

107. Jarvis C. McInnis, "'Behold the Land': W. E. B. Du Bois, Cotton Futures, and the Afterlife of the Plantation in the US South," *Global South* 10, no. 2 (2016): 70–98.

108. Toyohiko Kagawa, *Brotherhood Economics* (New York: Harper and Brothers, 1936), loc. 387, Kindle.

109. W. E. B. Du Bois, "The Economic Future of the Negro," *American Economic Association* 7, no. 1 (February 1906).

110. Charles Autrey and Roland Hall, *The Law of Cooperatives* (Chicago: The American Bar Association, 2009), 8–9.

111. Sara Smith's school was based on Calhoun Colored School, particularly according to Du Bois, on its "scheme of cooperative land buying." Founded in Alabama in 1892 by Mabel Dillingham and Charlotte Thornton, the Calhoun School was a venture Du Bois encountered while conducting a study of land tenantry in Lowndes County completed in 1906 for the U.S. Department of Labor, which later destroyed it.

112. W. E. B. Du Bois, *The Quest of the Silver Fleece: A Novel* (New York: Harlem Moon, 2004), 352.

113. Du Bois, 195, 198.

114. In an interview on the Great Dismal Swamp, archeologist Dan Sayers said, "They were using organic materials from the swamp. Except for the big stuff like cabins, it decomposes without leaving a trace." He then reveries: "Imagine it. Digging, chopping, bailing mud, working in chest-high water. One hundred degrees in summer, full of water moccasins, ungodly mosquitoes. Freezing cold in winter. Beatings, whippings. Deaths were fairly common." Richard Grant, "Deep in the Swamps, Archaeologists Are Finding How Fugitive Slaves Kept Their Freedom," *Smithsonian Magazine*, September 2016, https://www.smithsonianmag.com/history /deep-swamps-archaeologists-fugitive-slaves-kept-freedom-180960122/.

115. See Ralph Turner and Lewis Killian, *Collective Behavior*, 3rd ed. (Englewood Cliffs, NJ: Prentice-Hall, 1987), 8.

116. Du Bois, *Quest of the Silver Fleece*, 196.

117. Du Bois, 129.

118. Fred Moten, *Black and Blur* (Durham, NC: Duke University Press, 2016), 3; and Bill Brown, *Other Things* (Chicago: University of Chicago Press, 2015), 50.

119. Du Bois, *Quest of the Silver Fleece*, 105.

120. Eva Illouz, "Constructing the Romantic Utopia," in *Consuming the Romantic Utopia: Love and the Cultural Contradictions of Capitalism* (Berkeley: University of California Press, 1997).

121. Steven Seidman, "The Power of Desire of Eroticism and Love," in *Romantic Longings: Love in America, 1830–1980* (New York: Routledge, 1991).

122. Jean-Francois Lyotard, *Libidinal Economy*, trans. Iain Hamilton Grant (Bloomington: Indiana University Press, 1993), 215.

123. Lauren Berlant, *Desire/Love* (Brooklyn: Punctum Books, 2012), 86.

124. David Eng, "Colonial Object Relations," *Social Text* 34, no. 1 (March 2016): 7.

125. Eng, 11.

126. Harney and Moten, *Undercommons*, 105.

127. Harney and Moten, *Undercommons*, 106.

128. George Streator to W. E. B. Du Bois, April 18, 1935, W. E. B. Du Bois Papers, MS 312, Special Collections and University Archives, University of Massachusetts Amherst Libraries.

129. Du Bois, *Quest of the Silver Fleece*, 413.

130. W. E. B. Du Bois to George Streator, April 24, 1935, W. E. B. Du Bois Papers, MS 312, Special Collections and University Archives, University of Massachusetts Amherst Libraries.

131. Ian Baucom, *Specters of the Atlantic: Finance Capital, Slavery, and the Philosophy of History* (Durham, NC: Duke University Press, 2005), 217.

132. Erica Edwards, *Charisma and the Fictions of Black Leadership* (Minneapolis: University of Minnesota Press, 2013), 60; Claudia Tate was one of the first to open up this line of argumentation: "[Du Bois] seems to have experienced the emotional effect of laboring for racial uplift like the pleasure of libidinal satisfaction." Claudia Tate, *Psychoanalysis and Black Novels: Desire and the Protocols of Race* (New York: Oxford University Press, 1998), 51.

133. Du Bois, "The Economic Future of the Negro," 230.

134. David Levering Lewis, *W. E B. Du Bois, 1868–1919: Biography of a Race, 1868–1919* (New York: Owl Books, 1994), 159. Sigmund Freud, "Mourning and Melancholia," in *The Standard Edition of the Complete Psychological Works,* trans. James Strachey (London: Hogarth, 1974), 245.

135. W. E. B. Du Bois, "Separation," *Crisis* 1, no. 4 (1911): 20–21; W. E. B. Du Bois, "The Strength of Segregation," *Crisis* 7, no. 2 (1913): 84. "What can America do against a mass of people who move through their world but are not of it and stand as one unshaken group in their battle?" (84).

136. The image of the "vault" was seminal in Du Bois's short story "The Comet," where it appears in the first scene: "'Oh, that was Halley's,' said the president; 'this is a new comet, quite a stranger, they say—wonderful, wonderful! I saw it last night. Oh, by the way, Jim,' turning again to the messenger, 'I want you to go down into the lower vaults today.' The messenger followed the president silently. Of course, they wanted *him* to go down to the lower vaults. It was too dangerous for more valuable men. He smiled grimly and listened" (253).

137. Doug McAdam, *Political Process and the Development of Black Insurgency, 1930–1970,* 2nd ed. (Chicago: University of Chicago Press, 2010), 108.

138. W. E. B. Du Bois, "Winds of Time," *Pittsburgh Courier,* July 27, 1946, 15.

139. David Eng and David Kazanjian, "Introduction: Mourning Remains," in *Loss: The Politics of Mourning* (Berkeley: University of California Press, 2003), 3.

140. Eng and Kazanjian, 4.

141. For Freud mourning incurs a "loss of interest in the outside world—in so far as it does not recall him," "a loss of capacity to adopt a new object of love," "a turning away from any activity that is not connected to thoughts of him." Freud, "Mourning and Melancholia," 244.

142. David Levering Lewis, *W. E. B. Du Bois: Biography of a Race,* 89.

143. Josiah Royce, *The Basic Writings of Josiah Royce, Vol 2: Logic, Loyalty, and Community,* ed. John J. McDermott (New York: Fordham University Press, 2005), 968.

144. Sarah Ahmed, "Affective Economies," *Social Text* 22, no. 2 (2004): 117–39, 120.

145. For more on Du Bois's challenge of Spencerian positivism and idiosyncratic typologies, see Ronald A. T. Judy, "On W. E. B. Du Bois and Hyperbolic Thinking," *boundary* 2 27, no. 3 (2000): 1–36, 34.

146. W. E. B. Du Bois, *Some Efforts of American Negroes for Their Own Social Betterment: Report of an Investigation Under the Direction of Atlanta University; Together With the Proceedings of the Third Conference for the Study of the Negro Problems, Held at Atlanta University, May 25–26, 1898* (Atlanta: Atlanta University Press, 1898), 11.

147. W. E. B. Du Bois, 12.

148. W. E. B. Du Bois, 12.

149. W. E. B. Du Bois, 43.

150. W. E. B. Du Bois, 39–40.

151. W. E. B. Du Bois, "Sociology Hesitant," *boundary* 2 27, no. 3 (Fall 2000): 37–44, 39.

152. Emblematic of other studies like the *Philadelphia Negro* (1899), Du Bois's Lowndes County study was "a house to house canvas," where he decided to "go

personally and talk" with his subjects, "examine any documents they may have, and hear their stories" (Du Bois to The United States Bureau of Labor, October 1, 1906, MS 312, Special Collections and University Archives, University of Massachusetts Amherst Libraries).

153. W. E. B. Du Bois, "Sociology Hesitant," 44.

154. Fred Moten, "Uplift and Criminality," in *Next to the Color Line: Gender, Sexuality, and W. E. B. Du Bois*, ed. Susan Gillman and Alyn Eve Weinbaum (Minneapolis: University of Minnesota Press, 2007), n2.

155. W. E. B. Du Bois, *Some Efforts of American Negroes for Their Own Social Betterment*, 28.

156. "Editorial," *Crisis* 17, no. 3 (January 1, 1919): 111.

157. Oxford English Dictionary. He used the word "incident" as if he could foresee from an ashen plane without sound over bodies without tombs the after-light that fell from the lynching of Sam Hose in 1899 and struck from without his perception of his work. Remembering Hose, he was plangent: "at the very time when my studies were most successful, there cut across this plan, which I had as a scientist, a red-ray which could not be ignored." Sam Hose had been accused of murdering his landlord's wife, and Du Bois received the news of the lynching while walking to deliver at the Atlanta *Constitution* a "statement concerning the evident facts" of the case. Grief colored his work while he tried to recover not only the facts of cooperation, "the evident facts," but also, more broadly, the facts of Black life (*Dusk of Dawn*, 67).

Chapter 2

1. Ella Baker, "Oral History Interview with Ella Baker," by Casey Hayden and Sue Thrasher, *Southern Oral History Program Collection*, Interview G-0008, MP3, April 19, 1977, duration of quote 1:49:30–1:50:49. The official transcript inserts a comma after "you know" despite the absence of a pause in her speech, thus imposing a dolorous, wistful tone.

2. Raymond Williams, *Marxism and Literature* (Oxford: Oxford University Press, 1977), 144.

3. Nathaniel Mackey, "Cante Moro," *Black Out*, July 1991, https://my-blackout .com/2018/09/27/nathaniel-mackey-cante-moro/.

4. Nathaniel Mackey, *Nod House* (New York: New Directions, 2011), 34.

5. "Park Lincoln Apartments Pamphlet," New York Real Estate Brochures, item no. 1, call no. YR.1843.MH.001, Columbia University Archives.

6. George Schuyler to Mr. Cooley, "Consumers' Cooperation among American Negroes: A Summary of Accomplishments and Efforts before and since the Founding of the Young Negroes Co-operative League," 1932, box 8, folder 10, Ella Baker Papers, Schomburg Center for Research in Black Culture; Baker, "Youthful City Workers Turning to Cooperative Farming," *Amsterdam News*, May 11, 1935, 2.

7. NourbeSe Philip, MLA Presidential Plenary Presentation, Friday, January 8, 2021.

8. "What if black life is not so much about persistence? . . . What if persistence is but a tiny part of something else . . . something that cannot be trapped and held and certainly not by a word like persistence, something other, over there, can't you

see it, right there, on the horizon, splitting time?" "Exist, Insist, Resist," MLA Presidential Plenary Presentation, Friday, January 8, 2021.

9. "A place of settlement," *Oxford English Dictionary*. Pointing to the word's origins in the notion of empire, the *OED* quotes cartographer John Speed's *Theatre of the Empire of Great Britain*, which as the first atlas in English of the British Isles helped solidify the image of a coherent British empire. Fred Moten, MLA discussed such life as "ex-standing."

10. Fredric Jameson, *Valences of the Dialectic* (London: Verso, 2009), 392.

11. Deborah Gould, "Political Despair," in *Politics and Emotions: The Affective Turn in Contemporary Political Studies*, ed. Paul Hoggett and Simon Thompson (New York: Continuum, 2012), 95; David Scott, *Omens of Adversity: Tragedy, Time, Memory, Justice* (Durham, NC: Duke University Press, 2014), 6–11.

12. Nick Srnicek and Alex Williams, *Inventing the Future: Postcapitalism and a World Without Work* (New York: Verso, 2016), 5.

13. For defining a social movement as a longevity, "a sustained . . . challenge to authorities," see William Gamson and David Meyer, "Framing Political Opportunity," in *Comparative Perspectives on Social Movements: Political Opportunities, Mobilizing Structures, and Cultural Framings*, ed. Doug McAdam, John D. McCarthy, and Mayer Zald (New York: Cambridge University Press, 1996), 283; Kimberly Springer, *Living for the Revolution: Black Feminist Organizations, 1968–1980* (Durham, NC: Duke University Press, 2005), 15.

14. Jeffrey B. Leak ed., *Rac[e]ing to the Right: Selected Essay of George Schuyler* (Knoxville: University of Tennessee Press, 2001).

15. Marilyn Bordwell DeLaure, "Planting Seeds of Change: Ella Baker's Radical Rhetoric," *Women's Studies in Communication* 31, no. 1 (2008): 1–28, 16; Barbara Ransby, *Ella Baker and the Black Freedom Movement: A Radical Democratic Vision* (Chapel Hill: University of North Carolina Press, 2003), 143.

16. Charles Tilly, "Speaking Your Mind without Elections, Surveys, or Social Movements," *Public Opinion Quarterly* 47, no. 4 (1983): 464; Charles Tilly, "From Interactions to Outcomes in Social Movements," in *How Social Movements Matter*, ed. Giugni Marco, McAdam Doug, and Tilly Charles (Minneapolis: University of Minnesota Press, 1999).

17. Charles Tilly and Sidney G. Tarrow, *Contentious Politics*, 2nd rev. ed. (New York: Oxford University Press, 2015).

18. Ta-Nehisi Coates, *The Beautiful Struggle: A Father, Two Sons, and an Unlikely Road to Manhood* (New York: Spiegel & Grau, 2008).

19. Ta-Nehisi Coates, *We Were Eight Years in Power: An American Tragedy* (New York: One World, 2017), 14–15.

20. Elizabeth Povinelli, "On Suicide, and Other Forms of Social Extinguishment," in *Theory Aside*, ed. Jason Potts and Daniel Stout (Durham, NC: Duke, 2014), 84.

21. Brent Hayes Edwards, *Epistrophies: Jazz and the Literary Imagination* (Cambridge, MA: Harvard University Press, 2017), 28; Fred Moten, "Black Op.," *PMLS* 123, no. 5 (2008): 1745.

22. Barbara Ransby, *Ella Baker and the Black Freedom Movement: A Radical Democratic Vision* (Chapel Hill: University of North Carolina Press, 2003), 261.

23. Jeffrey B. Ferguson, *The Sage of Sugar Hill: George S. Schuyler and the Harlem Renaissance* (New Haven: Yale University Press, 2005), 123.

24. George Schuyler, "The Young Negro Cooperative League," *Crisis* 39, no. 1 (January 1932): 472; Ferguson, *The Sage of Sugar Hill*, 125; Floyd J. Calvin, "Let George Do It," *Philadelphia Tribune*, February 12, 1931, 9.

25. Baker, "Oral History Interview with Ella Baker," duration of quote 1:48:12–1:48:43.

26. Gayatri Chakravorty Spivak, "Critical Intimacy: An Interview with Gayatri Chakravorty Spivak," interview by Steve Paulson, 2016, https://lareviewofbooks .org/article/critical-intimacy-interview-gayatri-chakravorty-spivak/.

27. Flyer for joining YNCL, George Schuyler, "An Appeal to Young Negroes," 1930, box 2, folder 3, page 6, Ella Baker Papers, Schomburg Center for Research in Black Culture.

28. Baker, "Oral History Interview with Ella Baker."

29. Frank Crosswaith, "New Era of Cooperation Replacing Individualism," *Philadelphia Tribune*, July 11, 1929, 13.

30. Ella Baker, "Report of the First National Conference," box 2, folder 2, Ella Baker Papers, Schomburg Center for Research in Black Culture.

31. Editors, *Philadelphia Tribune,* May 26, 1932, 16.

32. "Introducing a Traitor," *Liberator* 3, no. 37 (July 1, 1932): 8.

33. George Schuyler, "The Economic Outlook for the Negro," *Forum Quarterly Review* (December 1932): 18–20.

34. Alex Gourevitch, *From Slavery to the Cooperative Commonwealth: Labor and Republican Liberty in the Nineteenth Century* (New York: Cambridge University Press, 2015), 17.

35. Vladislav Valentinov and Constantine Iliopoulos, "Economic Theories of Nonprofits and Agricultural Cooperatives Compared," *Nonprofit and Voluntary Sector Quarterly* 42, no. 1 (2013): 118.

36. Nathan Schneider, *Everything for Everyone: The Radical Tradition That Is Shaping the Next Economy* (New York: Nation Books, 2018), 6.

37. St. Clair Drake and Horace Cayton, *Black Metropolis: A Study of Negro Life in a Northern City* (New York: Harcourt, 1945).

38. Schuyler, "Consumers' Cooperation among American Negroes."

39. Schuyler, "Economic Outlook," 18–20.

40. "Arizona Negroes to Form Cooperative Organization," *Negro World* (New York, September 19, 1931), 8.

41. D. A. Cooper to Ella Baker, September 9 1944, box 2, folder 7, Ella Baker Papers, Schomburg Center for Research in Black Culture.

42. D. A. Cooper to Ella Baker.

43. Baker, "Oral History Interview with Ella Baker," duration of quote 01:52:09–01:52:12, transcript p. 42.

44. George Schuyler, An Open Letter to Young Negroes, c. 1930, Joann Grant Research Material, box 1, folder 17, Ella Baker Papers, Schomburg Center for Research in Black Culture, New York.

45. Schuyler, "Consumers' Cooperation among American Negroes," 3.

46. Ryan Glauser, "Race, Neighborhood, and Economic Self-Help: The Buffalo Cooperative Economic Society, 1934–1961," Undergraduate Senior Thesis, SUNY Buffalo State, Buffalo State Library Special Collections.

47. Mary Jenness, *Twelve Negro Americans* (New York: Friendship Press, 1936), 82.

48. Baker, "Oral History Interview with Ella Baker," duration of quote 01:52: 12–01:52:16, transcript p. 42.

49. Baker, "Oral History Interview with Ella Baker," duration of quote 1:52: 45–1:52:47, transcript p. 42.

50. In respect to the League's temporality, the phrase "something out" at first seems like a contradiction, but what I find fascinating is that it is not one. It is not say, a play of darkness and light, a meeting of pure opposites, but of semi- or, better yet, sometimes-opposites. The relationship between "something out" as an outage and "something out" as a release, between a finality and an extension, an end and creative act, is only sometimes an opposition. A sometimes-opposition is less a contradiction than it is a contrariness. In Aristotelian logic, a contradiction is a constant in both time and space. If it could speak it would say, "because one of these terms is always true, the other is always not." "Always" and "not-always" are its basic formal categories. As Paul North notes, because the law of noncontradiction "keeps eternal vigil over the line between the two ['always' and 'not-always']," because it allows no gradient, no in-between, no shades—because it really only speaks the higher principle of "always," the temporal structure of a contradiction is the same as eternity. A "contrariness," on the other hand, "admits degrees." This is again how Baker configures not in an eternity, but in an indefinite sempiternity, an eternity with a beginning and an indefinite end, and an indefinite since its definite ones are many.

51. David Toop, *Ocean of Sound: Ambient Sound and Radical Listening in the Age of Communication* (London: Serpent's Tail, 2018), 27.

52. C. L. R. James, "Dialectical Materialism and the Fate of Humanity," October 26, 2020 (1947), https://www.marxists.org/archive/james-clr/works/diamat/diamat47.htm.

53. If we were to give this movement a grammatical tense, we'd have to make one up, the past continuous complete, perhaps. None can capture it, only puns, coexistences, and grammatical breaks—yet another way this movement was at once im/possible.

54. Karen Brodkin, *Caring by the Hour: Women, Work, and Organizing at Duke Medical Center* (Urbana: University of Illinois Press, 1988); Belinda Robnett, *How Long? How Long? African American Women in the Struggle for Civil Rights* (New York: Oxford University Press, 1997).

55. The reliance on visible and familiar objects of sight in turn underlies the common explanation that movements arise when familiar and visible seats of power become available to actors. To address the context out of which a movement forms, sociologist Douglas McAdam theorized "opportunity structures": access to political and state institutions, McAdam contends, encourages actors to act.

56. Kevin Gillan, "Temporality in Social Movement Theory: Vectors and Events in the Neoliberal Landscape," *Social Movement Studies* 19, no. 5–6 (2020): 516–36, 520.

57. Paul North, *The Problem of Distraction* (Stanford: Stanford University Press, 2012), 157.

58. Katherine McKittrick, *Demonic Grounds: Black Women and the Cartographies of Struggle* (Minneapolis: University of Minnesota Press, 2006). For McKittrick, an "absented presence" is the erasure of Black feminist histories and geographies that are in fact here, and lived (33). It is the spatial conundrum of the "unrepresentability of black femininity" and of the "ways in which black women necessarily contribute to a re-presentation of human geography," a play on presence and absence (xxv–xxvi).

59. Harry McKinley Williams, "When Black Is Right: The Life and Writings of George Schuyler" (PhD diss., Brown University, 1988), 151.

60. Schuyler, "An Appeal."

61. Schuyler to "Colleague," November 1930, box 2, folder 2, Ella Baker Papers, Schomburg Center for Research in Black Culture.

62. Schuyler, "An Appeal," 5, 8.

63. "Schuyler's Movement 'Explains': Founder of Y.N.C.L. Plans to Retire as Soon as Program Is Definitely Launched," *Pittsburgh Courier*, February 28, 1931.

64. "Schuyler's Movement 'Explains.'"

65. Herbert Robinson, letter to *Crisis* editor, December 23, 1931, box 2, folder 2, Ella Baker Papers, Schomburg Center for Research in Black Culture.

66. Hannah Arendt, *On Revolution* (New York: Penguin, 2006), 224, Kindle.

67. Karl Marx, *Capital: Volume III*, trans. David Fernbach (London: Penguin, 1993), 571.

68. Henri Bergson, *Laughter: An Essay on the Meaning of the Comic* (Mansfield, CT: Martino, 2014), 143–44.

69. Chantal Mouffe and Ernesto Laclau, *Hegemony and Socialist Strategy: Towards a Radical Democratic Politics* (New York: Verso, 2001), 48–54.

70. Quoted in Barbara Ransby, "Ella Taught Me: Shattering the Myth of the Leaderless Movement," colorlines.com, June 12, 2015, www.colorlines.com/articles /ella-taught-me-shattering-myth-leaderless-movement.

71. Marina Sitrin, "Goals without Demands: The New Movements for Real Democracy," *South Atlantic Quarterly* 113, no. 2 (2014): 248; Heike Schaumberg, "'Disorganisation' as Social Movement Tactic: Reappropriating Politics during the Crisis of Neoliberal Capitalism," in *Marxism and Social Movements*, ed. Colin Barker et al. (Chicago: Haymarket Books, 2013), 378–400, 380. While being interviewed by Schaumberg, José "Pepino" Fernández, the leader of the former oil workers in Mosconi, Argentina, who formed the UTD ("Union of Unemployed Workers"), "pressed" her to state her definition of the UTD in light of his emphasis on their tactic of disorganization/unorganization. She told him she thought "it was definitely an organization, even if [she] struggled to define what kind," but "he rejected the idea" (389). That still she thought the tactic "seemed absurd" and retranslated it into a kind of order further begs the question of what kinds of common sense foreclose or forestall seeing such a tactic as necessary and sensible?

72. Stefano Harney and Fred Moten, *The Undercommons: Fugitive Planning and Black Study* (New York: Minor Compositions, 2013), 79.

73. Olga Cassels, "'Let's Get Going' on Consumers' Cooperation Plan, Writer Urges," *Pittsburgh Courier*, December 2, 1933, A2.

74. Judith Butler, *Undoing Gender* (New York: Routledge, 2004), 20.

75. Nick Tabor, "No Slouch," *Paris Review* (April 7, 2015): https://www.theparisreview.org/blog/2015/04/07/no-slouch.

76. A central tenet of Afro-Pessimism is that within the West the enslaved and the Black represent conditions of total fungibility and irreducible subjection. Operating as commodities rather than workers, they mark the absolute limit of unfreedom and the human and therefore share virtually synonymous subject-positions.

77. Lee Edelman, "Antagonism, Negativity, and the Subject of Queer Theory," *PMLA* 121, no. 3 (2006): 822; Christina Sharpe, *In the Wake: On Blackness and Being* (Durham, NC: Duke University Press, 2016), Kindle.

78. George Schuyler, "Views and Reviews," *Pittsburgh Courier*, October 25, 1930.

79. Nick Tabor, "No Slouch: The Widening Gyre of Heavy Handed Allusions to Yeats's 'A Second Coming'," *Paris Review* (April 7, 2015), https://www.theparisreview.org/blog/2015/04/07/no-slouch/.

80. Ella Baker, newsletter, box 2, folder 4, page 11, Ella Baker Papers, Schomburg Center for Research in Black Culture.

81. George Schuyler to Ella Baker, "My Dear Colleague," November 1930, box 8, folder 10, Ella Baker Papers, Schomburg Center for Research in Black Culture; Ella Baker, "My Dear Fellow Cooperator," ca. 1931, box 2, folder 3, Ella Baker Papers, Schomburg Center for Research in Black Culture.

82. Ferguson, *The Sage of Sugar Hill*, 122.

83. Kathi Weeks, *The Problem with Work: Feminism, Marxism, Antiwork Politics, and Postwork Imaginaries* (Durham, NC: Duke University Press, 2011), 135.

84. Quoted in Ransby, *Ella Baker and the Black Freedom Movement*, 95.

85. Bill Brown, *Other Things* (Chicago: University of Chicago Press, 2015), 51.

86. Ella Baker, syllabus, "The Consumer: His Problems and Their Remedies," box 2, folder 11, Ella Baker Papers, Schomburg Center for Research in Black Culture.

87. Julia Primoff to Ella Baker, April 30 1937, box 2, folder 11, Ella Baker Papers, Schomburg Center for Research in Black Culture.

88. Ella Baker, "Why Negroes Should Vote," handwritten speech, box 1, folder 6, Ella Baker Papers, Schomburg Center for Research in Black Culture.

89. Joanne Grant, *Ella Baker: Freedom Bound* (New York: Wiley, 1998), 230.

90. George Schuyler, "Views and Reviews," *Pittsburgh Courier*, November 15, 1930.

91. Cedric Robinson, *The Terms of Order: Political Science and the Myth of Leadership* (Chapel Hill: University of North Carolina Press), 160.

92. Harney and Moten, *Undercommons*, 76.

93. Harney and Moten, 76.

94. Schuyler, "Economic Outlook," 18–20.

95. George Schuyler, "Views and Reviews," *Pittsburgh Courier*, November 15, 1930.

96. George Schuyler, "The Negro Looks Ahead," *American Mercury* 19 (1930): 220.

97. Ella Baker, Newsletter (1932), box 2, folder 1, Ella Baker Papers, Schomburg Center for Research in Black Culture, Harlem, New York.

98. John Curl, *History of Work Cooperation in America: Cooperatives, Cooperative Movements, Collectivity, and Communalism from Early America to the Present* (Berkeley, CA: Homeward Press, 1980), 43.

99. Irvin Hunt, "Unco-Opted: Cooperative Economics as Counter-Surveillance, 1940–50," in *African American Literature in Transition*, ed. Lena Hill and Michael Hill (London: Cambridge University Press, 2019); see correspondence from Clark Foreman (adviser on economic status of Negroes) to George Schuyler, November 13, 1933, box 6, folder 9, Schuyler Family Papers, Schomburg Center for Research in Black Culture, Harlem, New York. Foreman to Schuyler (December 21): "It is probably a bad policy for the government to start such undertakings as you suggest. I believe, however, that the possibilities exist which could be taken advantage of if some group organized themselves in such a way as to fit into one of the existing schemes of Federal aid."

100. Lizabeth Cohen, *A Consumers' Republic: The Politics of Mass Consumption in Postwar America* (New York: Vintage, 2004), 19.

101. George Schuyler, "Views and Reviews," *Pittsburgh Courier*, November 15, 1930.

102. Hortense J. Spillers, "Interstices: A Small Drama of Words," in *Black, White, and in Color: Essays on American Literature and Culture* (Chicago: University of Chicago Press, 2003), 163.

103. Floyd B. McKissick Enterprises, Inc., *A Proposal to Develop Soul City: A New Town in North Carolina*, Submitted to the Department of Housing and Urban Development for Guarantees to Cover Land Acquisition and Development Costs, April 11, 1969, folder 6596, Floyd B. McKissick Papers, Special Collections, Manuscripts Department, Wilson Library, University of North Carolina, Chapel Hill, 13–14.

104. Floyd B. McKissick Enterprises, Inc., 16; Christopher Strain, "Soul City, North Carolina: Black Power, Utopia, and the African American Dream," *Journal of African American History* 89, no. 1 (2004): 57–74, 58.

105. Strain, "Soul City, North Carolina," 62.

106. Baker to Floyd McKissick, November 11, 1969, box 12, folder 19, Ella Baker Papers, Schomburg Center for Research in Black Culture; Floyd B. McKissick Enterprises, Inc., "Proposal to Develop Soul City," 1, 13.

107. Floyd B. McKissick Enterprises, Inc., *Proposal to Develop Soul City*, 5.

108. Ella Baker to Mr. Floyd B. McKissick, November 11, 1969, box 12, folder 19, Ella Baker Papers, Schomburg Center for Research in Black Culture, Harlem, New York.

109. Spillers, *Black, White, and in Color*, 167.

110. Strain, "Soul City, North Carolina," 64.

111. Floyd B. McKissick Enterprises, Inc., *Proposal to Develop Soul City*, 1.

112. Jared Sexton, *Black Men, Black Feminism: Lucifer's Nocturne* (Basel, Switzerland: Springer International, 2018), 94.

113. The intractability of their inherent contradiction some, on some level, already knew from the beginning. On a promotional brochure appeared a poem "Soul City: The Bold Alternative." "Imagine / A city without prejudice," it began.

"Where stars and moon are visible. . . . Well built, stylish housing. A master plan."
It depicts the city as straddling a tension that doubled as one between freedom from
patriarchy ("A master") and the seduction of it ("A master plan"). This tension then
occurs again under another between commerce and community:

> But not
> sterile a cold. For a city conceived with just an eye for bricks
> And mortar is a city without soul. Call the bold alternative
> SOUL CITY.

"Cold" contra "bold" and "bricks" contra "soul" are more than a nod to the bout
between spirituality and materialism in Du Bois's double-consciousness, which as
we know Du Bois plays out not between Black men and women, male chauvinism
and feminism, but between the Black men and their absented referent. Soul City
went right precisely where it went wrong: it attempted to resolve what brooks no
resolution.

114. Ella Baker, "Tent City: Freedom's Front Line," *Southern Patriot* 19 (February 1961): 1; Charles Payne, "Ella Baker and Models of Social Change," *Signs* 14, no. 4 (Summer 1989): 889.

115. Ella Baker, "Oral History," interview by John Britton, *Civil Rights Documentary Project*, transcript, June 19, 1968.

116. Michel Foucault, *The Order of Things: An Archaeology of the Human Sciences* (New York: Vintage Books, 1994), xxiv.

117. Denise Ferreira da Silva, "In the Raw," *E-flux* 93, (September 2018), https://www.e-flux.com/journal/93/215795/in-the-raw/.

118. Evenlyn Brooks Higgenbotham, *Righteous Discontent: The Women's Movement in the Black Baptist Church, 1880–1920* (Cambridge, MA: Harvard University Press, 1993). Here Higginbotham explored how Black propertied women and white philanthropists exhorted Black female laborers to adopt a similar ethic of thrift, to abstain from alcohol, premarital sex, and partying.

119. Saidiya Hartman, *Scenes of Subjection: Terror, Slavery, and Self-Making in Nineteenth-Century America* (Oxford: Oxford University Press, 1997), 127.

120. Clinton B. Fisk, *Plain Counsels for Freedmen in Sixteen Brief Lectures* (Boston: American Tract Society, 1886), 57.

121. Ella Baker, "Oral History," Interview by John Britton.

122. "Personal Thrift" by Ella Baker, n.d., box 2, folder 9, Ella Baker Papers, Sc MG 630, Schomburg Center for Research in Black Culture, Manuscripts, Archives and Rare Books Division, New York Public Library.

123. Fisk, *Plain Counsels for Freedmen*, 45.

124. Fisk, 12.

125. North, *Problem of Distraction*, 13.

126. Ferreira da Silva, "In the Raw."

127. Brent Edwards, *Epistrophies: Jazz and the Literary Imagination* (Cambridge, MA: Harvard University Press, 2017), 28.

128. Ella Baker to Lawrence Campbell, January 24, 1940, box 2, folder 2, page 16, Ella Baker Papers.

129. Edward Palmer Thompson, *The Making of the English Working Class* (New York: Open Road Integrated Media, 2016), Kindle.

130. George Schuyler, "On Being a Tired Radical," *Pittsburgh Courier*, December 10, 1932.

131. "Letter to George Schuyler," September 4, 1934, box 1, folder 13, Schuyler Family Papers, Schomburg Center for Research in Black Culture, Harlem, New York.

132. Jack Halberstam, *The Queer Art of Failure* (Durham, NC: Duke University Press, 2011), 174, 15, 28, 184, 3.

133. Søren Kierkegaard, *Concluding Unscientific Manuscript to Philosophical Crumbs*, trans. and ed. Alastair Hannay (New York: Cambridge University Press, 2009).

134. Alenka Zupančič, *The Odd One In: On Comedy* (Cambridge, MA: MIT Press, 2008), 135.

135. Zupančič, 140.

136. Quoted in Jessica Nembhard, *Collective Courage: A History of African American Cooperative Economic Thought and Practice* (University Park: Pennsylvania State University Press, 2014), 130.

137. Thomas Millay makes the same point about the entanglement between pragmatics and theory, the practicum and the dream, in "Always Historicize! On Fredric Jameson, the Tea Party, and Theological Pragmatics," *Other Journal: An Intersection of Theology and Culture*, no. 22 (2013): 46–57: "This is theory as pragmatics, not the philosophical school of pragmatism, but the practice of using theory to change the present world" (48).

138. For this idea I thank Germanist Anna Henke.

139. Ella Baker to Roy Wilkins, March 11, 1942, box 14, folder 16, Ella Baker Papers, Schomburg Center for Research in Black Culture.

140. Ransby, *Ella Baker and the Black Freedom Movement*, 80.

141. George Schuyler, "The Young Negro Cooperative League," *Crisis*, no. 38 (January 1932): 472.

142. Ella Baker, "Letter to the Editor 3," *Pittsburgh Courier*, May 9, 1931, p. A2

143. George Schuyler, "Views and Reviews," *Pittsburgh Courier*, November 23, 1935.

144. P. L. Prattis, "Questions and Answers," *Pittsburgh Courier*, May 15, 1937, a reply to a letter from Louise E. Kelley.

145. John Gruesser counters this scholarly bent by offering an interpretation of the novel as a trickster narrative. See Gruesser, "George S. Schuyler, Samuel I. Brooks, and Max Disher," Rev. of *Black Empire*, by George Schuyler, ed. Robert A. Hill and R. Kent Rasmussen, *African American Review* 27, no. 4 (1993): 679–86; Yogita Goyal, "Black Nationalist Hokum: George Schuyler's Transnational Critique," *African American Review* 47, no. 1 (2014): 26.

146. For framings of the novel as utopian romance, see Ivy Wilson, "'Are You Man Enough?' Imagining Ethiopia and Transnational Black Masculinity," *Callaloo* 33, no. 1 (2010): 265–77; Alexander Bain, "*Shocks Americana!* George Schuyler Serializes Black Internationalism," *American Literary History* 19, no. 4 (2007): 937–63; and Dora Ahmad, *Landscapes of Hope: Anti-Colonial Utopianism in America* (New York: Oxford University Press, 2009), 176–77.

147. Robert A. Hill and R. Kent Rasmussen, "Afterword," in *Black Empire* (Boston: Northeastern University Press, 1991), 261.

148. Hill and Rasmussen, 260.

149. George Schuyler, "Views and Reviews," *Pittsburgh Courier*, November 15, 1930.

150. George Schuyler, *Black Empire* (Boston: Northeastern University Press, 1991), 142.

151. Schuyler, 3.

152. Schuyler, 10.

153. For an illuminating treatment of Belsidus's disappearance, see Erica Edwards, *Charisma and the Fictions of Black Leadership* (Minneapolis: University of Minnesota Press, 2013).

154. Sigmund Freud, *Jokes and Their Relation to the Unconscious*, trans. James Strachey (New York: W. W. Norton, 1960), 222–23.

155. Schuyler, *Black Empire*, 6–7.

156. Zupančič, *Odd One In*, 137.

157. Karl Marx, *Capital: Volume I*, trans. Ben Fowkes (New York: Penguin, 2004), 449.

158. Marx, 6.

159. Kenneth Burke, *Attitudes toward History* (Berkeley: University of California Press, 1984), 308.

160. Fred Moten, "Black Mo'nin," in *Loss: The Politics of Mourning*, ed. David Eng and David Kazanjian (Berkeley: University of California Press, 2003), 65.

161. Freud, *Jokes and Their Relation to the Unconscious*, 210.

162. Schuyler, *Black Empire*, 7.

163. Ken Byrne and Stephen Healy, "Co-operative Subjects: Towards a Post-Fantasmatic Enjoyment of the Economy," *Rethinking Marxism* 18, no. 2 (2006): 243.

164. Quoted in Hill and Rasmussen, "Afterword," 267.

165. Edwards, *Charisma*, 185.

166. See Schuyler's "Courageous Leadership Needed," in "New Tactics for Aging Branches," 1938, National Association for the Advancement of Colored People Papers, Manuscript Division, Library of Congress, Washington, DC, 2. Schuyler reports that whereas the first national conference in 1931 was attended by "thirty delegates from six or seven states," the second narrowed to "twenty delegates from five states," but nowhere does he report the total number of attendees. See "Consumers' Co-operation among American Negroes."

167. Henry Williams, "When Black Is Right: The Life and Writings of George Schuyler" (PhD diss., Brown University, 1988), 153.

168. "YNCL Conference Program," box 1, George Schuyler Papers, Syracuse University, New York.

169. Jameson, *Valences of the Dialectic*, 372.

170. Stephen Best, *None Like Us: Blackness, Belonging, Aesthetic Life* (Durham, NC: Duke University Press, 2018), 132.

171. For this formulation, I am indebted to Jared Sexton ("Afro-Pessimism: The Unclear Word," *Rhizomes: Cultural Studies in Emerging Knowledge*, no. 29 [2016], doi.org/10.20415/rhiz/029.e02), who writes, "Coalitions tend systematically to render supposed common interests as the concealed particular interests of the most powerful and privileged elements of the alliance." No doubt, he meant to say the reverse (coalitions render particular interests common interests), but it is saying *something* that something in him could not.

172. Schuyler, "New Tactics," 2.

173. George Schuyler, "Consumer's Co-operation: The Negro's Economic Salvation," *Cooperation* 17 (August 1931): 145.

174. Schuyler, "New Tactics," 4.

175. Schuyler, 2.

176. Ransby, *Ella Baker and the Black Freedom Movement*, 112.

177. Ella Baker, "Report of Dept. of Branches," December 1941, Board of Directors Meeting, box C390, folder "Monthly Reports," National Association for the Advancement of Colored People Papers, Manuscript Division, Library of Congress, Washington, DC.

178. Ella Baker, "Board Report Number Six," 1941, NAACP Field Secretary Records, box 14, folder 10, Ella Baker Papers, Schomburg Center for Research in Black Culture.

179. James H. Robinson, "Twenty-Seventh Annual Conference Best in Years," *Crisis* 43, no. 8 (August 1936): 246–49.

180. Schuyler, *Black Empire*, 25.

181. The sensuality of labor was central to the League's intellectual genealogy. No study on cooperation was more important to Baker and Schuyler than James Peter Warbasse's *Co-operative Democracy* (1923). Warbasse was president of the largest cooperative organization in the country, the Cooperative League of America. Schuyler later reflected that during the late 1920s, "I was closely following the writings of Dr. Henry P. Warbasse" (George Schuyler, *Black and Conservative: The Autobiography of George S. Schuyler* [New York: Arlington House, 1966], 165). Not only was Warbasse's book listed first on the reading list given to League members, but Baker urged them in a newsletter to "Get a copy of 'Co-operative Democracy' by James Peter Warbasse from the Rand Book Store" ("Penny-a-Day Plan," Ella Baker Papers, Schomburg Center for Research and Black Culture, 4). Warbasse encouraged a sensual form of political activism.

> Love, honour, kindness, and helpfulness . . . are products of the mind—the brain—which is nourished by red blood, created out of bread and potatoes. All of the great virtues are manifestations of material things, as motion and noise are manifestations of the moving wheel. And love, honour, and kindness . . . are in vain unless they are absorbed—consumed—and physically affect the body of the consumer. (39)

Warbasse is reiterating Marx's practical materialism as articulated in the *Theses on Feuerbach* (1888), republished the year before Warbasse moved to Germany then

Vienna for his medical postgraduate work: "The chief defect of all hitherto existing materialism . . . is that the thing, the reality, sensuousness, is conceived only in the form of the *object or of contemplation,* but not as *sensuous human activity, practice*" (Karl Marx, *The Early Writings of Marx* [New York: International Publishers, 1975], 421). Whether or not Warbasse managed to read the theses in the German (the first English translation would not appear until 1938), he unearths an idea somewhat hidden in the practical materialism of the first volume of *Capital.* Not only, as Marx claimed, does "the mode of production of material life conditio[n] the general process of social, political and intellectual life," nor only, as Warbasse maintained, does "the development of the mind com[e] from man's contact with material things," but also, to return to Schuyler's "Appeal": production muddies the line between subjects and objects, subjective and objective being (Marx, *Capital: Volume 1,* 175). Warbasse moves from Marx's postulate that "all social life is essentially *practical*" to the notion that practical activity inverts then ambiguates the classical contents of subjecthood and objecthood: the abstract virtues (like "love") are not to be expressed through the enlightenment suppression of the senses, but absorbed ("consumed") through contact with nature. In Warbasse's schema the "ethics of co-operation," as he titles it, ambiguously stem, in a chain of causation, from the mind and the body, bearing their stamp on both. This is the stamp of ecstasy.

182. W. E. B. Du Bois, *Black Reconstruction in America, 1860–1880* (Oxford: Oxford University Press, 2007), 124.

183. Schuyler, *Black Empire,* 325.

184. Aliyyah I. Abdur-Rahman, "The Black Ecstatic," *GLQ* 24, no. 2–3 (2018): 345, 350.

185. José Muñoz, *Cruising Utopia* (New York: New York University Press, 2009), 185.

186. Abdur-Rahman, 345.

187. Muñoz, *Cruising Utopia,* 30

188. Muñoz, 32

189. Muñoz, 185.

190. Muñoz, 151

191. Abdur-Rahman, "Black Ecstatic," 344.

192. Abdur-Rahman, 344.

193. Saidiya Hartman, *Wayward Lives, Beautiful Experiments: Intimate Histories of Riotous Black Girls, Troublesome Women, and Queer Radicals* (New York: W. W. Norton, 2020), 324.

194. Fred Moten, "The Case of Blackness," *Criticism* 50, no. 2 (2008): 189.

195. Sharpe, *In the Wake.*

196. Michael Hardt and Antonio Negri, *Multitude: War and Democracy in the Age of Empire* (New York: Penguin, 2004), 108.

197. George Schuyler, "Views and Reviews," *Pittsburgh Courier,* January 10, 1931.

198. George Schuyler, "Views and Reviews," *Pittsburgh Courier,* November 8, 1930.

199. Schuyler, "Summary of Accomplishments," box 8, folder 10, page 3, Schuyler Family Papers, Schomburg Center for Research and Black Culture.

200. Quoted in Claudia Rankine, "The Condition of Black Life Is One of Mourning," *New York Times*, June 22, 2015.

201. Zupančič, *Odd One In*, 52.

202. Rankine, "Condition of Black Life."

203. Beatrice Potter, *The Co-operative Movement in Great Britain* (New York: Charles Scribner's Sons, 1893), 227, 87.

204. Fredric Jameson, *The Political Unconscious: Narrative as a Socially Symbolic Act* (London: Routledge, 2013), 88.

205. Jameson, 88.

206. Stephen Best and Saidiya Hartman, "Fugitive Justice," *Representations* 92, no. 1 (2005): 3.

207. Zupančič, *Odd One In*, 132.

Chapter 3

1. I've been inspired by Hamer's celestial imagery, her portrait of herself in Space: "My teacher used to tell me—I didn't get to go to school much—but she told me to hitch your wagon to a star, so I always hitch my wagon to a sun, so if I fall I can reach back at the moon." Hamer answers questions from audience at University of Wisconsin, n.d., Sweet Family Papers, audio file u1670a2_2, duration of quote 00:40–00:55, Sound Archive, Wisconsin Historical Society Archives, Madison, WI. When speaking at a rally on November 22, 1963, in Washington, DC, James Baldwin said that the freedom songs, with which the name Hamer was becoming almost as synonymous as Makeba, Simone, and "Mississippi Goddam," were "something of a miracle . . . the country's only hope." Moses Moon Collection, box 7, audio file AC0556-OT_N18, duration of quote 46:00–48:00, Smithsonian Institution, Archive Center of the National Museum of American History, Washington, DC.

2. Fannie Lou Hamer, "Status Report and Request for Funds," March 1973, Fannie Lou Hamer Papers, 1966–1978, box 11, folder 24, Amistad Research Center, Tulane University, New Orleans, LA.

3. Hamer, "Status Report and Request for Funds." As one newspaper reported, "Mrs. Fannie Lou Hamer of Ruleville believes . . . her people must buy land for cooperative farming and cooperative housing before her people are completely starved out," January 8, 1969, Madison Measure for Measure Records, 1965–1977, box 1, folder 21, page 9 in newspaper, page 73 in pdf, Wisconsin Historical Society Archives, Madison, WI.

4. John Dittmer, *Local People: The Struggle for Civil Rights in Mississippi* (Chicago: University of Illinois Press, 1995), 366.

5. Saidiya Hartman, *Wayward Lives, Beautiful Experiments: Intimate Histories of Social Upheaval* (New York: W. W. Norton, 2019), 308; Harriet Jacobs, *Incidents in the Life of a Slave Girl*, ed. Nellie Y. McKay and Frances Smith Foster (New York: W. W. Norton, 2001), 93.

6. Neil McMillen, "An Oral History with Fannie Lou Hamer," April 14, 1972, The Henry and Sue Lorenzie Sojourner Civil Rights Movement Collection, Digital

Collections: Center for Oral History and Cultural Heritage, University of Southern Mississippi. Audio recording from same repository.

7. Hamer, "Status Report and Request of Funds."

8. Fannie Lou Hamer, *To Praise Our Bridges: An Autobiography*, taped and edited by Julius Lester and Mary Varela (Jackson, MS: KIPCO, 1967), 9.

9. Walter Benjamin, "Awakening," in *The Arcades Project*, trans. Howard Eiland and Kevin McLaughlin (Cambridge, MA: Harvard University Press, 2002), 473, N9, 7.

10. Susan Buck-Morss, *The Dialectics of Seeing: Walter Benjamin and the Arcades Project* (Cambridge, MA: MIT Press, 1991), 210.

11. David Eng and David Kazanjian, "Mourning Remains," in *Loss: The Politics of Mourning* (Berkeley: University of California Press, 2003), 1–26.

12. Roderick Ferguson, "Conclusion: An Alternative Currency of Difference," in *The Reorder of Things: The University and Its Pedagogies of Minority Difference* (Minneapolis: University Minnesota Press, 2012), Kindle.

13. Benjamin, "Awakening," 462; N2a, 3.

14. Benjamin, 475; N10a, 3.

15. Benjamin, 474; N9a, 7.

16. Benjamin, 473; N9a, 1.

17. Fannie Lou Hamer, *The Speeches of Fannie Lou Hamer: To Tell It Like It Is*, ed. Meagan Parker Brooks and Davis W. Houck (Jackson: University Press of Mississippi, 2011), 71.

18. Fannie Lou Hamer, Speech delivered at University of Wisconsin, Madison, January 1971, Sweet Family Papers, 1970–77, box 7, audio file u1670a2_2, 11:10–11:26, Wisconsin Historical Society Archives, Madison WI.

19. Peter Fenves, *The Messianic Reduction: Walter Benjamin and the Shape of Time* (Stanford: Stanford University Press, 2011), 238.

20. Immanuel Kant, *Critique of Pure Reason*, trans. Paul Guyer and Alan Wood (Cambridge: Cambridge University Press, 1998), 258, B154.

21. I was introduced to this idea and its phrasing by Ben Lerner's novel *10:04* (New York: Farrar, Straus, and Giroux, 2014), 107.

22. Hamer, *To Praise Our Bridges*, 15.

23. Hamer, 16.

24. I am thinking of Frantz Wright's poem "A Happy Thought," which begins, "assuming this is the last day of my life / (which might mean it is almost the first) / I'm struck blind but my blindness is bright" (Robert Pinsky, ed., *The Best of the Best American Poetry* [New York: Scribner, 2013], 240). Ends and beginnings, death and life, blindness and insight, are contiguous here, whereas in Hamer they overlap.

25. National Council of Negro Women, Inc., "Self-Help Campaign against Hunger, Progress Report," June 1969, Madison Measure for Measure Records, 1965–1977, box 1, folder 15, page 4, Wisconsin Historical Society Archives, Madison, WI.

26. Jessica Gordon Nembhard, *Collective Courage: A History of African American Cooperative Economic Thought and Practice* (University Park: Pennsylvania State University Press, 2014), 12–13.

27. "Brief Historical Background of Freedom Farm Corporation," 1977, Fannie Lou Hamer Papers, 1966–1978, box 11, folder 1, page 3, Amistad Research Center, Tulane University, New Orleans, LA.

28. National Council of Negro Women, Inc., "Self-Help Campaign against Hunger," 3.

29. Angela Jill Cooley, "Freedom Farms: Activism and Sustenance in Rural Mississippi," in *Dethroning the Deceitful Pork Chop: Rethinking African American Foodways from Slavery to Obama*, ed. Jennifer Jensen Wallach (Fayetteville: University of Arkansas Press, 2015), 212.

30. Audio File, Operation Daily Bread, October 11, 1968, 34:00, National Archives for Black Women's History, transcript p. 13.

31. Loan Application to the Southern Cooperative Development Fund, June 1970, Fannie Lou Hamer Papers, box 11, folder 24, Amistad Research Center, Tulane University, New Orleans, LA; see Dorothy Height's statement, "'Maybe we could set up a pig bank,' I thought out loud," in her memoir *Open Wide the Freedom Gates: A Memoir* (Cambridge, MA: Perseus Books Group, 2003), 188.

32. Audio Recording of Presentation and Responses to Questions at the University of Wisconsin, Madison, January 29, 1976, Madison Measure for Measure Records, 1965–77, tape 782A, digitization file#: u782a1_2, comment made at the 7:00 minute mark, Wisconsin Historical Society Archives, Madison WI.

33. Nonprofit expert and Hamer's longtime ally Lester Salomon told me in an interview that they came up with the name Freedom Farm together one night on her porch. However, the name might have already been part of the cultural consciousness. In 1961 the buzz across the Black press through to the *New York Times* was the purchase by the National Baptist Convention of a 404-acre plot of land in Tennessee: Freedom Farm. Led by Joseph Harrison Jackson, the land was an emergency refuge, "equipped . . . with modern houses and farm equipment for the use of farmers who lost their homes and income because they sought to register and vote," in "Freedom Farm Makes a Profit," *Baltimore Afro-American*, September 15, 1962, 11. See also "Fayette County's 'Freedom Farm'—Dream Come True for Dr. J. H. Jackson," *Chicago Defender*, August 19, 1961, 1–2; "Freedom Farm Paid Up: Negro Baptists Buy in South to Help Sharecroppers," *New York Times*, August 1, 1961, 29; "Makes Plea for Faith: Baptist Leader Dedicates 404-Acre Freedom Farm," *Norfolk Journal and Guide*, April 1, 1961, 3; "Receive Deeds for Freedom Farm," July 8, 1961, *Philadelphia Tribune*, 9.

34. "Report on Operation Daily Bread," October 1968, Interreligious Foundation for Community Organization Records, Subject Files, box 48, folder 43, National Council of Negro Women, Schomburg Center for Research in Black Culture, New York Public Library, New York, NY.

35. Interviews with Fannie Lou Hamer about the Pig Bank, recording date 1973, Recording Transcription of National Council of Negro Women Records, National Archives for Black Women's History, Landover, MD, 3, corresponding audio file at 1:00 minute mark.

36. "Food is a weapon": Height, *Open Wide the Freedom Gates*, 188.

37. Monica Mills White, "A Pig and a Garden: Fannie Lou Hamer and the Freedom Farms Cooperative," *Food and Foodways* 25, no. 1 (2017): 20–39, 24.

38. James M. Fallows, "Mississippi Farmers Fight for Co-op," *Harvard Crimson*, January 27, 1969.

39. "Pig Project in Sunflower County" (October, n.d.), National Archives of Black Women's History, audio file, 17:00, transcript p. 6.

40. "Proposed Program of Mississippi Freedom Democratic Party," box 7, folder 13, page 3, Amistad Research Center, Tulane University, New Orleans, LA.

41. National Council of Negro Women, Inc., "Self-Help Campaign Against Hunger," June 1969, IFCO Subject Files, Interreligious Foundation for Community Organization records, 1966–1984, box 48, folder 43, Appendix A, page 9, Schomburg Center for Research in Black Culture, New York Public Library, New York, NY.

42. Fannie Lou Hamer, "It's in Your Hands," in *Black Women in White America: A Documentary History*, ed. Gerda Lerner (New York: Vintage, 1972), 612.

43. "At Freedom Farm Coop, when a vegetable crop needs picking, they just pass the word around and the people go and glean the crop. They went in and picked corn that way, and the Farm lost a lot of corn that way. People just tramp around on the plants, and they would tear back the husks on the corn to see if it was ripe, leaving it if it wasn't to their liking. Those cobs of corn then dried up and were not usable later." Martha's Report after Visit to Mississippi, December 5–11, 1972, "Sunflower Freedom Farm Coop and Fannie Lou Hamer's Situation," Madison Measure for Measure Records, 1965–77, box 1, folder 17, Wisconsin Historical Society Archives, Madison, WI.

44. Harry Belafonte, Fundraising Letter on behalf of Fannie Lou Hamer and Freedom Farm Cooperative, May 1969, Fannie Lou Hamer Papers, 1966–1978, box 1, Amistad Research Center, Tulane University, New Orleans, LA.

45. "Freedom Farm Corporation is owned and worked co-operatively by about 1,500 member families in Sunflower County. Founded by Mrs. Fannie Lou Hamer, nationally recognized civil rights leader, the co-op presently owns 692 acres, the main portion consisting of a 640-acre parcel bought in January 1971," "Madison Measure for Measure Brief on Freedom Farm Corporation and North Bolivar County Co-op Farm," n.d., Madison Measure for Measure Records, 1965–1977, box 1, folder 16, Wisconsin Historical Society Archives, Madison, WI.

46. "Life in Mississippi: An Interview with Fannie Lou Hamer," *Freedomways* (Second Quarter, Spring 1965): 231–242.

47. "Status Report and Request for Funds," March 1973, 10; "I'll say it again," Hamer told Paule Marshall, "America owes us a debt." "Hunger Has No Colour Line," *Vogue* 155, no. 10 (June 1970): 126, 191–92, 192.

48. "Measure for Measure General Meeting," February 17, 1974, Meeting Minutes, Eric Smith Papers, box 1, Wisconsin Historical Society Archives, Madison, WI.

49. Monica White, *Freedom Farmers: Agricultural Resistance and the Black Freedom Movement* (Chapel Hill: University of North Carolina Press, 2018), 78.

50. "Brief Historical Background of Freedom Farms Corporation," 4.

51. "Freedom Farm Corporation, Phone Call Information from Ron Thornton 9/4/73," Madison Measure for Measure Records, 1965–77, box 1, folder 17, page 67, Wisconsin Historical Society Archives, Madison, WI.

52. "All that remains in Freedom Farm's possession is 40 acres, a tractor, a combine, wagons, and the houses and their lots being supported under 240A." Measure for Measure General Meeting, January 20, 1974, Eric Smith Papers, box 1, Wisconsin Historical Society, Madison, WI.

53. Martha Smith, Report after Visit to Mississippi, December 5–11, 1972, "Sunflower Freedom Farm Coop and Fannie Lou Hamer's Situation," Madison Measure for Measure Records, 1965–77, box 1, folder 17, Wisconsin Historical Society Archives, Madison, WI.

54. Lester Salamon, *The Resilient Sector: The State of Nonprofit America* (Washington, DC: Brookings Institute Press, 2003), 20.

55. Y. Levi and P. Davis, "Cooperatives as the 'enfants terribles' of Economics: Some Implications for the Social Economy," *Journal of Socio-Economics* 37 (2008): 2178–88.

56. "An Oral History with Fannie Lou Hamer," Audio File.

57. Henry Hansmann, *The Ownership of Enterprise* (Cambridge, MA: Harvard University Press, 2000), 17.

58. *Hunger: Starvation in Affluent U.S.*, producer Dale Bell, Public Broadcast Laboratory episode #115, aired February 25, 1968, as part of the National Education Television network, WGBH Media Library and Archives, American Archive of Public Broadcasting, Boston, MA. See also Fannie Lou Hamer Papers, box 3, folder 16, page 7, film transcript, Amistad Research Center, Tulane University, New Orleans, LA.

59. "Bylaws: Freedom Farm Corporation," Fannie Lou Hamer Papers, box 11, folder 1, Amistad Research Center, Tulane University, New Orleans, LA.

60. Application to the Minority Group Self-Determination Fund, The Commission on Religion and Race, The United Methodist Church, Maryland, June 6, 1973, Fannie Lou Hamer Papers, box 11, folder 25, Amistad Research Center, Tulane University, New Orleans, LA.

61. "Campaign for Human Development, Application for Funding," 1973, Fannie Lou Hamer Papers, box 11, folder 25, Amistad Research Center, Tulane University, New Orleans, LA.

62. Imani Perry, *Vexy Thing: On Gender and Liberation* (Durham, NC: Duke University Press, 2018), "*State v. Mann*" section, Kindle.

63. "Brief Report," Fannie Lou Hamer Papers, box 11, folder 25, Amistad Research Center, Tulane University, New Orleans, LA.

64. By the 1970s, cooperatives were changing their face, which also complicates what running the organization as such indicates. In a traditional cooperative, returns on investment are limited and transferals of ownership are proscribed. Nonmembers do not usually contribute equity, yet the Freedom Farm received most of their money from outside donors. To meet the challenges of unsustainably limited capital, cooperatives adopted a model to better finance manufacturing, retail, or processing costs. They closed membership to a set number, obliged members to deliver a certain quantity of products (whereas before, this was up to them), required a fixed equity investment, and elasticized restrictions on the transferability of shares. These modified, corporate-lurching cooperatives have been variously

christened "new generation cooperatives," "new age cooperatives," or "value-added cooperatives." Precisely because of their distinctions, it is what these arrivistes retain that should give us pause to classify Freedom Farm as a cooperative in function, if not in name: the majority of shares are owned by the members, rather than the investors; dividends are distributed; and, again, each member has one vote. The hallmark of voting parity was questionable at best in the Farms, and the other two were totally absent. See Samira Nuhanovic-Ribic, Ermanno Tortia, and Vladislav Valentinov, "Agricultural Cooperatives: A Struggle for Identity," in *The Oxford Handbook of Mutual, Co-operative, and Co-owned Business,* ed. Jonathan Michie, Joseph Blasi, and Carlo Borzaga (New York: Oxford University Press, 2017), 165.

65. Derek Jones, "American Producer Cooperatives and Employee-Owned Firms: An Historical Perspective," in *Worker Cooperatives in America,* ed. Robert Jackall and Henry Levin (Berkeley: University of California Press, 1984), 37–56, 38–39.

66. Jones, 40–41.

67. Jones, 52.

68. United Nations Secretariat, *Rural Progress through Cooperatives: The Place of Cooperative Associations in Agricultural Development* (New York: UN, Department of Economic Affairs, 1954), 81–82.

69. Greta de Jong, *You Can't Eat Freedom: Southerners and Social Justice after the Civil Rights Movement* (Chapel Hill: University of North Carolina Press, 2016), 95.

70. Stuart Hall, "The Local and the Global: Globalization and Ethnicity," in *Culture, Globalization and the World System: Contemporary Conditions for the Representation of Identity,* ed. Anthony D. King (Minneapolis: University of Minnesota Press, 2000): 19–41, 31.

71. Hall, 35.

72. Hall, 36.

73. The Black Economic Development Conference, "Black Manifesto," April 26, 1969, https://episcopalarchives.org/church-awakens/files/original/c20bd83547dd3cf92e788041d7fddfa2.pdf.

74. Susan Johnson, "Fannie Lou Hamer: Mississippi Grassroots Organizer," *The Black Law Journal,* no. 155 (1972): 155–62, 160. See also Hamer, "America Is Sick and Man Is on the Critical List," in *The Speeches,* 117.

75. Michael Simanga, "Appendix E: 'Congress of African Peoples Ideological Statement,'" in *Amiri Baraka and the Congress of African People: History and Memory* (New York: Palgrave, 2015), 174–178, 173.

76. Elsie Boddie, "Adaptive Discrimination," *North Carolina Law Review* 94, no. 4 (2016): 1235–1313, 1273.

77. Nembhard, *Collective Courage,* 183.

78. Nembhard, 186.

79. Kay Mills, *This Little Light of Mine: The Life of Fannie Lou Hamer* (Lexington: University Press of Kentucky, 2007), 271.

80. "Perhaps," wrote Hamer, "the major problem of Freedom Farm Corporation is simply that it is not generating its own capital. The only thing Freedom Farm is

generating is food," to which she added "pride," "concern," "healing," "a chance to speak," "to learn," and for "the dying ones a chance to life." Fannie Lou Hamer to Leslie Dunbar, Field Foundation, November 16, 1971, Fannie Lou Hamer Papers, box 11, folder 24, Amistad Research Center, Tulane University, New Orleans, LA. In a "Status Report and Request for Funds," anonymously prepared in March 1973, a huge puzzle piece to Hamer's post-progressive map of history emerges on page 8: "Mrs. Hamer has always believed in helping a family today instead of making promises for tomorrow." Fannie Lou Hamer Papers, box 11, folder 24, Amistad Research Center, Tulane University, New Orleans, LA. Here's a slightly slimmer piece of evidence but worth mentioning. Mayor of Ruleville J. M. Robertson told a reporter, "I have no fuss with the organization, and I have no fuss with Fannie Lou . . . but they're throwing their money down a rathole. I've told Fannie Lou that to her face." When the reporter asked Hamer about Robertson's suggestion to invest instead in an industry, she didn't refute his claim: "We might have a chance for industry later . . . to provide jobs for all people. We've got the land for it." "Hunger Hikes Offer Hope for Mississippi Co-op," *Milwaukee Journal*, April 18, 1971, 10.

81. Nembhard, *Collective Courage*, 260.

82. Chris Myers Asch, *The Senator and the Sharecropper: The Freedom Struggles of James O. Eastland and Fannie Lou Hamer* (Chapel Hill: University of North Carolina Press, 2008), 259–60.

83. Henri Lefebvre, *The Explosion: Marxism and the French Upheaval*, trans. Alfred Ehrenfeld (New York: Monthly Review Press, 1969), 90, 86.

84. Paule Marshall writes, "the voice, blunt, direct, telling it like it is." Marshall, "Hunger Has No Colour Line," 126.

85. Rosetta E. Ross, *Witnessing and Testifying: Black Women, Religion, and Civil Rights* (Minneapolis: Fortress Press, 2003), 139.

86. Meagan Parker Brooks, "Oppositional Ethos: Fannie Lou Hamer and the Vernacular Persona," *Rhetoric & Public Affairs* 14, no. 3 (2011): 511–48, 530.

87. Brooks, 519.

88. Asch, *The Senator*, 250.

89. Marshall, "Hunger Has No Colour Line," 126. Video recording of Hamer's funeral, Mississippi Department of Archives and History, Reels 1–4, Patti Carr Black Film Collection, Jackson, MS.

90. Brittney Cooper, *Beyond Respectability: The Intellectual Thought of Race Women* (Chicago: University of Illinois Press, 2017), 10.

91. Franklynn Peterson, "Pig Banks Reap Dividends: Mississippi Blacks Develop Thriving Cooperative," *Dallas Morning News* 124, no. 123 (Wednesday, January 31, 1973).

92. "We are in the process of making application for tax-exempt status," they wrote in an application for funding, Campaign for Human Development, 1973, Fannie Lou Hamer Papers, box 11, folder 25, Amistad Research Center, Tulane University, New Orleans, LA.

93. Franklynn Peterson, *Sepia* 19, no. 2 (February 1970): 8–22, 17.

94. June Jordan, *Fannie Lou Hamer*, illustrated by Albert Williams (New York: Thomas Y. Crowell Company, 1972), 36.

95. Thomas Ward, *Out in the Rural: A Mississippi Health Center and Its War on Poverty* (New York: Oxford University Press, 2017), 119.

96. Darlene Hine, "Rape and the Inner Lives of Black Women in the Middle West: Preliminary Thoughts on the Culture of Dissemblance," *Signs* 14, no. 4 (Summer 1989): 912–20.

97. Dittmer, *Local People*, 366.

98. Richard Drayton, *Nature's Government: Science, Imperial Britain, and the Improvement of the World* (New Haven: Yale University Press, 2000), 51.

99. Alyosha Goldstein, "The Ground Not Given: Colonial Dispositions of Land, Race, and Hunger," *Social Text* 36, no. 2 (June 2018): 83–106, 87.

100. Goldstein, 91.

101. Goldstein, 83.

102. William Pease and Jane Pease, *Black Utopia: Negro Communal Experiments in America* (Madison: State Historical Society of Wisconsin, 1963), 19.

103. Pease and Pease, 19.

104. C. V. McTeer, "Northern Sunflower County Memorandum," 1971, Fannie Lou Hamer Papers, box 11, folder 22, page 6, Amistad Research Center, Tulane University, New Orleans, LA.

105. Averting my suspicion that the appearance was an effect of poor reproduction, curator Sarah Peterson wrote "only two publications . . . *Popular Science* and *Sepia*," where this photograph was printed, "reproduced his photos as they were meant to be seen." *Images from an Activist Lens, 1959–2008: Retrospective of the Art of Photography of Wisconsin's Own Franklynne Peterson*, ed. Judi K-Turkel, curated by Sarah Peterson (Madison: Center for Photography, Wisconsin Academy of Sciences, Arts, and Letters, 2014), 24.

106. Smith, "Sunflower Freedom Farm Coop." Regarding weather from 1972 to the "winter month" of '73, see "Status Report and Request for Funds," July 1973, Fannie Lou Hamer Papers, box 11, folder 24. On the early drought, see "Proposal for Funding," 1975, Fannie Lou Hamer Papers, box 11, folder 23; "Two disastrous draught years 1969 and 1970 with an existing drought pending for 1971," "Proposal," August 23, 1971, Fannie Lou Hamer Papers, box 11, folder 22, page 12, all from Amistad Research Center, Tulane University, New Orleans, LA.

107. "Certification of Losses Caused by Major or Natural Disaster," June 18, 1973, Fannie Lou Hamer Papers, box 11, folder 22, Amistad Research Center, Tulane University, New Orleans, LA.

108. Roland Barthes, *Camera Lucida: Reflections on Photography*, trans. Richard Howard (London: Vintage Classics, 2020), 115, 109.

109. Smith, "Sunflower Freedom Farm Coop."

110. Hamer, "If the Name of the Game Is Survive, Survive," in *The Speeches*, 142.

111. Priscilla McCutcheon, "Fannie Lou Hamer's Freedom Farms and Black Agrarian Geographies," *Antipode* 50, no. 1 (2019): 207–224, 219.

112. Karl Marx, *Capital: A Critique of Political Economy, Volume 1*, trans. Ben Fowkes (New York: Vintage, 1977), 928–29.

113. Marx, 310.

114. Etienne Balibar, "'Possessive Individualism' Reversed: From Locke to Derrida," *Constellations* 9, no. 3 (2002): 299–317, 310.

115. Walter Benjamin, "Theses on the Philosophy of History," in *Illuminations: Essays and Reflections*, trans. Harry Zohn (New York: Schocken, 1968), 263.

116. Benjamin, 262–63.

117. Hamer, "If the Name of the Game Is Survive, Survive," in *The Speeches*, 141.

118. Hamer, *To Praise Our Bridges*, 6.

119. Speech delivered at the University of Wisconsin, Madison, January 29, 1976, Sweet Family Papers, 1970–77, box 7, audio file u782a1_1.mp3, 9:05–9:21, Wisconsin Historical Society Archives, Madison, WI; Hartman, *Wayward Lives*, 28.

120. As researchers of cooperatives in Latin America have found, these economies by and large try to "integrate historically marginalized smallholders into global markets" by seeking to turn "economic gains into human and social capital." Another way of putting this is that, when they "flourish," they manage to balance business success with social uplift. By bringing property rights into intractable tension, Hamer conveyed the relationship between social flourishing and market demands as an unsuitable mésalliance. Marcela Vásquez-León and Brian Burke, "Cooperatives as Change Agents in Rural Latin America: Synthesizing Experiences across Countries," in *Cooperatives, Grassroots Development, and Social Change: Experiences from Rural Latin America*, ed. Marcela Vásquez-León, Brian J. Burke, and Timothy Finan (Tucson: University of Arizona Press, 2017), 203–19, 205, 207.

121. Recording of Fannie Lou Hamer and Matt Jones, Greenwood, MS, November 3, 1963, Moses Moon Collection, box 8, audio file AC0556-OT_N33, duration of quote 3:00–3:15, Smithsonian Institution, Archive Center of the National Museum of American History, Washington, DC.

122. Hamer, "I'm Sick and Tired of Being Sick and Tired," in *The Speeches*, 57.

123. Katherine McKittrick, *Demonic Grounds: Black Women and the Cartographies of Struggle* (Minneapolis: University of Minnesota Press, 2006), 14, 69.

124. Arjun Appadurai, *The Future as Cultural Fact: Essays on the Global Condition* (New York: Verso, 2013), 121.

125. Hamer, *To Praise Our Bridges*, 22.

126. L. C. Dorsey to Jack Geiger, August 5, 1971, Delta Health Center Records, 1956–1992, box 39, folder 292, Jack Greiger Collection, Wilson Library, University of North Carolina, Chapel Hill.

127. Speech delivered at University of Wisconsin, Madison, January 1971, Sweet Family Papers, 1970–77, box 7, audio file u1670a2_2, duration of quote 11:00–11:26, Wisconsin Historical Society Archives, Madison, WI.

128. Trinh T. Minh-ha, *Lovecidal: Walking with the Disappeared* (New York: Fordham University Press, 2016), 1.

129. Delta Health Center Records, "Delta Ministry Reports," February 1966, 1956–1992, box 59, Southern Historical Collection, University of North Carolina, Chapel Hill.

130. Delta Health Center Records, "New Community," box 59, Southern Historical Collection, University of North Carolina, Chapel Hill, 3.

131. Delta Health Center Records, "Freedom City Has Begun" (flyer), box 59, Southern Historical Collection, University of North Carolina, Chapel Hill.

132. "Brief Historical Background of Freedom Farm Corporation," 1977, 1; Madison Measure for Measure, box 1, folder 17, Wisconsin Historical Society Archives, Madison, WI.

133. John Locke, *Second Treatise of Government*, ed. C. B. Macpherson (Indianapolis: Hackett, 1980), paragraph 36, 23.

134. Balibar, "'Possessive Individualism' Reversed," 304.

135. Jeremy Waldron, "'To Bestow Stability Upon Possession': Hume's Alternative to Locke," in *Philosophical Foundations of Property Law*, ed. James Penner and Henry Smith (Oxford: Oxford University Press, 2013), 3.

136. Balibar, "'Possessive Individualism' Reversed," 303.

137. On how real property that one holds becomes, by way of Bentham's "permanent expectation," an abstract property that one expresses, see Cheryl Harris, "Whiteness as Property," *Harvard Law Review* 106, no. 1709 (1993), and Brenna Bhandar, "Property, Law, and Race: Modes of Abstraction," *UC Irvine Law Review* 4, no. 203 (2014): 203–18.

138. Locke, *Second Treatise*, 19 (emphasis mine).

139. Balibar, "'Possessive Individualism' Reversed," 304.

140. Bhandar, "Property, Law, and Race," 206.

141. Locke, *Second Treatise*, 46.

142. Peterson, "Pig Bank Reaps Dividends."

143. Lisa Lowe, *The Intimacies of Four Continents* (Durham, NC: Duke University Press, 2015), 21.

144. Toni Morrison, *The Bluest Eye* (New York: Vintage, 2007), 17.

145. McCutcheon, "Fannie Lou Hamer's Freedom Farms," 209.

146. Hamer, Speech delivered at University of Wisconsin, Madison, January 1971, 13:00–13:50.

147. Locke, *Second Treatise*, 21.

148. Buck-Morss, *The Dialectics of Seeing*, 210.

149. David S. Meyer and Sidney Tarrow, *The Social Movement Society: Contentious Politics for a New Century* (Lanham, MD: Rowman and Littlefield, 1998), 4.

150. Donatella della Porta and Mario Diani, *Social Movements: An Introduction* (New York: Wiley-Blackwell, 2006), 24, 138.

151. Rodrigo Nunes, *Organisation of the Organisationless: Collective Action after Networks* (Post-Media Lab and Mute Books, 2014), 15.

152. Nunes, 21.

153. "Group of compañeras, MTD Solano," in *Horizontalism: Voices of Popular Power in Argentina*, ed. Marina Sitrin (Oakland: AK Press, 2006), 99; Marina Sitrin, "Goals without Demands: The New Movements for Real Democracy," *South Atlantic Quarterly* (Spring 2014): 256.

154. McMillen, 43, along with audio recording.

155. Hartman, *Wayward Lives*, 46.

156. Robert Wright, Oral Interview of Fannie Lou Hamer, August 9, 1968, Moorland-Spingarn Research Center, Manuscript Division, Howard University.

157. "Tuesday Evening Meeting," June 27, 1967, Official Transcription, National Archives for Black Women's History, National Council of Negro Women Records.

158. I have inferred this total from the number of signatories on the "Position Statement by the Family and Friends of the Late Fannie Lou Hamer," July 15, 1978, Fannie Lou Hamer Papers, box 10, folder 15; and "Minutes of the Meeting," July 15, 1978, Fannie Lou Hamer Papers, box 11, bolder 14, both from Amistad Research Center, Tulane University, New Orleans, LA.

159. "Minutes of the Meeting," July 15, 1978, Fannie Lou Hamer Papers.

160. "Minutes of the Meeting."

161. Letter from Charles McLaurin, President of the Board, to Sarah Mae Ratliff, June 1, 1977, Fannie Lou Hamer Papers, box 10, folder 15, Amistad Research Center, Tulane University, New Orleans, LA.

162. Bobby Bounds, Secretary, to Hattie McGrover, May 2, 1978, Fannie Lou Hamer Papers, box 10, folder 15, Amistad Research Center, Tulane University, New Orleans, LA.

163. "Minutes of the Meeting," July 15, 1978, Fannie Lou Hamer Papers.

164. Bounds to McGrover.

165. Greg Patmore and Nikola Balnave, *A Global History of Co-operative Business* (New York: Routledge, 2018), 187–217, 197.

166. Dittmer, *Local People*, 366.

Conclusion

1. Jericho Brown, *The Tradition* (Port Townsend, WA: Copper Canyon Press, 2019).

2. Toni Morrison, "Hard, True, and Lasting," in *The Source of Self-Regard: Selected Essays, Speeches, and Meditations* (New York: Alfred A. Knopf, 2019), 223.

3. Frederic Jameson, *Valences of the Dialectic* (London: Verso, 2009), 42.

4. Jameson, *Valences of the Dialectic*, 49.

5. Kali Akuno, "Build and Fight: The Program and Strategy of Cooperation Jackson," in *Jackson Rising: The Struggle for Economic Democracy and Black Self-Determination in Jackson, Mississippi*, ed. Cooperation Jackson (Quebec, Canada: Daraja Press, 2017), 29.

6. Danielle M. Purifoy, "The Earthseed Land Collective and Black Freedom," *Southern Cultures* (2021, 2020).

7. Danez Smith, *Don't Call Us Dead: Poems* (Minneapolis: Graywolf Press, 2017).

8. Nahum Dimitri Chandler, *X—The Problem of the Negro as a Problem for Thought* (New York: Fordham University Press, 2014), 11.

9. Chandler, 1.

10. Chandler, 10.

11. Theodore Ward, "Our Lan'," in *Black Drama in America: An Anthology*, ed. Darwin T. Turner (Greenwich, CT: Fawcett Publications, 1971).

12. Ward, 134.

13. Ward, 134.

14. Ward, 198.

15. Chandler, *X—The Problem of the Negro*, 185.

16. Joshua Clover, *Riot. Strike. Riot. The New Era of Uprisings* (New York: Verso, 2016), 189.

17. Amy Dru Stanley, "Republic of Labor," *Dissent Magazine*, Fall 2015.

18. Clover, *Riot. Strike. Riot.*, 2.

19. Patrick Chamoiseau, Rose-Myriam Réjouis, and Val Vinokurov, *Texaco* (New York: Pantheon Books, 1997), 385.

20. Fred Moten, "Global Uprising: Racism, Racialization, Anti-Blackness," September 20, 2020, https://www.youtube.com/watch?v=kUoYD8j3av8&t=2629s.

21. Chandler, *X—The Problem of the Negro*, 7.

Afterword

1. Quotes from the interview are from a transcription in the author's possession.

2. Kali Akuno, "Build and Fight: The Program and Strategy of Cooperation Jackson," in *Jackson Rising: The Struggle for Economic Democracy and Black Self-Determination in Jackson, Mississippi*, ed. Cooperation Jackson (Quebec, Canada: Daraja Press, 2017), 30.

3. The Freedom Georgia Initiative, thefreedomgeorgiainitiative.com; Ashley Scott, "We're Creating a City in Georgia for Black People to Live without Racism," *Newsweek* (November 1, 2020).

4. Audre Lorde, "The Master's Tools Will Never Dismantle the Master's House," in *This Bridge Called My Back: Writings by Radical Women of Color*, ed. Cherríe Moraga and Gloria Anzaldúa (Albany: SUNY Press, 2015).

5. Joy James, "The Womb of Western Theory: Trauma, Time Theft, and the Captive Maternal," *Carceral Notebooks* 12 (2016): 253–96, 280–81.

6. Avery Gordon, "Some Thoughts on Haunting and Futurity," *Borderlands* 12, no. 2 (2011): 1–21, 16.

Index

Abdur-Rahman, Aliyyah, 131–33
absented presence, 88, 231n58
absent referent, 113, 234n112
aesthetics, Black cooperative, 5, 34–35, 110, 130–31, 197–98
affect, 17, 23, 52–54, 87, 94–95, 133; generational, 32; intimate, 64; political, 56; romantic longing, 61; unpredictable, 5, 44
"affectable I," 117
affective economy, 16, 60, 64
Afro-Asian alliance, 50–51
afro-pessimism, 45, 107, 232n76
aftermaths, 13–14, 45, 91, 103
agrarian cooperative, 5–6
agriculture, Euro-American uses of, 166–67
Ahmed, Sarah, 64
Akuno, Kali, 194
Ali, Omar, 5
allegory, 44, 60, 106, 124
Allen, Richard, 4
Allen, Sarah, 4
Allotment Act (1888), 166
allotments, 166
Althusser, Louis, 8, 72
altruism, 48, 65
American Cooperative League, 40
An American Dilemma (Carnegie Corporation), 35, 37
American Revolution, 91–92
anaphoric time, 51–52
anarchy, 18, 92, 95–102
Anthony, Lewis, 84
anti-Blackness, 10, 127
anti-capitalism, 2, 4, 28–29, 110
Appadurai, Arjun, 177

Appeal to the Colored Citizens of the World (Walker), 101–2
"An Appeal to the Young" (Kropotkin), 99
Appiah, Anthony, 64
appropriation: of land, 140, 170, 172–73; subject as process of, 182–83
Arab-Israeli War, 35
The Arcades Project (Benjamin), 141
Arendt, Hannah, 91–92
Argentina, autonomous movement in, 93, 186
artists, 2–3, 7, 74, 116–17, 161, 194–95
Aryan Path (journal), 51
Asch, Chris, 151, 161–62
asset lock, 29, 32
attention, 114–16
Austin, J. L., 38

Badiou, Alain, 53
Baker, Ella "Jo," 2–3, 5, 7, 18, 69–135, 198; and anarchy, 99–100; challenges to longevity, 73–74; comic approach, 122–23, 127–30; denial, gestures of, 78–79, 105, 111; and double absence, 104–5; "Double Duty Dollar" concept, 118; group-centered view, 80, 85–88, 93; on "honor, glory, and fame," 112–17; interviews, 69–70, 85; literary attention to, 3; as National Director of YNCL, 80, 90, 97; pan-point perspective, 86–87; recursion in, 112, 115, 117; on "simple lines," 109; and Soul City, 103–10; spatialization of, 74; university work in mid-1920s, 110

—works: "The Consumer: His Problems and Their Remedies" course, 99; "Personal Thrift" essay, 110–20; speech in Hattiesburg, Mississippi, 85, *86*; "Tent City: Freedom's Front Line" docu-essay, 107–10; "Why Negroes Should Vote" marginalia, 99–100. *See also* planned failure; Schuyler, George; Young Negroes' Cooperative League (YNCL)

Baldwin, James, 239n1

Balibar, Etienne, 172, 173, 181–82

"A Bank Fails for a Million" (Roddy), 31

banks: Black-owned, 31; cooperative, 8, 17, 84, 128

Baraka, Amiri, 159

bare citizenship, 177

Barret, Lindon, 97

Barthes, Roland, 169–70

Bay, Mia, 22, 218n8

beach/edge image, 131–32

beginning, 20–21, 37, 85, 92, 119, 210, 230n50; "again beginning," 31; continual, 5, 17, 31; "of bigger things," 24; prefiguration, 38; rebeginning, 34; transpersonal feedback loop, 39. *See also* sustained incipience

being, 7, 135, 182; "being-open," "being-open-*with*," 132; birth as state of, 21; collective, 87

Belafonte, Harry, 150

Beloved (Morrison), 127, 193, 199

Benevolent Daughters, 4, 173

Benjamin, Walter, 47, 140–41, 170, 185

Bergson, Henri, 93, 132

Berlant, Lauren, 58

Berry, Wendell, 210

"beside oneself," 94

Best, Stephen, 10, 16, 19, 117

"Between Memory and History: Les Lieux de Memoire Nora," 13

Bhabha, Homi, 16

Big White Fog (Ward), 197

Bion, Wilfred, 42

BIPOC land access convergence, 206–7

birth, as state of being, 21

Black cooperatives: as "advantage of the disadvantage," 42, 49; aesthetics of, 5, 34–35, 110, 130–31, 197–98; as alternatives to capitalism, 8, 11, 29, 33, 34–35, 96, 194–95; asset locks, 29, 32; backlash against, 21, 29, 209; banks, 8, 17, 84, 128; bylaws and charters, 4–5, 19, 140; capitalism, connection with, 7, 21, 26, 32, 46–47, 51, 79, 103, 108, 243–44n64; decline of in 1970s, 8, 191–92; disadvantages of, 61–64; dividends, 24, 29, 32; failure narratives of, 12, 88; genealogies of dispossession disrupted by, 159; generational solidarity, 32, 207; as historical break, 8–9; of homeless people, 107–10; 1900s newspaper accounts, 1–2; as non-dialectical, 46–51; as outside choices, 4, 7, 16, 49, 55, 72; present as dreamed by, 1, 7, 11, 16, 72, 131, 208; as type of motion, 28; vulnerability of, 22–23. *See also* cooperatives; federal funding for Black cooperatives; Freedom City (New Community); Freedom Farm Cooperative (Mississippi); Freedom Village/Tent City (Somerville, Tennessee); Negro Cooperative Guild; Soul City (North Carolina); Young Negroes' Cooperative League

Black Empire (Schuyler), 123–28, 130, 132–33

Black Feminism Reimagined (Nash), 53

Black Freedom Movement, 159

Black Lives Matter, 9, 93, 128

"Black Manifesto," 171

Blackness, 46, 75–77, 102, 182; disentangling from property, 88, 95

Black No More (Schuyler), 122

Black Panthers, 159

Black Reconstruction (Du Bois), 130

Black studies, 4, 13–14, 76, 130, 137, 199

Bluefield Colored Institute, 27, 40–46
The Bluest Eye (Morrison), 183
Boggs, Carl, 14, 38
Bounds, Bobby, 190–91
breath, 194–96
Britton, John, 86
Brody, Joseph, 120
"The Bronx Slave Market" (Cooke and Baker), 71
Brooks, Meagan, 161
Brotherhood Economics (Kagawa), 55
Brown, Jericho, 17, 193
Brown, Michael, 93
Buck-Morss, Susan, 140
Bunche, Ralph, 35–37, *36*
burial, 198–99
Burke, Kenneth, 125
burnout, 38, 52–53, 64, 73, 134
Butler, Judith, 94
Butler, Octavia, 195
bylaws and charters: Freedom Farm Cooperative, 19, 140; *Rochedale Rules*, 4–5
Byrne, Ken, 125–26

Calvin, Floyd J., 78
Campbell, Lawrence, 119
Campbell, Nora, 156, 190
Campt, Tina, 14, 15
capital, Black, 135–36
capitalism, 71, 112–14, 125–26, 133–34; Black cooperatives as alternative to, 8, 11, 29, *33*, 34–35, 96, 194–95; Black cooperatives' connection with, 7, 21, 26, 32, 46–47, 51, 79, 103, 108, 243–44n64; challenges to, 2–6, 20, 26, 29, 50–51, 81–82, 95; European, 50–51; global, 158; love as challenge to, 17, 53; planned obsolescence, 93, 209–10; queerness as alternative to, 121–22; romantic ideal of overthrow, 126
Capper-Volstead Act (1922), 8
captive maternal, 137–38
"Captive Maternal" (James), 207

Carmichael, Stokely, 162
Carnegie Corporation, 35–36
Carther, Sallie, 149
Cartmell, Samuel, 101
Cassels, Olga, 93
causality, 16, 27, 66, 68, 98, 238n181
Chambers-Letson, Joshua, 14–15
Chamoiseau, Patrick, 199
chance, 66–67
Chance the Rapper, 13
Chandler, Nahum, 195–200
charity and relief, 65–66
Cheah, Pheng, 39–40, 47
"Childs Play" (Sza and Chance the Rapper), 13
church, Black, 20, 65
Citizens' Co-Operative Society (Buffalo, New York), *80*, 80–81
citizenship, 215n20; bare, 177; citizen-subject, 100; and sovereignty, 198; and thrift, 113
civil rights movement, 12, 75, 158–59; and Baker, 4, 79; dominant narrative about, 141; Du Bois as architect of, 20; equal rights discourses deprioritized, 159; and Hamer, 4, 8, 136, 176, 187; women in, 10
clandestine maneuver, 7, 28
Clark, Robert, 136
class conflict, 11–12, 40, 47–48, 82, 101
Clifton, Lucille, 193
Clover, Joshua, 199
Coates, Ta-Nehisi, 75
Cohen, Lizabeth, 102
coherence, 4, 7, 10, 42, 78, 90, 114, 129, 183
Colbert, Soyica, 16
collective-action repertoire, 74
Collective Courage (Nembhard), 12
Collier, Jo-Etha, 173
colonialism, 6, 58–59, 203; anticolonial resistance, 13, 84, 159; colonial terror, 177–78, 207; and Locke's theory of property, 180–82; settler, 8, 19, 166, 195

"Colonial Object Relations" (Eng), 59

Colored Farmers Alliance Advocate, 218n7

Colored Farmers Alliance and Co-operative Union, 5–6, 7, 22

Colored Merchants Association (CMA), 81–82

Combahee Colony (Port Royal, South Carolina), 6

Combahee River Collective, 6

comedy/comic time, 93, 120–30, 135; in *Black Empire*, 123–28, 130, 132–33; in *Black No More*, 122–23; comic horror of sharecropping, 177, 184–85; discontinuity, 121–22; and fantasy of wholeness, 126–27; perspective by incongruity, 125; and present, 123–25; queer, 121; and tragic frame, 120–21; uncouth, the, 128–29; and Young Negroes' Cooperative League, 119–20, 123–31

"The Comet" (Du Bois), 44–46, 62, 226n136

Commercial Study Club (Washington, D.C.), 25

commodities, 5, 45–46, 64; Black subjects as, 45, 232n76; dialectical image as, 141–42

common good, 35, 155

common sense, 4, 63, 74–75, 231n71

commonwealth, cooperative, 31, 48, 63, 82, 90, 107, 123

communes, Black, 6

communes, utopian, 167

"Communism, Garveyism, Consumers' Cooperation" forum, 78

Communist Party, U.S., 101, 120, 128

communist states, 21, 48

Community Conservation Program, 206

confinement, 42, 49, 57, 61–62, 114, 196; discerning movement in, 137–38

Congress of African Peoples, 159

Congress of Racial Equality (CORE), 103

conjunction, 11, 21, 46–47, 50, 67

conservation trusts, 202

conservatism, Black, 75

consumers, 35, 42, 49–51, 78–82, 101–2, 111, 198; "consuming public," 8, 102; as producers, 98–99

contingency, 63, 121, 124, 126–27, 189

contractual relations, critique of, 148–49

Cooke, Marvel, 71

Cooper, Brittney, 3, 162

Cooper, D. A., 84

cooperation, 48; charity and relief, 65–66; disadvantages of, 61–62; as dual operation, 4; ethics of, 30; as lost and formless, 65–66; and love, 53, 55, 60; non-dialectical nature of, 50; as revolution, 101

Cooperation Jackson, 194, 195, 202

Co-operation: The Solution of the So-Called Negro Problem (Fowlkes), 2–3, 55

cooperative commonwealth, 31, 48, 63, 82, 90, 107, 123

The Cooperative Commonwealth in Its Outlines: An Exposition of Modern Socialism (Gronlund), 48, 82

Co-operative Democracy (Warbasse), 237–38n181

cooperative economics, 65, 159, 217n6

cooperative economies, 6, 28–29, 50, 193, 201

Cooperative League of America, 24, 79

cooperatives: 1930s prominence of, 30–31; as anti-capitalist, 2, 4, 28–29, 110; appeal of, 77–78; and confinement, 61; vs. "co-ops," 165; and cultural homogeneity, 157–58; emergence of in late 1800s, 5; horizontal structure, 34; vs. nonprofits, 155–57; openness to contingency, 125–26; "service instead of profit," 2; and state welfare responsibilities, 7–8; tendency toward autonomy, 50;

types, 155; voting rights in, 29, 32–34, 157. *See also* Black cooperatives

Cooperative Society of Bluefield Colored Institute, 27

Cooperative Wholesale Ltd. (Liverpool, Manchester, England), 82–84, *83*

coordination mechanism, 34

corporate model, 143, 157, 243–44n64

Country Life Commission, 8

credit system for farmers, 8

Crisis, 22–25, *23*, 27, 33–34, 41, 77–78, 129

Crosswaith, Frank, 81–82

Cruising Utopia (Muñoz), 15, 131

Cullors, Patrice, 93

cultural respect easements, 202

Dasein, 132

Dawes Act of 1887, 201

Dawn Settlement (Ontario, Canada), 6

death: corps and corpse, relation of, 77; death-worlds, 54; and historical materialism, 49–50; life and a living inside, 49; living dead, 54; and love, 53–54; of Man, 45; rates, 37, 44, 67

de Jong, Greta, 158

della Porta, Donatella, 186

Delta Housing Development Corporation, 151

democracy: agrarian, 166–67; and captive maternal, 137–38; direct, 34, 81, 161, 186; not spontaneous, 39; participatory, 90; Schuyler on, 123; timescale of, 51–52

Democratic National Convention (1964), 136

demutualization, 32

dent, image of, 137

Derrida, Jacques, 47, 49, 88

description, inquisitive practice of, 11

desidementation, 198

desire: and cooperative aesthetics, 34–35; economic crisis as crisis of,

126; history as what hurts, 135; and necromance, 64–65

desorganización, 93, 231–32n71

destruction: as remaking, 143; self-destruction, 55, 133; serialized, 178

Deyohahá:ge (Two Roads) repository, 205

dialectics, 5, 11, 21, 39–40, 82, 124; dialectical image, 141–42, 185; dialectical negativity, 85; non-dialectical time, 17, 46–51; at a standstill, 141, 177. *See also* Marxist approaches

Diani, Mario, 186

direct democracy, 34, 81, 161, 186

disability and ableism, 40–41

disappearance, 61, 75; of present, 13–16; willful, 79, 193

disaster, 44, 131, 137, 141–42, 177–78, 196–97

disjuncture, 124–25

disorganization/unorganization, 93, 231–32n71

dispossession, 76, 84, 118, 159, 172; of indigenous peoples, 180, 197, 206

dissemblance, 7, 165

distraction/diversion, 114–16, 118

distribution: according to need, 143, 150; by nonprofits, 155; of surplus, 3–4, 24, 28–29, 46, 55, 57, 92, 157–58. *See also* dividends

Dittmer, John, 166

diversionists, 114

dividends, 24, 29, 32, 155–56. *See also* distribution

"doomed to fly," 76, 199, 209

Dorsey, L. C., 177

double-consciousness, 103, 199–200, 234n112

Douglass, Frederick, 114, 217n7

Drayton, Richard, 166

dreaming the present, 1, 7, 11, 16, 72, 131, 208

Du, Soon Ja, 196

Du Bois, W. E. B., 3, 6, 20–68; break
with Marxist self, 21; comet image,
39, 44–46, 226n136; conference, 1918,
23–25; conjunction concept, 46–47,
67; double-consciousness, 199–200,
234n112; initial plans for cooperative
movement, 20–24; and institutions,
20, 29, 39–40, 65–66; intentions of,
24–30, 41, 46; "in the midst" as
concept, 46–47, 50; and Matney,
40–46; mystification used by, 24–25;
non-dialectical approach, 46–51;
optimism as untenable for, 61–62;
"out of this came" phrase, 26–28;
Pan-African conferences, 26, 35;
repetitive nature of activism, 21,
28–31; and Roddy's stores, 26–28,
32–34; self-doubt of as productive,
30–31; as shadow, 20; socialist vision
of, 17, 220n25; transgressive scar
in voice of, 29–30; and voluntary
segregation, 48–49, 61–62, 226n135;
word-eddy in language of, 26–27;
work toward resurgence of cooperative movement, 22–23
—works: "Basic American Negro
Creed," 46; *Black Reconstruction*, 130;
"The Comet," 44–46, 62, 226n136; *Dusk
of Dawn*, 37; *Economic Co-operation
among American Negroes*, 22–23,
134; 1907 study, 12, 226–27n152;
The Quest of the Silver Fleece, 17–18,
55–61, 64, 164; *Scorn*, 55; "Sociology
Hesitant," 66; *Some Efforts of American Negroes for Their Own Social
Betterment*, 65, 67–68; "The Union
of Color," 50–51. *See also* beginning;
Negro Cooperative Guild; Roddy's
Citizens' Co-operative Stores;
sustained incipience
duplicity, necessity of, 101–2
dwelling, 131–32

Earthseed Land Collective, 195
Eastland, James, 161–62

Ebony Magazine, 6
eco-grief, 201
*Economic Co-operation among American
Negroes* (Du Bois), 22–23, 134
ecstasy, 18, 93–95, 100, 130–35
Edwards, Brent, 76, 118
Edwards, Erica, 61, 77, 127
electoral politics, 187
emancipation, 21, 25, 96, 107, 128, 130;
"gradual," 167; narrative of, 5, 13,
65
empathic looking, 53
ends, politics of, 12, 21, 38, 99
Eng, David, 58, 63
Engels, Friedrich, 47
England (Liverpool) cooperatives,
82–84, *83*
equal rights claims, 159
Ethiopia, invasion of, 123
Evers, Charles, *86*
expressive culture, Black, 70

failure: beginning as not capable of, 31;
call to, 96; and haunting/ghostliness,
63; narratives of, 12, 88; and queerness, 121; of self, as excess, 134;
temporary, 35; two kinds of, 96–97.
See also planned failure
Farmers Home Administration, 151
Farm Service Administration, 166
fascism, 82
FBI, 28, 106
Federal Emergency Relief Association,
84
federal endorsements, 7–8
Federal Farm Loan Act (1916), 8
federal funding for Black cooperatives,
30, 84, 151, 163; Model Cities
Program, 105–6; proposals, 62–63,
233n99; proposals and applications,
102, 156–57; USDA loans, 165–66
"federal movement organization,"
220–21n37
Ferguson, Roderick, 41
Fernández, José "Pepino," 231–32n71

Ferreira da Silva, Denise, 108, 110, 116–17
15M (Spain), 186
Fisher, Ruth Anna, 24, 35
Fisk, Clifton, 111
Foreman, Clark, 233n99
Fortune Magazine, 6
forty acres and a mule, promise of, 150, 197–98
Foster, Myles, 143, 150, 155, 168–70, *169*
Foucault, Michel, 29, 75, 109
Fowlkes, Ben, 2–3, 55
Franklin, Benjamin, 114
Free African Society, 4
Freedmen's Bureau, 63, 111
freedmen's manuals, 110–12
freedom, 1; agri-power projects, 166–67; ongoing-ness of, 75–76; political, as prior to political organization, 99; security of, and time, 94–95; of self-severance, 55
Freedom City (New Community), 178–80, *179*
Freedom Farm Cooperative (Mississippi), 19, 137–38, 202, 242n43, 243–44n64; as both owned and not owned, 138–39, 143, 154, 155–56, 163–64, 171–72; and climactic extremes, 168–70, 183, 246n106; daycare center, *154*; decline of, 153–54, 190, 243n52; housing developments, *168*, 178–80, *179*; humanitarian aid by, 151; as "little co-op," 151, 154, 160, 162–65; membership criteria, 156–57; names for, 139, 163, 165–66, 241n33; as nonprofit, 19, 150, 155, 160, 245n92; photographs of, *144–47*, *154*, *168*; "Pig Bank," 143, 148–49; and plantation logics, 148–49; rent charged to tenants, 190–92; timeline of, 143–54. *See also* Hamer, Fannie Lou
Freedom Singers, 137
Freedom Village/Tent City (Somerville, Tennessee), 107–10

Freedomways journal, 151, *153*
Freud, Sigmund, 53–54, 61, 65, 124, 125, 226n141
fugitivity: and Baker, 70, 85, 95, 100; and Du Bois, 29–30, 48, 57–58
future, 56–57, 124, 194–95, 223n78; as already here, 135; as break from present, 47–48; deferral of protects hope, 39; as existing content, 15–16; "future real conditional," 14; futurity of hope, 1, 23; generations/members of, 32, 34, 50, 218n8; having and not having, 52; and impossibility, 17, 21, 48, 51–52, 73; living into, 208; multiplicity of, 88; prefiguration, 14–15, 38; in present, 40, 85, 131–33; "that must happen," 14, 37; time as lacking, 73; universalist conceptions of, 7, 15. *See also* sustained incipience; time

Gabbert, Elisa, 14
Garvey, Marcus, 100–101
gaze, return of, 103
generational solidarity, 32, 34, 218n8
Georgia Freedom Initiative, 202–3
Gillan, Kevin, 87
Glaser, Elton, 21
Glissant, Édouard, 199
global empire, 124–25, 133
globalization, 2, 8, 52, 158, 175–76, 246n120, 247n120; global and local, 157–59
Goldstein, Alyosha, 166
Gordon, Avery, 209
Gould, Deborah, 100
Gramsci, Antonio, 4, 101
Grange, the, 5
Great Depression, 2, 62, 70, 77, 84, 193
Great Dismal Swamp, 57, 224–25n114
Greenwood Mississippi voter registration campaign (1963), 12
Greiger, Jack, 165

grief/melancholy, 18, 25, 54, 56–57; and disadvantage, 61–64; eco-grief, 201; forethought of, 209–10; Freudian view of, 63–64; limits of sociology, 66–67; transvaluation of, 57, 217n5. *See also* loss

Gronlund, Laurence, 48, 82

guilds, 35

Halberstam, Jack, 121

Hall, Jacquelyn, 12

Hall, Stuart, 158–59, 176

Hamer, Fannie Lou Townsend, 1, 136–92, 244–45n80; and appropriation of land, 140, 170, 172–73; and civil rights movement, 4, 8, 136, 176, 187; and comic horror of sharecropping, 177, 184–85; concept of progress, 139–43; contractual relations, critique of, 148–49; and Freedom City, 178–80, *179*; health decline, 153–54; joins civil rights movement, 136; literary attention to, 3; local and global context, 157–59, 176; and Mississippi Democratic Party, 137; and Mississippi Freedom Democratic Party, 136, 150, 162; photographs of, *144*; pluripresence of, 7, 19, 140, 175–78, 183–89, 192, 239n1; poor academic reception of, 159–62; as timekeeper, 188–89; transnationalism of, 159; vernacular approaches to, 161 —works: "If the Name of the Game Is Survive, Survive" (Mississippi State Senate campaign speech), 170–71, 173–74; "I'm Sick and Tired of Being Sick and Tired" speech, 176. *See also* Freedom Farm Cooperative (Mississippi)

Hansmann, Henry, 155

hapticality, 59–60

Hardt, Michael, 39, 50, 53–54, 61, 93

Harlem Economic Forum, 78

Harlins, Latasha, 196

Harney, Stefano, 59, 100

Harris, Joseph "Joe," 139, 150, 155, 156, 169

Hartman, Saidiya, 45, 92, 111, 130–31, 137–38, 175, 187

Harvey, Juanita, 155

Hatch, John, 165

Haudenosaunee citizenship, 204

haunting/ghostliness, 6, 35, 58, 66–67, 113, 163, 198; and failure, 63; and Matney, 42; in *Quest of the Silver Fleece*, 56–57; "something out somewhere else," 85, 88, 230n50. *See also* necromance; shadow, image of

Hayden, Casey, 69–70, 85

Healy, Stephen, 125–26

Heidegger, Martin, 132

Height, Dorothy, 148

Helms, Jesse, 106

Henderson, William, 78

historical materialism, 13, 47, 49, 194, 234n112, 237–38n181; organization as central principle of, 39–40

historical time, 45, 64, 114, 135, 199, 223n83

holding, 207

Holiday, Billie, 70

home, as perspective, 102–3

"home industry," 62–63

Homestead Act (1862), 166

hooks, bell, 53

Hoover, J. Edgar, 28

hope, 14, 17, 52, 57, 95, 135, 141, 175; and dialectical reason, 49–50; displacement of, 109; and dwelling, 132; futurity of, 1, 23; protected by deferral of future, 39, 42

horizontal collaboration, 34

Hose, Sam, 29, 227n157

Houck, Davis, 161

housing. *See* Freedom City (New Community); Freedom Farm Cooperative (Mississippi); Freedom Village/Tent City (Somerville, Tennessee); Soul City (North Carolina)

"how-it-were-to-be," "how it used to was," 14
Hughes, Langston, 197
humor, 120–21
hunger, as political weapon, 143–44, 149–50
Hunger: Starvation in Affluent U.S. (documentary), 156
"hush-shops," 119
Husserl, Edmund, 117

I, "affectable," 117
I, "transparent," 116–17
"I can't breathe" slogan, 194
I-Exist, 176–77
imperialism, 8, 51, 123–26, 166–67, 178
impossible, the, 17, 21, 48, 51–52, 73
"improvement," 166, 181, 185
incident, as term, 68
inclusion, politics of, 157
Incontinence of the Void (Žižek), 54
Indigenous Consultation and Partnerships Program, 206
Indigenous peoples, 166, 180, 201–10; Sixties Scoop assimilation programs, 204; sovereignty, 167, 195, 198, 202
individual, 65; collective as, 171; individualized, 172; individual ownership by, 180–84; "self-possessed," 59–60; and sustained incipience, 29, 58–59; "total individual ownership," 171, 173, 175, 184
individualism, 96, 167, 182
"infancies of light," 21, 23
influenza pandemic of 1918, 44
In Praise of Love (Badiou), 53
instability, recovery of, 199
insurgency, Black, 74
intentional communities, Black, 105–6
International Cooperative Alliance, 3, 30
International Labor Defense, 120
"Interstices: A Small Drama of Words" (Spillers), 103
interstitiality, 109–10

In the Days of the Comet (Wells), 44
"into," as term, 208
"Introducing a Traitor" *(The Liberator)*, 82
Irish War of Independence, 94–95

Jackson, Joseph Harrison, 241n33
Jackson, Zakiyyah Iman, 11, 16, 117
Jacobs, Harriet, 138
Jamaica, 84, 100–101
James, C. L. R., 11, 85
James, Joy, 137–38, 207
Jameson, Frederic, 49, 73, 135, 194
Jay Treaty, 204
jazz and blues, 70
Jefferson, John, 20
Jefferson, Thomas, 166–67
Jehlen, Myra, 10
Johnson, Andrew, 197
Johnson, John Harold, 6
Johnson, Lyndon, 171
Jones, Absalom, 4
Jones, Derek, 157–58
Jordan, George, 155
Jordan, June, 164–65
Journal of Negro Education, 8
judicial system, 53

Kagawa, Toyohiko, 55
Kant, Immanuel, 181
Kazanjian, David, 63
Keeling, Kara, 14, 15
Keiser, Samuel, 31
Kelley, Robin, 12
Kierkegaard, Soren, 121
King, Rodney, 196
Klein, Melanie, 59
knowledge, subjugated, 59
Kotef, Hagar, 6–7
Kropotkin, Peter, 48, 99, 101

land trusts, 201–10; planned obsolescence, 209–10; types of, 202
Lane, Charles, 25
"last," 70–71

Latimer, Ira, 30

Latin American cooperatives, 247n120

law: and chance, 67; deployment of by Hamer, 140; equal rights claims, 159; and pluripresence, 19

leadership: "bridge leaders," 9, 10, 86; fluid, 41–42; group-centered, 80, 93; horizontal, 34, 72, 78, 93, 128; leaderless movements, 9, 11; metonymic with base, 39, 44–46, 87; "old Negroes have failed," 95–96; spontaneous and planned action, 39; top-down planning, 72, 100; welcoming of "trouble" by, 128–29

Lefebvre, Henri, 161

LeFlore Massacre, 22, 218n7

leftist movements: arc-view (wave form) of, 38, 52, 53, 87; failure narrative of, 88; and love, 54–55

Leiken, Steve, 215n20

Lemert, Charles, 223n83

Lenin, Vladimir, 9

Lewis, David Levering, 20, 64

Lewis, Ira, 126

The Liberator, 82

life, existence in place of, 176–77

light, concept of, 16, 172; "flash" of the image, 139–41, 169, 177; "incident," 68; "infancies of," 21; "something out somewhere else," 85, 88, 230n50; and temporality, 142–43; vision of, 40

liminality, 109

Lincoln, Abraham, 112, 114

literary concerns, 3–5, 22

Livingstone, David, 114

"The Local and the Global" (Hall), 158

Locke, John, 19, 180–83, 185

longevity, 38, 73, 97, 149, 158, 160, 228n13

Lorde, Audre, 203

Los Angeles riots of 1992, 196, 198

loss, 22, 61–65, 95, 139–41, 198–99, 201; of boundaries, 185; cooperatives as sites of, 65; of life, 49; seizure of,

141; transvaluation of, 57. *See also* grief/melancholy

love, 140, 237–38n181; colonial divisions enforced by, 58–59; as counter capital affect, 17, 53; and death, 53–54; as hapticality, 59–60; historical notion of, 52–53; inter- and inner-subjective nature, 58; and leftist movements, 54–55; as life-taking, 17, 58; "love-politics," 53; nineteenth-century marriage plots, 56; redemptive powers of, 52–54; reparative, 58–60; and transvaluation of loss, 57–58. *See also* necromance

Lowe, Lisa, 183

loyalty, 34, 64, 221n44

Luxemburg, Rosa, 6, 109

lynchings, 22, 218n7, 218n8, 227n157

Mackey, Nathaniel, 1, 16, 51, 69, 70, 136, 190

Macpherson, C. B., 182

The Making of the English Working Class (Thompson), 11

Marshall, Paule, 162

Marx, Karl, 47, 92, 172, 173, 181, 237–38n181

Marxist approaches, 11, 47, 82, 194. *See also* dialectics; historical materialism

"The Master's Tools Will Never Dismantle the Master's House" (Lorde), 203

materialism. *See* historical materialism

Matney, William Clarence (W. C.), 40–46; Harvard Business School application, 40–41; as "nucleus," 41–44

Mbembe, Achille, 38, 54–55, 223n78

McAdam, Douglas, 62, 230n55

McCutcheon, Priscilla, 171, 183

McGrover, Hattie, 190–91

McKissick, Floyd, 103–7

McKittrick, Katherine, 88, 176–77, 231n58

McLaurin, Charles, 190
McMillen, Neil, 155, 187
McTeer, C. V., 168
means, politics of, 12, 38
Measure for Measure (charity), 150, 165
Meeks, Kathi, 47
memory, 13–14; of memories, 67
Messenger, 71
messianic time, 39, 44–45, 88, 173
metaleptic history, 16
metropolis, Black, 82–83
Mills, Kay, 160
Mississippi: as disaster area, 177; Greenwood voter registration, 12; state-imposed starvation, 143–44, 148–49; Sunflower County, 151, *152*; voter suppression, 136–37, 143, 148, 176. *See also* Freedom Farm Cooperative (Mississippi)
Mississippi Democratic Party, 137
Mississippi Freedom Democratic Party, 79, 136, 150, 162
Mitchel, George, 25
modernity, 94–95
Mondragon, 3
Moreland, Eloise, 148
Morningstar, Stephanie, 201–10
Morrison, Toni, 73; *Beloved*, 127, 193, 199; *The Bluest Eye*, 183; "Recitatif," 113; *Song of Solomon*, 1
Moss, Thomas, 22
Moten, Fred, 59, 76, 93, 100, 125, 134, 199; "chromatic saturation," 133; on Du Bois's voice, 29–30
Movement for Black Lives, 93
Mullen, Bill, 20, 51
Muñoz, José, 13, 15, 16, 131–32
Mutual Aid: A Factor in Evolution (Kropotkin), 48, 99
mutual aid societies, 4, 6–7, 77; secret passwords, 7, 68

NAACP, 48, 79, 84, 128, 219n19
Nash, Jennifer, 53
Nashoba Commune (Tennessee), 167

National Colored Farmers Alliance, 81
National Council of Negro Women, 143, 148, 189
National Industrial Recovery Act, 102
nationalisms, Black, 102
National Negro Business League, 27, 32, 81
National Women's Political Caucus, 137
Nation Magazine, 79
nation-state, 102, 113, 197
necessity, 93
necromance, 17–18, 51–68; as non-subjective, 58; in *Quest of the Silver Fleece*, 55–61; as resource for activism, 57, 64–65; shadow, image of, 64–67
necromancy, 17, 57, 59
necropower, 54–55
need, self-limitation of, 34–35
negation, 46–51, 94–95; of negation, 79
Negri, Antonio, 39, 50, 53–54, 61
"Negro-Art Hokum" (Schuyler), 116–17
Negro Betterment and Interracial Organizations (Bunche), 35
Negro Cooperative Guild, 10, 17; Bunche's writing on, 35–37, *36*; establishment of, 23–25; failure to pinpoint beginning of, 24–25, *36*, 37; study clubs, 25–26; three-point program, *36*, 37. *See also* Du Bois, W. E. B; Roddy's Citizens' Co-operative Stores
Negro Playwrights' Company, 197
Nembhard, Jessica, 12, 27, 30, 160
network-system, 186
New Communities Land Trust, 202
New Deal, 8, 30, 62, 102
"New Era of Cooperation Replacing Individualism" (Crosswaith), 81–82
New Negro, 97–98
New York-based collectives, 202
New York State Climate Action Council, 202
Nichols, Frederick, 40
Nixon, Richard, 105

Nod House (Mackey), 1

nonprofits, 150; cooperatives vs., 155–57, 158

nonprogressivism, 4, 5, 10–11, 16, 99, 200

Nora, Pierre, 13

North, Paul, 87, 115, 230n50

North Bolivar County Farm Cooperative, 137, 160–61, 165, 177

Northeast Farmers of Color Land Trust (NEFOC), 201–10

North Hampton Association of Education and Industry (Florence, Massachusetts), 167

nowhere to go, 137–38

now-politics, 38

nucleus metaphor, 41–42, 44–45, 216n28

Nunes, Rodrigo, 186

Occupy, 9, 186

odd, as term, 114–15

Office of Economic Opportunity, 158

oil crisis of 1974, 106

"Oppositional Ethos" (Brooks), 161

optimism, 61–62, 77, 95, 133

organization: Bake's view, 86–87; as central principle of historical materialism, 39–40; emphasis on, 9–10; political freedom as only prior to, 99; work of done by women, 86

Our Lan' (Ward), 197

Owen, Robert, 119

pan-point perspective, 86–87

Parable of the Sower and *Parable of the Talents* (Butler), 195

past, 13–17, 73, 124, 132; "how it used to was," 14; memory, 13–14; as no-longer-conscious, 15; within present, 28, 31

patriarchy, 13, 53, 104–5, 107, 108, 110, 234n112; agriculture linked to, 166–67; and property ownership, 157

Payne, Charles, 12

"The Peace of Wild Things" (Berry), 210

"penny-a-week" schools, 119

People's Grocery Store (Memphis, Tennessee), 22, 218n8

Pereyra, Gabriela, 202, 207

performative utterance, 38

Perry, Imani, 157

persistence, 9, 17, 21, 227–28n8; and planned failure, 70, 72; and sustained incipience, 42, 51, 72

"Personal Thrift" (Baker), 110–20

Peterson, Franklynn, 162–64, 168–70, *169*

Philadelphia Tribune, 78, 81–82

Philip, M. NourbeSe, 72

"Pig Bank" (Freedom Farm Cooperative), 143, 148–49

Pilgrim, John H., 26

Pittsburgh Courier, 62, 77, 90, 100, 122, 123

Plain Counsels for Freedmen in Sixteen Brief Lectures (Fisk), 111

planned failure, 7; and Black public sphere, 18, 81, 95, 96, 98; and comic time, 120–30; context and action negated, 92–93; and ecstasy, 93–95, 130–35; endings, 70; foundation for, 110; as generative gesture, 133; and revolution, 120–21; slippage, 74–75; "things fall apart," 94–95; and tragic frame, 73, 88, 93, 120–21, 126, 135. *See also* Baker, Ella "Jo"; failure; Schuyler, George; Young Negroes' Cooperative League (YNCL)

planned obsolescence, 209–10

pluripresence, 7, 19, 140, 175–78, 183–89, 192, 220n37; and social movement theory, 186–87. *See also* Hamer, Fannie Lou

political economies, 50–51

political time, 1, 8, 19, 110, 194

Poor People's Corporation, 137

populism, Black, 5

position, war of, 101, 129

possessive individualism, 182

potentiality, 15, 28, 42, 63, 75, 82,
131–32; of self-government, 99–100
Potter, Beatrice, 134–35
Pound, Ezra, 8
poverty, 166; endemic hunger, 149–50;
hunger as political weapon, 143–44,
149–50; persistence through, 173; and
voter suppression, 136–37, 143, 148
Povinelli, Elizabeth, 75–76
power relations, 29, 53–55, 63, 75–76;
agri-power projects, 166–67;
necropower, 54–55
pragmatism, 122, 235n137
praxis, 4–5; problematic, 127–28
prefiguration, 12, 14–15, 38
presencing, 209
present, 5; as accumulation of aftermaths, 13, 45; and comic time,
123–25; as container for time, 15;
disappearance of, 13–16; and double
absence, 104–5; dreaming, 1, 7, 11, 16,
72, 131, 208; expanded, 131; future in,
40, 85, 131–33; as impasse, 13, 131;
living into, 208–10; and local time,
189; long-form nowness, 119; and
negation, 48; past divorced from,
13–14; past within, 28, 31; and
pluripresence, 176; and queerness,
121, 131–32; seizure of, 138, 141; as
stalled, 73; twenty-first-century
cooperatives, 193–95, 201, 208; as
waiting for the future, 131–32
privacy, 140, 183–84
problematic, concept of, 127–28
producer cooperatives, 30, 157–58
progress: avoiding pretentions of, 1;
Hamer's concept of, 139–43; narrowing of arenas for freedom, 52;
necessity of countering, 93; nonprogressivism vs., 4, 5, 10–11, 16, 99,
200; planned failure as counter to,
93; universalist logic of, 15
property ownership, 19, 139–40,
155–60, 203; collective property, 172;
"cooperative" and "individual,"
171–72; individual against itself, 173;
individual made by, 181–82; individual ownership by individuals,
180–84; Locke's labor theory of,
19, 181; mutually exclusive rights,
140; opposing forms of, 142, 156,
159–60, 171–72; reinvention of,
170–73; "total individual ownership,"
171, 173, 175, 184
property relations: domination over
nonpersons, 157; ecstatic disobedience to logics of, 130; Hamer's
critique of, 148; new modes of
having, 139–40; nonprofits vs.
cooperatives, 155–57; suspended by
necromance, 57; unraveling Blackness from, 88, 94, 95–96
prosperity, perils of, 22
protests, 74, 86
Proudhon, Pierre-Joseph, 100
provincialization, 61
psyche, economic model of, 53–54
psychoanalysis, 42, 61, 126
public sphere, Black, 18, 81, 95, 96, 98

The Queer Art of Failure (Halberstam),
121
queerness, 121, 131–32
Queer Times, Black Futures (Keeling), 15
question mark, as alternative punctuation, 127
The Quest of the Silver Fleece (Du Bois),
17–18, 55–61, 64, 164
quicksilver aesthetic, 5

racial disadvantage, behavioral thesis
of, 75
radical, as term, 100
railroad strikes of 1877, 48
Randolph, A. Philip, 71
Rand School of Social Science, 99
Ransby, Barbara, 6, 73, 76, 78, 122, 129
Rasberry, Vaughn, 21
rational choice models, sexism in, 9
rationality, emphasis on, 9–10

Ratliff, Sarah Mae, 190–91
Reagon, Bernice Johnson, 136
reciprocity, 32, 48, 100, 150, 160, 200, 206
"Recitatif" (Morrison), 113
reclamation, 72, 103, 138, 188, 196, 198
Reconstruction, 63, 106, 142, 150, 197–98
recursions, 8, 28, 45, 223n83; in Baker's writing, 112, 115, 117
Red Summer of 1919, 44
refusal, right to, 79
"regulatory affirmation" of the minoritized, 41
remains, 63, 110, 141, 168, 195, 199–200
reparation, 171; and love, 58–60
Republicans, 82
Republic of New Afrika, 106
resistance, 28–29, 38, 52, 55; anticapitalist, 95, 101; conjunctive, 50; distraction/diversion as, 114–16; and space, 6–7; two registers of, 75
resource sharing, 32, 65
revel, as term, 121
revolution, 12; concept of, 73; cooperation as, 101; as momentary "flash," 140; and planned failure, 120–21; as romantic longing, 61; "world revolution," 17, 20, 84, 101, 217n2
"revolutionary spirit," 91–92
riot, 199; Los Angeles riots of 1992, 196, 198
Riot. Strike. Riot: The New Era of Uprisings (Clover), 199
Le Rire (Bergson), 93
Robeson, Paul, 197
Robinson, Cedric, 5, 77, 87, 99, 100
Robinson, Corre, 195
Robinson, Herbert, 91
Robinson, Justin, 195
Robnett, Belinda, 9, 10, 86
Rochdale Rules, 3–4
Rochdale Society of Equitable Pioneers (England), 3, 82–84, 119
Roddy, Bert M., 24, 26, 31–35

Roddy's Citizens' Co-operative Stores, 26–28, *28*, 31–35, *33*. *See also* Negro Cooperative Guild
Roosevelt, Franklin D., 8, 102
Roosevelt, Theodore, 8
Rosenthal, Naomi, 39, 220–21n37
Royce, Josiah, 64

Sack, Karen, 86
Salomon, Lester, 241n33
Sayers, Dan, 57, 224–25n114
Schuyler, George, 2–4, 18, 69–135; as anarchist, 95–102; Baker answers call for militants, 77–78; and Barbadian magazine, 81, 84; comic approach to activism, 120–30; early years on left, 73; ego of, 78; international travel, 81, 82–84, *83*; mismanagement admission, 88; NAACP address, 1938, 128; wholesale cooperatives, interest in, 82–84, 91
—works: "An Appeal to Young Negroes," *89*, 89–90, 93–95, 99, 101; *Black Empire*, 123–28, 130, 132–33; *Black No More*, 122; "Negro-Art Hokum," 116–17; "Views and Reviews" column, 76. *See also* Baker, Ella "Jo"; planned failure; Young Negroes' Cooperative League
Schwartz, Michael, 39, 220–21n37
Scott, David, 13
Scott, Jones W., 25–26
Scottsboro Case, 120
"The Second Coming" (Yeats), 94–95, 96
Second Treatise on Government (Locke), 180–83, 185
secret passwords, 7, 68
secret societies, 66–68, 81
Sedgwick, Eve, 117
segregation, voluntary, 48–49, 61–62, 226n135
self: failure of as excess, 134; ownership of, 182; voluntary negation of, 79. *See also* subjectivity
self-dependence, 118

self-government, 84, 99
self-help, 110–20, 134–35; as self-dependence, 118; as self-help-now, 119; as
self-reliance, 111, 113, 116–18
selflessness, radical, 208
self-possession, 59–60
self-reliance, 111, 113, 116–18
self-sufficiency, 100, 117, 123, 159
The Senator and the Sharecropper
(Asch), 161–62
settlement, place of, 72, 228n9
settler colonialism, 8, 19, 166, 195
Sexton, Jared, 107, 128, 237n171
shadow, image of, 16, 20, 64–68, 85, 87,
88, 102, 168, 189. *See also* haunting/
ghostliness
sharecropping, 178, 188–89; comic
horror of, 184–85
Sharpe, Christina, 196
Sherman, William Tecumseh, 197
Sherrod, Shirley, 202
Shirley, Aaron, 150
short story form, 44
Sims, Richard Page, 24, 35
Six Nations, 204–6
Six Nations Polytechnic, 205
slavery, 17, 19, 56, 125, 148, 171, 217n7,
223n83
Smith, Danez, 195
socialism, 7, 194, 217n2; Black, 163;
Du Bois's view, 17, 20, 21, 48, 50, 62
Socialist Party, 82, 101
social movements: about beginning, 21;
arc-view- (wave form), 38, 52, 53, 87;
burnout, 38, 52–53, 64, 134; collective-action repertoire, 74; day-to-day
work of, 134; definitions, 9; end
rather than means as focus, 12; and
invisibility, 86–87; language of, 4–5;
as leaderless, 9, 11; longevity
question, 38; perpetual beginning
sustains hope, 39, 42; pulse and
resonance of, 76–77; repeated public
displays, 74; and self-transformation,
81; structure and spontaneity, 39

social movement theory, 11, 17;
necromance, significance of for,
64–65; and pluripresence, 186–87;
spaces prioritized, 74; spatial
tradition of, 6–7
social movement time, 4, 8–12, 38;
bringing time to a standstill, 140–41,
177
sociology, 18, 65–67, 68, 74; Spencerian, 65, 67
Solvent Savings Bank and Trust Co., 31
*Some Efforts of American Negroes for
Their Own Social Betterment* (Du Bois
and research team), 65, 67–68
Song of Solomon (Morrison), 1
Soul City (North Carolina), 103–10,
233–34n112
Soultech 1 industrial and business
center, 105, 106
Southern Christian Leadership Conference (SCLC), 86, 109
Southern Tenant Farmers' Union, 102
Southwest Alabama Farmers Cooperative Association, 158
sovereignty, 98, 100, 108, 114–15;
indigenous, 167, 195, 198, 202
space, 16–17, 19, 74; both rooted and
shifty, 85; for living, 102–10; return of
the gaze, 103; and social movements,
6–7; terra nullius, 108; time separated from, 132
Specters of Marx (Derrida), 47
Spencer, Herbert, 65, 67
Spillers, Hortense, 103, 109
Spinoza, Benedict, 53
Spivak, Gayatri, 79
spontaneity, 9, 17, 39
Srnicek, Nick, 38, 52, 73
Stanley, Amy Dru, 198
state, the, 28, 50, 81, 100–102, 108, 113;
welfare responsibilities offloaded,
7–8; legitimacy of questioned, 6,
18, 100; nation-state, 102, 113, 197;
structure, 9, 149
Strain, Christopher, 105–6

Streator, George, 60

Street Fighter (Nintendo game), 13–14

Student Nonviolent Coordinating Committee (SNCC), 10, 76, 109, 136, 189

subaltern, 110, 113–14, 117

subjectivity, 42, 57, 60, 63, 139, 181–83; "ideal of humanity," 117; normative, 19; without subjects, 99. *See also* self

success, 22, 73, 197; capitalist standards of, 160–61; as ruse, 121

Sugar Hill (Harlem), 71

Sunflower County, Mississippi, 151, 152

Sunflower County Cooperative League, 155

"Sunflowers Don't Grow in Sunflower County" (Peterson), 163–64

surplus, 201, 208; distribution of, 3–4, 24, 28–29, 46, 55, 57, 92, 157–58; riot as, 199

survival, 174–75, 207; captivity within, 138

sustained incipience, 7, 10; as alternative to prefiguration, 38; comet image, 39, 44–46, 226n136; and deferral of hope, 39, 42; defined, 21; as fugitivity, 29; as inconspicuous, 31; as individual, 29, 58–59; "infancies of light," 21, 23; necroromance, 17–18, 51–54; non-dialectical time, 17, 46–51; nucleus metaphor, 41–42, 44–45, 216n28; organized beginnings, 20–21; "out of this came," 26–28; prefigured future vs., 38; return, 21, 26–27, 52; tomorrow again, 28–31. *See also* beginning; Du Bois, W. E. B; Roddy's Citizens' Co-operative Stores

swamps, 6, 56–57

synesthesia, social, 133

Sza, 13

Tabor, Nick, 96

Tarrow, Sidney, 74

Tate, Claudia, 225n132

teleology, 16, 21, 45, 73, 130, 133, 182, 194

Tennessee Valley Authority (TVA), 62

tense, use of, 14

Tent City/Freedom Village (Somerville, Tennessee), 107–10

terror, colonial, 177–78, 207

Texaco (Glissant), 199

This Bridge Called My Back (Moraga and Anzaldua), 203

Thomas, Norman, 82

Thompson, E. P., 11

Thrasher, Sue, 69–70, 85

thrift, 110–20, 134–35, 234n118; "of time," 112–20

Tilly, Charles, 74

time, 4–5; anaphoric, 51–52; causeless, 45; comic, 93, 120–30; as cycloid, 142; as dubious, 45; duration, 9, 31, 35, 37–38, 73, 143, 182; entryway of, 139–40; escape, moments of, 113–14; future as lacking, 73; Hamer as timekeeper, 188–89; Heideggerian, 132; historical, 45, 64, 114, 135, 199, 223n83; linearity of, 4, 15–16, 45, 48, 108, 116, 124, 133, 142, 182–83; longevity, 38, 73, 97, 149, 158, 160, 228n13; messianic, 39, 44–45, 88, 173; non-dialectical, 17, 46–51; "odd moments," 112–18; "ordinary," 8, 72; political, 1, 8, 110, 194; as pre-memory, 14; present as container for, 15; present-present continuous, 27, 46; reclamation of, 72, 138, 188, 196, 198; recursions, 8, 28, 45, 112, 115, 117, 223n83; social movement, 4, 8, 38, 140–41, 177; teleological, 16, 21, 45, 73, 130, 133, 182, 194; in "The Second Coming," 94–95; "thrift of," 112–20; vectors, 87; waiting, 140; "waiting without expectation," 88. *See also* future; planned failure; pluripresence; social movement time; sustained incipience

Time and Free Will (Bergson), 132

Toop, David, 85

Toward a Global Idea of Race (Ferreira da Silva), 116

Townsend, Pascal, 150–51

tragic frame, 10, 18, 43; and planned failure, 73, 88, 93, 120–21, 126, 135

transgression, fugitivity as, 29–30

"transparent I," 116–17

transpersonal feedback loop, 39

trauma, racialized, 205

trust, 207–8

Truth, Sojourner, 167

Tubman, Harriet, 6, 162

UJAMAA (cooperative economics), 159

Uncle Tom's Cabin (Stowe), 120

The Undercommons (Moten and Harney), 59, 93

unemployment, Black, 30, 84, 137

"The Union of Color" (Du Bois), 50–51

United Nations survey of cooperatives, 158

United Negro Improvement Association, 100–101

"The Unreality of Time" (Gabbert), 14

urban workers, 84

UTD ("Union of Unemployed Workers"), 231–32n71

utopian communes, nineteenth century, 167

vanguard, concept of, 11

Van Wienen, Mark, 50, 51

vault, image of, 62, 226n136

vector, concept of, 87

Vexy Thing (Perry), 157

violence: against Black cooperatives, 22–23, 23; as defining, 175; lynchings, 22, 218n7, 218n8; normalized, 29, 176; persistence of racial, 75; productive force of, 29; retaliation against Black success, 22–23, 218n8; tragic pathos attributed to public, 120; transgressive scar, 30

visuality, 97

voice, 29–30, 70

voter registration campaign, Greenwood Mississippi (1963), 12

voter suppression, 136–37, 143, 148, 176

voting rights in cooperatives, 29, 32–34, 157

Wagner-Lewis Relief Act, 30

Walcott, Derek, 69

Walker, A'lelia, 131

Walker, Alice, 139, 165

Walker, David, 101–2

Walker, Madame C. J., 131

Warbasse, James Peter, 24, 41, 237–38n181

Ward, Theodore, 197

Ward, Thomas, 165

Ward, William Hates, 219n19

Weeks, Kathi, 98

Wells, H. G., 44

Wells, Ida B., 22

West, Cornel, 79

West India Co-Operative Bank, 84

West Indies, 81, 84

What Is to Be Done? Burning Questions of Our Movement (Lenin), 9

white historiography, 13

whiteness, self-reliance as instrument of, 113

white supremacy, 45, 76, 209

wholeness, as fantasy, 126–27

wholesale cooperatives, 82–84, 91

Wilkins, Roy, 122

Williams, Alex, 52, 73

Williams, Henry, 128

Wilson, Woodrow, 8

women: privacy, need for, 140, 183–84; and work of organization, 86. *See also* Baker, Ella "Jo"; Hamer, Fannie Lou Townsend; specific women's organizations

Workers Education Project, oo

world revolution, 17, 20, 84, 101, 217n2

Wright, Francis, 167

Wright, Frantz, 240n24

Wright, Michelle, 16
Wright, Richard, 197
Wright, Robert, 188–89
Wyndham, Olivia, 130

Yeats, William Butler, 94–95, 96
Young, Andrew J., 187
Young Negro, as category, 97–98
Young Negroes' Cooperative League
(YNCL), 2, 8, 10, 69–72, 97–103; age
requirements, 18, 90–92, 97; "An
Appeal to Young Negroes" flyer, 89,
89–90, 93–94, 101; Baker as National
Director, 80, 97; biography of, 77–88;
bizarre elements of, 88–90; bylaws,
90–92; Citizens' Co-Operative
Society (Buffalo, New York), 80,
80–81; and comic time, 119–20,
123–31; conferences, 80, 127–28, 130,
236n166; consumption and production, 98–99; council system, 81, 84,
109; decentralization planned for,
84, 97, 109; dissolved as centralized
body, 84–85; issues, problematic of,
127–28; members as "shock troops,"
133–34; National Director position,
80, 90; National Office, 97; projects
of, 80–81; "something out somewhere else," 85, 88, 230n50; space
of, 85. *See also* Baker, Ella
Yvaire, Çaca, 202, 206–7

Žižek, Slavoj, 21, 54
Zupančič, Alenka, 121, 122, 124, 134

CPSIA information can be obtained
at www.ICGtesting.com
Printed in the USA
LVHW091926180322
713721LV00013B/1193